THE ECONOMIC ANALYSIS OF CAPITAL EXPENDITURES FOR MANAGERS AND ENGINEERS

G.T. Stevens, Jr.

GINN PRESS
160 Gould Street
Needham Heights, MA 02194

D1089661

10 9 8 7 6 5 4 3 2 1

ISBN 0–536–58346–3
BA 7538

 GINN PRESS
160 Gould Street/Needham Heights, MA 02194
Simon & Schuster Higher Education Publishing Group

CONTENTS

APPENDICES

INDEX   485

PREFACE

This book is intended for use as a text in economic analysis. It is primarily concerned with the techniques for evaluating and comparing capital investments. There are many books that consider these techniques, and from this standpoint this book is not unique. However, it does have some features that are not usually included in a book of this type. These are (1) explicit definitions of equity, operating, and total cash flows; and (2) a detailed discussion of minimum annual revenue requirements and their use in the evaluation of projects. This book also includes certain new tax regulations that are related to capital investments.

This book is intended for students of accounting, economics, engineering, and finance. From a mathematical standpoint, Chapters 1 through 12 only require algebra with the exception of the discussion of nonlinear break-even analysis in Chapter 8 which requires some very basic calculus. Chapters 13 through 15 require a basic course in probability and statistics. Included in the appendices are interest tables, a computer program for determining the internal rate of return, a computer program for determining minimum annual revenue requirements, and some probability tables. In recent times, there have been some discussions about the desirability of including interest tables in a text of this type. There are some who contend that with the capabilities of the hand-calculator, interest tables are not required. This book takes a middle-of-the-road approach in this regard. Some problems and examples allow the use of the interest tables; other problems and examples require the numerical evaluation of the interest factors.

I would like to take this opportunity to thank my wife Jane and our children Bob and Bartlett for their patience and encouragement during this venture. I would also like to thank Christie Murphy and Ann von der Heide for their understanding and diligence during the typing of the final manuscript.

G. T. STEVENS, JR.
University of Texas at Arlington

1

INTRODUCTION

Today, most business and engineering college curriculums require courses that involve a study of the techniques used to evaluate capital investments. These courses are taught under such names as managerial economics, finance, and engineering economy. Whatever the name, it is generally recognized that the study of capital investment analysis is an important part in the education of a business or engineering student. At some point in their careers, business and engineering graduates will be faced with the responsibility of evaluating capital investments.

THE NATURE AND SCOPE
OF CAPITAL INVESTMENT ANALYSIS

Private companies produce products and provide services for one basic reason. This reason is the expectation of some economic gain. Companies do not engage in scientific or engineering activities simply to achieve some scientific breakthrough or demonstrate their engineering capabilities. They engage in these and other activities in the belief that they will realize, at some point in time, an economic advantage. Also, companies do not employ people simply to provide them with an income. Companies employ people as a needed resource for the attainment of the company's economic goals. Basically, a company requires and expects that the economic value of the output resulting from their activities will be larger than the economic value of their inputs. Stated another way, a company requires their economic efficiency (output divided by input) to be greater than 100%. The techniques used to measure this economic efficiency are the primary concern of this book; more specifically, the techniques used to measure (evaluate) the economic desirability of capital investments (expenditures). Capital investment decisions are concerned with answering such questions as the following:

1. Should a company produce a new product?
2. Should a company replace some of its existing equipment?
3. Should a company increase its manufacturing capabilities?
4. What are the investment alternatives and which ones should be chosen?

Capital investments are a critical business decision. Errors in the evaluation of capital investments can result in high costs because evaluation errors are largely irredeemable once the capital is committed. The cost of correcting a capital investment error is greater than the cost of simply "putting up" with the error. Consequently, it is important that economically sound techniques be used to evaluate capital investments. It is the purpose of this book to present some of the accepted techniques for evaluating capital investments. However, it must be understood that regardless of the technique used there is always some degree of risk in the evaluation of a proposed capital investment. The evaluation of proposed capital investments involves the estimation of many variables over long periods of time. Consequently, an incorrect evaluation should not discredit an economically sound evaluation technique. More often an incorrect evaluation is a result of incorrect estimates or omitted considerations. Also, a given evaluation technique, in itself, does not make the decision to undertake an investment. There is always the need for a decision-maker. The evaluation of a capital investment only provides an indicator of possible economic worth of an investment, and the evaluation is only as good as the input data (estimates). The decision-maker must always weigh the evaluation of a particular capital investment against other considerations. A capital investment decision is not an independent decision. The investment of capital is related to financing (debt-equity ratios) decisions and dividend decisions. The decision-maker must also consider any intangible (qualitative) factors—factors that cannot be expressed in monetary terms.

In the future, capital investments will continue to be a critical business decision due to the increasing complexity of technology and demands for greater productivity. Large commitments of capital will be required over long periods of time before expected returns will be realized. Consequently, it is most important that capital investment continue to be evaluated using the best techniques available.

THE OBJECTIVES OF A COMPANY

This book takes the point of view that the basic objectives of a company are (1) survival and (2) the maximization of the stockholder's wealth. The first objective is understandable. The second objective, from the standpoint of evaluating a capital investment, is equivalent to the maximization of the net present value (an evaluation technique discussed in Chapter 5). It is sometimes true that short-term considerations such as liquidity requirements and/or governmental restrictions override the objective of maximizing the stockholder's wealth. However, within these and possibly other constraints, the objective of making the stockholder's wealth is a sound basis on which to evaluate capital investments.

AN OVERVIEW OF THE BOOK

The chapters in this book have been sequenced such that the topics in one chapter serve as a foundation for the discussion of the topics in the following chapter. Chapter 2 is a fundamental chapter that discusses the concepts of time value of money, interest, interest rates, and equivalence. These concepts are used throughout this text.

Depreciation and depreciation models are discussed early in this book, Chapter 3, because of their relationship to the topic of federal income taxes discussed in Chapter 4 and the concept of capital recovery used in Chapters 6, 8, 9, and 10. Federal income taxes and the other tax regulations discussed in Chapter 4 serve as a foundation for the discussion of after-tax cash flows in Chapter 5. These after-tax cash flows (total, operating, and equity) are a basic requirement for discussing, in Chapter 5, the techniques (internal rate of return, net present value, payback period, and benefit-cost ratio) used to evaluate capital investments.

Chapter 6 discusses minimum annual revenue requirements as a technique for the economic evaluation of a single capital investment.

Chapter 7 discusses capital budgeting and uses as a foundation the internal rate of return and net present value techniques presented in Chapter 5. Chapter 8 discusses break-even models and the relationship of profit and net cash flow. The topics discussed in Chapter 5 serve as a foundation for the topics in Chapter 8.

Chapters 9 and 10 discuss cost comparisons and replacement analysis and use largely the discussion in Chapter 5.

Chapters 11 and 12 expand some of the topics discussed in earlier chapters. Chapter 11 provides a method for including working capital changes in the determination of revenue requirements. Chapter 12 is an expansion of cost of capital considerations including the capital asset pricing model (CAPM).

Chapters 13 through 15 include risk and uncertainty topics. Chapter 13 discusses probabilistic cash flow models, expected loss, and Monte Carlo simulation of cash flows. Chapter 14 is a discussion of cardinal utility theory and its uses. Chapter 15 is a discussion of approaches to uncertainty.

2

INTEREST AND
INTEREST FACTORS

Most people realize, intuitively at least, that a dollar today is more desirable than a dollar five years from now and this is true even if inflation is disregarded. This implies that the value of money is related to time. Or stated more succinctly, there exists *a time value of money*. This time value of money is a result of earnings (returns) that might be realized over time if money is available today. Consequently, it is directly related to the concepts of interest and interest rates. Interest is a payment for the use of money and as such can be considered in two ways. To the lender, interest is a return but to the borrower, interest is a cost. Corporations and institutions are also borrowers and lenders of money (usually referred to as capital in this context). They, in effect, loan money whenever they build a new plant, expand production facilities, buy a new piece of equipment, etc. In addition, corporations borrow money through the sale of stocks and bonds as well as from banks and insurance companies. In all of these transactions, the interest (sometimes given a different name) received or paid is an important economic consideration. Consequently, a discussion of interest, interest rates, and interest factors is fundamental in any text concerned with economic analysis.

SIMPLE INTEREST

Simple interest (sometimes referred to as add-on interest) occurs when interest is paid (or received) only on the principal. It is calculated using the equation

$$I = Pni \qquad (2\text{-}1)$$

where

$$
\begin{aligned}
I &= \text{simple interest} \\
P &= \text{the principal (amount borrowed or lent)} \\
n &= \text{number of interest periods} \\
i &= \text{simple interest rate expressed as a decimal}
\end{aligned}
$$

The final amount, F, due (or received) on a simple interest transaction is

$$F = P + I = P + Pni \qquad (2\text{-}2)$$

Example 2-1

What is the interest and amount due at the end of five years if $4,000 is borrowed at 8% per year simple interest?

Using Eqs. (2-1) and (2-2), the interest is

$$I = (4,000)\ (5)\ (0.08) = \$1,600$$

and the total amount due is

$$F = 4,000 + 1,600 = \$5,600$$

COMPOUND INTEREST

Compound interest occurs when interest is paid (or received) on accumulated interest and principal. For example, if the interest rate in Example 2-1 is compounded annually, the situation shown in Table 2-1 is the result.

The results in Table 2-1 can be put in the general form shown in Table 2-2. This table indicates that the amount due, F, at the end of a particular year, n, is given by the relationship

$$F = P\ (1 + i)^n \tag{2-3}$$

For example, using the values in Table 2-1 and Eq. (2-3) gives

$$F = 4,000\ (1 + 0.08)^5 = \$5,877.32$$

TABLE 2-1

Compound Interest Calculations

End of Year	Amount Borrowed	Interest		Amount Due	
0	$4,000	—		—	
1		4,000 (0.08)	= $320.00	4,000 + 320	= $4,320.00
2		4,320 (0.08)	= $345.60	4,320 + 345.60	= $4,665.60
3		4,665.60 (0.08)	= $373.25	4,665.60 + 373.25	= $5,038.85
4		5,038.85 (0.08)	= $403.11	5,038.85 + 403.11	= $5,441.96
5		5,441.96 (0.08)	= $435.36	5,441.96 + 435.36	= $5,877.32

for the amount due at the end of the fifth year, and

$$F = 4,000\ (1 + 0.08)^3 = \$5,038.85$$

for the amount due at the end of the third year. These are the same values given in Table 2-1.

The term $(1 + i)^n$ in Eq. (2-3) is referred to as an *interest factor*. Consequently, a general discussion of interest factors at this point is required. Initially this discussion of interest factors is limited to discrete interest rates compounded annually and time periods measured in years. Other compounding periods (semiannually, quarterly, etc.) and time periods (months, weeks, etc.) are discussed later in this chapter. Also initially, this discussion is largely approached on the basis of borrowing (or lending) money because this provides a familiar setting that facilitates an understanding of interest factors. The nomenclature used in this discussion is

i = interest rate compounded per interest period (initially, the interest period is a year)

n = number of interest periods (initially, the number of years)

P = an amount at the present time (often called the initial amount or principal)

F = an amount at the end of n interest periods (a future amount)

A = a series of equal amounts occurring at the end of each interest period

Single Payment Compound Amount Factor   This interest factor is the term mentioned earlier; namely, $(1 + i)^n$. It is designated as

$$(F/P \ i,n) = (1 + i)^n \tag{2-4}$$

TABLE 2-2

General Form for Table 2-1

End of Year	Amount Borrowed	Interest	Amount Due	
0	P	—	—	
1		$P(i)$	$P + P(i)$	$= P(1 + i)$
2		$P(1 + i)(i)$	$P(1 + i) + P(1 + i)(i)$	$= P(1 + i)^2$
3		$P(1 + i)^2 (i)$	$P(1 + i)^2 + P(1 + i)^2 (i)$	$= P(1 + i)^3$
.		.	.	
.		.	.	
.				
n		$P(1 + i)^{n-1} (i)$	$P(1 + i)^n$	

and is used in the formulation

$$F = P \, (F/P \; i,n) \qquad\qquad (2\text{-}5)$$

Eq. (2-5) determines the amount of principal and interest (F) that accumulates over n years at an annual compound interest rate (i) if an initial amount (P) is deposited. The relationship between F, P, n, and i is shown in Figure 2-1.

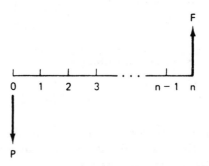

FIGURE 2-1 The Time Relationship Between F and P

Values for the F/P factor are obtained from the tables given in Appendix A. For example, the F/P factor for an interest rate of 8% and 5 years is

$$(F/P \; 8,5) = 1.469$$

Example 2-2 _____

If \$5,000 is borrowed at an interest rate of 10% compounded annually, determine the amount due at the end of six years and the amount of interest paid.

Using Eq. (2-5), the amount due is

$$\begin{aligned} F \; &= 5,000 \, (F/P \; 10,6) \\ &= 5,000 \, (1.772) \\ &= \$8,860 \end{aligned}$$

and the amount of interest paid is

$$I = F - P \qquad\qquad (2\text{-}6)$$
$$= 8,860 - 5,000$$
$$= \$3,860$$

Single Payment Present Worth Factor   The reciprocal of the single payment compound amount factor is the single payment present worth factor. Mathematically, it is

$$(P/F \ i,n) = \frac{1}{(1 + i)^n} \qquad\qquad (2\text{-}7)$$

and is used in the formulation

$$P = F(P/F \ i,n) \qquad\qquad (2\text{-}8)$$

In financial circles (and in this text) the P/F factor is often referred to as the *discount factor* and has wide application to topics considered later in this text.

Example 2-3 _____

How much money must be deposited in a savings account that earns 6% compounded annually in order to have \$10,000 after seven years?

Using Eq. (2-8), the deposit amount is

$$P = 10,000 \ (P/F \ 6,7)$$
$$= 10,000 \ (0.6651)$$
$$= \$6,651$$

where the value 0.6651 is obtained from the interest tables in Appendix A.

Uniform Series Compound Amount (Future Worth) Factor   If an equal amount is deposited at the end of successive years as shown in Figure 2-2, the future amount can be determined in the following manner.

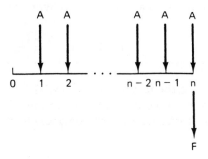

FIGURE 2-2   Uniform Series Amounts

$$F = A(1 + i)^{n-1} + A(1 + i)^{n-2} + \ldots + A(1 + i) + A(1 + i)^0 \qquad (2\text{-}9)$$

or in terms of the F/P factor

$$F = A(F/P\ i, (n - 1)) + A(F/P\ i, (n - 2))$$
$$+ \ldots + A(F/P\ i,1) + A(F/P\ i,0) \qquad (2\text{-}10)$$

Such an approach can be tedious. Consequently, another interest factor can be defined which simplifies the determination of the future amount (F).

Multiplying Eq. (2-9) by the term $(1 + i)$ gives

$$F(1 + i) = A(1 + i)^n + A(1 + i)^{n-1} + \ldots + A(1 + i) \qquad (2\text{-}11)$$

and subtracting Eq. (2-9) from this result gives

$$F(1 + i) - F = A(1 + i)^n - A \qquad (2\text{-}12)$$

Rearranging Eq. (2-12) gives

$$F = A\left(\frac{(1 + i)^n - 1}{i}\right) \qquad (2\text{-}13)$$

The term in the parentheses in Eq. (2-13) is called the uniform series compound amount (future worth) factor. It is designated as

$$(F/A \ i,n) = \frac{(1 + i)^n - 1}{i} \tag{2-14}$$

and used in the formulation

$$F = A \ (F/A \ i,n) \tag{2-15}$$

Example 2-4

Determine the accumulated amount of money in an account and the interest earned at the end of ten years if equal deposits of $2,000 are made each year, assuming the account pays 8% compounded annually and the first deposit occurs one year from now.

Using Eq. (2-15), the accumulated amount is

$$F = 2,000 \ (F/A \ 8,10)$$
$$= 2,000 \ (14.487)$$
$$= \$28,974$$

and the interest earned is

$$I = 28,974 - 2,000 \ (10)$$
$$= \$8,974$$

A Comment   The scheme of deposits shown in Figure 2-2 may seem impractical. That is, why not start the deposits now? Also, why make a deposit in the last year since it earns no interest? The answer to these questions is that some convention must be used when establishing uniform series factors. The usual convention is the one shown in Figure 2-2. This convention choice, however, does not result in any limitations. Beginning-of-the-year deposit problems can be solved with a slight extension as shown in Example 2-5.

Example 2-5

Rework Example 2-4 on the basis that the first of the ten deposits is made now.

This example implies the deposits shown in Figure 2-3 and can be solved in the following manner.

$$F = 2,000 \ (F/A \ 8,10) \ (F/P \ 8,1)$$
$$= 2,000 \ (14.487) \ (1.08)$$
$$= \$31,291.92$$

The interest earned is

$$I = 31,291.92 - 2,000 \ (10)$$
$$= \$11,291.92$$

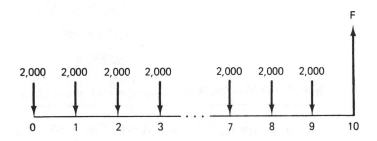

FIGURE 2-3 Deposits for Example 2-5

Uniform Series Sinking Fund Factor This factor, often abbreviated to sinking fund factor, is the reciprocal of the uniform series compound amount (future worth) factor

$$(A/F \ i,n) = \frac{i}{(1 + i)^n - 1} \tag{2-16}$$

It is used in the formulation

$$A = F(A/F \ i,n) \tag{2-17}$$

Example 2-6

A woman is setting up a retirement fund and believes she must have $100,000 available ten years from now. If she finds a fund that pays 8% compounded annually, what is her equal annual deposit for ten years assuming the first deposit is made one year from now?

Using Eq. (2-17), the annual amount is

$$A = 100,000 \ (A/F \ 8,10)$$
$$= 100,000 \ (0.0690)$$
$$= \$6,900$$

It should be noted that this result assumes the first deposit is made one year hence. If it is decided to make the first deposit now, but still only ten deposits, then each deposit required is

$$A' = A(P/F \ i,n)$$
$$A' = 6,900 \ (P/F \ 8,1)$$
$$= 6,900 \ (0.9259)$$
$$= \$6,388.71$$

in order to have the $100,000 at the end of ten years.

Uniform Series Present Worth Factor   This interest factor allows the determination of the present amount required for a uniform series of withdrawals. This situation is depicted in Figure 2-4.

P can be determined by finding the future amount at the end of year n and then discounting this amount back to the present. Expressed mathematically,

$$P = A(F/A \ i,n) \ (P/F \ i,n) \tag{2-18}$$

By considering the two interest factors in Eq. (2-18), the uniform series present worth factor is defined; namely,

$$(P/A \ i,n) = (F/A \ i,n)(P/F \ i,n) \tag{2-19}$$

$$= \frac{(1+i)^n - 1}{i(1+i)^n}$$

It is used in the formulation

$$P = A(P/A \ i,n) \qquad\qquad (2\text{-}20)$$

Example 2-7 _____

A person has a certain debt obligation where $1,000 a year is required over the next five years. How much must be deposited into an account that pays 6% compounded annually in order to just meet these debt obligations?

Using Eq. (2-20), the deposit is

$$P = 1,000 \ (P/A \ 6,5)$$
$$= 1,000 \ (4.2124)$$
$$= \$4,212.40$$

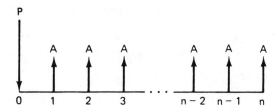

FIGURE 2-4   Present Worth of a Uniform Series

Uniform Series Capital Recovery Factor   This factor is the reciprocal of the uniform series present worth factor

$$(A/P \ i,n) = \frac{i(1+i)^n}{(1+i)^n - 1}$$

$$(2\text{-}21)$$

and is used in the formulation

$$A = P(A/P\ i,n) \tag{2-22}$$

Example 2-8

If $8,000 is deposited into an account that pays 8% compounded, what equal annual withdrawal can be made over the next six years?

Using Eq. (2-22), the withdrawal is

$$A = 8,000\ (A/P\ 8,6)$$

$$= 8,000\ (0.2163)$$

$$= \$1,730.40$$

Gradient Conversion Factor Situations often occur where the withdrawals (or payments) increase or decrease by a constant amount. Such a situation is shown in Figure 2-5. If it is desired to find the present amount that makes possible the series of withdrawals shown in Figure 2-5, one method ($i = 10\%$) is

$$P = 100\ (P/F\ 10,1) + 150\ (P/F\ 10,2) + 200\ (P/F\ 10,3)$$

$$+ 250\ (P/F\ 10,4) + 300\ (P/F\ 10,5)$$

$$= \$722.17$$

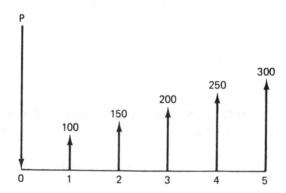

FIGURE 2-5 A Constantly Increasing Series of Withdrawals

This solution is not difficult but could be tedious for a long series of constantly increasing withdrawals. Consequently, another interest factor is defined that simplifies calculations involving a uniformly increasing series.

If the series of withdrawals shown in Figure 2-5 is considered, it can be seen that there are two parts: a constant amount (A_1) and a uniformly increasing amount (A_2). For example in Figure 2-5,

$$A_1 = \$100$$

$$A_2 = (n-1)(50)$$

where n is the year number. In general, the yearly withdrawal, A_n is

$$A_n = 100 + (n-1)(50)$$

or in more general form

$$A_n = A_1 + (n-1)(G) \tag{2-23}$$

where G is the annual gradient.

The second part of Eq. (2-23), called A_x, is shown in Table 2-3. Each item in column A, in Table 2-3 is a constant amount. Therefore the future amount of all of these items is

$$F = G(F/A\, i, (n-1) + F/A\ i,(n-2) + \ldots + F/A\ i,1) \tag{2-24}$$

or

$$F = G\left(\frac{(1+i)^{n-1}-1}{i} + \frac{(1+i)^{n-2}-1}{i} + \ldots + \frac{(1+i)-1}{i}\right)$$

$$= \frac{G}{i}\left((1+i)^{n-1} - 1 + (1+i)^{n-2} - 1 + \ldots + (1+i) - 1\right)$$

$$= \frac{G}{i}\left((1+i)^{n-1} + (1+i)^{n-2} + \ldots + (1+i) - (n-1)\right)$$

$$= \frac{G}{i}\left((1+i)^{n-1} + (1+i)^{n-2} + \ldots + (1+i) + 1\right) - \frac{nG}{i} \tag{2-25}$$

TABLE 2-3

An Increasing Gradient

End of Year	Amount (A_x)	Expanded Amount
0	—	—
1	0	0
2	G	G
3	$2G$	$G + G$
4	$3G$	$G + G + G$
.	.	.
.	.	.
.	.	.
$n - 1$	$(n - 2)(G)$	$G + G + \ldots + G + G$
n	$(n - 1)(G)$	$G + G + \ldots + G + G + G$

Now in Eq. (2-25) the terms in the parentheses define the F/A factor. Consequently, Eq. (2-25) can be written as

$$F = \frac{G}{i}\left(\frac{(1 + i)^n - 1}{i}\right) - \frac{nG}{i}$$

(2-26)

Eq. (2-26) can be converted to an annual amount by multiplying it by an A/F factor, which gives

$$A_x = \left\{\frac{G}{i}\left(\frac{(1 + i)^n - 1}{i}\right) - \frac{nG}{i}\right\}\left(\frac{i}{(1 + i)^n - 1}\right)$$

$$= G\left(\frac{1}{i} - \frac{n}{i}(A/F\ i,n)\right)$$

(2-27)

The expression in the parentheses in Eq. (2-27) is the gradient conversion factor and is designated as

$$(A/G\ i,n) = \left(\frac{1}{i} - \frac{n}{i}(A/F\ i,n)\right)$$

(2-28)

and is used in the formulation

$$A = A_1 \pm G\ (A/G\ i,n)$$

(2-29)

In Eq. (2-29) the plus sign is used for an increasing series and the negative sign for a decreasing series.

Example 2-9

In this example the present amount is determined for the withdrawals given in Figure 2-5 using the gradient conversion factor.

$$P = (100 + 50 \, (A/G \ 10,5)) \, (P/A \ 10,5)$$
$$= (100 + 50 \, (1.8101)) \, (3.7908)$$
$$= \$722.17$$

A Comment   In all of the examples presented up to this point, values for $F, P,$ and A are determined with given values for i and n. This is not always the case. There are many situations where either i or n is required. For example, if $F, A,$ and n are given, i can be determined. In fact in later discussions the determination of i is a prime consideration.

Example 2-10

If \$2,000 a year is deposited into an account and there is \$12,706 in the account at the end of five years, what rate of interest did the account pay?

Since an annual and future amount are involved, this implies an F/A (or A/F) factor; namely,

$$F = A \, (F/A \ i,n)$$
$$12,706 = 2,000 \, (F/A \ i,5)$$
$$(F/A \ i,5) = 6.353$$

With the value 6.353, the interest tables are searched for an F/A factor with the same value at $n = 5$. The same value is found in the 12% interest table. Consequently, the answer is 12% compounded annually.

LINEAR INTERPOLATION

In Example 2-10, the exact value 6.353 is in the interest tables. This is not always the case. Consequently, it is sometimes necessary to use interpolation. *Linear* interpolation, in these cases, is considered sufficient as long as the increments between values are small. Also, it is applicable to continuous interest factors (discussed later) as well as discrete interest factors.

Example 2-11 _____

Suppose in Example 2-10 the amount in the account after five years is $14,000; what is the rate of interest paid?

The solution to this problem takes the same form as that given in Example 2-10, only now

$$(F/A \ \ i,5) = 7.000$$

In searching the interest tables there is no interest rate for an F/A factor of 7.000. Consequently, interpolation is necessary. The interest tables indicate that the interest rate is somewhere between 20% and 15% since the corresponding interest factors are 7.442 and 6.742. This information is shown in Table 2-4 and is the basis for the following calculations.

$$X \ = \ 15 + \frac{7.000 - 6.742}{7.442 - 6.742}(20 - 15)$$

$$= \ 15 + (0.369)\,(5)$$

$$= \ 15 + 1.85$$

$$= \ 16.85\% \text{ compounded yearly}$$

NOMINAL AND EFFECTIVE INTEREST

The prior discussion of interest factors and rates has been limited to an annual compounding period. However, interest rates are often specified with compounding periods other than one year. An interest rate is completely defined if *two time periods* are specified (or at least understood). For example, 8% per year compounded per year is a completely defined interest rate. However, it is common to specify this rate as 8% compounded per year. The first *per year* phrase is understood. As another example, an interest rate might be specified as 12% compounded semiannually. This interest rate implies 12% per year compounded semiannually. Again, the per year phrase is understood. It is not unusual to see an interest rate specified as 1% per month. This usually means 12% per year compounded monthly. As a result of these considerations it is important at this point to define effective *annual* interest rate, effective interest rate, and nominal interest rate.

Effective Annual Interest Rate When both time periods are expressed on an *annual* basis, this is an effective annual rate. For example, 8% per year compounded per year is an effective annual interest rate. As mentioned previously, this is often abbreviated to 8% compounded annually.

TABLE 2-4

Interpolation Values for Example 2-11

Interest Rate	F/A Value
20%	7.442
X	7.000
15%	6.742

Effective Interest Rate When both time periods are the same, this is an effective interest rate. For example 3% per month compounded per month is an effective interest rate. It should be noted that with this definition an effective annual interest rate is always an effective interest rate. However, the reverse is not true.

Nominal Interest Rate When the time units are not the same but the first time period is per year, this defines a nominal interest rate. For example, 12% per year compounded semiannually is a nominal interest rate and is usually abbreviated to 12% compounded semiannually. The phrase per year is understood. With this definition the conversion of effective rates to nominal rates can be accomplished by the relationship

$$\text{effective} = \frac{\text{nominal rate}}{c}$$

(2-30)

where c is the number of compounding periods per year. For example, 8% compounded semiannually (remember the per year phrase is understood) is equivalent to an effective interest rate of 4% semiannually compounded semiannually ($c = 2$). An effective interest rate of 1% per month compounded monthly is equivalent to a nominal rate of 12% compounded monthly ($c = 12$).

Converting a nominal rate to an effective annual rate is accomplished by using the relationship

$$\begin{pmatrix} \text{effective annual} \\ \text{interest rate} \end{pmatrix} = \left(1 + \frac{r}{c}\right)^c - 1$$

(2-31)

where r is the nominal rate and c is the number of compounding periods per year. For example, 12% compounded monthly is an effective annual rate of

$$\left(1 + \frac{.12}{12}\right)^{12} - 1 = 0.1268$$

$$= 12.68\%$$

In this text the convention is to omit the first per year phrase when specifying effective annual and nominal interest rates. Also when an interest rate is simply specified as 8%, this implies, in this text, an interest rate of 8% compounded annually.

In conjunction with the previous discussion of effective annual, effective, and nominal interest rates, the relation between the compounding period and the timing of the payments (receipts, withdrawals, etc.) must be considered. The basic approach in these situations is to convert the interest rate to an effective rate with time units that agree with the timing of the payments and to convert the number of years (n) to the number of interest periods. When only single amounts (F or P) are involved, these conversions are relatively simple.

Example 2-12 _____

If a person deposits $5,000 into an account that pays 8% compounded quarterly, how much money is in the account after five years?
　　The solution to this problem is

$$F = P\,(F/P\ i,n)$$

$$= \ 5{,}000\,(F/P\tfrac{8}{4},4\,(5))$$

$$= \ 5{,}000\,(F/P\ 2{,}20)$$

$$= \ 5{,}000\,(1.486)$$

$$= \ \$7{,}430$$

It should be noted that in the solution to Example 2-12 the interest rate is converted to an effective rate in accordance with Eq. (2-30) and the number of years is converted to the number of interest periods (20).
　　When equal amounts (A) are involved in a problem, the necessary conversions may be slightly more involved.

Example 2-13 _____

A person makes an equal quarterly deposit of $4,000 in an account for a period of five years. Determine the amount in the account after five years if:

a. The interest rate is 12% compounded quarterly.
b. The interest rate is 12% compounded semiannually.

The solution for Part a is

$$F = \ 4{,}000\,(F/A\tfrac{12}{4},4\,(5))$$

$$= \ 4{,}000\,(F/A\ 3{,}20)$$

$$= \ 4{,}000\,(26.870)$$

$$= \ \$107{,}480$$

It should be noted that all the time units agree. That is, the deposits are quarterly, the interest rate (3%) is per quarter compounded quarterly, and there are 20 quarters in the five-year period.

There might be a tendency to solve this part of the problem in the following manner:

$$F = 4,000(4)(F/A\ 12,5)$$

$$= 16,000(6.353)$$

$$= \$101,648$$

This solution is *incorrect* because it does not fully take into account the time value of money. That is, interest is being earned each *quarter* on the quarterly amounts being deposited.

The solution to Part b is a little more involved since the compound period (semiannually) for the given interest rate does not agree with the timing of the deposits. The procedure in this case is to first convert the interest rate to an effective annual rate. Using Eq. (2-31), this is

$$\left(1 + \frac{.12}{2}\right)^2 - 1 = 0.1236 = 12.36\% \text{ compounded annually}$$

Next, this result is converted to a nominal rate with a compounding period that agrees with the deposit (quarterly, c = 4). This is also accomplished using Eq. (2-31):

$$0.1236 = \left(1 + \frac{r}{4}\right)^4 - 1$$

$$\frac{r}{4} = (1.1236)^{0.25} - 1$$

$$= 0.0296$$

$$r = 4\ (0.0296)$$

$$= 0.1184$$

$$= 11.84\% \text{ compounded quarterly}$$

With this result, the solution to Part b is

$$F = 4,000 \left(F/A \; \frac{11.84}{4}, 4\,(5) \right)$$

$$= 4,000 \; (F/A \; 2.96, 20)$$

$$= 4,000 \; (26.761)$$

$$= \$107,044$$

The value for the F/A factor in this solution can be obtained either by interpolation or by direct evaluation of the mathematical expression for the F/A factor. This is the approach in the example; namely,

$$F/A \; 2.96,20 = \frac{(1 + 0.0296)^{20} - 1}{0.0296}$$

$$= 26.761$$

CONTINUOUS INTEREST FACTORS

Interest rates are sometimes specified on the basis of continuous compounding. An interest rate with continuous compounding is a *nominal* rate. For example, 10% compounded continuously implies 10% *per year* compounded continuously. Continuous interest also requires different interest factors than those previously given.

Single Payment Compound Amount Factor   For discrete interest rates, the formulation involving the F/P factor is

$$F = P \; (F/P \; i,n) \tag{2-32}$$

and writing this in terms of a nominal rate gives

$$F = P \left(F/P \frac{r}{c} cn \right) \tag{2-33}$$

Substituting the mathematical term for the F/P factor in Eq. (2-33) gives

$$F = P \left(1 + \frac{r}{c}\right)^{cn}$$

(2-34)

which can be written as

$$F = P \left[\left(1 + \frac{r}{c}\right)^{\frac{c}{r}}\right]^{rn}$$

Taking the limit of Eq. (2-35) as c approaches infinity gives

$$F = P e^{rn}$$

(2-36)

With continuous compounding, the single payment compound amount factor is the expression e^{rn} in Eq. (2-36) and is designated $[F/P \ r,n]$. It is used in the formulation

$$F = P[F/P \ r,n]$$

(2-37)

It should be noted that continuous interest factors use brackets in order to distinguish them from discrete interest factors which use parentheses.

Example 2-14

If $2,000 is deposited into an account that pays 8% compounded continuously, the final amount in the account at the end of five years is

$$
\begin{aligned}
F &= 2,000 \ [F/P \ 8,5] \\
&= 2,000 \ [1.492] \\
&= \$2,984
\end{aligned}
$$

The value 1.492 is obtained from the continuous interest tables given in Appendix C.

Single Payment Present Worth Factor   This factor is the reciprocal of the F/P factor and consequently is designated as a P/F factor.

$$[P/F \ r,n] = \frac{1}{e^m} \qquad (2\text{-}38)$$

It is used in the formulation

$$P = F [P/F \ r,n] \qquad (2\text{-}39)$$

Uniform Series Compound Amount (Future Worth) Factor   If the series of uniform deposits in Figure 2-2 is considered, the future amount with *continuous* interest is

$$F = A[F/P \ r,(n - 1) + F/P \ r,(n - 2) + \dots$$
$$+ F/P \ r,2 + F/P \ r,1 + F/P \ r,0] \qquad (2\text{-}40)$$

Substituting the mathematical expressions for the F/P factors in Eq. (2-40) gives

$$F = A \left[e^{r(n-1)} + e^{r(n-2)} + \dots e^{2r} + e^r + 1 \right] \qquad (2\text{-}41)$$

The terms in the brackets in Eq. (2-41) form a geometric series with a common ratio of e^r. Therefore, the sum of n terms is

$$\frac{e^m - 1}{e^r - 1} \qquad (2\text{-}42)$$

This expression is designated as $[F/A \ r,n]$ and is the uniform series compound amount (future worth) factor for continuous compounding. It is used in the formulation

$$F = A [F/A \ r,n] \qquad (2\text{-}43)$$

Example 2-15 _____

An account pays 8% compounded continuously. Determine the amount in the account after three years if:

a. $1,000 is deposited every year.
b. $1,000 is deposited semiannually.

The solution to Part a is obtained using Eq. (2-43)

$$F = 1,000 \, [F/A \, 8,3]$$
$$= 1,000 \, [3.257]$$
$$= \$3,257$$

The solution to Part b is also obtained using Eq. (2-43). However certain modifications must be made because the deposits are semiannual. The solution is

$$F = 1,000 \left[F/A \frac{8}{2} \, 2 \, (3) \right]$$
$$= 1,000 \, [F/A \, 4,6]$$
$$= 1,000 \, [6.647]$$
$$= \$6,647$$

This solution converts the yearly continuous compounding rate to a semiannual continuous compounding rate.

Uniform Series Sinking Fund Factor   This factor is the reciprocal of the F/A factor; namely,

$$[A/F \; r,n \,] = \frac{e^r - 1}{e^m - 1} \qquad (2\text{-}44)$$

It is used in the formulation

$$A = F \, [A/F \; r,n \,]$$

Uniform Series Present Worth Factor   This factor is a combination of the previously defined F/A and P/F factors. Mathematically, it is

$$[P/A \ r,n] = [F/A \ r,n][P/F \ r,n]$$

$$= \left[\frac{e^{rn}-1}{e^r - 1}\right]\left[\frac{1}{e^m}\right]$$

$$= \frac{1 - e^{-rn}}{e^r - 1} \tag{2-45}$$

and is used in the formulation

$$P = A [P/A \ r,n] \tag{2-46}$$

Example 2-16

What minimum initial amount must be put into an account that pays 8% compounded continuously if it is desired to withdraw from this same account

a. $1,000 per year for five years?
b. $1,000 quarterly for five years?

The solution to Part a is

$$P = 1,000 [P/A \ 8,5]$$

$$= 1,000 [3.9584]$$

$$= \$3,958.40$$

and the solution to Part b is

$$P = 1,000 \left[P/A \frac{8}{4}, 4(5)\right]$$

$$= 1,000 [P/A \ 2,20]$$

$$= 1,000 [16.3197]$$

$$= \$16,319.70$$

Uniform Series Capital Recovery Factor   This factor is the inverse of the P/A factor. Consequently, it is defined as

$$[A/P \ r,n \ ] = \frac{e^r - 1}{1 - e^{-m}} \qquad (2\text{-}47)$$

and is used in the formulation

$$A = P[A/P \ r,n \ ] \qquad (2\text{-}48)$$

Example 2-17 _____

A person deposits $6,000 into an account that pays 12% compounded continuously. What is the maximum equal monthly withdrawal that can be made for two years?

The solution to this problem is obtained using Eq. (2-48)

$$A = 6,000 \left[A/P \ \frac{12}{12}, \ 12 \ (2) \right]$$

$$= 6,000 [A/P \ 1,24 \ ]$$

$$= 6,000 [0.0471]$$

$$= \$282.60$$

A CONTINUOUS RATE TO AN ANNUAL RATE

A continuous interest rate can be converted to an effective annual rate using the equation

$$\text{effective annual rate} = e^r - 1 \qquad (2\text{-}49)$$

For example, the effective annual rate for 8% compounded continuously is 8.33%.

FUNDS-FLOW FACTOR AND CONTINUOUS CASH TRANSACTIONS

In previous discussions, the cash transactions are assumed to be discrete. That is, the cash transactions occur at particular points in time. Another approach is to consider that the cash transactions flow at a uniform rate during the time period.

One approach that is often taken in discussions of continuous cash transactions is to define another set of interest factors and tables. Another approach is to convert the continuous cash flow to a discrete amount, then use the continuous interest factors and tables. This latter approach is the one used in this text.

A uniform continuous cash transaction, $\overline{A}$, in a year may be considered as a series of X equal amounts spaced at the end of equal time periods as shown in Figure 2-6. Now, the future sum, F', of these equal amounts at the end of one year using a continuous interest rate, r, is

$$F' = X\left[\frac{\left(1+\frac{r}{c}\right)^{c}-1}{\frac{r}{c}}\right] \tag{2-50}$$

Since $X = \dfrac{\overline{A}}{c}$, Eq. (2-50) can be written as

$$F' = \frac{\overline{A}}{c}\left[\frac{\left(1+\frac{r}{c}\right)^{c}-1}{\frac{r}{c}}\right]$$

$$F' = \frac{\overline{A}}{r}\left(1+\frac{r}{c}\right)^{c}-\frac{\overline{A}}{r}$$

Substituting $k = \dfrac{c}{r}$ gives

$$F' = \frac{\overline{A}}{r}\left[\left(1+\frac{1}{k}\right)^{k}\right]^{r}-\frac{\overline{A}}{r} \tag{2-51}$$

If c approaches infinity, then k approaches infinity and the limit of the term in the brackets is e. Consequently, Eq. (2-50) can be written as

$$F' = \frac{\overline{A}}{r}e^r - \frac{\overline{A}}{r}$$

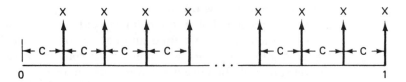

FIGURE 2-6   Continuous Cash Transactions in One Year

$$F' = \overline{A}\left[\frac{e^r - 1}{r}\right] \qquad (2\text{-}52)$$

Equation (2-52), in effect, converts the yearly continuous transaction to a discrete amount at the end of the year. Consequently, if there are n years of a uniform continuous cash transaction, the term in the brackets can convert these continuous transactions to a series of equal annual *discrete* amounts that occur at the end of each year. Therefore at the end of n years, the future amount is

$$F = F'[F/A \; r,n \;]$$

$$F = \overline{A}\left[\frac{e^r - 1}{r}\right][F/A \; r,n] \qquad (2\text{-}53)$$

The first bracketed term in Eq. (2-53) is called the funds-flow conversion factor and is designated as

$$\left[A/\overline{A}r\right] = \frac{e^r - 1}{r} \qquad (2\text{-}54)$$

Values for this factor are available in Appendix D. Substituting Eq. (2-54) into Eq. (2-53) gives

$$F = \bar{A}\,[A/\bar{A}\,r]\,[F/A\;r,n\,]\qquad\qquad(2\text{-}55)$$

If the continuous transaction, $\bar{A}$, is desired, Eq. (2-55) can be modified to

$$\bar{A} = F\frac{[A/F\;r,n]}{A/\bar{A}r}\qquad\qquad(2\text{-}56)$$

The present amount of a uniform continuous transaction can be obtained by

$$P = \bar{A}\,[A/\bar{A}\,r]\,[P/A\;r,n\,]\qquad\qquad(2\text{-}57)$$

or if P is given, $\bar{A}$ can be obtained by

$$\bar{A} = P\frac{[A/P\;r,n]}{A/\bar{A}r}\qquad\qquad(2\text{-}58)$$

As mentioned earlier in this section, some texts algebraically combine the two interest factors in Eqs. (2-55) through (2-58) and define a new set of interest factors. For example, Eq. (2-55) could be written as

$$F = \bar{A}\left[\frac{e^{r}-1}{r}\right]\left[\frac{e^{m}-1}{e^{r}-1}\right]$$

$$F = \bar{A}\left[\frac{e^{m}-1}{r}\right]\qquad\qquad(2\text{-}59)$$

The term in the brackets is designated as

$$[F/A\;r,n] = \left[\frac{e^{m}-1}{r}\right]\qquad\qquad(2\text{-}60)$$

and used in the formulation

$$F = \overline{A}\left[F/\overline{A}\ r,n\right]$$

(2-61)

Similar factors can be defined for Eqs. (2-56), (2-57), and (2-58). This approach is not taken in this text.

Example 2-18

If the interest rate is 8% compounded continuously, what is the final amount after five years of:

a. A continuous cash transaction of $1,000 a year?
b. A continuous cash transaction of $1,000 per quarter?

The solution to Part a is obtained using Eq. (2-55)

$$
\begin{aligned}
F &= 1,000\,[A\,/\overline{A}\ 8]\,[F/A\ 8,5] \\
&= 1,000\,[1.041088][5.905] \\
&= \$6,147.62
\end{aligned}
$$

In the case of Part b two solution methods are possible. The first is

$$
\begin{aligned}
F &= 1,000\,(4)\,[A\,/\overline{A}\ 8]\,[F/A\ 8,5] \\
&= 4,000\,[1.041088][5.905] \\
&= \$24,590.50
\end{aligned}
$$

and the second is

$$
\begin{aligned}
F &= 1,000\left[A\,/\overline{A}\ \frac{8}{4}\right]\left[F/A\frac{8}{4},\,4(5)\right] \\
&= 1,000\,[A\,/\overline{A}\ 2]\,[F/A\ 2,20] \\
&= \$24,591.04
\end{aligned}
$$

The difference in these two answers is due to rounding off. Theoretically, these two methods are the same and would give the same results if the two F/A factors were carried out to more significant figures.

The two solution methods used in Part b of Example 2-18 require a word of caution. The first solution in Part b converts the quarterly flow to a yearly flow by multiplying by the number of quarters in a year, then the factors are evaluated on the basis of an annual rate with continuous compounding. This approach is *only* valid in case of continuous transactions. It is *not valid* in the discrete case. The reason it is possible in the continuous flow case is due to the relationship between the funds-flow and continuous interest factors. For example, in Part b the interest factors in the second solution method can be written as

$$\left[A / \overline{A} \, \frac{8}{4} \right] \left[F / A \frac{8}{4}, 4(5) \right] = \left[\frac{e^{\frac{.08}{4}} - 1}{\frac{.08}{4}} \right] \left[\frac{e^{\frac{.08}{4}(4)(5)} - 1}{e^{\frac{.08}{4}} - 1} \right]$$

$$= 4 \left[\frac{e^{.08(5)} - 1}{.08} \right]$$

which is exactly the same as the combined effect of the interest factors in the first solution method; namely,

$$4 \left[A / A \, 8 \right] \left[F / A \, 8, 5 \right] = 4 \left[\frac{e^{.08} - 1}{.08} \right] \left[\frac{e^{.08(5)} - 1}{e^{.08} - 1} \right]$$

$$= 4 \left[\frac{e^{.08(5)} - 1}{.08} \right]$$

EQUIVALENCE

Many comparisons of economic alternatives require the comparisons of receipts and disbursements of money occurring at different times. In these situations, the receipts and disbursements must be placed on an *equivalent basis* in order to make a valid comparison. In order to put receipts and disbursements on an equivalent basis, the magnitude, interest rate, and timing of the receipts and disbursements must be considered. As a result, equivalence calculations involve an application of the interest factors in order to obtain either an equivalent present amount, an equivalent future amount, or an equivalent annual amount. The meaning of *equivalence* should be clearly understood. An equivalent amount does not imply an actual cash transaction. It is an amount that has the same monetary effect, taking into account interest and timing, as the actual cash transaction. For example, $1,000 today is equivalent to $1,539 five years from now at an interest rate of 9% compounded annually. Theoretically, a decision-maker is indifferent between these two amounts assuming, of course, that the decision-maker believes 9% is an accurate representation of the time value of money.

Example 2-19

Given the series of disbursements shown in Table 2-5 and an interest rate of 8% compounded annually, determine:

a. An equivalent present amount.
b. An equivalent future amount.
c. An equivalent annual amount.

The solution to Part a is obtained by discounting all of the disbursements back to year zero. This could be accomplished by multiplying each disbursement by an appropriate P/F factor. However, this would involve ten factors. A more direct solution is to employ the P/A in the following manner.

$$
\begin{aligned}
P &= 200 \,(P/A\ 8{,}6) + 400 \,(P/A\ 8{,}4)(P/F\ 8{,}6) \\
&= 200 \,(4.6229) + 400 \,(3.3121)(0.6302) \\
&= \$1{,}759.49
\end{aligned}
$$

TABLE 2-5

Data for Example 2-19

End of Year	Disbursement
0	—
1	200
2	200
3	200
4	200
5	200
6	200
7	400
8	400
9	400
10	400

The solution to Part b can be obtained by carrying the answer to Part a forward ten years.

$$F = 1{,}759.49(F/P\ 8{,}10)$$
$$= 1{,}759.49(2.159)$$
$$= \$3{,}798.74$$

If the answer to Part a is not available and only the future amount is required, a direct solution is

$$F = 200\ (F/A\ 8{,}6)(F/P\ 8{,}4) + 400(F/A\ 8{,}4)$$
$$= 200\ (7.336)(1.360) + 400(4.506)$$
$$= \$3{,}797.79$$

The difference in these two answers (\$0.95) is due to rounding off the interest factor values. Using the previous results, the equivalent annual amount is

$$A = P\,(A/P\ i{,}n\ )$$
$$= 1{,}759.49(A/P\ 8{,}10)$$
$$= 1{,}759.49(0.1490)$$
$$= \$262.16$$

or if the future amount is used

$$A = F(A/F\ i{,}n)$$
$$= 3{,}798.74(A/F\ 8{,}10)$$
$$= 3{,}798.74(0.0690)$$
$$= \$262.11$$

Again, the difference is due to rounding off the interest factor values.

In general, it is usually necessary to first determine either an equivalent present or future amount before an equivalent annual amount can be determined.

SOME SPECIAL CONSIDERATIONS

At this point, some special topics are considered. These topics are (1) automobile loans, (2) house mortgages, (3) bonds, and (4) inflation. These topics are considered because there usually is wide interest in them. Also, they provide additional examples of applications of the concepts presented earlier in this chapter.

Automobile Loans   Quite often the interest rates that are quoted on automobile loans are simple (add-on) interest rates. The monthly car payment is calculated by dividing the future amount, based on simple interest, by the number of monthly payments. This procedure results in a considerably larger annual compound rate than the simple interest rate. The specifics of this procedure are shown in the next example.

Example 2-20 _____

A person borrows $6,000 for an automobile loan that is to be paid back over 30 months. The loan agency quotes a simple (often, not specifically stated) interest rate of 8%. What is the effective annual compound rate paid on this automobile loan?

The monthly payment is calculated in the following manner,

$$\text{monthly payment} = \frac{P + P(n)(i)}{\text{number of months}} \qquad (2\text{-}62)$$

$$= \frac{6{,}000 + 6{,}000(2.5)(.08)}{30}$$

$$= \$240$$

The following formulation is used to calculate the effective rate

$$P = A(P/A\,i,n)$$

$$6{,}000 = 240\,(P/A\,i,30)$$

$$(P/A\,i,30) = 25$$

$$i = 1.23\% \text{ per month compounded per month}$$

Therefore, the nominal rate is

$$r = 1.23\,(12) = 14.76\% \text{ compounded monthly}$$

and the effective annual rate is

$$i = \left(1 + \frac{.1476}{12}\right)^{12} - 1$$

$$= 0.158 = 15.8\% \text{ compounded yearly}$$

House Mortgages   The manner in which house payments work
is best explained with a numerical example.

Example 2-21 _____

A person borrows $60,000 for a house loan (mortgage) that is to be
paid back in monthly payments over a period of 24 years. The
interest rate quoted on this loan is 12%. Answer the following
questions:

a. What is the monthly payment?
b. How much of the monthly payment determined in Part a is
   interest and how much is principal?

First, it is usual for the interest rate quoted on house loans to be a
nominal rate. Therefore, the 12% in this example is compounded
monthly, and the answer to Part a is

$$A = P\,(A/P\ i,n\ )$$

$$= 60,000\left(A/P\frac{12}{12}, 12(24)\right)$$

$$= 60,000\,(A/P\ 1,288\ )$$

$$= 60,000\,(0.0106)$$

$$= \$636$$

The value for the interest factor (0.0106) is not available in the interest tables and is determined in the following manner.

$$(A/P \; 1,288) \; = \; \frac{(0.01)(1+0.01)^{288}}{(1+0.01)^{288}-1}$$

The answers and calculations for Part b are shown in Table 2-6 for the first ten months. As an extension to Example 2-21, the unpaid principal at the end of the k payments, B_k, can be calculated using the relationship

$$B_k \; = \; P\,(F/P \; i,k) - A\,(F/A \; i,k) \qquad (2\text{-}63)$$

For example, the unpaid principal at the end of the tenth payment is

$$B_{10} \; = \; 60{,}000\,(F/P \; 1{,}10) - 636\,(F/A \; 1{,}10)$$

$$= \; 60{,}000\,(1.104622) - 636\,(10.4622)$$

$$= \; \$59{,}623.36$$

TABLE 2-6

Interest and Principal Payments for Example 2-21

End of Month	Payment	Interest Paid	Principal Paid	Unpaid Principal
0	—	—	—	60,000
1	636	60,000 (.01) = 600.00	636 − 600.00 = 36.00	60,000 − 36.00 = 59,964.00
2	636	59,964 (.01) = 599.64	636 − 599.64 = 36.36	59,964 − 36.36 = 59,927.64
3	636	59,927.64 (.01) = 599.28	636 − 599.28 = 36.72	59,927.64 − 36.72 = 59,890.92
4	636	59,890.92 (.01) = 598.91	636 − 598.91 = 37.09	59,890.92 − 37.09 = 59,853.83
5	636	59,853.83 (.01) = 598.54	636 − 598.54 = 37.46	59,853.83 − 37.46 = 59,816.37
6	636	59,816.37 (.01) = 598.16	636 − 598.16 = 37.84	59,816.37 − 37.84 = 59,778.53
7	636	59,778.53 (.01) = 597.79	636 − 597.79 = 38.21	59,778.53 − 38.21 = 59,740.32
8	636	59,740.32 (.01) = 597.40	636 − 597.40 = 38.60	59,740.32 − 38.60 = 59,701.72
9	636	59,701.72 (.01) = 597.02	636 − 597.02 = 38.98	59,701.72 − 38.98 = 59,662.74
10	636	59,662.74 (.01) = 596.63	636 − 596.63 = 39.37	59,662.74 − 39.37 = 59,623.37
Σ	6,360	5,983.37	376.63	—

The interest factors used in this calculation have been calculated using their respective formulas in order that rounding off errors will not be significant.

The principal paid at the end of k payments, C_k, can be calculated using

$$C_k = P - B_k \qquad (2\text{-}64)$$

For this example, the total principal paid at the end of the payments is

$$C_{10} = 60,000 - 59,623.36$$

$$= \$376.64$$

The total interest paid at the end of k payments, I_k, is given by

$$I_k = A(k) - C_k \qquad (2\text{-}65)$$

and for this example is

$$I_{10} = 636(10) - 376.64$$

$$= \$5,983.36$$

The slight differences in these answers and the values in Table 2-6 are due to rounding off various values.

Bonds   Bonds are financial instruments issued by private corporations, nonprofit organizations, and governmental organizations to obtain funds. From the standpoint of an issuing institution, a bond is a debt. From the standpoint of purchaser, a bond is an investment. Bonds are issued on the basis of a face (par or stated) value which is to be paid at the bond's maturity date (a specified number of years). In addition, certain amounts of money are paid between the time the bond is issued and its maturity date. This amount of money is usually paid either annually, semiannually, or quarterly and is a function of a contractual (bond) rate and the face value. The cash transactions resulting from the purchase of a bond are shown in Table 2-7. The negative signs in

TABLE 2-7
Cash Transactions Resulting from the
Purchase of a Bond

End of Period	Cash
0	$-P$
1	$+\dfrac{kV}{c}$
2	$+\dfrac{kV}{c}$
3	$+\dfrac{kV}{c}$
.	.
.	.
.	.
n	$+\dfrac{kV}{c} + V$

Table 2-7 indicate a cash disbursement and the positive signs indicate cash receipts. The nomenclature used in Table 2-7 is

P = the purchase price of the bond

V = the face value of the bond

k = bond contractual rate

$\dfrac{kV}{c}$ = amount (interest) received (paid) per period

c = number of periods per year

n = number of years to maturity

If the equivalent present amount of the cash receipts is set equal to the purchase price the result is

$$P = \frac{kV}{c}\left(P/A\, \frac{r}{c}, cn\right) + V\left(P/F\frac{r}{c}, cn\right)$$

(2-66)

where r is the earned nominal rate with c compounding periods.

Example 2-22

A $1,000, ten-year, 12% semiannual bond is purchased. Determine the rate of interest earned if the bond is purchased for (a) $1,000 and (b) $900.

For Part a the data is substituted into Eq. (2-66) which gives

$$1,000 = \frac{(0.12)(1,000)}{2}\left(P/A\, \frac{r}{2}, 2(10)\right) + 1,000\left(P/F\frac{r}{2}, 2(10)\right)$$

$$1,000 = 60\left(P/A\, \frac{r}{2}, 20\right) + 1,000\left(P/F\frac{r}{2}, 20\right)$$

(2-67)

In order to determine r, a trial-and-error solution is required. If r is estimated to be 12% compounded semiannually, Eq. (2-67) gives

$$1,000 = 60\ (P/A\ 6,20) + 1,000\ (P/F\ 6,20)$$
$$= 60\ (11.4699) + 1,000\ (0.3118)$$
$$= 1,000$$

This result indicates that the estimated interest rate is correct and consequently the rate of interest earned is 12% compounded semiannually (or 12.36% compounded annually). At this point, a generalization can be made. That is, if the purchase price is equal to the face value, the contractual rate (k) and the rate earned (r) are equal.

For Part b, the formulation, using Eq. (2-66), is

$$900 = \frac{(0.12)(1,000)}{2}\left(P/A\frac{r}{2}, 2(10)\right) + 1,000\left(P/F\frac{r}{2}, 20\right)$$

$$900 = 60\left(P/A\, \frac{r}{2}, 20\right) + 1,000\left(P/F\frac{r}{2}, 20\right)$$

The approach in a trial-and-error solution is to bracket the value on the left-hand side of the equality sign with values of the right-hand side at different interest rates. In the solution to Part a it is shown that at 12% compounded semiannually the value of the right-hand side is $1,000. If 14% compounded semiannually is used, the right-hand side has a value of $894.04. Consequently, using linear interpolation, the rate earned is

$$X = 12 + \frac{1,000 - 900.00}{1,000 - 894.04} \quad (2)$$

$$= 13.88\% \text{ compounded semiannually}$$

or 14.36% compounded annually. Two more generalizations can be made: (1) if $P < V$, then $r > k$ and (2) if $P > V$, then $r < k$. These generalizations provide guidelines in making initial estimates of the earned rate.

In Example 2-22 reference is made to the rate earned by the purchase of the bond. This same rate can also be interpreted as a cost to the seller of the bond. That is, in this example the seller is paying 12% compounded semiannually if the bond is sold for $1,000 or paying 13.88% compounded semiannually if the bond is sold for $900.

Inflation   As a result of economic trends in past years, the inclusion of the effects of inflation in economic analyses has received considerable attention in the literature. There are two basic methods used to include inflation in economic analyses. These methods depend on the basis upon which future dollars are estimated. They can be estimated either on the basis of (1) *actual* or (2) *real* dollars. Actual dollars, sometimes referred to as *then-current* dollars, are the actual currency (paper) transactions that are estimated to occur at some point in time. In this case, the inclusion of inflationary effects is accomplished through the use of a combined inflation and interest rate. Real dollars, sometimes referred to as *constant-worth* dollars, are dollars with the same purchasing (or payment) value as the dollars at some reference point in time which, in economic analysis, is the present time. In this case, inflation has implicitly been included. Consequently, the interest rate without adjustment for inflation is used. These definitions of actual and real dollars imply the following relationship between the two types of dollars

$$A_t = R_t (1 + e)^t \qquad (2\text{-}68)$$

where

$$A_t = \text{actual dollars at the end of } t \text{ periods}$$

$$R_t = \text{real dollars at the end of } t \text{ periods}$$

$$e = \text{inflation rate}$$

It should be noted that Eq. (2-68) assumes that the inflation rate, e, is a constant rate over t periods. With this assumption and Eq. (2-68), an equivalent present amount for a series of cash transactions based on actual dollars is

$$P = \sum_{t=0}^{n} A_t (1 + e)^{-t} (1 + i)^{-t} \qquad (2\text{-}69)$$

$$\sum_{t=0}^{n} A_t (1 + e + i + ei)^{-t} \qquad (2\text{-}70)$$

$$\sum_{t=0}^{n} A_t (1 + f)^{-t}$$

where

$$f = e + i + ei \qquad (2\text{-}71)$$

and is the combined inflation and interest rate. If real dollars are used, the equivalent present amount is

$$P = \sum_{t=0}^{n} R_t (1 + i)^{-t} \qquad (2\text{-}72)$$

Example 2-23

In order to illustrate the previous discussion of inflation, the following examples are worked. Suppose the cash transactions shown in Table 2-8 are in terms of actual dollars and it is desired to

TABLE 2-8

Cash Transactions for Example 2-23

End of Year	Cash Transaction in Actual Dollars
0	−8,000
1	3,000
2	3,500
3	4,000
4	5,000

calculate an equivalent present amount using an inflation rate of 8% and an interest (discount) rate of 15%.

Using Eq. (2-71) the combined interest and inflation rate is

$$f = 0.08 + 0.15 + (0.08)(0.15)$$

$$= 0.242$$

$$= 24.2\%$$

and using Eq. (2-70) the present worth is

$$P = -8,000 + 3,000(1 + 0.242)^{-1} + 3,500(1 + 0.242)^{-2}$$

$$+ 4,000(1 + 0.242)^{-3} + 5,000(1 + 0.242)^{-4}$$

$$= \$873$$

If the actual cash transactions given in Table 2-8 are converted to real cash transactions as shown in Table 2-9, the present worth using Eq. (2-72) is

$$P = -8,000 + 2,778(1 + 0.15)^{-1} + 3,001(1 + 0.15)^{-2}$$

$$+ 3,175(1 + 0.15)^{-3} + 3,675(1 + 0.15)^{-4}$$

$$= \$873$$

which shows that both methods give the same results.

If the inflation is not considered and the actual cash transactions are used, the equivalent present worth is

$$P = -8{,}000 + 3{,}000 (1 + 0.15)^{-1} + 3{,}500 (1 + 0.15)^{-2}$$
$$+ 4{,}000 (1 + 0.15)^{-3} + 5{,}000 (1 + 0.15)^{-4}$$
$$= \$2{,}745$$

This value of P is considerably larger than the previously obtained values and points out that in some situations the exclusion of inflationary effects could lead to incorrect decisions.

From a calculation standpoint, neither actual nor real dollars offer strong advantage at this point when including inflationary effects in economic analyses. However, whichever method is used it must be clearly understood whether estimates are in terms of actual or real dollars. The previous discussions in this chapter did not specifically mention inflation. This was done in order to facilitate the presentation of the topics considered. It can be assumed, therefore, that either the cash transactions were in the form of actual dollars and the associated interest rate included an inflation component or the cash transactions were real dollars and the associated interest rate was not adjusted for inflation.

TABLE 2-9
Conversion of Actual to Real Cash Transactions

End of Year	Actual Cash Transaction	Inflation Factor $(1 + e)^{-t}$	Real Cash Transaction
0	−8,000	1.0000	−8,000
1	3,000	0.9259	2,778
2	3,500	0.8573	3,001
3	4,000	0.7938	3,175
4	5,000	0.7350	3,675

In the previous discussion of inflation, it was assumed that the inflation and interest (discount) rate were both constant rates. Of course, these rates can change from one period to the next. If this is the case, the present value, in terms of actual dollars, is given by

$$P = \sum_{t=0}^{n} A_t \prod_{x=0}^{t} (1+e_x)^{-1} (1+i_x)^{-1} \tag{2-73}$$

Although the use of Eq. (2-73) is not difficult, it can be tedious. It also requires an estimation of the inflation and interest rates for each period. The use of Eq. (2-73) is shown in the next example.

Example 2-24

Given the data in Table 2-10, determine the present value of the actual dollar transactions.

Using Eq. (2-73) gives

$$P = 1{,}000 \ (1 + 0.05)^{-1}(1 + 0.10)^{-1}$$
$$+ 2{,}000 \ (1 + 0.06)^{-1} (1 + 0.12)^{-1} (1 + 0.05)^{-1} (1 + 0.10)^{-1}$$
$$+ 2{,}500 \ (1 + 0.07)^{-1} (1 + 0.15)^{-1} (1 + 0.06)^{-1} (1 + 0.12)^{-1}$$
$$(1 + 0.05)^{-1} (1 + 0.10)^{-1}$$
$$= \$3{,}806$$

which shows that calculations involving Eq. (2-73) can be tedious.

TABLE 2-10
Data for Example 2-24

End of Year	Actual Dollar Transaction	Inflation Rate, %	Interest Rate, %
0	—	—	—
1	1,000	5	10
2	2,000	6	12
3	2,500	7	15

Explicitly including inflation in economic analyses is a debatable issue. Some argue that differences in economic alternatives are the same with or without inflation. Or, they argue that estimates of cash transactions and the discount rate implicitly include inflationary effects. Consequently, inflationary effects can explicitly be ignored. These arguments do have merit. However, care should be taken before inflationary effects are dismissed in economic analyses.

Some additional points are required in this discussion of inflation. First, different components in an economic analysis may have different inflation rates. For example, labor costs may have a different escalation rate than, say, fuel costs. Second, there are some components that are unresponsive to inflation; namely, depreciation, lease fees, and interest charges resulting from loan agreements. Such unresponsive components are an important consideration in after-tax economic analysis.

PROBLEMS

 2-1. If a person borrows $4,000 at a simple interest rate of 8% per year, how much will be owed at the end of three years? How much of this amount is interest?

2-2. A person is informed that if he borrows $8,000 now, $10,000 will be due after four years. What simple interest rate is implied?

 2-3. If a person borrows $2,000 at a simple interest rate of 10% per year, how much will be owed at the end of six months? How much of this amount is interest?

 2-4. A person desires to have $50,000 in an account at the end of eight years. If the account pays 7% compounded annually, how much money must be deposited now?

2-5. If a person places $1,000 into an account that pays 6% compounded annually, how much money will be in the account after five years?

 2-6. In how many years will a deposit in an account that pays 6% compounded, double in value?

2-7.   If a person puts $1,000 in an account and has $1,500 in the account after five years, what compound rate of interest was earned?

 2-8.   What is the final accumulated amount resulting from a series of equal annual deposits of $3,000 for eight years if the interest rate is 10% compounded per year? Assume the first deposit is made one year from now.

 2-9.   Repeat Problem 2-8 assuming the first deposit is made now. Note, there are still only eight deposits.

 2-10.   If a person wishes to have available at the end of ten years $10,000, what equal annual deposit must be made, for ten years, into an account that pays 5% compounded annually? Assume the first deposit is made one year from now.

 2-11.   Repeat Problem 2-10 but assume that the first deposit is made now. Note, there are still only ten deposits.

 2-12.   How much money should be deposited in an account that pays 8% compounded annually in order to make six equal annual withdrawals of $2,000 with the last withdrawal exhausting the account?

2-13.   A deposit of $6,000 is made into an account that pays 6% compounded annually. What equal annual withdrawal for five years can be made with the last withdrawal exhausting the account?

 2-14.   Four years ago a person borrowed $10,000 at an interest rate of 8% compounded annually and agreed to pay it back in equal payments over a ten-year period. This same person now wants to pay off the remaining amount of the loan. How much should this person pay? Assume he has just made the fourth payment.

 2-15.   A person is considering depositing some money in a savings account. Several local banks pay different interest rates on savings accounts. If the interest rates are those given below, which bank should be chosen?
(a) 5.5% compounded per year.

(b)   5.0% compounded continuously.
(c)   5.2% compounded quarterly.
(d)   5.3% compounded semiannually.

2-16.   A local department store charges 1 1/2% per month on credit accounts. What effective annual rate is being charged?

2-17.   A person deposits $10,000 into an account that pays 8% compounded quarterly. How much money will be in the account after five years?

2-18.   Repeat Problem 2-17 assuming that the interest rate is:
(a)   8% compounded semiannually.
(b)   8% compounded continuously.

2-19.   A person wishes to have $5,000 in an account after six years. How much money must be deposited in the account now in order to have this amount if the account pays:
(a)   10% compounded quarterly.
(b)   10% compounded weekly.

2-20.   If a person borrows $2,000 and agrees to pay it back in 24 monthly installments of $105.74, determine:
(a)   The nominal interest rate paid.
(b)   The effective annual interest rate paid.
(c)   The amount of interest paid.

2-21.   What is the accumulated amount resulting from a series of equal quarterly deposits of $1,000 for five years if the interest rate is 8% compounded quarterly? Assume the first deposit is made three months from now.

2-22.   As a result of a certain debt obligation, a company must pay $10,000 a year for the next eight years. The next payment is due one year from now. The company now wants to cancel this debt over the next three years. If the interest rate is 12% compounded annually, what is the payment for the next three years?

2-23. What is an equivalent present amount for a series of equal annual amounts of $1,000 for five years if the interest rate is:
(a) 6% compounded semiannually?
(b) 6% compounded continuously?

2-24. If an equal quarterly deposit of $400 is made into an account for five years with the first deposit made three months from now, determine the amount in the account if:
(a) The interest rate is 12% compounded per quarter.
(b) The interest rate is 12% compounded continuously.

2-25. If a deposit of $4,000 is made into an account, determine the amount in the account after five years if the interest rate is:
(a) 10% compounded semiannually.
(b) 10% compounded continuously.

2-26. Determine an equivalent annual amount for the series of payments shown below using an interest rate of 9% compounded annually.

End of Year	Payment
0	1,000
1	1,000
2	1,000
3	1,000
4	2,000
5	3,000
6	4,000
7	4,000
8	4,000
9	500
10	500
11	500
12	500

2-27. Determine the equivalent present amount of a series of equal quarterly amounts of $10,000 for five years if the interest rate is 12% compounded semiannually.

2-28. If a person deposits $1,000 into an account that pays 8% compounded annually one year from now and then increases his deposits by $200 each year for the next ten years, determine the amount of money that will be in the account at the end of the ten years.

2-29. What is the equivalent present amount of an eight-year series of decreasing amounts if the interest rate is 10% compounded annually, the first year amount is $20,000, and the rate of decrease is $800 per year?

2-30. Find an equivalent present amount for the series of cash disbursements following using an interest rate of 12% compounded annually.

End of Year	Cash Disbursement
0	—
1	3,000
2	3,000
3	3,000
4	4,000
5	5,000
6	5,000
7	5,000
8	5,000

2-31. Find an equivalent present amount for the series of cash disbursements shown using the following:
(a) An interest rate of 10% compounded annually.
(b) An interest rate of 10% compounded continuously.
(c) An interest rate of 10% compounded semiannually.

End of Year	Cash Disbursement
0	—
1	5,000
2	5,000
3	5,000
4	5,000
5	8,000
6	8,000
7	8,000

2-32.   Convert the series shown below to an equivalent five-year equal amount series using an interest rate of 10% compounded annually with the first amount occurring one year from now.

End of Year	Amount
0	1,000
1	1,000
2	1,000
3	1,000
4	5,000
5	6,000
6	6,000
7	6,000
8	6,000
9	3,000
10	4,000

2-33.   A company borrows $10 million and agrees to pay it back in 20 equal yearly installments at an interest rate of 10% compounded annually. Determine the amount of interest and principal paid in each year for the first four payments.

2-34.   What is the equivalent quarterly funds-flow series for a present amount of $60,000 over ten years if the interest rate is 12% compounded continuously.

2-35.   Determine the future amount for the following funds-flow series using an interest rate of 10% compounded continuously.
(a) $2,000 per year for six years.
(b) $2,000 semiannually for five years.

2-36.   A person borrows $12,000 in order to buy an expensive automobile. If the bank makes the loan at a simple (add-on) rate of 8% for 30 equal monthly payments, determine:
(a) The monthly payment.
(b) The effective annual interest rate.

2-37.   A person pays $1,600 for a $2,000, 10% bond that matures in ten years. If the bond pays interest annually, what rate of interest does the person receive?

2-38. A $3,000 bond matures in ten years. The bond rate of interest is 12% paid quarterly. If a person buys the bond for $2,300, what effective annual rate of interest will the person receive?

2-39. A $1,000 bond that pays 8% semiannually and matures in 15 years is for sale. What is the maximum amount that should be paid for the bond if:
  (a) 12% compounded semiannually is required on bond investments?
  (b) 15% compounded annually is required on bond investments?

2-40. Given the cash transactions shown below, an inflation rate of 8% per year, and an interest rate of 10%, determine an equivalent present amount if:
  (a) The cash transactions are in terms of real dollars.
  (b) The cash transactions are in terms of actual dollars.

End of Year	Cash Transactions
0	1,000
1	1,000
2	1,000
3	1,000
4	2,000
5	2,000
6	2,000

3

DEPRECIATION

In this chapter depreciation and depreciation models are discussed. Depreciation is introduced at this point because of its relationship to taxes (discussed in the next chapter) and other future topics.

Depreciation may be considered as the reduction in value of an asset as a result of wear, deterioration, or obsolescence. Depreciation can also be considered as a procedure for the systematic recovery of capital invested in an asset (a viewpoint usually taken by the accountant). In either case, depreciation must be taken into account in economic analyses.

The estimation of *yearly* depreciation amounts either for tax or capital recovery purposes is accomplished through the use of *depreciation models*. These models are discussed in this chapter using the following nomenclature:

$P =$ capital investment (first cost, initial investment, or capital expenditure)

$n =$ depreciation life (usually in years); this is sometimes called the estimated life, useful life, or depreciation period

$L =$ salvage value; this occurs at the end of the depreciation life; it is sometimes called the final value, terminal value, or final worth

$D_j =$ depreciation amount (charge) for the year j; it can also be considered as an estimate of the capital recovered during the year j

$B_j =$ book value (unrecovered capital or undepreciated balance) at the end of year j

STRAIGHT-LINE DEPRECIATION

The straight-line depreciation model gives a constant yearly depreciation amount, and as a result, the book value decreases at a constant rate. The depreciation amount in any year, D_j is

$$D_j = \frac{(P-L)}{n} \tag{3-1}$$

and the book value at the end of year j is

$$B_j = P - \frac{j}{n}(P-L) \tag{3-2}$$

Example 3-1 _____

Using a straight-line depreciation model determine the depreciation schedule (yearly depreciation amounts and book values) for a capital asset that costs $100,000 and has a salvage value of $10,000 and a depreciation life of eight years.

Using Eq. (3-1), the yearly depreciation amounts are

$$D_j = \frac{100,000 - 10,000}{8}$$

$$= \$11,250$$

The book values are determined using Eq. (3-2) and for the first two years are

$$B_1 = 100,000 - \frac{1}{8}(100,000 - 10,000)$$

$$= \$88,750$$

$$B_2 = 100,000 - \frac{2}{8}(100,000 - 10,000)$$

$$= \$77,500$$

The entire depreciation schedule is given in Table 3-1.

TABLE 3-1
Straight Line Depreciation Schedule for Example 3-1

End of Year	Depreciation Amount	Book Value
0	—	$100,000
1	$11,250	88,750
2	11,250	77,500
3	11,250	66,250
4	11,250	55,000
5	11,250	43,750
6	11,250	32,500
7	11,250	21,250
8	11,250	10,000

At this point two useful expressions are introduced that relate depreciation amounts and book values; namely,

$$D_j = B_{j-1} - B_j \qquad (3\text{-}3)$$

$$B_j = P - \sum_{x=1}^{j} D_x \qquad (3\text{-}4)$$

These two equations are applicable regardless of the depreciation model and can be helpful when generating an entire depreciation schedule.

The term $\displaystyle\sum_{x=1}^{j} D_x$ in Eq. (3-4) represents the total accumulated depreciation through the end of the year j.

SUM-OF-THE-YEARS-DIGITS DEPRECIATION

The sum-of-the-years-digits (SYD) depreciation model provides an *accelerated* depreciation schedule. That is, yearly depreciation amounts decrease with time. The depreciation amount for the year j is given by the expression

$$D_j = \frac{(n-j+1)(P-L)}{\dfrac{n(n+1)}{2}} \qquad (3\text{-}5)$$

and the book value is given by

$$B_j = (P-L)\left(\frac{n-j}{n}\right)\left(\frac{n-j+1}{n+1}\right) + L \qquad (3\text{-}6)$$

The denominator in Eq. (3-5) provides the basis of the name sum-of-the-years-digits. For, the sum of the digits $1 + 2 + 3 + \ldots + n$ is equal to $n(n+1)/2$.

Example 3-2

Using the data given in Example 3-1 determine the depreciation schedule using the SYD depreciation model. The depreciation schedule is obtained using Eqs. (3-5) and (3-6) and is shown in Table 3-2. As examples, the depreciation amounts for the first two years are

$$D_1 = \frac{8-1+1}{8(9)/2}(100{,}000 - 10{,}000)$$
$$= \$20{,}000$$

$$D_2 = \frac{8-2+1}{8(9)/2}(100{,}000 - 10{,}000)$$
$$= \$17{,}500$$

and the book values are

$$B_1 = (100{,}000 - 10{,}000)\left(\frac{8-1}{8}\right)\left(\frac{8-1+1}{8+1}\right) + 10{,}000$$

$$= \$80{,}000$$

$$B_2 = (100{,}000 - 10{,}000)\left(\frac{8-2}{8}\right)\left(\frac{8-2+1}{8+1}\right) + 10{,}000$$

$$= \$62{,}500$$

TABLE 3-2
Sum-of-the-Years Depreciation Schedule for Example 3-2

End of Year	Depreciation Amount	Book Value
0	—	$100,000
1	$20,000	80,000
2	17,500	62,500
3	15,000	47,500
4	12,500	35,000
5	10,000	25,000
6	7,500	17,500
7	5,000	12,500
8	2,500	10,000

DECLINING-BALANCE DEPRECIATION

The declining-balance depreciation model is sometimes referred to as the *fixed-percentage* depreciation model. It is another accelerated depreciation model. In the declining-balance depreciation model the yearly depreciation amounts are determined by multiplying the book value at the beginning of the year by a constant fraction. Expressed mathematically, the depreciation amount is

$$D_j = a\, B_{j-1} \tag{3-7}$$

where a is the constant fraction. The book value at the end of year j is

$$B_j = (1 - a)^j P \qquad\qquad (3\text{-}8)$$

The yearly depreciation amounts can be directly determined by the equation

$$D_j = aP (1 - a)^{j-1} \qquad\qquad (3\text{-}9)$$

which is a result of substituting Eq. (3-8) into Eq. (3-7).

Values for a   Values for the constant fraction, a, are determined in two ways. The first way is to determine a value that will give a book value at the end of the depreciation life equal to the salvage value. Expressed mathematically, this is

$$L = (1 - a)^n P$$

which is usually written as

$$a = 1 - \sqrt[n]{\frac{L}{P}} \qquad\qquad (3\text{-}10)$$

Eq. (3-10) has some weaknesses. It cannot be used to depreciate an asset to a salvage value of zero. Also, if the salvage value is very small compared to the initial cost of the asset, the depreciation amounts in the early years can be unreasonably large. These weaknesses are not serious and can be partially overcome by the second method for determining values for a. A reasonable rate may be taken from tax regulations as long as the maximum yearly depreciation does not exceed an amount given by twice (200%) the straight-line rate. This implies that the maximum tax depreciation in any year is

$$\frac{2}{n} (P) \qquad\qquad (3\text{-}11)$$

since the straight-line rate is $1/n$. Consequently, it is common to set the value of a equal to $2/n$. If this is done, it is called a *double declining-balance* (DDB) depreciation model. Under certain circumstances specified in the tax regulations, twice the straight-line rate is not allowed. In these circumstances the rate is limited to 150% or 125% of the straight-line rate. In these cases the values of a, respectively, are $1.50/n$ and $1.25/n$. This second method also has a weakness in that it does not guarantee that the salvage value will be obtained at the end of the depreciation life. A systematic method to overcome this weakness, when it exists, is to switch over to straight-line depreciation. The switch to straight-line is made whenever the straight-line depreciation, based on the remaining undepreciated amount and life, is greater than the depreciation amount given by the double declining-balance model. This can be expressed mathematically as

$$\frac{B_{j-1}-L}{n-(j-1)} > aB_{j-1}$$

(3-12)

The basis of Eq. (3-12) is related to the present worth of taxes paid and is discussed in greater detail in the next chapter.

Example 3-3

A capital asset has an initial cost of $100,000, a salvage value of $20,000, and a depreciation life of eight years. Determine the depreciation schedule for this asset using the declining-balance model with the following rates:

a. The rate defined by Eq. (3-10).
b. The double declining rate.
c. The 125% rate with switch over to straight-line depreciation.

Using Eq. (3-10), the rate for Part a is

$$a = 1 - \sqrt[8]{\frac{20,000}{100,000}} = 0.18223$$

With this rate and Eqs. (3-7), (3-8), and (3-9) the depreciation schedule shown in Table 3-3 is obtained. For example, the depreciation amounts for the first two years are

$$D_1 = 0.18223 \ (100{,}000)$$

$$= \$18{,}223$$

TABLE 3-3

Declining-Balance Depreciation
a = 0.18223

End of Year	Depreciation Amount	Book Value
0	—	$100,000
1	$18,223	81,777
2	14,902	66,875
3	12,187	54,688
4	9,966	44,722
5	8,150	36,572
6	6,665	29,907
7	5,450	24,457
8	4,457	20,000

$$D_2 = 0.18223 \ (1 - 0.18223)^1 \ (100{,}000)$$

$$= \$14{,}902$$

and the book values are

$$B_1 = (1 - 0.18223)(100{,}000)$$

$$= \$81{,}777$$

$$B_2 = (1 - 0.18223)^2 (100{,}000)$$

$$= \$66{,}875$$

For Part b, the rate is

$$a = \frac{2}{n}$$

$$= \frac{2}{8}$$

$$= 0.2500$$

The depreciation schedule using this rate is shown in Table 3-4. Note that the depreciation amount given in year six is not the amount given by Eq. (3-7) since this equation gives

$$D_6 = 0.2500 \, (23,730)$$

$$= \$5,933$$

If this value is used for D_6 the salvage value in year six would be less than \$20,000. Consequently, the depreciation in year six is limited to the amount necessary to obtain the salvage value (\$3,730 in this case). This implies that the asset is fully depreciated at the end of six years and no further depreciation is taken. Consequently,

TABLE 3-4
Double Declining-Balance Depreciation
a = 0.2500

End of Year	Depreciation Amount	Book Value
0	—	\$100,000
1	\$25,000	75,000
2	18,750	56,250
3	14,063	42,187
4	10,547	31,640
5	7,910	23,730
6	3,730	20,000
7	—	20,000
8	—	20,000

the asset would maintain a book value equal to its salvage value (\$20,000) for the remainder of its life. Another point, quite often when DDB depreciation is used, a switch to straight-line depreciation is in order. From the standpoint of the present worth of taxes, there is no advantage in switching to straight-line depreciation if the book value at the end of an asset's depreciation life, calculated using Eq. (3-8), is less than the salvage value. Using Eq. (3-8), the book value at the end of the eighth year is

$$B_8 = (1 - 0.2500)^8 \, (100{,}000)$$

$$= \$10{,}011$$

which is less than the salvage value. In these cases, the approach is to adjust the depreciation in order to obtain the salvage value as shown in this example. However, if the book value at the end of the depreciation life is greater than the salvage value, there is a present worth advantage in switching to straight-line depreciation. This is the case in Part c.

The rate for Part c is

$$a = \frac{1.25}{8}$$

$$= 0.1563$$

Using this rate and Eq. (3-8), the book value at the end of the depreciation life is

$$B_8 = (1 - 0.1563)^8 \, (100{,}000)$$

$$= \$25{,}675$$

Since this value is greater than the salvage value, a switch to straight-line depreciation is in order. As mentioned earlier, the year that this switch is made is given by Eq. (3-12). The depreciation amounts and book values for this part of the example are given in Table 3-5. This table shows that the switch to straight-line depreciation occurs in the sixth year. The declining-balance depreciation amounts are calculated using Eq. (3-9) and the straight-line amounts are calculated using the left-hand side of

Eq. (3-12). For example, the straight-line amounts for the first two years are

$$\frac{100,000 - 20,000}{8} = \$10,000$$

$$\frac{84,370 - 20,000}{7} = \$9,196$$

SINKING-FUND DEPRECIATION

Sinking-fund depreciation is based on a series of equal annual deposits over the depreciation life that are equal to the

TABLE 3-5

Declining-Balance Depreciation with Switchover to Straight-Line Depreciation

$a = 0.1563$

End of Year	Depreciation Comparison		Final Depreciation	Book Value
	Declining-Balance	Straight Line		
0	—	—	—	$100,000
1	$15,630	$10,000	$15,630	84,370
2	13,187	9,196	13,187	71,183
3	11,126	8,531	11,126	60,057
4	9,387	8,011	9,387	50,670
5	7,921	7,668	7,921	42,749
6	6,682	7,583	7,583	35,166
7	—	—	7,583	27,583
8	—	—	7,583	20,000

depreciable amount (initial cost minus salvage). That is, an equal annual amount, A, that is equal to

$$A = (P - L)(A/F \ i,n) \tag{3-13}$$

where n is the depreciation life and i is some specified interest rate. The depreciation amount in any year consists of the sinking-fund deposit given by Eq. (3-13) and interest on the accumulated fund. The resulting expression, after algebraic simplification is,

$$D_j = (P - L)\ (A/F\ i,n)\ (F/P\ i,\ (j-1)) \qquad (3\text{-}14)$$

The book value is given by

$$B_j = P - (P - L)\ (A/F\ i,n)\ (F/A\ i,j) \qquad (3\text{-}15)$$

The sinking-fund depreciation model assumes that an asset depreciates at an increasing rate. Consequently, it is rarely used for tax computations. However, it is used on occasion by governmental agencies and thus is included in this text.

Example 3-4

Determine the depreciation schedule for an asset that has an initial cost of $100,000, a salvage value of $10,000, and a depreciation life of eight years using sinking-fund depreciation and an interest rate of 12%.

The depreciation schedule is calculated using Eqs. (3-14) and (3-15) and is shown in Table 3-6.

Sample calculations follow for the first two years.

$$D_1 = (100,000 - 10,000)\ (A/F\ 12,8)(F/P\ 12,0)$$

$$= (90,000)(0.0813)(1.000)$$

$$= \$7,317$$

$$D_2 = (100,000 - 10,000)(A/F\ 12,8)(F/P\ 12,1)$$

$$= 90,000\ (0.0813)\ (1.12)$$

$$= \$8,195$$

TABLE 3-6
Sinking-Fund Depreciation

End of Year	Depreciation Amount	Book Value
0	—	$100,000
1	$7,317	92,683
2	8,195	84,488
3	9,176	75,312
4	10,280	65,032
5	11,517	53,515
6	12,893	40,622
7	14,444	26,178
8	16,178	10,000

USAGE DEPRECIATION

In the previous depreciation models, depreciation is based entirely on time. In some instances, depreciation models are based on usage. In these instances, the yearly depreciation amount is calculated by

$$D_j = \frac{P - L}{U} (U_j)$$

$$(3-16)$$

where U is the total usage expected during the lifetime of the asset and U_j is the usage during the year j. The units of U and U_j depend on the type of asset. For example, earth-moving equipment often uses cubic yards. For tax purposes, depreciation amounts are calculated at the end of a particular year since U_j must be the *actual* usage. If a depreciation schedule is to be determined from the standpoint of estimating capital recovery, then yearly values for U_j must be estimated.

Example 3-5

A certain piece of earth-moving equipment has an initial cost of $75,000, a salvage value of $10,000, and an estimated lifetime usage of two million cubic yards of earth. Determine the depreciation amount for a particular year if the usage is 80,000 cubic yards.

The depreciation amount using Eq. (3-16) is

$$D_j = \frac{75,000 - 10,000}{2,000,000} (80,000)$$

$$= \$2,600$$

CAPITAL RECOVERY AND RETURN

In economic analyses the recovery of the invested capital and a return on the yearly unrecovered capital must be included. This is analogous to loaning money. The principal (invested capital) must be recovered as well as interest (a return). If it is assumed that the yearly depreciation amounts equal the yearly amounts of capital recovered, then the yearly capital recovery and return $(CR)_j$ is

$$(CR)_j = D_j + (i)B_{j-1} \tag{3-17}$$

where i is the rate of return on the unrecovered capital. If Eq. (3-17) and a 10% return are applied to the values given in Table 3-1, the results shown in Table 3-7 are obtained. An equivalent annual amount of the capital recovery and return ECR, is

$$\begin{aligned} ECR = \ &(21,250 \, (P/F \ 10,1) + 20,125 \, (P/F \ 10,2) \\ &+ \ldots + 13,375 \, (P/F \ 10,8)) \, (A/P10,8) \end{aligned}$$

$$= (95,335)(0.1875)$$

$$= \$17,875$$

If this same approach is taken with the values given in Table 3-2, the results given in Table 3-8 are obtained. The equivalent annual amount for the capital recovery and return amounts in Table 3-8 is

$$\begin{aligned} ECR = \ &(30,000 \, (P/F \ 10,1) + 25,500 \, (P/F \ 10,2) \\ &+ \ldots + 3,750 \, (P/F \ 10,8)) \, (A/P \ 10,8) \end{aligned}$$

$$= \$17,875$$

TABLE 3-7

Capital Recovery and Return
(Straight-Line Depreciation)

End of Year	Capital Recovery (Depreciation)	Capital Unrecovered (Book Value)	Return on Unrecovered Capital	Capital Recovery and Return
0	—	$100,000	—	—
1	$11,250	88,750	$10,000	$21,250
2	11,250	77,500	8,875	20,125
3	11,250	66,250	7,750	19,000
4	11,250	55,000	6,625	17,875
5	11,250	43,750	5,500	16,750
6	11,250	32,500	4,375	15,625
7	11,250	21,250	3,250	14,500
8	11,250	10,000	2,125	13,375

TABLE 3-8

Capital Recovery and Return
(SYD Depreciation)

End of Year	Capital Recovery (Depreciation)	Capital Unrecovered (Book Value)	Return on Unrecovered Capital	Capital Recovery and Return
0	—	$100,000	—	—
1	$20,000	80,000	$10,000	$30,000
2	17,500	62,500	8,000	25,500
3	15,000	47,500	6,250	21,250
4	12,500	35,000	4,750	17,250
5	10,000	25,000	3,500	13,500
6	7,500	17,500	2,500	10,000
7	5,000	12,500	1,750	6,750
8	2,500	10,000	1,250	3,750

which is the same value obtained using straight-line depreciation. Further, if the ECR is calculated using the relationship

$$ECR = (P - L)(A/P \ i,n) + L(i) \qquad (3\text{-}18)$$

the result is

$$ECR = (100,000 - 10,000)(A/P \ 10,8) + 10,000 \ (.10)$$
$$= 90,000 \ (0.1875) + 1,000$$
$$= \$17,875$$

which also gives the same result as the previous two cases. In fact, the same result (\$17,875) is obtained regardless of the depreciation model. That is, Eq. (3-18) *is independent of the depreciation model.* Consequently, Eq. (3-18) provides a convenient method for determining the *equivalent* annual amount of capital recovery and return. Eq. (3-18) is particularly useful in making cost comparisons and replacement studies (topics discussed later). It is introduced at this point because of its relationship to depreciation.

PROBLEMS

3-1.   Using straight-line depreciation, determine the depreciation schedule for an asset that has an initial cost of \$80,000, a salvage value of \$8,000, and a depreciation life of nine years.

3-2.   Using straight-line depreciation, determine the depreciation schedule for an asset that has an initial cost of \$64,000, a salvage value of zero, and a depreciation life of eight years.

3-3.   Using sum-of-the-years-digits depreciation, determine the depreciation schedule for an asset that has an initial cost of \$100,000, a salvage value of \$10,000, and a depreciation life of nine years.

3-4.   Using sum-of-the-years-digits depreciation, determine the depreciation schedule for an asset that has an initial cost of \$165,000, a salvage value of zero, and a depreciation life of ten years.

3-5. Using sinking-fund depreciation, determine the depreciation schedule for an asset that has an initial cost of $90,000, a salvage value of $9,000, and a depreciation life of eight years. Assume $i = 12\%$.

3-6. Repeat Problem 3-5 using a salvage value of zero.

3-7. Using declining-balance depreciation, determine the depreciation schedule for an asset that has an initial cost of $80,000, a salvage value of $10,000, and depreciation life of ten years. Use Eq. (3-10) for the rate.

3-8. Repeat Problem 3-7 using double declining-balance depreciation and a switch to straight-line depreciation on the basis of Eq. (3-12).

3-9. Using double declining-balance depreciation, determine the depreciation schedule for an asset that has an initial cost of $80,000, a salvage value of zero, and a depreciation life of ten years. Switch to straight-line depreciation on the basis of Eq. (3-12).

3-10. Using usage depreciation and the estimated yearly usage given below, determine the depreciation schedule for an asset that has an initial cost of $100,000, a salvage value of $10,000, and an estimated lifetime usage of 5.5 million pounds.

Year	Estimated Usage (Pounds)
1	1,000,000
2	2,000,000
3	500,000
4	1,000,000
5	1,000,000

3-11. If an asset has an initial cost of $30,000, a salvage value of $6,000, and a depreciation life of 20 years, determine the depreciation amount for the fourth year using:
(a) Straight-line depreciation.
(b) Sum-of-the-years-digits depreciation.
(c) Sinking-fund depreciation with $i = 10\%$.

(d) Declining-balance depreciation using Eq. (3-10) for the rate.

(e) Double declining-balance depreciation.

3-12. Determine the book values at the end of the fourth year using the data given in Problem 3-11.

3-13. Determine the estimated annual amounts of capital recovery plus a 12% return for the data given in Problem 3-5. Using these results, calculate an equivalent annual amount and check this result with the value obtained from Eq. (3-18).

3-14. Repeat Problem 3-13 using the data given in Problem 3-8 and a return of 10%.

3-15. Repeat Problem 3-13 using the data given in Problem 3-9 and a return of 10%.

3-16. Repeat Problem 3-13 using the data given in Problem 3-10 and a return of 10%.

3-17. If an asset has an initial cost of $100,000, a salvage value of $10,000, and a depreciation life of ten years, determine the following:

(a) The estimated capital recovery plus a 10% return for the fourth year assuming sum-of-the-years-digits depreciation.

(b) The equivalent capital recovery plus a 10% return for the fourth year assuming sum-of-the-years-digits depreciation.

4

SOME TAX
CONSIDERATIONS

This chapter presents some tax considerations that have a direct influence on some of the topics and calculations in subsequent chapters. It is not meant to be an all—inclusive discussion of taxes, but, rather, a foundation on which to include (or, at least, approximate) some of the more pertinent tax effects in economic studies.

There are considerable similarities between the basic tax regulations for individuals and corporations. However, at the same time, there are considerable differences. This chapter emphasizes the tax regulations as related to corporations. It does not consider tax regulations pertaining to individuals.

Tax regulations change from year to year. Consequently, the current tax regulations should be consulted to determine the applicability of some of the topics and values discussed and used in this chapter.

FEDERAL TAXES

Income Taxes   Federal income taxes are assessed on the taxable income (net earnings) of corporations. At present the tax rates are

15% for taxable income of $50,000 or less
25% for taxable income over $50,000 and up to $75,000
34% for taxable income over $75,000 and up to 100,000
39% for taxable income over $100,000 up to 335,000
34% for taxable income over 335,000

For example, the tax on a taxable income of $60,000 is

$$t = 50,000 \ (.15) + (60,000 - 50,000) \ (.25) = \$10,000$$

which implies an overall tax rate, T, of

$$T = \frac{10,000}{60,000} = .1667 = 16.67\%$$

The tax on $200,000 is

$$
\begin{aligned}
t &= 50,000 \ (.15) + 25,000 \ (.25) + 25,000 \ (.34) \\
&\quad + (200,000 - 100,000) \ (.39) \\
\\
&= \$61,250
\end{aligned}
$$

and implies an overall tax rate of

$$T = \frac{61,250}{200,000} = .30625 = 30.625\%$$

It should be noted that a taxable income above $335,000 implies an overall (flat) tax rate of 34%. For example, the taxes on $400,000 are

$$
\begin{aligned}
t &= 50,000 \ (.15) + 25,000 \ (.25) + 25,000 \ (.34) \\
&\quad + (335,000 - 100,000) \ (.39) \\
&\quad + (400,000 - 335,000) \ (.34) \\
\\
&= \$136,000
\end{aligned}
$$

This same value ($136,000) could be obtained by simply multiplying the taxable income of $400,000 by 34%.

Perhaps the more difficult aspect of corporate income taxes is the determination of the taxable income. For the purposes of this text, it is sufficient to say that taxable income, I_f, is

$$I_f = (G - C - D_t - I) \qquad (4\text{-}1)$$

where

G = gross income (receipts, sales, revenue)

C = cost of goods sold and other deductions; the cost of goods sold includes labor, materials, and other costs associated with the items sold. Other deductions might include certain taxes, advertising costs, executive salaries, etc.

D_t = tax depreciation allowance

I = interest paid on debt obligations (mortgages, bonds, etc.)

The cost of goods sold (C) implies just that. That is, the costs associated only with the items sold and not, necessarily, the total costs in the tax period. For example, if a company manufactures 10,000 items in a particular tax period but only sells 8,000 of these items, then only the costs "directly" associated with these 8,000 items are deductible in computing the taxable income. The other 2,000 items become a part of the company's finished-goods inventories, and when they are sold their associated costs are deductible. Actually, the cost of goods sold is related to the problem of the valuation of inventories. A problem that is discussed quite extensively in most accounting texts, and consequently, is not discussed further in this text. Also, the 2,000 items not sold in this example may result in a net increase in the working capital requirements of the company. The concept of working capital and its inclusion in economic studies is discussed in later chapters.

CAPITAL GAINS AND LOSSES

Under present federal tax regulations, certain types of property, called capital assets, are given special (not, necessarily, desirable) tax treatment when sold. Capital assets include nondepreciable assets, stocks, bonds, securities, etc. Essentially, capital assets are property but do not include the following:

1. Inventories
2. Property held primarily for sale to customers in the ordinary course of the taxpayer's trade or business
3. Depreciable business property
4. Real property used in business (business real estate)

The tax regulations concerning some of the preceding four exclusions are discussed later.

When capital assets are sold for more or less than their original cost, a capital gain or loss occurs. If the capital asset is held for one year or less, it is called a short-term gain or loss. If the asset is held for over a year, it is called a long-term capital gain or loss.

Long-term gains and losses are determined for each sale of a capital asset and then added together to determine whether a net long-term gain or loss is the result. Short-term gains and losses are treated in the same manner. The net results of these two combinations are then merged to determine the tax treatment of the gains and losses. Obviously, there are several combinations of gains and losses that can occur. These combinations and their tax treatment are shown in Table 4-1.

TABLE 4-1
Tax Treatment of Capital Gains and Losses

Result of Long-Term Transactions	Result of Short-Term Transactions	Net Result	Capital Gain	Capital Loss	Ordinary Income
Long-term loss	None	Long-term loss		X	
	Short-term gain	Long-term loss		X	
		or			
		Short-term gain			X
	Short-term loss	Long-term loss		X	
		and			
		Short-term loss		X	
Long-term gain	None	Long-term gain	X		
	Short-term gain	Long-term gain	X		
		and			
		Short-term gain			X
	Short-term loss	Long-term gain	X		
		or			
		Short-term loss		X	
None	Short-term gain	Short-term gain			X
	Short-term loss	Short-term loss		X	

For corporations, a net result denoted as a capital gain in Table 4-1 means the net result can be treated either as ordinary income and taxed at the corporation's income tax rate or the net result can be taxed at a maximum rate of 34%. The choice is up to the corporation. For corporations having a taxable income less than $335,000 a comparison of the two possibilities must be made to determine which provides the least taxes. Corporations having a taxable income greater than $335,000 will choose the 34%.

For corporations, the difference between long- and short-term capital gains has little effect. At present, all capital gains (short or long term) are taxed at a corporation's regular tax rate with a maximum rate of 34% as applied to the gains.

A corporation can offset its capital gains with losses. If in a particular year there is a loss, it is only applicable to other gains. That is, the loss is subject to the carryback (three years) and carryover (five years) provisions and can only be applied to capital gains in those years. When carried back or forward, the loss is treated as a short-term loss regardless of whether it was a short- or long-term loss when it actually occurred. There are some exceptions (Secs. 1245 & 1250 property) to these tax regulations that are discussed in the next section.

At this point and in later discussions, a question that might be asked is, why continue the definitions of long- and short-term gains and losses if both long- and short-term gains are taxed at the same rate? One answer to this question is, by maintaining the long- and short-term classification in the tax regulations, it facilitates rate changes in the future.

Example 4-1 _____

If a corporation has a taxable income of $50,000 before the following long-term and short-term capital transactions, determine the total tax. Values in parentheses indicate losses.

Transaction	Long-Term	Short-Term
1	$10,000	—
2	5,000	—
3	(3,000)	—
4	4,000	—
5	—	6,000
6	—	(7,000)

The result of the long-term transactions is a net gain of $16,000 and the result of short-term transactions is a net loss of $1,000. Therefore, the net result is a capital gain of $15,000. The tax can be computed two ways:

Solution 1:
total taxable income = 50,000 + 15,000 = $65,000
tax = 50,000 (.15) + (65,000 – 50,000) (.25) = $11,250

Solution 2:
tax = (50,000) (.15) + (15,000) (.34)
= $12,600

Obviously, the corporation would choose Solution 1 since the taxes are the least. As another example, consider the data given previously except the corporation's taxable income is $400,000. In this case, the taxes are

$$
\begin{aligned}
t \quad = \quad & 50,000 \,(.15) + 25,000 \,(.25) + 25,000 \,(.34) \\
& + (335,000 - 100,000) \,(.39) + (400,000 - 335,000) \,(.34) \\
& + 15,000 \,(.34) \\
\\
= \quad & \$141,100
\end{aligned}
$$

which is the same result that would be obtained if the $15,000 is considered to be ordinary income (a taxable income of $415,000).

DISPOSAL OF DEPRECIABLE PROPERTY AND BUSINESS REAL ESTATE

The gains and losses from the disposal of depreciable property used in a business (company) can be an important tax consideration in economic studies. These types of gains and losses for a corporation are treated differently than the capital gains and losses discussed previously. The tax treatment on gains and losses from the disposal of depreciable property depends on three sections of the tax laws. These sections are Sec. 1245 Property, Sec. 1250 Property, and Sec. 1231 Assets.

Section 1245 property is depreciable property that is either (1) personal property (tangible or intangible), or (2) other tangible property (not including a building or its structural components) used as an integral part of (a) manufacturing, (b) production, (c) extraction, or (d) the furnishing of transportation, communications, electrical energy, gas, water, or sewage disposal services. This definition implies that the vast majority of equipment, facilities, and property included in the usual analysis of investment alternatives is 1245 property. The exceptions are buildings and their structural components.

Basically, the tax treatments of gains and losses from Sec. 1245 property are shown in Figure 4-1. The meaning of this figure is explained in the following example.

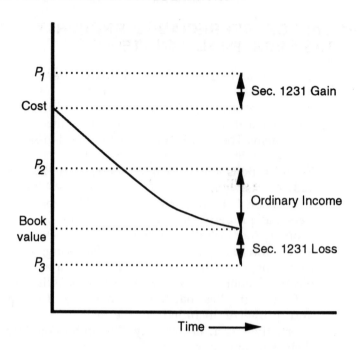

FIGURE 4-1   Gains and Losses from Section 1245 Property

Example 4-2

Suppose a Sec. 1245 asset was purchased January 1, 1987 for $100,000 and the total depreciation taken for tax purposes in years 1987 through 1990 was $42,000; determine the tax effects if the selling price is $65,000, $110,000, and $40,000. The present tax book value for this asset is

$$100,000 - 42,000 = \$58,000$$

Therefore, in the case of a selling price of $65,000, the following amount is taxable as ordinary income

$$65,000 - 58,000 = \$7,000$$

Actually, the tax regulations define the amount taxable as ordinary income as the "excess of depreciation deducted" and implies the following calculation: The present book value should be the selling price ($65,000). Therefore, the total depreciation for years 1987 through 1990 should have been

$$100,000 - 65,000 = \$35,000$$

Consequently, the excess depreciation is

$$42,000 - 35,000 = \$7,000$$

In either case, the result ($7,000) is the same.
    If the selling price is $110,000, then the amount

$$100,000 - 58,000 = \$42,000$$

is classified as ordinary income and the amount

$$110,000 - 100,000 = \$10,000$$

is classified as a Sec. 1231 gain.
    If the selling price is $40,000, then the amount

$$58,000 - 40,000 = \$18,000$$

is classified as a Sec. 1231 loss. This loss ($18,000) under Sec. 1231 is discussed later.

Section 1250 property basically includes buildings and their structural components and also all other property not considered as Sec. 1245 property. Basically, the tax regulations state that any "excess depreciation" plus a 20% recapture is taxed as ordinary income and any remaining amount is taxed as a Sec. 1231 gain. These regulations are explained in the following example.

Example 4-3

A company completes construction of a new building (1250 property) at a cost of $1,000,000 and chooses sum-of-the-years depreciation with a life of 30 years and a salvage of $100,000. Determine the tax effect if the building is sold after 4 years for $850,000, $950,000, and $600,000.

TABLE 4-2

Year	Depreciation Deduction	Straight-Line Depreciation	Excess Depreciation
1	$58,065	$30,000	$28,065
2	56,129	30,000	26,129
3	54,194	30,000	24,194
4	52,258	30,000	22,258
Total	220,646	120,000	100,646

First determine the depreciation amounts that have been deducted using sum-of-the-years depreciation. These amounts are shown as the second column in Table 4-2. The next step is to determine the depreciation amounts based on straight-line depreciation. This value is

$$\frac{1,000,000 - 100,000}{30} = \$30,000$$

The excess depreciation in Table 4-2 is the difference between the actual depreciation deducted and the straight-line depreciation.

The book value for the building is

$$1,000,000 - 220,646 = \$779,354$$

Therefore, the gain on the selling price of $850,000 is

$$850,000 - 779,354 = \$70,646$$

This total amount, $70,646, would be ordinary income since the gain is less than the total of the excess depreciation ($100,646).

Now, if the selling price is $950,000, the gain is

$$950,000 - 779,354 = \$170,646$$

Of this gain, $100,646 plus the 20% recapture, shown below, would be

$$\text{recapture} = (170,646 - 100,646)\,(.2)$$

$$= \$14,000$$

classified as ordinary income ($114,646). The remaining amount would be a Sec. 1231 gain

$$Sec. \ 1231 \ gain = 170{,}646 - 114{,}646$$

$$= \$56{,}000.$$

If the selling price is $600,000, then the amount

$$779{,}354 - 600{,}000 = \$179{,}354$$

is considered a Sec. 1231 loss.

Section 1231 The tax regulations contain special provisions for depreciable business property and business real estate. Under this section, all Sec. 1231 gains and losses are separately grouped. If the gains exceed the losses, each gain and loss is treated as though it were derived from the sale of a long-term capital asset. If the gains do not exceed the losses, each gain and loss is treated as though it were not derived from the sale of a capital asset. In effect, this allows the net 1231 gains on the disposal of properties used in trade or business to be treated as long-term capital gains. On the other hand, when Sec. 1231 losses exceed the Sec. 1231 gains, the net loss is a deduction in ordinary income.

Example 4-4

A company purchased a Section 1245 asset for $120,000, and after five years the same asset had a book value of $80,000. If the company's current taxable income is $400,000 before consideration of the gains and losses from the sale of this asset, determine the company's total taxes for the following selling prices of the 1245 asset: (a) $100,000, (b) $70,000, and (c) $200,000.

The taxes on the current taxable income are

$$t = 400{,}000 \ (.34) = \$136{,}000$$

For Part a, a selling price of $100,000 means a gain of

$$100{,}000 - 80{,}000 = 20{,}000$$

This gain is treated as ordinary income (see Figure 4-1). Consequently, the total taxes are

$$t = 136{,}000 + 20{,}000 \,(.34)$$

$$= \$142{,}800$$

An incremental tax rate of 34% is used since the company's current taxable income is greater than \$335,000.

For Part b, a selling price of \$70,000 means a loss of

$$80{,}000 - 70{,}000 = \$10{,}000$$

Since this is Section 1245 property, Section 1231 applies and this loss can be taken as an ordinary loss. Consequently, the company's taxes are

$$t = 136{,}000 - 10{,}000 \,(.34)$$

$$= \$132{,}600$$

For part c, a selling price of 200,000 means a Section 1231 gain of

$$200{,}000 - 120{,}000 = \$80{,}000$$

and ordinary income of

$$120{,}000 - 80{,}000 = \$40{,}000$$

Consequently, the company's taxes are

$$t = 136{,}000 + 40{,}000 \,(.34) + 80{,}000 \,(.34)$$

$$= \$176{,}800$$

The Section 1231 gain of \$80,000 is taxed at a 34% rate since it is the current capital gains rate. The difference between the original cost (\$120,000) and the book value (\$80,000) is taxed as ordinary income due to the requirements of Section 1245. It is difficult to show the implications of Section 1231 gains since the current tax rate for ordinary income and capital gains are currently the same (34%), assuming a taxable income over $335,000. To show the implications of 1231 gains, suppose the capital gains rate is 28% (it was, some time back). The taxes for Part c of this would be

$$t = 136,000 + 40,000 (.34) + 80,000 (.28)$$

$$= \$172,000$$

In this example, the taxes are calculated on the basis that only one Section 1245 asset was sold. If more than one is sold, the Section 1231 gains and losses are combined to determine the tax treatment.

Since it is very unlikely (if not impossible) to know future Sec. 1231 transactions, a convention is used in this text. This convention treats 1231 gains as long-term capital gains and 1231 losses as deductions from ordinary income

TAX DEPRECIATION

Depreciation is deductible when calculating taxable income. It provides an allowance for the wear and tear of property used in the production of income. Depreciation is not allowed for property used for pleasure, inventories, stock-in-trade, or land. Over the years, tax regulations regarding depreciation allowances have undergone several changes. During more recent times, depreciation allowances have evolved from the Class Life Asset Depreciation Range System (ADR) through the Accelerated Cost Recovery System (ACRS) to the present modified Accelerated Cost Recovery System (MACRS).

Modified Accelerated Cost Recovery System (MACRS) The MACRS is required for most tangible depreciable property placed in service after 1986. It establishes depreciation periods of 3, 5, 7, 10, 15, 20, 27.5, and 31.5 years. The depreciation period depends on the type of property and the ADR class life (midpoint of the ADR range) as of January 1, 1986. Table 4-3 gives the MACRS depreciation periods for various types of property.

Under MACRS, property is depreciated over the periods given in Table 4-3 using the applicable convention for the first year's depreciation. Basically, depreciation for 3, 5, 7, and 10 years uses 200% (double) declining balance with a switch to straight line and a zero salvage value. For 15 and 20 years, the MACRS uses 150%

TABLE 4-3
MACRS Depreciation Periods

MACRS Period	ADR Midpoint (M)	Some Examples
3	$M \leq 4$	special devices and tools for the manufacture of various products
5	$4 < M < 10$	computers and peripheral equipment manufacture of knitted goods manufacture of chemicals manufacture of electronic products
7	$10 \leq M < 16$	office furniture and fixtures manufacture of tobacco manufacture of wood products manufacture of rubber products manufacture of motor vehicles manufacture of aerospace products
10	$20 \leq M < 25$	manufacture of primary steel mill products petroleum refining manufacture of sugar manufacture of grain
15	$20 \leq M < 25$	manufacture of cement telephone control office equipment electric utility nuclear production plants liquified natural gas plants pipeline transportation
20	$20 \leq M < 25$	manufacture gas production plants electric utility steam production plants water utilities municipal sewers
27.5	M not applicable	residential real property
31.5	$M \geq 27.5$	non-residential real property

declining balance with a switch to straight line and a zero salvage value. Years 27.5 and 31.5 use straight line depreciation with a zero salvage value. With these depreciation methods, the depreciation rates shown in Table 4-4 are given in the tax regulations. The ranges in Table 4-4 use the half-year convention for the first year's depreciation. There are other conventions for the first year. Especially, if more than 40% of the property is placed in service during the last three months of the tax year. These other conventions are not provided in this book but are available in the tax regulations. Also, in Table 4-4, only the ranges for 5, 7, 10, and 15-year property are provided since these are considered to be most applicable for future discussions.

TABLE 4-4
MACRS Depreciation Rates

Year	5 Years	7 Years	10 years	15 years
1	20.00	14.29	10.00	5.00
2	32.00	24.49	18.00	9.50
3	19.20	17.49	14.40	8.55
4	11.52	12.49	11.52	7.70
5	11.52	8.93	9.22	6.93
6	5.76	8.92	7.37	6.23
7	–	8.93	6.55	5.90
8	–	4.46	6.55	5.90
9	–	–	6.56	5.91
10	–	–	6.55	5.90
11	–	–	3.28	5.91
12	–	–	–	5.90
13	–	–	–	5.91
14	–	–	–	5.90
15	–	–	–	5.91
16	–	–	–	2.95

Example 4-5

If certain equipment is classified as 5-year property and its initial cost is $200,000, determine the yearly depreciation amounts and book values under MACRS. Using Table 4-4, the required values are shown in Table 4-5.

INVESTMENT TAX CREDIT

As in the case of depreciation procedures, the investment tax credit has undergone changes in recent years. *In fact, the investment tax credit has been repealed for property placed in service after 1985.* However, it is possible that it may be resurrected in the future. Consequently, some basics of past investment tax credit regulations are presented at this point. Also in future discussions, the investment tax credit may be included. In these ways, if the investment tax credit reappears, a method for including it in the calculation of cash flows and revenue requirements (discussed later) is available.

TABLE 4-5
Solution for Example 4-5

Year	Depreciation	Book Value
0	–	$200,000
1	.20 (200,000) = 40,000	160,000
2	.32 (200,000) = 64,000	96,000
3	.192 (200,000) = 38,400	57,600
4	.1152 (200,000) = 23,040	34,560
5	.1152 (200,000) = 23,040	11,520
6	.0576 (200,000) = 11,520	0

TABLE 4-6
Investment Tax Credit (1981)

Life	Proportion of Full Allowance (10%)
7 Years of More	Full
5 and 6	$\frac{2}{3}$
3 and 4	$\frac{1}{3}$
Less than 3	None

TABLE 4-7
Investment Tax Credit Allowances (1985)

Life	Proportion of Full Allowance (10%)	Alternative Allowance
5 Years or More	Full	8%
4 and 3	60%	4%
Less than 3	0	0%

In the past, there was a credit against federal income tax for qualified property (Sec. 38 property). The credit was, in general, 10% of the qualified property. In order to qualify for the full 10% credit, the life of the depreciable property had to be seven years at one time and five years for later tax regulations. For lives less than seven or five years, only a certain proportion was allowed. Tables 4-6 and 4-7 show these proportions. If the property qualified under Table 4-6, the depreciation basis for the property was not reduced. However, if the property qualified under Table 4-7, a choice was available. The investment tax credit could be taken as 10% (assuming five years) by reducing the depreciable basis by one-half of the investment tax credit. Or, the investment tax credit could be taken as 8% without reducing the depreciable basis.

In addition to an investment tax credit, there was the possibility of an investment tax penalty if Sec. 38 property was disposed of before the end of its useful life. Under the tax laws, the tax for the year of disposal was increased by the difference between the originally allowed investment tax credit and the investment tax credit that would have been allowed with the shorter useful life. As an example (using Table 4-6), an asset that is sold after 4 years of service that originally cost $12,000 and had a 10-year useful life would result in a tax increase of $800 in the year it is sold as a result of the investment tax penalty. This value of $800 is based on the difference between the investment tax credit originally taken, $(0.10)(12,000) = \$1,200$, and the credit that should have been taken, $(0.10)(1/3)(12,000) = \$400$, because of a useful life of only four years. The possibility of an investment tax penalty was an important consideration in replacement analysis.

OTHER TAXES

In many economic studies, it is not unusual to find income tax rates that are higher than a company's incremental federal tax rate. This is done for two major reasons. One reason is to protect against possible increases in future tax rates. The other reason is to provide an approximation for some of the following tax effects.

State Income Taxes   The assessment of state taxes on corporate income varies from state to state; not only do the rates vary, but also the computation of the taxable base. However, it is desirable to include (or, at least, approximate) state income taxes in economic studies since these taxes are, now, a significant proportion of a company's costs. The usual procedure (and the one taken in this text) is to use a composite rate that reflects both state and federal income tax.

Property Taxes (Ad Valorem Taxes)   These taxes can be levied by states, counties, cities, and school districts. The tax is usually a percentage of the property's assessed valuation. The assessed valuation may or may not be the initial investment due to adjustments for nontaxable items. In economic studies, the usual procedure is to estimate property taxes as a constant percentage of the initial investment. The applicable percentage is, of course, dependent on the geographical location of the property.

Sales Taxes   Sales taxes are paid by a company on material and equipment purchases. The amount of the tax will vary with location. In many economic studies, sales taxes are omitted because the amount of these taxes are relatively small in comparison to other amounts in the study.

Franchise Taxes   Franchise taxes are assessed on the basis of a constant percentage of gross revenues (income). In economic studies such as cost comparisons that assume equal incomes, franchise taxes are usually omitted because they are the same for all alternatives. If gross revenues are not the same, then franchise taxes should be included (strictly speaking). However, they are often omitted because, they too, are relatively small when compared to other costs.

Payroll Taxes   The payroll component of operating and maintenance expenses is subject to taxes for Social Security, unemployment insurance, and Worker's Compensation. These taxes can be as high (maybe higher by now) as 30% of regular labor costs. The usual procedure is to include these taxes as a part of labor and maintenance overhead. Therefore, since overhead is a part of labor and maintenance estimates, these taxes are usually implied in economic studies. In general, these taxes are deductible in computing federal taxes. However, they may or may not be deductible in computing state taxes depending upon whether or not federal taxes are deductible in computing state taxes.

ECONOMIC STUDIES AND TAXES

The majority of economic studies concerns the evaluation and comparison of projects (investments). In this text, this evaluation and comparison is based on the concept that each new expenditure of money must, in some manner, justify itself, implying an *incremental analysis*. Consequently, it is from this standpoint that taxes are included in future problems and examples—the incremental changes in taxes that may occur as a result of the projects under consideration.

To some extent, an incremental approach simplifies the introduction of taxes into economic studies, i.e., federal and state income taxes, investment tax credit. However, there are other tax considerations where this is not the case. For example, the true tax effect from the retirement of a particular item of depreciable property (Sec. 1245 or 1250 property) depends on such things as the gains and losses from the retirements of property other than the particular item under consideration, past gains and losses, and whether or not the retirement is classified as an ordinary or extraordinary retirement. As a result of these considerations, it is necessary, at times, to use certain conventions and assumptions when including taxes in economic studies. These assumptions and conventions are stated when specific topics are discussed in later chapters.

TAXES AND DEPRECIATION

It can be seen from Eq. (4-1) that the amount of depreciation deducted has a direct effect on the amount of taxes paid in a particular year. Consequently, accelerated depreciation models offer an advantage because the depreciation amounts in the earlier years are greater than in later years and, thereby, reduce the *present worth* of taxes paid. This point is illustrated in Tables 4-8, 4-9, and 4-10. Note that the total taxes paid are the same over the six-year period. However, the present worth of the taxes are different. Tables 4-8, 4-9, and 4-10 use a depreciation life of five years, an initial cost of $12,000 and a zero salvage value. Because the half-year convention is used, the depreciation amounts extend over a period of six years. An arbitrary discount rate of 12% is used in these tables to calculate the present worth of the taxes.

TABLE 4-8
Income Taxes Using Straight-Line Depreciation

End of Year	Depreciation	Taxable Income Before Depr.	Taxable Income	Tax T = 34%
0	–	–	–	–
1	1,200	4,000	2,800	952
2	2,400	4,000	1,600	544
3	2,400	4,000	1,600	544
4	2,400	4,000	1,600	544
5	2,400	4,000	1,600	544
6	1,200	4,000	2,800	952
Σ	12,000	–	–	4,080

Present Worth of Taxes = $2,808

TABLE 4-9
Income Taxes Using MACRS Depreciation

End of Year	Depreciation	Taxable Income Before Depr.	Taxable Income	Tax T = 34%
0	–	–	–	–
1	2,400	4,000	1,600	544
2	3,840	4,000	160	54
3	2,304	4,000	1,696	577
4	1,382	4,000	2,618	890
5	1,382	4,000	2,618	890
6	692	4,000	3,308	1,125
Σ	12,000	–	–	4,080

Present Worth of Taxes = $2,581

TABLE 4-10
Income Taxes Using Sum-of-Year Depreciation

End of Year	Depreciation	Taxable Income Before Depr.	Taxable Income	Tax T = 34%
0	–	–	–	–
1	2,000	4,000	2,000	680
2	3,600	4,000	400	136
3	2,800	4,000	1,200	408
4	2,000	4,000	2,000	680
5	1,200	4,000	2,800	952
6	400	4,000	3,600	1,224
Σ	12,000	–	–	4,080

Present Worth of Taxes = $2,598

TAXES AND INTEREST

The interest paid on externally borrowed funds is deductible as a business expense in computing company income taxes. The net effect is to reduce the actual cost of borrowed funds. For example, if a company has a taxable income of $500,000, its taxes are

$$t = 500,000(.34)$$
$$= \$170,000$$

Now, if the company borrows $100,000 at 10% for one year, its interest is $10,000 and its taxes are reduced to

$$t = 170,000 - 10,000(.34) = \$166,600$$

Consequently, the actual cost of the borrowed money is

$$10,000 - (170,000 - 166,600) = \$6,600$$

meaning that the actual (after tax) interest rate on the borrowed money is

$$\frac{6,600}{100,000} = .066 = 6.6\%$$

This same result can also be obtained in the following manner,

$$10(1 - .34) = 6.6\%.$$

This simple example points out that the "cost" of borrowed funds is appreciably reduced because interest is deductible in computing taxes.

PROBLEMS

4-1. At the end of a tax year, the ABC Company has the following data:

gross receipts (sales)	$100,000
cost of goods sold	25,000
tax depreciation	6,000
book depreciation	5,000
interest on debt	1,000

Determine the company's tax liability and effective tax rate.

4-2. Repeat problem 4-1 only multiply all given values by ten.

4-3. What is a company's tax liability and effective tax rate for a taxable income of $300,000?

4-4.   A company has a taxable income of $500,000 before
        consideration of long-term and short-term transactions.
        With the transactions shown in the table below, determine
        the following (not Sec. 1245 or 1250 property):
        (a) Total tax liability for the year
        (b) The tax liability if the $4000 and $3000 amounts under
            short-term are losses.
        (c) The tax liability if the $4000, $3000, and $8000
            amounts under long-term are losses.
        (d) The tax liability if all long-term transactions are
            losses.

Transaction	Long-Term	Short-Term
1	$4,000	—
2	3,000	—
3	8,000	—
4	1,000	—
5	6,000	—
6	—	$4,000
7	—	3,000
8	—	2,000
9	—	1,000

4-5.   A company establishes a depreciation account for an asset
        that is classified as Sec. 1245 property. The account is based
        on the MACRS with a life of seven years and an initial cost
        of $150,000. Without consideration of the sale of this asset,
        the company's taxable income is $700,000. Determine the
        following if the asset is sold after four years:
        (a) the federal tax liability if the asset is sold for
            $100,000
        (b) same as part (a) only the selling price is $30,000
        (c) same as part (a) only the selling price is $160,000

4-6.   For the situation described in Problem 4-5 with the
        exception that the asset is classified as Sec. 1250 property,
        determine the following:
        (a) the federal tax liability if the asset is sold for $70,000
        (b) the federal tax liability if the asset is sold for $30,000

(c) the federal tax liability if the asset is sold for $85,000 and assuming there are no past Sec. 1231 losses

4-7.   Using the 1981 investment tax credit, determine the following:
(a) the investment credit for $15,000,000 of qualified (Sec. 38) assets with a 10-year life
(b) the investment tax penalty if the asset is sold after four years

4-8.   Repeat Problem 4-7 only use the 1985 investment tax credit assuming the company will reduce its depreciable basis by one-half the investment tax credit.

5

THE ECONOMIC EVALUATION OF A SINGLE PROJECT

This chapter discusses various methods for determining the economic desirability of a *single* project (investment). That is, the decision alternative is either *accept* or *not accept* the project. Methods for choosing alternatives in problems that involve a comparison (ranking) of competing projects (cost comparisons, replacement analysis, and capital budgeting) are discussed in later chapters.

The specific methods discussed in this chapter for determining the economic desirability of a project are internal rate of return (IRR), net present value (NPV), and payout (payback) period. There are other methods proposed to economically evaluate projects such as the benefit-cost ratio. A review of some of these methods is also presented in this chapter.

Basically the methods for evaluating the economic desirability of a single investment are very similar to the evaluation of a loan. A company loans money, usually called *invested capital*, to a project, and the project, in turn, returns the monetary surplus of the incomes and various costs resulting from the project's activities to the company. This monetary surplus is called *net cash flow*. The net cash flow and invested capital are transformed into a rate of return (or some other criterion). This rate of return is then compared to a *required* rate of return called the *minimum acceptable (attractive) rate of return* (MARR) or *the hurdle rate*. In general, if MARR is less than the project's rate of return, the project is economically desirable.

THE MINIMUM ACCEPTABLE RATE OF RETURN

A company obtains its capital (funds) to invest in projects from primarily two sources: (1) debt sources and (2) equity sources. Debt capital is obtained by borrowing money from institutions (banks and insurance companies) *external* to the company and from the sale of company bonds. Equity capital is obtained through the sale of common stock and retained earnings (profits not paid in the form of dividends to stockholders). Each of these two types of capital has an associated cost. These costs are referred to as the *cost of debt capital* and the *cost of equity capital* and are usually expressed as an interest rate. In general, the cost of equity capital is larger than the cost of debt capital. These two costs of capital are combined to define a *weighted before-tax cost of capital*. Expressed mathematically, this weighted cost of capital is

$$k_b = w_e k_e + w_d k_d \qquad (5\text{-}1)$$

where

$$
\begin{aligned}
k_b &= \text{before-tax weighted cost of capital} \\
k_e &= \text{cost of equity capital} \\
k_d &= \text{cost of debt capital} \\
w_e &= \text{proportion of equity capital} \\
w_d &= \text{proportion of debt capital}
\end{aligned}
$$

Since the interest paid on debt capital is a tax deduction, a weighted after-tax cost of capital, k_a, can be defined as

$$k_a = w_e k_e + (1-T) w_d k_d \qquad (5\text{-}2)$$

where T is the company's incremental tax rate. *From the standpoint of evaluating proposed (new) projects*, the costs of capital and proportions indicated in Eqs. (5-1) and (5-2) should be based on a company's plans for raising capital to finance new projects over some finite planning period. The basis should not be current or past values unless current proportions and capital costs are considered to be a true representation of future financing policy. When Eq. (5-2) is used as a basis for establishing a MARR value that is to be used in the economic evaluation of projects, the inclusion of the term $(1-T)$ implies certain assumptions regarding the method of debt payment. These assumptions are discussed later.

Equations (5-1) and (5-2) are often written in terms of a debt ratio (c) where the debt ratio is the proportion of debt capital to be raised for a group of projects. That is, c is substituted for w_d, and since only two sources of capital are considered

$$w_d + w_e = 1.00 \qquad (5\text{-}3)$$

and therefore

$$w_e = 1 - c \qquad (5\text{-}4)$$

consequently, Eq. (5-1) can be written as

$$k_b = (1-c)\,k_e + c\,k_d \qquad (5\text{-}5)$$

and similar substitutions can be made in Eq. (5-2).

An Important Point (Assumption)   The previous discussion of cost of capital and debt ratio provides in part a foundation for a discussion of the debt ratio as it relates to the manner in which a *particular* project is financed. A *particular project* may be financed entirely by debt capital, entirely by equity capital, or some combination of debt and equity capital that is *not in agreement* with the debt ratio of the total monies being obtained for *a group of new projects*. In these cases, the question is, what debt ratio should be used for purposes of evaluating the economic desirability of a particular project? One answer might be the debt ratio of the project, and another might be the planned debt ratio of the total capital being raised for all new projects. In actuality, both answers are correct. For a company could obtain, for a period of time, the debt ratio of the total capital funds required for a group of projects by financing early projects entirely by debt and later projects by equity (or vice versa). Or a company could finance each project strictly in accordance with the debt ratio of the total capital being raised. Both approaches give the same result; namely, the desired debt ratio of the total capital committed to a group of projects at the end of some period of time. However, many times capital used to finance new projects is raised in "blocks" of money, and the proportions of debt and equity money used to finance a particular project are not known. In these cases the planned debt ratio of the total capital funds should be used in the evaluation of a particular project so long as the debt ratio remains constant. If the debt ratio is changed at some point in time (when another block of money is obtained), a revised debt ratio is used. Since using the debt ratio of the total capital avoids the problem of determining how a particular project is financed, the convention taken in this text is to use the debt ratio that represents the planned debt ratio of the total capital being raised for all projects. In capital budgeting problems that involve the comparison of acceptable projects this convention is highly desirable. It allows the comparison of projects on an equitable basis, namely, the same debt ratio. In practice the debt ratio is not difficult to determine because many companies raise money in accordance with their existing debt ratios. This approach of using a planned debt ratio does not preclude the actual use of a different combination of debt and equity capital once a project is determined to be acceptable (assuming there are no undesirable short-term effects such as interim dividend payments).

The Cost of Debt Capital The cost of debt capital is the interest rate paid for externally borrowed money. It is relatively easy to determine since it is usually explicitly stated when a loan is made or it can be calculated knowing the amount borrowed and the payment schedule (see Examples 2-20 and 2-22). Some care must be taken when determining the cost of debt capital. It must be the *actual* cost of the debt capital. Many times, the stated interest rate on a loan and the actual rate being paid are not the same due to the procedure of discounting loans. Also, the cost of debt capital should be expressed as an effective annual rate since it is in this context that it is most often used.

The Cost of Equity Capital   The cost of equity capital is more conceptual than the cost of debt capital. Furthermore, a great deal of controversy exists concerning the determination of the cost of equity capital, and it appears unlikely that complete unanimity will ever exist. However, it is generally accepted that there *is* a cost of equity capital and its purpose is to make economic decisions in the best interest of the stockholders. It is used to achieve one of the basic objectives of a company's management; namely, the maximization of the stockholders' wealth. One often cited approximation for determining the cost of equity capital is the Gordon-Shapiro growth model. (See references at the end of the chapter.) This model is a dividend valuation model that incorporates a growth factor and can be expressed mathematically as

$$k_e = \frac{d}{p} + br$$

(5-6)

where

$$k_e = \text{cost of equity capital}$$

$$d = \text{current dividends per share of common stock}$$

$$p = \text{current market value per share of common stock}$$

$$b = \text{proportion of earnings retained} = \frac{y - d}{y}$$

$$y = \text{after-tax earnings per share}$$

$$r = \text{return on book value} = \frac{y}{B}$$

$$B = \text{book value per share of common stock}$$

$$br = \text{growth factor}$$

Example 5-1

A company is currently paying a dividend of $5.00 per share, and the current market value for a share of its common stock is $40.00. In addition, the company's current financial report shows the following data:

$$
\begin{aligned}
\text{after-tax earnings} &= \$\ 3{,}500{,}000 \\
\text{total assets} &= \$20{,}000{,}000 \\
\text{liabilities} &= \$\ 5{,}000{,}000 \\
\text{number of common stock} &= \quad 500{,}000
\end{aligned}
$$

Determine the company's cost of equity capital.
The earnings per share are

$$
y = \frac{3{,}500{,}000}{500{,}000}
$$

$$
= \$7.00
$$

and the book value per share is

$$
B = \frac{\$20{,}000{,}000 - 5{,}000{,}000}{500{,}000}
$$

$$
= \$30.00
$$

The return on book value is

$$
r = \frac{7.00}{30.00}
$$

$$
= 0.233
$$

and the proportion of retained earnings is

$$
b = \frac{7.00 - 5.00}{7.00}
$$

$$
= 0.286
$$

Using Eq. (5-6), the return on equity is

$$k_e = \frac{5}{40} + (0.286)(0.233)$$

$$= 0.192$$

$$= 19.2\%$$

The cost of capital serves as a practical foundation upon which the MARR is based. In practice the cost of capital is adjusted (increased) to obtain the MARR. This adjustment is a result of risk considerations. The amount of the adjustment is often a result of the type of project under consideration. Consequently, it is not unusual to find a company with different MARR values for different types of projects. For example, a company might have a higher MARR value for projects involving new products than the MARR value for the expansion of existing production facilities.

The previous discussion of the cost of capital and MARR is not meant to be a comprehensive discussion. In actuality the theories and methods for determining the cost of capital and MARR are far beyond the scope of this text. In this text the discussion of cost of capital introduces the concepts of debt and equity capital to show how they are involved in the economic analysis of projects, once their cost values are determined. For an in-depth discussion of cost of capital the references at the end of this chapter should be consulted.

NET CASH FLOW

All of the methods mentioned earlier for evaluating the economic desirability of a project are related to the concept of net cash flow. It is important at this point to define net cash flow. From the standpoint of evaluating a project, the net cash flow is the algebraic sum of money estimated to flow in and out of a company over some period of time as a result of a particular project. *Incremental* cash flows occur as a result of the project. The sign convention used in this chapter is to designate cash inflows positive and cash outflows negative. The net cash flows are usually evaluated for each year of the project's life. It is then assumed that these yearly amounts occur as discrete amounts at the end of their respective year (end-of-year convention). This assumption allows the use of discrete interest factors and introduces very little, if any, error in the evaluation.

Net cash flows can be defined in three ways. The first way defines cash flows on the basis of returns to equity capital. The second way defines cash flows on the basis of returns to the total investment and the third way defines cash flows as operating cash flows. These three definitions, under certain circumstances, can be used to determine the economic desirability of projects. Mathematically, the equity net cash flows can be defined as

$$X_{ej} = (G_j - C_j - I_j) - (G_j - C_j - I_j - D_j)T$$
$$- K_j + L_j + B_j - P_j \pm W_j + V_j \tag{5-7}$$

The total cash flows can be defined as

$$X_j = (G_j - C_j) - (G_j - C_j - D_j)T$$
$$- K_j + L_j \pm W_j + V_j \tag{5-8}$$

and the operating cash flows can be defined as

$$X_{oj} = (G_j - C_j) - (G_j - C_j - D_j - I_j)T$$
$$- K_j + L_j \pm W_j + V_j \tag{5-9}$$

The components in Eqs. (5-7), (5-8), and (5-9) are defined as follows:

X_{ej} , X_j and X_{oj} are, respectively, the net equity, total, and operating cash flows at the end of year j. The basic difference between these cash flows is that Eq. (5-7) provides for the explicit recovery of debt capital while Eqs. (5-8) and (5-9) seemingly (but not actually) omit debt capital. Also, interest is included in the tax term in Eq. (5-9).

G_j = gross income (savings, receipts, revenues) at the end of year j. Gross income could be the result of the selling price per unit multiplied by the expected volume of sales in year j. It should be clearly understood that the G_j, used in the cash flow definitions, is expected to be *actually realized*. It is subject to taxation after applicable tax deductions (interest, depreciation, costs, etc.). In Eqs. (5-7), (5-8), and (5-9), G_j does *not represent potential gross income* such as in finished-goods inventories, which are a working capital consideration (discussed later).

C_j = *the total yearly cost associated with the gross income* (G_j). As used in Eqs. (5-7), (5-8), and (5-9), the yearly cost *does not include depreciation* since it is not a cash flow. It includes such items as labor, material, and applicable overhead expenses that are associated with the realization of the corresponding income (G_j). The value used for a C_j is not necessarily the total of all the costs incurred in the year j. For example, some of the costs incurred in a given year might be the result of the purchase of raw materials expected to be needed by the project under consideration in later years. In this case only the cost of the raw materials associated with G_j is included in C_j. The remaining amount is a working capital consideration. Also, *debt interest is not included* in C_j since it is considered separately.

W_j = *net increase (or decrease) in working capital in year* j. This value is negative if a particular project requires a net increase in working capital. It is positive if a project results in a net decrease in working capital or if there is a recovery of working capital. Many types of projects require significant changes in working capital as a result of meeting payrolls, paying other current costs, accounts receivable, and inventories (raw materials, in-process, and finished goods). The usual case is to have working capital requirements increase cash outflows in the beginning years of a project. The exception is to have some project that decreases working capital requirements as a result of increased efficiency. The inclusion of working capital considerations in cash flows is important since its omission can lead to incorrect conclusions regarding the desirability of a project.

I_j = *debt interest paid in year* j. This is the increase in debt interest as a result of the project under consideration. It is directly related to the amount borrowed (B_j) to finance the project and the principal payments (P_j). This text considers four methods for the repayment of borrowed money. They are (1) a single payment of principal and interest, (2) a constant interest payment, (3) a constant principal payment, and (4) a constant yearly payment of interest and principal. In order to use Eqs. (5-7) and (5-9) the specific yearly amounts of interest and principal must be separated and known since interest is a tax deductible item and principal is not tax deductible. In order to show the four methods for repayment of debt the following example is worked.

V_j = *investment tax credit in year* j. This is included when tax laws allow and the amount is based on the tax depreciation period.

Example 5-2 _____

If $40,000 is borrowed for five years at an interest rate of 10%, determine the yearly interest and principal payments for the following methods of repayment:

a. Single payment of principal and interest.
b. Constant interest payment.
c. Constant principal payment.
d. Constant payment.

In Part a the total payment at the end of five years is

$$40,000 \ (F/P \ \ 10,5)$$

$$40,000 \ (1.611) \ = \ \$64,440$$

which means that the interest and principal payments in year five are

$$P_5 = \$40,000$$

$$I_5 = \$64,440 - 40,000$$

$$= \$24,440$$

and the interest and principal payments in years one through four are zero. The interest and principal payment schedule is shown in Table 5-1.

In Part b the constant interest paid in years one through five is

$$40,000 \ (0.10) \ = \ \$4,000$$

and the principal is paid in one lump sum ($40,000) in year five. The interest and principal payment schedule is shown in Table 5-1.

TABLE 5-1
Four Methods for Debt Payment

End of Year	Interest Payment	Principal Payment	Total Payment	End of Year	Interest Payment	Principal Payment	Total Payment
0	$0	$0	$0	0	$0	$0	$0
1	0	0	0	1	4,000	0	4,000
2	0	0	0	2	4,000	0	4,000
3	0	0	0	3	4,000	0	4,000
4	0	0	0	4	4,000	0	4,000
5	24,440	40,000	64,440	5	4,000	40,000	44,000

a. Single Payment of Debt and Interest				b. Constant Interest Payment			

End of Year	Interest Payment	Principal Payment	Total Payment	End of Year	Interest Payment	Principal Payment	Total Payment
0	$0	$0	$0	0	$0	$0	$0
1	4,000	8,000	12,000	1	4,000	6,552	10,552
2	3,200	8,000	11,200	2	3,345	7,207	10,552
3	2,400	8,000	10,400	3	2,624	7,928	10,552
4	1,600	8,000	9,600	4	1,831	8,721	10,552
5	800	8,000	8,800	5	959	9,593	10,552

c. Constant Principal Payment				d. Constant Payment			

In Part c, the constant principal payment is

$$\frac{40,000}{5} = \$8,000 \text{ per year}$$

and the interest is assessed on the unpaid principal. Consequently, the interest for years one and two are

$$I_1 = 40,000 \ (0.10)$$
$$= \$4,000$$
$$I_2 = (40,000 - 8,000)(0.10)$$
$$= \$3,200$$

The method used in determining the specific yearly interest and principal payment for Part d is basically the same as the method used for house mortgages (see Example 2-21). However, in this example it is done on a yearly basis rather than the monthly basis used in the house mortgage example. The total constant yearly payment of interest and principal is

$$40{,}000 \ (A/P \ 10{,}5)$$

$$40{,}000 \ (0.2638) = \$10{,}552$$

The interest for the first year is

$$40{,}000 \ (0.10) = \$4{,}000$$

and the principal payment is

$$10{,}552 - 4{,}000 = \$6{,}552$$

Similarly, the interest for the second year is

$$(40{,}000 - 6{,}552) \ (0.10) \ = \ \$3{,}345$$

and the principal paid is

$$10{,}552 - 3{,}345 = \$7{,}207$$

The remaining values for principal and interest are given in Table 5-1.

D_j = *tax depreciation amount for year j*. The tax depreciation schedule must be determined. Various depreciation models are discussed in Chapter 3.

K_j = *total capital expenditure (investment, cost) in year j*. This is the total amount of money spent on capital assets that are required by the project in year j.

T = *incremental tax rate*. In the cash flow equations, the tax rate is assumed to be constant over the life of the project. This is the usual assumption. However, this assumption is not required. The tax rate could be varied if considered applicable. In practice the tax rate is often adjusted in order to approximate both federal and state income taxes.

L_j = *salvage value received in year j.* This is the salvage value of the capital assets. It is usually assumed that these values are recoverable at the end of the depreciation period except in cases where the tax depreciation period is shorter than the life of the project. In these cases another convention is used. This convention is shown and discussed in a later example.

B_j = *the amount of borrowed money received in year j.* This is the amount of money borrowed from external sources (loans from bank, sale of company bonds, etc.) used to finance the capital expenditure. As mentioned earlier, in the context of evaluating the incremental equity cash flows, B_j is directly related to I_j and P_j. B_j is often referred to as the *debt capital* required by the project. The *equity capital* required by the project in year j, K_{ej}, is the difference between the total capital, K_j and the borrowed money. That is,

$$K_{ej} = K_j - B_j \qquad (5\text{-}10)$$

P_j = *the principal payment provision in year j.* This is often referred to as the recovery of the debt capital (B_j) required by the project. In actuality the payment (reduction) of the principal may or may not be made. This is a management decision. However, a provision for the recovery of the debt capital must be *explicitly* included in the definition of net cash flow if *equity* cash flows are used.

c = *debt ratio.* This is not specifically included in the cash flow definitions; however, it is implied. The debt ratio expresses the amount of total capital (K_j) that is financed by debt as a percentage. That is,

$$B_j = c K_j \qquad (5\text{-}11)$$

and, consequently,

$$K_{ej} = (1-c)K_j \qquad (5\text{-}12)$$

Eqs. (5-11) and (5-12) imply the convention mentioned previously regarding the debt ratio; that is, to use the debt ratio of the total capital funds as the basis for separating debt and equity capital when evaluating a particular project.

THE INTERNAL RATE OF RETURN

The internal rate of return (IRR) is the interest rate that makes the sum of the discounted cash flows equal zero. This definition is true for the three definitions of cash flow. However, the interpretation of the IRR is different for the three definitions of cash flow (discussed later). Mathematically, the IRR is determined from the equation

$$0 = \sum_{j=0}^{n} \frac{X'_j}{(1 + i)^j}$$

(5-13)

where

$$
\begin{aligned}
X'_j &= \text{net cash flow in year } j \text{ defined by either} \\
&\quad \text{Eq. (5-7), (5-8), or (5-9)} \\
n &= \text{number of years of cash flow} \\
j &= \text{the year in which the cash flow, } X'_j \\
&\quad \text{occurs} \\
i &= \text{IRR} = \text{the internal rate of return}
\end{aligned}
$$

Example 5-3 _____

A company is considering a project that has an initial expenditure of $100,000 and a salvage value of $10,000 at the end of ten years. It is estimated that this initial expenditure will increase gross incomes and costs by, respectively, $40,000 and $10,000 per year for the next ten years. The company's tax rate is 40%; and for tax purposes the initial expenditure will be depreciated on a straight-line basis. Assuming no working capital considerations or investment tax credit, determine the following:

a. The yearly total cash flows and the corresponding internal rate of return.
b. The yearly equity cash flows and the corresponding internal rate of return. Assume the debt ratio is 40% and the debt is to be paid in ten equal principal installments with interest assessed on the unpaid balance at a cost of 10%.

For Part a, Eq. (5-8) is used to define the cash flows. Since straight-line depreciation is specified, the tax depreciation is a constant yearly value of

$$D_j = \frac{100,000 - 10,000}{10}$$

$$= \$9,000$$

Applying Eq. (5-8) to the data gives the cash flow for year zero (the beginning of the first year) as

$$X_0 = -\$100,000$$

For year one, the cash flow is

$$X_1 = (40,000 - 10,000) - (40,000 - 10,000 - 9,000)(.40)$$

$$= \$21,600$$

The remaining cash flows are given in Table 5-2. In order to solve for the internal rate of return, Eq. (5-13) is applied to the cash flows in Table 5-2.

$$0 = -100,000 + 21,600 (1 + i)^{-1} + \ldots$$
$$+ 21,600 (1 + i)^{-10} + 10,000 (1 + i)^{-10}$$

Since in this case most of the cash flows are constant, a more efficient way to solve for the internal rate of return is by the formulation

$$0 = -100,000 + 21,600 (P/A \ i,10) + 10,000 (P/F \ i,10)$$

which gives

$$i = IRR = 17.91\%$$

TABLE 5-2
Total Net Cash Flows for Example 5-3

End of Year	Capital Exp. & Salvage	Gross Income	Costs	Depreciation	Total Cash Flows
0	$100,000	—	—	—	–$100,000
1	—	$40,000	$10,000	$9,000	21,600
2	—	40,000	10,000	9,000	21,600
3	—	40,000	10,000	9,000	21,600
4	—	40,000	10,000	9,000	21,600
5	—	40,000	10,000	9,000	21,600
6	—	40,000	10,000	9,000	21,600
7	—	40,000	10,000	9,000	21,600
8	—	40,000	10,000	9,000	21,600
9	—	40,000	10,000	9,000	21,600
10	10,000	40,000	10,000	9,000	21,600 + 10,000

In order to obtain this value (17.91%) a trial-and-error procedure is used. This procedure involves "bracketing" the internal rate of return. That is, determining two interest rates that give positive and negative results for Eq. (5-13) and then using linear interpolation to obtain the IRR. Of course, the closer these two interest rates are, the better the approximation. Using this case as an example, 15% gives

$$-100,000 + 21,600 \ (P/A \ 15,10) + 10,000 \ (P/F \ 15,10) = \$10,878$$

and 20% gives

$$-100,000 + 21,600 \ (P/A \ 20,10) + 10,000 \ (P/F \ 20,10) = \$-7,827$$

Therefore, the IRR is between 15% and 20% and using linear interpolation, the IRR is

15%	10,878
IRR	0
20%	–7,827

$$IRR = 15 + \frac{10,878}{18,705} \quad (5)$$

$$= 17.91\%$$

For Part b, Eq. (5-7) is used to define the cash flows. The problem statement indicates that the amount of debt money is

$$B_0 = 100,000 \ (0.4)$$
$$= \$40,000$$

Therefore, the principal payments in years one through ten are

$$P = \frac{40,000}{10}$$
$$= \$4,000$$

and the interest amounts for the first two years are

$$I_1 = 40,000 \ (0.10)$$
$$= \$4,000$$
$$I_2 = (40,000 - 4,000)(0.10)$$
$$= \$3,600$$

The interest payments for the remaining years are given in Table 5-3. With this data and the depreciation schedule obtained in Part a, the equity cash flows are determined. For example, the equity cash flows in years zero and one are

$$X_{e0} = -100,000 + 40,000$$
$$= -\$60,000$$
$$X_{e1} = (40,000 - 10,000 - 4,000) -$$
$$(40,000 - 10,000 - 4,000 - 9,000)(.40)$$
$$- 4,000$$
$$= \$15,200$$

TABLE 5-3
Net Equity Cash Flows for Example 5-3

End of Year	Capital Expenditure and Salvage	Gross Income.	Costs	Depre-ciation	Debt Money	Debt Recovery	Interest	Equity Cash Flows
0	$100,000	—	—	—	$40,000	—	—	$60,000
1	—	$40,000	$10,000	$9,000	—	$4,000	$4,000	15,200
2	—	40,000	10,000	9,000	—	4,000	3,600	15,440
3	—	40,000	10,000	9,000	—	4,000	3,200	15,680
4	—	40,000	10,000	9,000	—	4,000	2,800	15,920
5	—	40,000	10,000	9,000	—	4,000	2,400	16,160
6	—	40,000	10,000	9,000	—	4,000	2,000	16,400
7	—	40,000	10,000	9,000	—	4,000	1,600	16,640
8	—	40,000	10,000	9,000	—	4,000	1,200	16,880
9	—	40,000	10,000	9,000	—	4,000	800	17,120
10	10,000	40,000	10,000	9,000	—	4,000	400	27,360[a]

[a]includes $10,000 salvage value

The remaining equity cash flows are given in Table 5–3. The internal rate of return is

$$0 = -60,000 + 15,200 \ (P/F \ i,1) + \ldots + 27,360 \ (P/F \ i,10)$$

where

$$i = IRR$$

$$= 23.94\%$$

Decision Criterion for the IRR
The economic desirability of a project (capital investment) is determined by making a comparison of the IRR and the MARR. In making this comparison a very important point must be realized. *The correct MARR value to use in the comparison and the definition of cash flow is dependent.* The MARR value could be based on a weighted cost of capital as defined either by Eq. (5-1) or Eq. (5-2). The MARR value could also be based strictly on the cost of equity capital (k_e). If equity cash flows are used, Eq. (5-7), the resulting IRR is the *return on equity capital.* Consequently, it must be compared with a MARR that is based on

the *required* return on equity (equity cost of capital). If total cash flows, Eq. (5-8), are used, the resulting IRR is the return on the *total investment* and should be compared to a MARR value based on a cost of capital defined by Eq. (5-2). However, if Eq. (5-2) is used in conjunction with total cash flows, certain assumptions, suggested earlier, are implied as a result of the $(1 - T)$ term included in Eq. (5-2). The implied assumptions are (1) the payment of the debt obligation is spread over the life of the project and (2) the interest is a constant yearly amount. Consequently, the after-tax cost of capital defined by Eq. (5-2) is only an *approximation* for other methods of debt payment. This point must be realized since the return on equity does vary with the manner in which debt payments (interest and principal) are made. It is possible, therefore, for the return on equity and return on total investment to give conflicting results regarding the acceptability of a project. If operating cash flows are used, the MARR value should be based on a cost of capital given by Eq. (5-5). Since operating cash flows explicitly include interest in the tax term, the use of Eq. (5-2) for operating cash flows would result in taking the interest deduction twice. This dependency between definitions of cash flow and MARR must be clearly understood.

The manner in which the MARR and IRR values are compared for decision purposes depends on the form of the cash flow series under consideration. This book chooses to distinguish between a traditional and a nontraditional cash flow series. *A traditional cash flow series* is defined as a series of cash flows comprised of at least one negative cash flow *followed* by at least one positive cash flow and whose algebraic total, at a discount rate of zero, is positive. Note that this definition of a traditional cash flow series allows only *one sign change* in the cash flow series. A *nontraditional cash flow series* is defined as a series of cash flows that do not qualify as a traditional cash flow series. Although the definition of a traditional cash flow series may appear limiting, a series of traditional cash flows is by far the most usual case in the analysis of capital investments. For decision purposes an investment giving a series of traditional cash flows is considered acceptable if the IRR is equal to or greater than MARR (IRR $\geq$ MARR). Otherwise, the investment is unacceptable. This decision criterion does imply the assumption (condition) that the capital required by the investment could be invested in other economic endeavors and earn the value of MARR. The decision criterion for a nontraditional cash flow series is discussed later.

This text takes the point of view that equity cash flows should be the basic criterion for the evaluation of capital projects either from the standpoint of IRR or net present value (discussed later). This point of view is taken because, as previously stated, the principal objective of a company's management is to maximize the equity shareholder's wealth (in conjunction with the objective of survival). Consequently, the critical figure in the economic analysis of investments is the return on equity capital. It is true that the use of equity cash flows requires some knowledge (approximation) regarding the manner in which the debt obligation is recovered. However, this is not a difficult problem. Any one of the methods for debt payment shown in Table 5-1 could be used. Some might be more appropriate than others. For example, if the debt funds are largely a result of a bond issue, then the constant interest method might be applicable. If the debt funds are largely a result of borrowing from institutions (banks, insurance companies) or mortgages, then the constant payment or constant principal methods might be applicable. In general, it would be a rare circumstance for the single payment method to be applicable except in cases of short-term debt obligations. From the combined standpoints of separating and calculating interest and principal payments and providing for an *annual* recovery of the debt capital, the constant principal method is perhaps the easiest and the most appropriate.

A final point in regard to Example 5-3. The IRR for the equity cash flows (23.94%) is higher than the IRR for the total cash flows (17.91%). This result can be generalized. That is, if the quantities G_j, C_j, D_j, K_j and L_j remain the same, the return on equity will be higher. This also implies that as the debt ratio increases, the return on equity will increase. This is one reason why companies are inclined to use some mix of debt and equity capital to finance projects even though the companies might have the money to finance projects entirely by equity funds.

Another Interpretation of the IRR   Equation (5-13) provides a mathematical definition of the IRR. A better insight to the meaning of the IRR is obtained by considering the calculations in Table 5-4. If the IRR is calculated for the cash flows in Table 5-4, the result is

$$0 = -20,000 + 4,463 \, (P/A \, i,6) + 1,000 \, (P/F \, i,6)$$
$$i = \text{IRR}$$
$$= 10\%$$

Using this IRR as the return on the yearly unrecovered capital, the total capital is recovered over the six-year period as shown in Table 5-4. Thus, another interpretation of the IRR is that it is the rate of return earned each year on the unrecovered capital which allows for the full recovery of the capital over the life of the project. Another way of interpreting the IRR is that it is the rate of return earned on the company's "loan" of $20,000 to the project and the project's return of the net cash flows to the company.

There exists a persistent misconception regarding the IRR. Namely, that in order to earn the IRR, the cash flows must be reinvested at the IRR. This is an incorrect statement. By comparison, if a person loans $20,000 and is paid back the cash flows in Table 5-4, the person earns 10% on his or her loan regardless of what is done with the yearly cash flows. This is what happens when a company invests in a project. In effect a company "loans" money (capital) to the project, and the project in turn returns money in the form of positive cash flows to the company. Consequently, there is no assumption regarding the reinvestment of *the cash flows*. The IRR is generated internally as a result of the cash flows. This is the reason the word *internal* is used in conjunction with the words *rate of return*. As stated previously, the investment assumption that is made is that the required capital could be invested at the value of MARR in other economic endeavors.

TABLE 5-4
The Meaning of the Internal Rate of Return

End of Year	Net Cash Flow	Return on Unre-covered Capital	Capital Recovered	Unrecovered Capital
0	−$20,000	—	—	$−20,000
1	4,463	0.1(−20,000) = $−2,000	4,463−2,000 = $2,463	−20,000+2,463 = −17,537
2	4,463	0.1(−17,537) = −1,754	4,463−1,754 = 2,709	−17,537+2,709 = −14,828
3	4,463	0.1(−14,828) = −1,483	4,463−1,483 = 2,980	−14,828+2,980 = −11,848
4	4,463	0.1(−11,848) = −1,185	4,463−1,185 = 3,278	−11,848+3,278 = − 8,570
5	4,463	0.1(− 8,570) = − 857	4,463− 857 = 3,606	− 8,570+3,606 = − 4,964
6	1,000[a] +4,463	0.1(− 4,964) = − 496	5,463[c]− 496 = 4,967	− 4,964+4,967 = 0[b]

[a] Salvage value.
[b] Actual difference is +3 which is due to rounding-off error.
[c] Includes salvage value.

CASH FLOW EXTENSIONS
AND CONVENTIONS

Determining the cash flows in Example 5-3 was a relatively simple matter since there was only one capital expenditure and most of the variables were constants. Also there were no working capital or investment tax credit considerations. In this section a more comprehensive cash flow example is worked and certain conventions used in generating cash flows are discussed.

Example 5-4

For a particular project the data shown in Tables 5-5 and 5-6 has been estimated. Determine the equity cash flows using the additional information given below:

1. The tax rate is 40%.
2. The investment tax credit is applicable.
3. Depreciation for tax purposes is straight-line.
4. The debt ratio is 40%.
5. All debt capital is to be paid back in ten equal principal installments, and the cost of debt capital is 10% on the unpaid principal.

The first step in generating the equity cash flows is to determine the yearly tax depreciation amounts for each depreciable asset. These amounts are shown in Table 5-7. The convention used in Table 5-7 is to begin the depreciation amounts following the year in which the capital expenditure (K_j) occurs. There is another convention that is sometimes used in determining the yearly tax depreciation amounts. In this other way, the depreciation begins after all capital is expended. This would imply the depreciation amounts shown in Table 5-8. In this table the building and equipment depreciation amounts all begin in year four. The depreciation schedules for the building and equipment are separated because they have different lives. Also, the building is, in all probability, Section 1250 Property and the equipment is Section 1245 Property. The depreciation lives are decided by tax regulations. Both of the depreciation conventions shown in Tables 5-7 and 5-8 are correct under certain circumstances. The question from the standpoint of tax regulations is, Are the assets ready for service? If an asset is ready for service, depreciation deductions can

TABLE 5-5
Capital Requirement Data for Example 5-4

End of Year	Capital Requirement	Use	Tax Depreciation Life in Years	Salvage	Working Capital Requirement
0	$ 500,000	Land	—	—	—
1	2,000,000	Building	25	200,000	600,000
2	3,000,000	Equipment	15	300,000	800,000
3	6,000,000	Equipment	15	600,000	1,000,000

TABLE 5-6
Gross Income and Cost Data for Example 5-4

End of Year	Gross Income	Costs	G – C
0	—	—	—
1	—	—	—
2	—	—	—
3	—	—	—
4	500,000	1,000,000	−500,000
5	1,500,000	1,000,000	500,000
6	5,000,000	1,000,000	4,000,000
.	.	.	.
.	.	.	.
.	.	.	.
20	5,000,000	1,000,000	4,000,000

TABLE 5-7
Depreciation Amounts for Example 5-4

End of Year	Building $2(10)^6$	Equipment $3(10)^6$	Equipment $6(10)^6$	Total Depreciation
0	—	—	—	—
1	—	—	—	—
2	72,000	—	—	72,000
3	72,000	180,000	—	252,000
4	72,000	180,000	360,000	612,000
5	72,000	180,000	360,000	612,000
6	72,000	180,000	360,000	612,000
7	72,000	180,000	360,000	612,000
8	72,000	180,000	360,000	612,000
9	72,000	180,000	360,000	612,000
10	72,000	180,000	360,000	612,000
11	72,000	180,000	360,000	612,000
12	72,000	180,000	360,000	612,000
13	72,000	180,000	360,000	612,000
14	72,000	180,000	360,000	612,000
15	72,000	180,000	360,000	612,000
16	72,000	180,000	360,000	612,000
17	72,000	180,000	360,000	612,000
18	72,000	—	360,000	432,000
19	72,000	—	—	72,000
.	.	.	.	.
.	.	.	.	.
26	72,000	—	—	72,000

TABLE 5-8
Another Depreciation Schedule for Example 5-4

End of Year	Building $2(10)^6$	Equipment $9(10)^6$	Total Depreciation
0	—	—	—
1	—	—	—
2	—	—	—
3	—	—	—
4	72,000	540,000	612,000
5	72,000	540,000	612,000
6	72,000	540,000	612,000
.	.	.	.
.	.	.	.
.	.	.	.
18	72,000	540,000	612,000
19	72,000	—	72,000
.	.	.	.
.	.	.	.
.	.	.	.
28	72,000	—	72,000

start as shown in Table 5-7. If assets are dependent (the entire facility must be completed before it is ready for use), then the depreciation convention in Table 5-8 is more applicable. It should be noted that the tax regulation is based on *ready* for service. It is not based on being in actual use. In general the depreciation convention shown in Table 5-7 is used in this text. Also, this example uses straight-line depreciation for tax purposes. This is merely for convenience. In practice the tax depreciation model would most likely be an acceptable tax depreciation model.

The next step is to calculate the amount of debt capital and corresponding recovery and interest amounts. As mentioned earlier, the approach taken in this text is to use the convention that the amount of debt money is a function of the debt ratio. Therefore, the debt capital for each year is

$$B_0 = (0.4)(500,000)$$

$$= \$200,000$$

$$B_1 = (0.4)(2,000,000 + 600,000)$$

$$= \$1,040,000$$

$$B_2 = (0.4) (3,000,000 + 800,000)$$

$$= \$1,520,000$$

$$B_3 = (0.4) (6,000,000 + 1,000,000)$$

$$= \$2,800,000$$

where the values in parentheses are the capital expenditures and working capital requirements given in Table 5-5. The debt recovery and interest amounts are shown in Table 5-9. Note that the recovery

TABLE 5-9
Principal and Interest Payments for Example 5-4

End of Year	$B_0 = \$200,000$ Principal	Interest	$B_1 = \$1,040,000$ Principal	Interest	$B_2 = \$1,520,000$ Principal	Interest	$B_3 = \$2,800,000$ Principal	Interest	Total Principal	Interest
0	—	—	—	—	—	—	—	—	—	—
1	$20,000	$20,000	—	—	—	—	—	—	$ 20,000	$ 20,000
2	20,000	18,000	$104,000	$104,000	—	—	—	—	124,000	122,000
3	20,000	16,000	104,000	93,600	$152,000	$152,000	—	—	276,000	261,600
4	20,000	14,000	104,000	83,200	152,000	136,800	$280,000	$280,000	556,000	514,000
5	20,000	12,000	104,000	72,800	152,000	121,600	280,000	252,000	556,000	458,400
6	20,000	10,000	104,000	62,400	152,000	106,400	280,000	224,000	556,000	402,800
7	20,000	8,000	104,000	52,000	152,000	91,200	280,000	196,000	556,000	347,200
8	20,000	6,000	104,000	41,600	152,000	76,000	280,000	168,000	556,000	291,600
9	20,000	4,000	104,000	31,200	152,000	60,800	280,000	140,000	556,000	236,000
10	20,000	2,000	104,000	20,800	152,000	45,600	280,000	112,000	556,000	180,400
11	—	—	104,000	10,400	152,000	30,400	280,000	84,000	536,000	124,800
12	—	—	—	—	152,000	15,200	280,000	56,000	432,000	71,200
13	—	—	—	—	—	—	280,000	28,000	280,000	28,000

and interest start in the year following the borrowed amount and are based, as stated in the problem, on ten equal installments with interest (10%) assessed on the unpaid balance. With the data in Tables 5-5, 5-6, 5-7, 5-9, and Eq. (5-7), it is possible to determine the annual net equity cash flows. The calculations and results are shown in Table 5-10. In determining the cash flows in Table 5-10 certain conventions are used. A discussion of these conventions follows:

1.   Land is not depreciable. However, it does represent a negative cash flow when it is purchased. In this example, the land is purchased in year zero. The usual convention is to assume that money spent for land is recoverable in the year that the cash flows resulting from the project end. Consequently, in this example, the value of the land ($500,000) is added in year 26.

2.   It is assumed in generating the cash flows that there are sufficient incomes from other company endeavors to allow for the full deductions of costs and depreciation amounts in years where the project itself is not generating sufficient incomes to cover these items. Also, the building will continue to be depreciated after the gross income stops.

3.   The investment tax credit (10%) is taken in the years following the associated capital expenditures. For example, the investment tax credit for the $3,000,000 worth of equipment purchased in year 2 is taken in year 3. This is merely the convention used in this text. Valid arguments can be made for taking the investment tax credit in the same year as the year in which the equipment is purchased. The full 10% credit is taken since the life of the equipment is over seven years. No investment tax credit is provided for the land or building. In general, land and buildings do not qualify for the investment tax credit.

4.   The net increases in working capital are deducted in the appropriate years. The usual convention is to assume that the increases in working capital required by a project are recovered in the last year of the gross income. Consequently, the total working capital ($2,400,000) is added to the cash flow in year 20. If it is estimated that the working capital is recovered over some period of years, then the yearly amounts should be added in the appropriate years. Note that the working capital is taken in year 20 as an equity cash flow since the recovery of the debt-financed portion of the working capital is provided for in the recovery amounts.

5.   The two equipment salvage values are added in year 20. It might be argued that these values should be added in the year when the asset is fully depreciated. In this example this would be year 17 for the $3,000,000 equipment and year 18 for the $6,000,000 equipment. This text takes the point of view that it is more realistic to assume that the earliest these salvage values can be

TABLE 5-10
Equity Cash Flows for Example 5-4

End of year			
0	X_0 =	-500,000 + 200,000	= \$ -300,000
1	X_1 =	(-20,000) - (-20,000)(0.40) - 2,000,000 - 600,000 + 1,040,000 - 20,000	= -1,592,000
2	X_2 =	(-122,000) - (-122,000 - 72,000)(0.40) - 3,000,000 - 800,000 + 1,520,000 - 124,000	= -2,448,400
3	X_3 =	(-261,600) - (-261,600 - 252,000)(0.40) - 6,000,000 - 1,000,000 + 2,800,000 -276,000 + 300,000[a]	= -4,232,160
4	X_4 =	(-500,000 - 514,000) - (500,00 - 514,000 - 612,000)(0.40) - 556,000 + 600,000[a]	= -319,600
5	X_5 =	(500,000 - 458,400) - (500,000 - 458,400 - 612,000)(0.40) - 556,000	= -286,240
6	X_6 =	(4,000,000 - 402,800) - (500,000 - 458,400 - 612,000)(0.40) - 556,000	= 1,847,120
7	X_7 =	(4,000,000 - 347,200) - (4,000,000 - 347,200 - 612,000)(0.40) - 556,000	= 1,880,480
8	X_8 =	(4,000,000 - 291,600) - (4,000,000 - 291,600- 612,000)(0.40) - 556,000	= 1,913,840
9	X_9 =	(4,000,000 - 236,000) - (4,000,000 - 236,000 - 612,000)(0.40) - 556,000	= 1,947,200
10	X_{10} =	(4,000,000 - 180,400) - (4,000,000 - 180,400 - 612,000)(0.40) - 556,000	= 1,980,560
11	X_{11} =	(4,000,000 - 124,800) - (4,000,000 - 124,800 - 612,000)(0.40) - 536,000	= 2,033,920
12	X_{12} =	(4,000,000 - 71,200) - (4,000,000 - 71,200 - 612,000)(0.40) - 432,000	= 2,170,080
13	X_{13} =	(4,000,000 - 28,000) - (4,000,000 - 28,000 - 612,000)(0.40) - 280,000	= 2,348,000
14	X_{14} =	(4,000,000) - (4,000,000 - 612,000)(0.40)	= 2,644,800
15	X_{15} =	(4,000,000) - (4,000,000 - 612,000)(0.40)	= 2,644,800
16	X_{16} =	(4,000,000) - (4,000,000 - 612,000)(0.40)	= 2,644,800
17	X_{17} =	(4,000,000) - (4,000,000 - 612,000)(0.40)	= 2,644,800
18	X_{18} =	(4,000,000) - (4,000,000 - 432,000)(0.40)	= 2,572,800
19	X_{19} =	(4,000,000) - (4,000,000 - 72,000)(0.40)	= 2,428,800
20	X_{20} =	(4,000,000) - (4,000,000 - 72,000)(0.40) + 300,000[b] + 600,000[c] + 2,400,000[d]	= 5,728,800
21	X_{21} =	-(-72,000)(0.40)	= 28,800
22	X_{22} =	-(-72,000)(0.40)	= 28,800
23	X_{23} =	-(-72,000)(0.40)	= 28,800
24	X_{24} =	-(-72,000)(0.40)	= 28,800
25	X_{25} =	-(-72,000)(0.40)	= 28,800
26	X_{26} =	-(-72,000)(0.40) + 200,000[e] + 500,000[f]	= 728,800

[a] Investment tax credit = (0.10)(3,000,000) = \$300,000.
[a] Investment tax credit = (0.10)(6,000,000) = \$600,000.
[b] Salvage value.
[c] Salvage value.
[d] Working capital recovery.
[e] Salvage value of building.
[f] Recovery of land.

realized is in the year the gross income ceases since this implies that production stops at that time. If there is an estimated decrease in production activity and this makes possible the realization of salvage values, then the appropriate salvage values should be added in the years in which they can be realized. If an asset becomes fully depreciated *after* the gross income stops, the convention used in this text is to assume the salvage value can be realized in the year in which the asset becomes fully depreciated. It must be remembered that depreciation lives for tax purposes are dictated by tax regulations. These regulations may or may not agree with the expected life of the project. Also in relation to the recovery of salvage values and the land, it should be understood that the project can provide these cash flows to the company. Whether or not the company actually realizes these cash flows is dependent upon the alternatives and situation at the time it is possible to retire the assets. For example, some of the equipment might be used for another project or other purposes. However, the project under consideration does provide these cash flows. Consequently, the project should be credited with these cash flows regardless of the actual disposition of these assets.

6. In this example the tax salvage values are given (estimated) for each depreciable component (building and equipment) of the total investment. Salvage values for each investment component are not always known or estimated. Often, only the total salvage values for similar components of the capital investment are estimated. For example, a salvage value for the building might be estimated and only a total salvage value for all the equipment might be estimated. This is consistent since in this example the building is considered to be Section 1250 Property and the equipment is considered to be Section 1245 Property, and thus separate depreciation accounts would be maintained. If depreciation begins after the total equipment expenditure as shown in Table 5-8, there is no problem with a total salvage value for the total equipment expenditures. However, if depreciation begins following the expenditure of a particular capital component as shown in Table 5-7 (this implies separate depreciation accounts), the total salvage value must be allocated to the various investment components. This allocation of the total salvage value between various investment components is usually assumed to be in direct proportion to the dollar expenditure of the investment component.

That is,

$$L_x = \frac{K_x}{K_T}(L_T)$$

(5-14)

where

L_x = salvage value for investment component x

K_x = investment expenditure of component x

K_T = total capital investment

L_T = total salvage for K_T

Suppose in Example 5-4 that only a total salvage value of $900,000 is given for the total equipment investment ($9,000,000). The salvage value for the $3,000,000 equipment component using Eq. (5-14) is

$$L_x = \frac{3,000,000}{9,000,000}(900,000)$$

$$= \$300,000$$

This is the same value given in Table 5-5. However, it should not be concluded, because these salvage values are the same, that the salvage values for each investment component should always be in direct proportion to the investment component. Eq. (5-14) is simply a *convenient method* for determining component salvage values *when only the total salvage value is estimated*. If salvage values are estimated independently for each component, Eq. (5-14) does not necessarily have to be satisfied. Also, Eq. (5-14) is only applicable if the various components have the same depreciation life. It is not applicable if the depreciation lives of the components are different since this requires different depreciation accounts, which in turn would require the determination of salvage values for each component (depreciation account).

7. The assumption is implied, in regard to salvage values and the land, that no gains or losses occur. That is, the value actually realized from the disposition of these assets exactly equals the tax salvage value. Consequently, there are no gains or losses and

therefore no possible tax effects. This is the usual assumption (convention) for cash flow calculations because of the problem of estimating actual realizable salvage values that occur in the distant future. This assumption can also be usually justified on the practical consideration that any difference between actual realizable salvage values and tax salvage values and the possible resulting tax effects contribute very little in the economic evaluation of a project due to the discounting process. That is, in the usual practical situation, salvage values are discounted over a long period of time and consequently have little effect in determining the internal rate of return or net present value.

8. Mathematically, it is not difficult to determine the IRR. However, this example does suggest that determining the IRR for a series of cash flows such as those given in Table 5-10 could be tedious. A computer program for determining the IRR is provided in the appendices.

Some Additional Tax Effects in Cash Flow Calculations

In spite of the practical arguments for disregarding possible differences between actual realizable salvage values and tax salvage values presented in Example 5-4, this section presents a method for approximating tax effects in the cash flows calculations when there are estimated differences between actual realizable salvage values and tax salvage values. This presentation is provided for purposes of completeness and providing a project evaluator with an appreciation for the possible magnitude of these effects.

Salvage values used in determining tax depreciation amounts are based on tax considerations and regulations. They may or may not be representative of the actual realizable salvage value. When there are estimated differences between the realizable salvage value and tax salvage value, it is possible to approximate tax effects if it is believed the property will actually be sold and not used for some other purpose (project). This discussion of tax effects relating to salvage values is limited to Sec. 1245 property with realizable salvage values below the original purchase price of the property (no Sec. 1231 gains).

The approximation of tax effects is accomplished by subtracting the realizable salvage value from the tax book value at the same point in time. If this difference is positive, it is taxed as ordinary income (Sec. 1245 property). If the difference is negative, it is a Sec. 1231 loss. For example, suppose in Example 5-4 that the actual realizable salvage values for the equipment in year 20 are $240,000 and $700,000, respectively, K_2 and K_3. With these values and the tax book values in year 20 of $300,000 and $600,000 (see Table 5-5), there is a loss of $60,000 and a gain of $100,000. Therefore, the cash flow for year 20 is

$$
\begin{aligned}
X_{20} &= (4{,}000{,}000) - (4{,}000{,}000 - 72{,}000)\,(0.40) \\
&\quad + 2{,}400{,}000 + 240{,}000 + 700{,}000 \\
&\quad - (40{,}000)\,(0.40) \\
&= \$5{,}752{,}800
\end{aligned}
$$

The (40,000) (0.40) term is a net tax result. There is a gain of $100,000 from the disposal of the K_3 equipment (700,000 - 600,000) which is taxable as ordinary income (Sec. 1245). The disposal of the K_2 equipment results in Sec. 1231 loss of $60,000. Since there are no offsetting Sec. 1231 gains, this loss is taken as a reduction in ordinary income and the net of these gains and losses is treated as a taxable ordinary gain of $40,000.

If the losses exceed the gains, there is reduction in taxes. For example suppose in the previous example, the realized salvage for K_2 is $170,000. This is a loss of $130,000 and when combined with the $100,000 gain is a net loss of $30,000. In this case, the net cash flow for year 20 is

$$
\begin{aligned}
X_{20} &= (4{,}000{,}000) - (4{,}000{,}000 - 72{,}000)\,(0.40) \\
&\quad + 2{,}400{,}000 + 170{,}000 + 700{,}000 \\
&\quad + (30{,}000)\,(0.40) \\
&= \$5{,}710{,}800
\end{aligned}
$$

It should be noted that the tax effect, (30,000)(0.40), is a positive cash flow since the loss results in a decrease in taxes. These discussions of tax effects are only approximations. The true tax effects would depend on gains and losses from the disposal of other assets in the same year. That is, the tax effects in these examples are based on the assumption that they are the *only* gains and losses.

NET PRESENT VALUE

The net present value is the algebraic sum of the net cash flows discounted at the minimum acceptable rate of return (MARR), to time zero. Mathematically, the net present value is

$$NPV = \sum_{j=0}^{n} \frac{X'_j}{(1 + k)^j}$$

(5-15)

where

NPV = net present value

X'_j = net cash flow in year j defined by either Eq. (5-7), (5-8), or (5-9)

n = number of years of cash flow

j = the year in which the cash flow X'_j occurs

k = MARR = the minimum acceptable rate of return

As in the case of the IRR, k is dependent upon the definition used for the cash flows. If equity cash flows are used, it must be based on an acceptable (required) return on only equity funds. If total cash flows are used, it must be based on Eq. (5-2). If operating cash flows are used, it must be based on Eq. (5-5).

Example 5-5

Calculate the net present value for the cash flows given in Tables 5-2 and 5-3 assuming the minimum acceptable rate of return is 12% for total cash flows.

Using Eq. (5-15), the net present value for total cash flows is

$$NPV = -100,000 + 21,600 \ (P/A \ 12,10) + 10,000 \ (P/F \ 12,10)$$

$$= \$25,264$$

Since the MARR for total (debt and equity) funds is 12%, this implies that the MARR for equity funds, k_e, based on Eq. (5-2) is

$$12 = (0.60)k_e + (1 - .40)(0.40)(10)$$

$$k_e = 16\%$$

Therefore, the net present value for the equity funds is

$$
\begin{aligned}
\text{NPV} \ = \ & -60{,}000 + 15{,}200(P/F\ 16{,}1) + 15{,}440(P/F\ 16{,}2) \\
& + 15{,}680\ (P/F\ 16{,}3) + \ldots + 27{,}360\ (P/F\ 16{,}10) \\
= \ & \$19{,}584
\end{aligned}
$$

Decision Criterion for the NPV   Using the net present value, a project is economically desirable if the NPV ≥ 0 and undesirable if NPV < 0. Consequently, in Example 5-5, the project is acceptable for both cash flow definitions. However, the result that both cash flow definitions gave the same decision should not be generalized. As mentioned in the discussion of the decision criterion for the IRR, equity cash flows can give a different decision than total cash flows as a result of the manner in which the debt obligation is paid.

The NPV decision criterion makes the same investment assumption that is stated in the discussion of the IRR decision criterion. That is, the capital required by a particular project could be invested in some other economic endeavor that would earn the value of MARR (NPV = 0).

Another Interpretation of the NPV   If the cash flows given in Table 5-4 are used and the MARR is equal to 8%, the net present value is

$$
\begin{aligned}
\text{NPV} \ = \ & -20{,}000 + 4{,}463\ (P/A\ 8{,}6) + 1{,}000\ (P/F\ 8{,}6) \\
= \ & \$1{,}262
\end{aligned}
$$

Now if the procedure shown in Table 5-4 is repeated with the exception that the MARR is used in place of the IRR, the results in Table 5-11 are obtained. The results in Table 5-11 indicate that all the capital is recovered somewhere between the fifth and six year with a yearly return of 8% on the unrecovered capital. Also a surplus of $2,003 is realized in the sixth year. If this surplus is discounted to time zero at the MARR, the result is

$$2,003 \ (P/F \ 8,6) = \$1,262$$

which is the NPV. Consequently, a *positive* NPV can be interpreted as a surplus or a "bonus," measured in present dollars, that a project provides in addition to the recovery of all capital and a return of MARR on the unrecovered capital. A negative NPV indicates the capital is not recovered, in present dollars, at the value of MARR. If equity cash flows are used to calculate the net present value, a positive NPV "belongs" to the equity stockholder (an increase in wealth). If total cash flows are used, the NPV is a return to the combined pool of debt and equity capital.

THE RELATIONSHIP BETWEEN THE NPV AND THE IRR

The internal rate of return and net present value give the same decision regarding the economic desirability of a *single project with traditional cash flows*. That is, a project that is acceptable using the IRR criterion is also acceptable using the NPV criterion. Conversely, if it is unacceptable using the IRR, it is unacceptable using the NPV. This relationship can be seen by plotting the net present value profile for a series of *traditional cash flows*. The net present value profile for a series of traditional cash flows is shown in Figure 5-1. This figure is basically a plot of the NPV and the MARR (indicated as i in Figure 5-1). It is obtained for a particular series of cash flows by assuming various MARR values, calculating the corresponding NPV, and plotting these results.

TABLE 5-11
The Meaning of the Net Present Value

End of Year	Net Cash Flow	Return on Unrecovered Capital	Capital Recovered	Unrecovered Capital
0	−20,000	—	—	−20,000
1	4,463	$0.08(-20,000) = \$-1,600$	$4,463 - 1,600 = \$2,863$	$-20,000 + 2,863 = \$-17,137$
2	4,463	$0.08(-17,137) = -1,371$	$4,463 - 1,371 = 3,092$	$-17,137 + 3,092 = -14,045$
3	4,463	$0.08(-14,045) = -1,124$	$4,463 - 1,124 = 3,339$	$-14,045 + 3,339 = -10,706$
4	4,463	$0.08(-10,706) = -856$	$4,463 - 856 = 3,607$	$-10,706 + 3,607 = -7,099$
5	4,463	$0.08(-7,099) = -568$	$4,463 - 568 = 3,895$	$-7,099 + 3,895 = -3,204$
6	1,000[a] + 4,463	$0.08(-3,204) = -256$	$5,463[b] - 256 = 5,207$	$-3,204 + 5,207 = +2,003$

[a] Salvage value.
[b] Includes salvage value.

If Figure 5-1 is considered, it can be seen that if MARR is i_1 the NPV is positive, which indicates that the MARR is less than the IRR. If MARR is i_2, the NPV is negative, which indicates that the MARR is greater than the IRR. These results substantiate the earlier statement that the IRR and NPV give the same decision. However, it should be noted that this is *only true for traditional cash flows*.

NONTRADITIONAL CASH FLOWS

A series of nontraditional cash flows can give multiple rates of return. This occurrence is a result of Descartes "rule of signs" which states that the number of real positive roots is never greater than the number of sign changes for an nth-degree polynomial. The applicability of this rule to finding a rate of return can be seen by expanding Eq. (5-13). That is.

$$0 = X_0 + aX_1 = a^2X_2 + \ldots + a^nX_n \qquad (5\text{-}16)$$

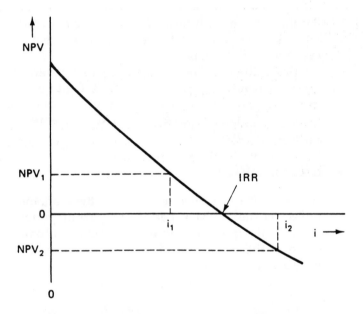

FIGURE 5-1 Net Present Value Profile for Traditional Cash Flows

where

$$a = \frac{1}{(1 + i)} \qquad (5\text{-}17)$$

Equation (5-16) is an nth-degree polynomial. Therefore, if the number of sign changes in Eq. (5-16) is two or more, then there *may* be more than one rate of return. Two or more sign changes in the cash flows is a *necessary* condition but not a *sufficient* condition for the existence of more than one rate of return. There are numerous examples of cash flows that give more than one rate of return. Some of these examples are given in G. T. Stevens' *Economic and Financial Analysis of Capital Investments* (see References). When more than one rate of return exists for a series of cash flows, the net present value and its related decision criterion should be used to determine the economic desirability of the cash flows.

Example 5-6

For the series of cash flows shown in Table 5-12, determine the net present value profile and determine under what circumstances the cash flows are acceptable.

Calculating the net present values for various interest rates gives the results shown in Table 5-13. Plotting these results gives Figure 5-2. Figure 5-2 indicates that the series of cash flows given in Table 5-12 is acceptable if the MARR is between 0% and 20% or between 50% and 100%.

THE PAYBACK PERIOD

A method that is sometimes used for the economic evaluation of a project is the payback period (or payout period). The payback period is the number of years required for incoming cash flows to balance the cash outflows. Expressed mathematically, the payback period, p, is

$$0 = \sum_{j=0}^{p} X_j \qquad (5\text{-}18)$$

TABLE 5-12
Cash Flows for Example 5-6

End of Year	Cash Flow
0	-500
1	2,350
2	-3,600
3	1,800

TABLE 5-13
Net Present Values for Example 5-6

i	NPV
10	50
20	0
30	-30
50	0
70	3
100	0

Equation (5-18) is one definition of the payback period. There is another definition that employs a discounting procedure. However, Eq. (5-18) is the definition most often used in practice.

Example 5-7

Determine the payback period for the series of cash flows given in Table 5-14.

Using Eq. (5-18), the sum of the cash flows for the first five years is

$$-20,000 - 7,000 - 5,000 + 8,000 + 9,000 + 9,000 = \$-6,000$$

and for the first six years is

$$-20,000 - 7,000 - 5,000 + 8,000 + 9,000 + 9,000 + 10,000 = \$4,000$$

which implies the payback period is between five and six years. Using linear interpolation the payback period is

$$p = 5 + \frac{6,000}{10,000}$$

$$= 5.6 \text{ years}$$

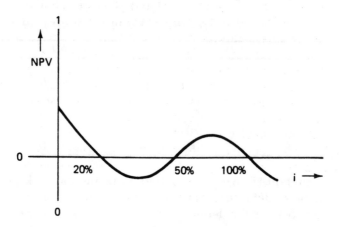

FIGURE 5-2   Net Present Value Profile for Example 5-6

TABLE 5-14
Cash Flows for Example 5-7

End of Year	Net Cash Flow
0	−20,000
1	− 7,000
2	− 5,000
3	8,000
4	9,000
5	9,000
6	10,000
7	10,000
8	10,000

Decision Criterion   The usual approach used with the payback period is to compare a project's payback period with some predetermined payback period. If a project's payback period is equal to or less than the predetermined period, the project is acceptable. Otherwise, the project is unacceptable.

There are serious drawbacks to using the payback period as a procedure for evaluating the economic desirability of a project. It is a simple task to provide examples of cash flows that are acceptable using the IRR or NPV but are unacceptable using the payback criterion. Conversely, examples are possible where a series of cash flows is acceptable based on the payback period but are unacceptable from the standpoints of the IRR and NPV. These conflicts occur because the payback period does not consider the time value of money nor does it consider what the cash flows are after the payback period.

The payback period may have some merit as a secondary criterion. Once a project is considered acceptable on the basis of NPV or IRR, the payback might be used as a rough indicator of a project's effect on a company's liquidity requirements.

OTHER MEASURES OF A PROJECT'S ECONOMIC WORTH

In addition to the methods already presented in this chapter for evaluating the economic desirability of a project, there are other methods that are sometimes proposed. Some of these methods are (1) proceeds per dollar of outlay, (2) average proceeds per dollar of outlay, (3) average income on investment, and (4) average income on average book value. None of these methods consider the time value of money and are not considered, in this text, acceptable as measures of a project's economic worth. Hence, they are not discussed further.

The Benefit-Cost Ratio   Another method for the evaluation of projects is the benefit-cost ratio (B/C). This method has received wide attention particularly in the evaluation of projects in the public (government) sector. For a particular project, the basic definition of the B/C ratio is

$$B/C = \frac{\sum\limits_{j=0}^{n} B_j (1+k)^{-j}}{\sum\limits_{j=0}^{n} C_j (1+k)^{-j}} \qquad (5\text{-}19)$$

where

$$B_j \; = \; \text{project benefits in the year } j$$

$$C_j \; = \; \text{project costs in the year } j$$

$$k \; = \; \text{MARR}$$

The decision criterion used in conjunction with the B/C ratio defined by Eq. (5-19) is to accept the project if the B/C ratio is equal to or greater than one and reject the project if the ratio is less than one. Now, there is a problem with the B/C ratio. This problem revolves around the definitions of benefit and cost and can be shown numerically by considering the data in Table 5-15. This table shows cash flow data for a particular project. In applying Eq. (5-19) to the data in Table 5-15, one approach might be to define the benefits as positive net cash flows and the costs as negative net cash flows. That is, assuming MARR equals 15%, the discounted benefits and costs are

$$B \; = \; 59{,}000 \; (P/A \; 15{,}3)(P/F \; 15{,}1) + 69{,}000 \; (P/F \; 15{,}5)$$

$$= \; \$151{,}450$$

$$C \; = \; 100{,}000 + 31{,}000 \; (P/F \; 15{,}1)$$

$$= \; \$126{,}958$$

which gives a B/C ratio of

$$B/C \; = \frac{151{,}450}{126{,}958}$$

$$= 1.193$$

Another approach might be to define the denominator of the B/C ratio in terms of the required capital investments (K_0 and K_1) and omit the capital investment in the cash flow result. With this approach the discounted benefits and costs are

$$B \; = \; 49{,}000 \; (P/F \; 15{,}1) + 59{,}000 \; (P/A \; 15{,}3)(P/F \; 15{,}1)$$

$$+ \; 69{,}000 \; (P/F \; 15{,}5)$$

$$= \; \$194{,}060$$

$$C = 100{,}000 + 80{,}000 \ (P/F \ 15{,}1)$$

$$= \$169{,}568$$

TABLE 5-15
Cash Flows for B/C Ratio

End of Year	Capital Investments	Salvage Value	Total Depreciation[b]	Gross Income	Annual Costs	Taxes (T = 50%)	Net Cash Flows[c]
0	−$100,000	—	—	—	—	—	−$100,000
1	− 80,000	—	$18,000	$100,000	$20,000	$31,000	−$ 31,000
2	—	—	38,000	100,000	20,000	21,000	59,000
3	—	—	38,000	100,000	20,000	21,000	59,000
4	—	—	38,000	100,000	20,000	21,000	59,000
5	—	$10,000[a]	38,000	100,000	20,000	21,000	69,000[d]

[a] The salvage value for K_0 is $10,000 and for K_1 zero.
[b] Straight-line depreciation is used for both K_0 and K_1 with depreciation lives of five and four years, respectively.
[c] Based on Eq. (5-8).
[d] Includes $10,000 salvage.

and the B/C ratio is

$$B/C = \frac{194{,}060}{169{,}568}$$

$$= 1.144$$

A third approach, and the final one considered, is to define all positive (inflow) cash flow components as benefits and all negative (outflow) components as costs. This approach gives

$$B = 100{,}000 \ (P/A \ 15{,}5) + 10{,}000 \ (P/F \ 15{,}5)$$

$$= \$340{,}192$$

$$C = 100{,}000 + 80{,}000 \ (P/F \ 15{,}1) + 20{,}000 \ (P/A \ 15{,}5) + 31{,}000 \ (P/F \ 15{,}1) + 21{,}000 \ (P/A \ 15{,}4)(P/F \ 15{,}1)$$

$$= \$315{,}707$$

and a B/C ratio of

$$B/C = \frac{340,192}{315,707}$$

$$= 1.078$$

These three approaches all give different values and point out that the B/C ratio depends on how the benefits and costs are defined. It is true that if the B/C ratio is greater than one for a particular project, the NPV for the same project is positive. However, since the B/C ratio does not provide any computational advantages over the NPV and since it is weakened by its dependency on the definitions of benefits and costs, it is not used further in this text.

REFERENCES

Gordon, M. J. *The Investment, Financing, and Valuation of the Corporation*. Homewood, Ill.: Richard D. Irwin, 1962.

Gordon, M. J., and Shapiro, E. "Capital Equipment Analysis: The Required Rate of Profit." *Management Science* 3 (October 1956): 102–10.

Haley, C. W., and Schall, L. D. *The Theory of Financial Decisions*. New York: McGraw-Hill Book Co., 1973.

Lewellen, Wilbur G. *The Cost of Capital*. Belmont, Calif.: Wadsworth Publishing Co., 1969.

Robichek, A. A., and Myers, S. C. *Optimal Financial Decisions*. Englewood Cliffs, N.J.: Prentice-Hall, 1965.

Stevens, G. T., Jr. *Economic and Financial Analysis of Capital Investments*. New York: John Wiley & Sons, 1979.

Solomon, Ezra. "Measuring a Company's Cost of Capital." *Journal of Business* (October 1955).

VanHorne, James C. *Financial Management and Policy*. 2d ed. Englewood Cliffs, N.J.: Prentice-Hall, 1971.

Weston, J. F., and Brighan, E. F. *Essentials of Managerial Finance*. 3d ed. Hinsdale, Ill.: Dryden Press, 1974.

PROBLEMS

5-1. For the net cash flows given below, determine the following:
  (a) The net present value if MARR equals 12%.
  (b) The internal rate of return.
  (c) The payback period.

End of Year	Net Cash Flow
0	−200,000
1	−300,000
2	100,000
3	100,000
4	100,000
5	100,000
6	100,000
7	100,000
8	100,000
9	100,000
10	100,000

5-2. For the net cash flows given below, determine the following:
  (a) The net present value if MARR equals 15%.
  (b) The internal rate of return.
  (c) The payback period.

End of Year	Net Cash Flow
0	− 50,000
1	− 70,000
2	−100,000
3	30,000
4	50,000
5	70,000
6	100,000
7	100,000
8	100,000
9	100,000
10	100,000
11	100,000
12	100,000

5-3. A company uses a minimum acceptable rate of return of 20% for total cash flows. If the company's debt ratio is 40%, tax rate is 40%, and the cost of debt capital is 15%, what is the company's implied required return on equity capital?

5-4. A company is considering certain modifications to one of its production systems. The modifications will require an initial expenditure of $500,000 for equipment. It is estimated that the modifications will provide gross savings of $300,000 per year for ten years and the annual costs for operating the new equipment are a total of $100,000 per year. For tax purposes, the company uses straight-line depreciation, a salvage value of zero, and a life of ten years for evaluating projects of this type. The company's tax rate is 40% and the investment tax credit is to be neglected. If the minimum acceptable rate of return is 20% for total cash flows, are the modifications economically justified?

5-5. Repeat Problem 5-4 on the basis of equity cash flows. Assume the debt ratio is 40%, the cost of debt is 15%, and the debt obligation is to be paid back in ten equal installments of principal with interest payments assessed on the unpaid balance.

5-6. Repeat Problem 5-4 using operating cash flows and the interest amounts established in Problem 5-5.

5-7. Repeat Problem 5-5 using the following methods of debt payment:

(a) Constant principal payment over a five-year period.
(b) Constant interest.
(c) Constant yearly payment of interest and principal.

5-8. Based on the results obtained in the solutions to Problems 5-4, 5-5, 5-6, and 5-7, what comments are possible in relation to the use of equity, operating, and total cash flows? Suppose in Problem 5-5 a debt ratio of zero is used. What does this imply? What would the cash flows be?

5-9. Determine the yearly interest and principal payments using the four methods of debt payment shown in Table 5-1 if the amount borrowed is $100,000, the loan is to be paid back in eight years, and the loan interest rate is 10%. Also determine the total present value of principal and interest for the four methods using the following discount rates: (a) 5%, (b) 10%, and (c) 15%. Using these results, are any generalizations possible?

5-10. A particular investment requires a capital expenditure of $300,000. It is expected that this investment will provide a gross income of $200,000 per year for ten years and costs of $100,000 for the same period of time. The tax depreciation is based on a straight-line model, a life of ten years, and a salvage value of zero. The tax rate is 40%. Determine the following:
  (a) The net present value profile for the total cash flows.
  (b) The net present value profile for the equity cash flows assuming a debt ratio of 30%, a 10% cost of debt capital, and the debt is paid back in ten equal installments of principal with interest assessed on the unpaid principal.

5-11. Repeat Problem 5-10 but use the following depreciation models for tax purposes:
  (a) Sum-of-the-years-digits.
  (b) Five year MACRS depreciation.

5-12. Based on the results obtained in the solution of Problems 5-10 and 5-11, what generalizations are possible?

5-13. For cash flows given below plot the net present value profile.

End of Year	Net Cash Flow
0	-
1	80
2	80
3	80
4	80
5	80
6	-1,400
7	200
8	200
9	200
10	200
11	200
12	200

 5-14. A company is considering a project line. It is estimated that this new product line will require the following capital expenditures and increases in working capital:

End of year	Capital Expenditure	Use	Depreciation Life	Salvage Value	Working Capital
0	$200,000	Land	—	—	—
1	500,000	Building	20	40,000	100,000
2	800,000	Equipment	15	50,000	150,000
3	500,000	Equipment	15	20,000	200,000

As a result of this new product line, it is estimated that gross incomes and costs will increase by the amounts shown below:

End of Year	Gross Income	Cost
0	—	—
1	—	$400,000
2	—	400,000
3	300,000	400,000
4	500,000	400,000
5	1,000,000	400,000
6	1,000,000	400,000
7	1,000,000	400,000
8	1,000,000	400,000
9	1,000,000	400,000
10	1,000,000	400,000
11	1,000,000	400,000
12	1,000,000	400,000
13	1,000,000	400,000
14	1,000,000	400,000
15	1,000,000	400,000

Determine if this new product line is economically justified assuming the company's required return on equity is 15% and the following additional points are considered:

1. The company's debt ratio is 30%, and this is not expected to change.
2. All debt funds are to be paid back in ten equal installments of principal with interest paid yearly on the unpaid principal at a rate of 10%.
3. Tax depreciation for each capital expenditure component begins immediately following the capital and is based on a straight-line depreciation model.
4. The investment tax credit (10%) is applicable for the equipment.
5. The tax rate is 40%.
6. There is sufficient taxable income from the company's other activities to take advantage of any depreciation or interest deductions that are not offset by the taxable incomes from this project.

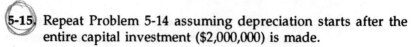 **5-15.** Repeat Problem 5-14 assuming depreciation starts after the entire capital investment ($2,000,000) is made.

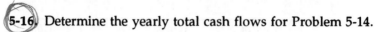 **5-16.** Determine the yearly total cash flows for Problem 5-14.

5-17. Determine the yearly total cash flows for Problem 5-15.

6

MINIMUM ANNUAL REVENUE REQUIREMENTS

Minimum annual revenue requirements provide another method for the economic evaluation of a project. Basically, minimum annual revenue requirements are the *minimum* yearly gross incomes that provide for the recovery of invested capital, all costs, and a return on the yearly unrecovered capital.

Minimum annual revenue requirements can be expressed mathematically as

$$R_j = D_{lj} + F_{ej} + I_j + C_j + t_j \qquad (6\text{-}1)$$

where the components in Eq. (6-1) are defined as:

$R_j = $ *the minimum annual revenue requirement for year j.*

This can also be considered as the minimum gross income or the annual costs with a required return on equity.

D_{bj} = *the total capital recovered in year j.* This is the amount of the total investment (capital) recovered in year j. It is usually estimated on the basis of a depreciation model and is often referred to as the book depreciation. The book depreciation may or may not be the same as the tax depreciation. There is no requirement that they be the same. Since the book depreciation is based on the total investment (not just the equity portion), the assumption is implied in generating revenue requirements that any debt portion of the investment is being recovered over the book depreciation life. Further, the capital recovered (book depreciation) in the year j is proportional between the recovery of the debt capital, D_{dj}, and equity capital, D_{ej}, in accordance with the debt ratio, c. That is,

$$D_{dj} = cD_{bj} + cL_j \qquad (6\text{-}2)$$

$$D_{ej} = (1-c)D_{bj} + (1-c)L_j \qquad (6\text{-}3)$$

F_{ej} = *return on equity in year j.* Mathematically, this is determined by

$$F_{ej} = (1-c)(k_e)(B_j - 1) \qquad (6\text{-}4)$$

where k_e is the minimum required return (MARR) on equity and B_{j-1} is the book value for the year $(j - 1)$ based on the book depreciation method. The value of k_e is usually assumed to be a constant over the life of the project.

I_j = *debt interest cost in year j.* Mathematically, this is determined by the equation

$$I_j = (c)(k_d)(B_{j-1}) \qquad (6\text{-}5)$$

where k_d is the cost of debt capital and assumed to be constant over the life of the project. Equations (6-4) and (6-5) are sometimes added to define an overall return, F_{oj}, as

$$F_{oj} = F_{ej} + I_j = [(1-c)k_e + ck_d]B_{j-1} \qquad (6\text{-}6)$$

using Eq. (5-5), Eq. (6-6) can be written as

$$F_{oj} = k_b(B_{j-1})$$ (6-7)

This text prefers to keep the returns on equity and debt interest separate and not use Eq. (6-7) since it is believed that the separation of these quantities facilitates an understanding of minimum annual revenue requirements.

C_j = *annual costs in year j.* These are the annual costs of operation and maintenance. They could also be the costs of labor and materials but they do not include depreciation.

t_j= *taxes paid in year j.* An expression for the annual taxes can be obtained by considering the basic equation for the incremental taxes; namely,

$$t_j = (G_j - C_j - I_j - D_j)T$$ (6-8)

Since the minimum annual revenue requirements are the minimum gross incomes, Eq. (6-1) is substituted in Eq. (6-8) for G_j. The result is

$$t_j = (D_{bj} + F_{ej} - D_j + t_j)T$$ (6-9)

which can be written as

$$t_j - t_j T = (D_{bj} + F_{ej} - D_j)T$$ (6-10)

and rearranged to give

$$t_j = \frac{T}{1-T}(D_{bj} + F_{ej} - D_j)$$ (6-11)

Example 6-1

Using the data given below, generate the annual revenue requirements.

Initial cost of the project	=	$100,000
Book depreciation	=	straight-line model
salvage	=	$20,000
life	=	10 years

Tax depreciation	=	sum of years–digits model
salvage	=	$10,000
life	=	8 years
Required return on equity	=	30%
Cost of debt capital	=	15%
Debt ratio	=	1/3
Tax rate	=	40%
Total costs	=	$7,000 per year

The minimum annual revenue requirements for this data are given in Table 6-1. Some sample calculations follow:

The book depreciation amounts are

$$D_b = \frac{100,000 - 20,000}{10} = \$8,000$$

since straight-line depreciation is specified. The tax depreciation amounts for the first two years are

$P.60$

$$D_1 = \frac{8}{36}(100,000 - 10,000) = \$20,000$$

$$D_2 = \frac{7}{36}(100,000 - 10,000) = \$17,500$$

It should be noted that in generating the minimum annual revenue requirements it is not required that the tax and book depreciation models, including life and salvage, be the same.

The equity returns for the first two years using Eq. (6-4) are

$$F_{e1} = \left(1 - \frac{1}{3}\right)(0.30)(100,000) = \$20,000$$

$$F_{e2} = \left(1 - \frac{1}{3}\right)(0.30)(92,000) = \$18,400$$

TABLE 6-1
Minimum Annual Revenue Requirements for Example 6-1

End of Year	Book Depreciation D_b	Tax Depreciation D	Book Value B	Equity Return F_e	Debt Interest I	Tax t	Annual Costs C	Minimum Annual Revenue Requirement R
0	—	—	$100,000	—	—	—	—	—
1	$8,000	$20,000	92,000	$20,000	$5,000	$5,334	$7,000	$45,334
2	8,000	17,500	84,000	18,400	$4,600	5,934	7,000	43,934
3	8,000	15,000	76,000	16,800	4,200	6,534	7,000	42,534
4	8,000	12,500	68,000	15,200	3,800	7,134	7,000	41,134
5	8,000	10,000	60,000	13,600	3,400	7,734	7,000	39,734
6	8,000	7,500	52,000	12,000	3,000	8,334	7,000	38,334
7	8,000	5,000	44,000	10,400	2,600	8,934	7,000	36,934
8	8,000	2,500	36,000	8,800	2,200	9,534	7,000	35,534
9	8,000	—	28,000	7,200	1,800	10,134	7,000	34,134
10	8,000	—	20,000	5,600	1,400	9,067	7,000	31,067

and debt interest for the first two years, using Eq. (6-5) are

$$I_1 = \left(\frac{1}{3}\right)(0.15)(100{,}000) = \$5{,}000$$

$$I_2 = \left(\frac{1}{3}\right)(0.15)(92{,}000) = \$4{,}600$$

Using Eq. (6-11), the taxes for the first two years are

$$t_1 = \left(\frac{0.40}{1-0.40}\right)(8{,}000 + 20{,}000 - 20{,}000) = \$5{,}334$$

$$t_2 = \left(\frac{0.40}{1-0.40}\right)(8{,}000 + 18{,}400 - 17{,}500) = \$5{,}934$$

The revenue requirements for the first two years, using Eq. (6-1), are

$$R_1 = 8{,}000 + 20{,}000 + 5{,}000 + 7{,}000 + 5{,}334 = \$45{,}334$$

$$R_2 = 8{,}000 + 18{,}400 + 4{,}600 + 7{,}000 + 5{,}934 = \$43{,}934$$

It is instructive, at this point, to see if the taxes given by Eq. (6-11) are the same as the taxes given by Eq. (6-8). Using the R_j values as the gross incomes, the taxes given by Eq. (6-8) for the first two years are

$$t_1 = (45{,}334 - 7{,}000 - 5{,}000 - 20{,}000)(0.40) = \$5{,}334$$

$$t_2 = (43{,}934 - 7{,}000 - 4{,}600 - 17{,}500)(0.40) = \$5{,}934$$

which are the same as the taxes given by Eq. (6-11).

___

The Investment-Tax Credit   In the formulation of the annual revenue requirements, a provision for the investment tax credit is not included. This was done, initially, to facilitate the presentation. However, it is a relatively easy matter to include a provision for the investment tax credit. This is accomplished by adding the term

$$- \frac{V}{1-T}$$

(6-12)

to the revenue requirements (or the tax equation) *for just the first year*. The value V is the investment tax credit. Equation (6-12) is based on the fact that for a decrease in taxes, the equivalent reduction in gross income is $G(I - T)$. As an example of the use of Eq. (6-12), suppose a 10% investment tax credit is applicable in Example 6-1. The revenue requirement in year one is changed to

$$R_1 = 45,334 - \frac{100,000 \, (0.10)}{1 - 0.40} = \$28,667$$

and the other revenue requirements are the same as those given in Table 6-1. Another approach to including the investment tax credit is to add Eq. (6-12) to Eq. (6-11). That is

$$t_1 = \frac{0.40}{1 - 0.40} \, (8,000 + 20,000 - 20,000) - \frac{100,000 \, (0.10)}{1 - 0.40}$$

$$= -\$11,333$$

Either approach gives the same answer for R_1. As a check, the taxes for year one with the investment tax credit, and using Eq. (6-8) are

$$t_1 = (28,667 - 7,000 - 5,000 - 20,000) \, (0.40) - 10,000$$

$$= -\$11,333$$

The negative result for the taxes simply implies the assumption that there is sufficient income from other company operations to take the full investment tax credit. It shows that the investment tax credit can have a significant short-term effect and can be a definite factor in the decision process.

Decision Criterion for Minimum Annual Revenue Requirements An economic evaluation of a project can be determined by Eq. (6-13)

$$NPV_x = (1-T) \sum_{j=1}^{n} (G_j - R_j) \, (P/F \, k_x, j) \qquad (6\text{-}13)$$

where

NPV_x = the net present value of after—tax cash flows. This value can be the net present value of equity, total, or operating cash flows depending on the discount rate (k_x) used.

k_x = $k_e, k_a,$ or k_b depending on implied definition of cash flow (equity, total, or operating)

G_j = the expected gross revenues (incomes) for the year j

R_j = minimum annual revenue requirements for the year j

T = tax rate

The basic decision criterion for Eq. (6-13) is the same as given in Chapter 5. That is, if the NPV is positive, the project is acceptable. If negative, the project is unacceptable.

Revenue requirements also allow a project to be evaluated on an attribute basis as opposed to a numerical determination of the NPV. That is, are the yearly expected gross revenues all greater than the corresponding minimum annual revenue requirements $(G_j > R_j)$? If the answer is yes, the project is acceptable since the NPV given by Eq. (6-13) is positive. If all the expected gross revenues are less than the revenue requirements $(G_j < R_j)$, the project is unacceptable. If some of the revenue requirements are less than the expected revenues and others are greater, the project can be evaluated using Eq. (6-13).

Example 6-2

Suppose in Example 6-1 the expected annual revenues (incomes) are yearly constant values of $60,000, $31,000, and $47,000 and it is desired to determine the project's acceptability. In the case of the $60,000 value, the project is acceptable since this value is greater than all the minimum annual revenue requirements. Similarly in the case of the $31,000 amount, the project is unacceptable since this value is less than all the revenue requirements. Of course if a numerical value for the NPV is desired for these expected amounts, Eq. (6-13) can be used. This procedure is shown in the case of the $47,000 amount using equity cash flow as the basis. Substituting into Eq. (6-13) gives

$$
\begin{aligned}
NPV_e &= (1 - 0.40) \left[(47,000 - 45,334) \, (P/F \ 30,1) \right] \\
&\quad + (47,000 - 43,934)(P/F \ 30,2) \\
&\quad + (47,000 - 42,534)(P/F \ 30,3) \\
&\quad + \ldots + (47,000 - 31,067)(P/F \ 30,10) \\
&= (0.60)(16,311) \\
&= \$ \, 9,787
\end{aligned}
$$

which indicates the project is acceptable since the NPV_e is positive. It should be noted that the use of equity cash flows as the evaluation basis establishes the value (30%) for k_x in Eq. (6-13) since it is the required equity return (k_e) given in Example 6-1. If the net present value for total cash flows, NPV, is desired, the discount rate in Eq. (6-13) is k_a defined in Chapter 5 and for this example is

$$
\begin{aligned}
k_a &= \frac{1}{3} (1 - .40)(15) + \frac{2}{3}(30) \\
&= 23\%
\end{aligned}
$$

If this value (23%) is used in Eq. (6-13), the result is NPV = $13,193. The net present value of the operating cash flows is $12,066 using k_b (25%) as the discount rate.

THE RELATIONSHIP BETWEEN REVENUE REQUIREMENTS AND CASH FLOW DEFINITIONS

The basis of Eq. (6-13) can be shown by some examples. These same examples also show *numerically* the relationships between the definitions of cash flow and MARR discussed in Chapter 5.

If the revenue data given in Table 6-1 and a yearly expected gross revenue of $47,000 per year (Example 6-2) are used to determine the equity cash flows, the results given in Table 6-2 are obtained. The net present value of the equity cash flows in Table 6-2 is

$$\text{NPV}_e = -66,667 + 26,333 \ (P/F \ 30,1) + \ldots + 33,826(P/F \ 30,10)$$

$$= \$9,787$$

which is the same result obtained using Eq. (6-13).

TABLE 6-2
Equity Cash Flows

Year j	Cap. Exp. & Salvage K_j, L_j	Gross Revenue G_j	Annual Costs C_j	Debt Interest I_j	Tax Depreciation D_j	Taxes t_j	Borrowed Capital B_j	Recovery of Debt Capital P_j^*	Equity Cash Flow X_{ej}
0	$100,000	—	—	—	—	—	$33,333	—	-$66,667
1		$47,000	$7,000	$5,000	$20,000	$6,000	—	$2,667	26,333
2		47,000	7,000	4,600	17,500	7,160	—	2,667	25,573
3		47,000	7,000	4,200	15,000	8,320	—	2,667	24,813
4		47,000	7,000	3,800	12,500	9,480	—	2,667	24,053
5		47,000	7,000	3,400	10,000	10,640	—	2,667	23,293
6		47,000	7,000	3,000	7,500	11,800	—	2,667	22,533
7		47,000	7,000	2,600	5,000	12,960	—	2,667	21,773
8		47,000	7,000	2,200	2,500	14,120	—	2,667	21,013
9		47,000	7,000	1,800	—	15,280	—	2,667	20,253
10	L = 20,000	47,000	7,000	1,400	—	15,440	—	2,667 + 6,667	33,826

*These values are based on Eq. (6-2)

If this same procedure for total cash flows is used, the results in Table 6-3 are obtained. The NPV of these cash flows is

TABLE 6-3
Total Cash Flows

End of Year j	Cap. Exp. & Salvage K_j, L_j	Gross Revenues G_j	Annual Costs C_j	Tax Depreciation D_j	Taxes t_j	Total Cash Flow X_j
0	$100,000	—	—	—	—	−$100,000
1	—	$47,000	$7,000	$20,000	$8,000	32,000
2	—	47,000	7,000	17,500	9,000	31,000
3	—	47,000	7,000	15,000	10,000	30,000
4	—	47,000	7,000	12,500	11,000	29,000
5	—	47,000	7,000	10,000	12,000	28,000
6	—	47,000	7,000	7,500	13,000	27,000
7	—	47,000	7,000	5,000	14,000	26,000
8	—	47,000	7,000	2,500	15,000	25,000
9	—	47,000	7,000	—	16,000	24,000
10	$L = 20,000$	47,000	7,000	—	16,000	44,000

$$
\begin{aligned}
\text{NPV} &= -100,000 + 32,000 \, (P/F \ 23,1) + \ldots \\
&\quad + 44,000 \, (P/F \ 23,10) \\
&= \$13,193
\end{aligned}
$$

which is the same result obtained by Eq. (6-13) given in Example 6-2. If the operating cash flows are determined, the results shown in Table 6-4 are obtained.

TABLE 6-4
Operating Cash Flows

End of Year j	Cap. Exp. & Salvage K_j, L_j	Gross Revenues G_j	Annual Costs C_j	Tax Depreciation D_j	Debt Interest I_j	Taxes t_j	Operating Cash Flow X_{oj}
0	$100,000	—	—	—	—	—	–$100,000
1	—	$47,000	$7,000	$20,000	$5,000	$6,000	34,000
2	—	47,000	7,000	17,500	4,600	7,160	32,840
3	—	47,000	7,000	15,000	4,200	8,320	31,680
4	—	47,000	7,000	12,500	3,800	9,480	30,520
5	—	47,000	7,000	10,000	3,400	10,640	29,360
6	—	47,000	7,000	7,500	3,000	11,800	28,200
7	—	47,000	7,000	5,000	2,600	12,960	27,040
8	—	47,000	7,000	2,500	2,200	14,120	25,880
9	—	47,000	7,000	—	1,800	15,280	24,720
10	L = 20,000	47,000	7,000	—	1,400	15,440	44,560

The discount rate for operating cash flows is k_b and for this example is

$$k_b = \frac{1}{3}(15) + \frac{2}{3}(30)$$

$$= 25\%$$

Using this discount rate (25%), the net present value of the operating cash flows is

$$NPV = -100{,}000 + 34{,}000\,(P/F\ 25{,}1) + \ldots + 44{,}560\,(P/F\ 25{,}10)$$

$$= \$12{,}066$$

which is the same result given in Example 6-2.

THE RELATIONSHIP BETWEEN CASH FLOW DEFINITIONS AND MARR

Revenue requirements can be used to show *numerically* the relationship between the definitions of cash flow and MARR discussed in Chapter 5. For example if the revenue requirements in Table 6-1 are used as the expected gross revenues (Gj), the total cash

TABLE 6-5
Total Cash Flows
for $Gj = Rj$

End of Year	Total Cash Flows
0	−$100,000
1	31,000
2	29,160
3	27,320
4	25,480
5	23,640
6	21,800
7	19,960
8	18,120
9	16,280
10	34,440[a]

[a]includes salvage value of $20,000

flows in Table 6-5 are obtained. As sample calculations, the total cash flows for years 0, 1, and 2 are

$$X_0 = -\$100,000$$

$$X_1 = (45,334 - 7,000) - (45,334 - 7,000 - 20,000)(.40)$$

$$= \$31,000$$

$$X_2 = (43,934 - 7,000) - (43,934 - 7,000 - 17,500)(.40)$$

$$= \$29,160$$

Calculating the internal rate of return, IRR, for the cash flows in Table 6-5 gives

$$0 = -100{,}000 + 31{,}000 \, (P/F \, i{,}1) + \ldots + 34{,}440 \, (P/F \, i{,}10)$$

$$i = \text{IRR}$$

$$= 0.23$$

$$= 23\%$$

which is exactly equal to the MARR defined by Eq. (5-2); namely,

$$k_a = \frac{1}{3} (15) (1 - .40) + \frac{2}{3} (30)$$

$$= 23\%$$

Taking the same approach only calculating the equity cash flows gives the results shown in Table 6-6. Some sample calculations for the values in Table 6-6 follow:

TABLE 6-6
Equity Cash Flows For $Gj = Rj$

End of Year	Equity Flow
0	−$66,667
1	25,333
2	23,733
3	22,133
4	20,533
5	18,933
6	17,333
7	15,733
8	14,133
9	12,533
10	24,267

$$X_0 = -100{,}000 + \frac{1}{3}(100{,}000)$$

$$= \$-66{,}667$$

$$X_1 = (45{,}334 - 7{,}000 - 5{,}000)$$

$$- (45{,}334 - 7{,}000 - 5{,}000 - 20{,}000)(.40) - 1/3(8{,}000)$$

$$= \$25{,}333$$

$$X_2 = 43{,}934 - 7{,}000 - 4{,}600)$$

$$- (43{,}934 - 7{,}000 - 4{,}600 - 17{,}500)(.40) - 1/3(8{,}000)$$

$$= \$23{,}733$$

$$X_{10} = (31{,}067 - 7{,}000 - 1{,}400) - (31{,}067 - 7{,}000 - 1{,}400)(.40)$$

$$- 1/3(8{,}000) - 1/3(20{,}000) + 20{,}000$$

$$= \$24{,}267$$

Calculating the internal rate of return for the cash flows in Table 6-6 gives

$$0 = -66{,}667 + 25{,}333\,(P/F\ i,1) + \ldots + 24{,}267\,(P/F\ i,10)$$

$$i = \text{IRR}$$

$$= 30\%$$

which is exactly the required return on equity (k_e). This same approach using operating cash flows gives the results in Table 6-7. Some sample calculations follow:

$$X_0 = -\$100{,}000$$

$$X_1 = (45{,}334 - 7{,}000)$$

$$- (45{,}334 - 7{,}000 - 5{,}000 - 20{,}000)(.40)$$

$$= \$33{,}000$$

$$X_2 = (43,934 - 7,000)$$

$$- (43,934 - 7,000 - 4,600 - 17,500)(.40)$$

$$= \$31,000$$

TABLE 6–7
Operating Cash Flow For $G_j = R_j$

End of Year	Operating Cash Flow
0	$-100,000
1	33,000
2	31,000
3	29,000
4	27,000
5	25,000
6	23,000
7	21,000
8	19,000
9	17,000
10	35,000

The internal rate of return for the operating cash flows in Table 6-7 is

$$0 = -100,000 + 33,000 \, (P/F \ i,1) + \ldots + 35,000 \, (P/F \ i,10)$$

$$i = IRR$$

$$= 0.25$$

$$= 25\%$$

which is exactly equal to the cost of capital defined by Eq. (5-5); namely,

$$k_b = \frac{1}{3}(15) + \frac{2}{3}(30)$$

$$= 25\%$$

Now the results of IRR = 23% for total cash flows, IRR = 30% for equity cash flows, and IRR = 25% for operating cash flows are not surprising. In fact, these results are expected since these returns are "built into" the minimum revenue requirements in Table 6-1. The results do show the basis of the decision criterion used with minimum annual revenue requirements. If the expected revenues are less than the minimum revenue requirements, this will give an IRR less than MARR or a negative NPV. Further, these results show *the dependency between the definitions of cash flow and MARR.* In both cases the NPV equals zero since IRR = MARR. However, an NPV of zero is not obtained if a cash flow definition is used with an incorrect definition of MARR.

Levelized Minimum Annual Revenue Requirements: This is another name for an equivalent annual amount of the minimum annual revenue requirements. It can be used as an alternative to Eq. (6-13) to determine the acceptability of a project. The basic procedure is to determine the equivalent annual (levelized) amounts of the minimum annual revenue requirements (R_j) and expected (yearly) revenues (G_j) and compare these two values. If the equivalent annual amount of the expected revenues is greater than the equivalent annual amount of the minimum annual revenue requirements, the project is acceptable. Otherwise, the project is unacceptable. The discount rate to use in determining the levelized amounts is the same as already discussed in this chapter. That is, if equity cash flows are implied, the discount rate should be k_e. If total cash flows are implied, the discount rate should be k_a. If operating cash flows are implied, the discount rate should be k_b.

A MINIMUM REVENUE REQUIREMENT EXTENSION

In the previous discussions of minimum annual revenue requirements, a convention is used where the total investment (capital expenditure) required by the project occurs at one point in time $(j = 0)$. This convention is satisfactory for projects requiring a short construction period. However, there are many cases where the total capital expenditure is spread over several years. This is particularly true for major projects. In these cases, this convention becomes unacceptable. Consequently, it is the purpose of this section to provide a method for determining minimum annual revenue requirements for the case of extended construction periods. In actuality there are two methods presented. The method to use is dependent upon how the capital recovery (book depreciation) and tax depreciation schedules are approached. One depreciation approach is to begin the depreciation amount the year after a particular capital expenditure. This is the approach used for the depreciation schedules in Table 5-7. The other approach is to begin the depreciation schedules after the total amount of capital is expended. This is the approach used for the depreciation amounts in Table 5-8. As mentioned in the discussion of these two different depreciation schedules in Chapter 5, the basic question is, when are the components represented by the associated capital expenditure ready for service? If they are ready for service after each capital expenditure, then the approach given in Table 5-7 is applicable. If service can only begin after the commitment of all capital, the approach in Table 5-8 is applicable. The methods for determining the minimum annual revenue requirements for these two depreciation approaches are shown in the following example.

Example 6-3

Determine the minimum annual revenue requirements for the data given below assuming (a) depreciation amounts begin after each expenditure of capital and (b) depreciation begins after all the capital is expended.

Capital expenditure at ($j = 0$)	=	$100,000
Book depreciation	=	straight-line
life	=	10 years
salvage	=	$20,000
Tax depreciation	=	SYD
life	=	8 years
salvage	=	$10,000

Capital expenditure at $(j = 1)$ = $80,000

    Book depreciation   =   straight-line

        life   =   10 years

        salvage   = $4,000

    Tax depreciation   =   SYD

        life   =   8 years

        salvage   = $8,000

Capital expenditure at $(j = 2)$ = $60,000

    Book depreciation   =   straight-line

        life   =   10 years

        salvage   = $5,000

    Tax depreciation   =   SYD

        life   =   8 years

        salvage   = $6,000

    Required return on equity =   30%

    Cost of debt capital   =   15%

    Debt ratio   =   1/3

    Tax rate   =   40%

    Annual costs   = $7,000

For Part a, the method that is most straight-forward is to determine the minimum annual revenue requirements *excluding the annual costs* for each capital expenditure component as though they are independent and then combine these results in the appropriate years. At this point, the annual costs are also added in the years that are estimated to be appropriate. The minimum annual revenue requirements, excluding annual costs, for each of the capital expenditure components are given in Tables 6-8, 6-9, and 6-10.

In adding the component revenue requirements to obtain the total revenue requirements for the project, it must be remembered that the revenue requirement in year one for the capital expenditure occurring in year one actually occurs in year two when

TABLE 6-8
Minimum Annual Revenue Requirements for the Capital Expenditure at $j = 0$

End of Year j	Book Depreciation D_b	Tax Depreciation D_t	Book Value B	Equity Return F_e	Debt Interest I	Taxes t	Costs C	Minimum Annual Revenue Requirement R
0	—	—	$100,000	—	—	—	—	—
1	$8,000	$20,000	92,000	$20,000	$5,000	$5,334	—	$38,334
2	8,000	17,500	84,000	18,400	4,600	5,934	—	36,934
3	8,000	15,000	76,000	16,800	4,200	6,534	—	35,534
4	8,000	12,500	68,000	15,200	3,800	7,134	—	34,134
5	8,000	10,000	60,000	13,600	3,400	7,734	—	32,734
6	8,000	7,500	52,000	12,000	3,000	8,334	—	31,334
7	8,000	5,000	44,000	10,400	2,600	8,934	—	29,934
8	8,000	2,500	36,000	8,800	2,200	9,534	—	28,534
9	8,000	—	28,000	7,200	1,800	10,134	—	27,134
10	8,000	—	20,000	5,600	1,400	9,067	—	24,067

TABLE 6-9
Minimum Annual Revenue Requirements for the Capital Expenditure at j = 1

End of Year j	Book Depreciation D_b	Tax Depreciation D_t	Book Value B	Equity Return F_e	Debt Interest I	Taxes t	Costs C	Minimum Annual Revenue Requirement R
0	—	—	$80,000	—	—	—	—	—
1	$7,600	$16,000	72,400	$16,000	$4,000	$5,067	—	$32,667
2	7,600	14,000	64,800	14,480	3,620	5,387	—	31,087
3	7,600	12,000	57,200	12,960	3,240	5,707	—	29,507
4	7,600	10,000	49,600	11,440	2,860	6,207	—	27,927
5	7,600	8,000	42,000	9,920	2,480	6,347	—	26,347
6	7,600	6,000	34,400	8,400	2,100	6,667	—	24,767
7	7,600	4,000	26,800	6,880	1,720	6,987	—	23,187
8	7,600	2,000	19,200	5,360	1,340	7,307	—	21,607
9	7,600	—	11,600	3,840	960	7,627	—	20,027
10	7,600	—	4,000	2,320	580	6,614	—	17,114

TABLE 6-10
Minimum Annual Revenue Requirements for the
Capital Expenditure at j = 2

End of Year j	Book Depreciation D_b	Tax Depreciation D_t	Book Value B	Equity Return F_e	Debt Interest I	Taxes t	Costs C	Minimum Annual Revenue Requirement R
0	—	—	$60,000	—	—	—	—	—
1	$5,500	$12,000	54,500	$12,000	$3,000	$3,667	—	$24,167
2	5,500	10,500	49,000	10,900	2,725	3,934	—	23,059
3	5,500	9,000	43,500	9,800	2,450	4,200	—	21,950
4	5,500	7,500	38,000	8,700	2,175	4,467	—	20,842
5	5,500	6,000	32,500	7,600	1,900	4,734	—	19,734
6	5,500	4,500	27,000	6,500	1,625	5,000	—	18,625
7	5,500	3,000	21,500	5,400	1,350	5,267	—	17,517
8	5,500	1,500	16,000	4,300	1,075	5,534	—	16,409
9	5,500	—	10,500	3,200	800	5,800	—	15,300
10	5,500	—	5,000	2,100	525	5,067	—	13,192

adding the revenue requirements of the components. Similarly, the revenue requirement in year one for the capital expenditure occurring in year two actually occurs in year three. The addition of the revenue requirements and annual costs is shown in Table 6-11. In Table 6-11, the annual costs are added in years three through twelve. This is arbitrary. In actuality, the years in which the annual costs are applicable must be estimated for the particular project under consideration.

TABLE 6-11
Total Minimum Revenue Requirements
for Example 6-3

End of Year	Minimum Annual for Capital $j = 0$	Revenue Expenditures $j = 1$	Requirements at $j = 2$	Costs	Total Minimum Revenue Requirements
0	—	—	—	—	—
1	$38,334	—	—	—	$38,334
2	36,934	$32,667	—	—	69,601
3	35,534	31,087	$24,167	$7,000	97,788
4	34,134	29,507	23,059	7,000	93,700
5	32,734	27,927	21,950	7,000	89,611
6	31,334	26,347	20,842	7,000	85,523
7	29,934	24,767	19,734	7,000	81,435
8	28,534	23,187	18,625	7,000	77,346
9	27,134	21,607	17,517	7,000	73,258
10	24,067	20,027	16,409	7,000	67,503
11	—	17,114	15,300	7,000	39,414
12	—	—	13,192	7,000	20,192

In this example, the tax and book salvage values are given (estimated) for each component of the total capital investment ($240,000). As pointed out in Chapter 5, these values are not always given (estimated). Often, only the total salvage value is given (estimated). The usual approach in these cases is the same as that discussed in Chapter 5. That is, proportion the total salvage value between the various capital expenditure components using Eq. (5-14).

For Part b, the method for determining the minimum annual revenue requirements is different than the method used in Part (a). The depreciation amounts begin in the year after the total amount of capital is expended and are based on the total investment and total salvage. In this example, this is year three and the book depreciation is

$$D_b = \frac{240,000 - 29,000}{10} = \$21,100$$

for years three through twelve. The tax depreciation amounts for years three and four are

$$D_{t_3} = \frac{8}{36}(240,000 - 24,000) = \$48,000$$

$$D_{t_4} = \frac{7}{36}(240,000 - 24,000) = \$42,000$$

The remaining tax depreciation amounts are given in Table 6-12.

The book values given in Table 6-12 are the cumulative totals of the capital expenditure components. These values do not begin to decrease until year three when the recovery of capital (book depreciation) begins. The other values given in Table 6-12 are determined using the equations previously given in this chapter. For example, the equity returns for years one and two, using Eq. (6-4) are

$$F_{e_1} = \left(\frac{2}{3}\right)(0.30)(100,000) = \$20,000$$

$$F_{e_2} = \left(\frac{2}{3}\right)(0.30)(180,000) = \$36,000$$

and the debt interest for the same years, using Eq. (6-5), is

$$I_1 = \left(\frac{1}{3}\right)(0.15)(100,000) = \$5,000$$

$$I_2 = \left(\frac{1}{3}\right)(0.15)(180,000) = \$9,000$$

TABLE 6-12
Minimum Annual Revenue Requirements
for Part B of Example 6-3

End of Year	Book Depr. D_b	Tax Depr. D_t	Book Value B	Equity Return F_e	Debt Interest I	Tax t	Costs C	Minimum Annual Revenue Requirement R
0	—	—	$100,000	—	—	—	—	—
1	—	—	180,000	$20,000	$5,000	$13,334	—	$38,334
2	—	—	240,000	36,000	9,000	24,000	—	69,000
3	$21,100	$48,000	218,900	48,000	12,000	14,067	$7,000	102,167
4	21,100	42,000	197,800	43,780	10,945	15,254	7,000	98,079
5	21,100	36,000	176,700	39,560	9,890	16,441	7,000	93,991
6	21,100	30,000	155,600	35,340	8,835	17,628	7,000	89,903
7	21,100	24,000	134,500	31,120	7,780	18,814	7,000	85,814
8	21,100	18,000	113,400	26,900	6,725	20,001	7,000	81,726
9	21,100	12,000	92,300	22,680	5,670	21,188	7,000	77,638
10	21,100	6,000	71,200	18,460	4,615	22,374	7,000	73,549
11	21,100	—	50,100	14,240	3,560	23,561	7,000	69,461
12	21,100	—	29,000	10,020	2,505	20,748	7,000	61,373

Using Eq. (6-11), the taxes for the first two years are

$$t_1 = \frac{0.40}{1-0.40}(20,000) = \$13,334$$

$$t_2 = \frac{0.40}{1-0.40}(36,000) = \$24,000$$

and using Eq. (6-1), the minimum annual revenue requirements for the first two years are

$$R_1 = 20,000 + 5,000 + 13,334 = \$38,334$$

$$R_2 = 36,000 + 9,000 + 24,000 = \$69,000$$

The costs (\$7,000) are not added in determining these two values because it is assumed that these costs begin in year three. As in Part a, this is arbitrary. Where the annual costs begin must be estimated.

SUMMARY

This chapter has presented the concept of minimum annual revenue requirements for purposes of evaluating a single project (investment). The generation of revenue requirements for this purpose is not difficult. However, it can be tedious, especially, when the capital recovery period (book depreciation life) is more representative (longer) than the periods used in this chapter's examples. Consequently, a computer program is provided in the appendices for generating the minimum annual revenue requirements.

The method given in this chapter for generating revenue requirements is known as the *flow-through method* because it follows the concept of cash flow from the standpoint of accounting for costs and incomes at the time of their estimated occurrence. Another method, not discussed in this book, for generating revenue requirements is possible. This method is known as the *normalizing method* and is widely used by public utility companies because of its similarities to their accounting procedures. A detailed discussion of the normalizing method is given in reference [6] listed in Chapter 5.

PROBLEMS _____

6-1. Determine the minimum annual revenue requirements for the
following data:

initial investment	= $60,000
book depreciation	= straight-line
life	= 8 years
salvage	= $4,000
tax depreciation	= sum of years-digits
life	= 5 years
salvage	= $0
debt ratio	= 25%
cost of debt capital	= 12%
required return on equity	= 20%
tax rate	= 40%
annual costs	= $5,000

6-2. What are the minimum revenue requirements in Problem 6-1 if
the investment tax credit is 10%?

6-3. Repeat Problem 6-1 only assume that the tax depreciation
model is five years under MACRS.

6-4. Calculate the minimum annual revenue requirements for the
data given below:

initial cost	= $40,000
tax and book depreciation	= sum of years-digits
life	= 8 years
salvage value	= $4,000
annual costs	= $3,000
required return on equity	= 25%

cost of debt	=	15%
debt ratio	=	40%
tax rate	=	40%

6-5. Using the data given below, determine the minimum annual revenue requirements on the basis that the book and tax depreciation begins in the year following a particular capital expenditure.

Total investment	=	$250,000
capital expenditure at $(j = 0)$	=	$40,000
capital expenditure at $(j = 1)$	=	$160,000
capital expenditure at $(j = 2)$	=	$50,000
Total salvage value for both tax and book purposes	=	$50,000
Required return on equity	=	20%
Debt interest	=	10%
Debt ratio	=	40%
Tax rate	=	40%
Life for both tax and book depreciation purposes	=	8 years
Depreciation method for tax purposes	=	sum of years-digits
Depreciation method for book (capital recovery) purposes	=	straight-line
Annual costs	=	$10,000 beginning in

the third year and ending in year ten.

6-6. Repeat Problem 6-5 only assume that the depreciation begins after the total capital is expended.

6-7 If an investment tax credit of 10% is applicable, what are the revenue requirements in Problems 6-5 and 6-6?

6-8. If the estimated annual gross revenues (income) in Problem 6-1 are (a) $30,000, (b) $17,000, (c) $25,000, and (d) $20,000, is the project acceptable? Assume equity cash flows are the basis of the evaluation.

6-9. Suppose in Problem 6-2, the estimated gross revenues are as shown below. What is the net present value of the equity cash flows?

End of Year	Estimated Gross Revenues
1	$13,000
2	20,000
3	24,000
4	24,000
5	25,000
6	30,000
7	30,000
8	30,000

6-10. A company is considering buying a particular machine for $840,000. It is estimated that the annual cost of operating (power and labor) this machine is $50,000. The company's practice is to depreciate, for tax purpose, this type of machine on the basis of sum of the years-digits, a seven-year life, and a zero salvage value. For capital recovery purposes, the company uses straight-line depreciation and the same life and salvage as that used for tax depreciation. For this type of machine, the company's required return on equity is 25%. The company believes that a 15% cost of debt capital and a tax rate of 40% is applicable for the next seven years. The company currently operates with a 30% debt ratio and does not expect this ratio to change in the future. If the company can lease the same machine for $250,000 per year, should the company purchase or lease the machine? Assume equity cash flows as the basis.

6-11. A company is considering revising their current materials handling system over the next two years. The total cost of the equipment for the contemplated revisions is $600,000 which is estimated to be split in the following manner: an initial expenditure of $200,000, an expenditure of $250,000 one year from now, and an expenditure of $150,000 two years from now. It is estimated that the annual cost of operating and maintaining the new equipment is $25,000 beginning in the third year. The company requires a return on equity capital of 30% and uses a 15% interest rate for debt capital. It currently has a debt ratio of 1/3 and this ratio is expected to be maintained in the future. The company uses the same depreciation model for tax and capital recovery purposes. For this equipment, sum of the years-digits depreciation is used with a total salvage value of $60,000 and a life of eight years. Because of the nature of the material handling equipment, service of the equipment cannot be realized until all the revisions are made. All new materials handling equipment required by this project is eligible for the investment tax credit (10%) and the company's tax rate is 40%. Calculate the minimum annual revenue requirements for this project and determine if the project is economically desirable assuming that the annual gross savings resulting from this project are $400,000 a year for the first eight years the project is in service. Assume equity cash flows.

6-12. Using the data given in Problem 6-2 and assuming $G_j = R_j$ determine the yearly equity and total cash flows. Use Eqs. (6-2) and (6-3) to determine the debt recovery (P).

7

CAPITAL BUDGETING

In Chapters 5 and 6 the primary concern is the acceptability of a single project (investment). In this chapter the concern is with the problem of choosing a single project or group of projects from a larger group of *individually acceptable* projects. This problem is referred to as the *capital budgeting problem*. It is a result of a group of acceptable projects competing for some restricted (constrained) resource (capital, manpower, materials, etc.) that does not allow all the projects to be chosen.

Before a solution to the capital budgeting problem can be formulated, a correct criterion for ranking projects must be established. In this text, this criterion is based on the financial objective of maximizing the wealth of the stockholders. Also in establishing this criterion two conditions are imposed that are consistent with this financial objective. These conditions are (1) every additional requirement of capital must be justified and (2) an acceptable project today is preferred over the speculation that a better project might be available in the future.

For the discussions in this chapter, the initial starting point is with the cash flows already determined for each project. This is done to facilitate these discussions. However, it should be understood that determining the cash flows for each project is, in actuality, the first step. These cash flows are determined in accordance with the procedures discussed in Chapter 5. In the capital budgeting problem, a relative comparison of the projects' cash flows is made. The cash flows for each project must be determined on a consistent basis in order to insure an equitable comparison. The following points must be maintained when comparing cash flows:

1. The cash flow definition for all projects must be the same. It is not acceptable to mix cash flow definitions in the same capital budgeting problem. Also, it must be remembered that it is assumed that any debt obligation is recovered over the life of the project when total or operating cash flows are used.
2. If equity cash flows are used, the debt ratio should be the same for all projects. This is *only for purposes of providing a consistent basis* for the comparison of the projects in a particular capital budgeting problem. It does not preclude a particular project, once selected, from being financed in some manner that is not in accordance with the debt ratio used in the analysis. This point and approach are discussed in Chapter 5.
3. Since the NPV and IRR for equity cash flows vary with the method used to pay the debt obligation, the debt payment method in a particular capital budgeting problem should be the same for each project. This debt payment method should be based on the manner in which a company has decided to obtain a majority of its new debt capital. This point is similar to the situation discussed in Chapter 5 in regard to a single project.

In addition to the preceding three points, two other conditions are imposed on the discussions of capital budgeting problems in this chapter. These two conditions are (1) risk is not a consideration and (2) the projects in a particular capital budgeting problem are all independent.

Because it is stated in Chapter 5 that the NPV and IRR give the same decision regarding the acceptability of a project, it might be assumed that either the NPV or IRR is acceptable as a ranking criterion. This is not the case. In capital budgeting problems, the NPV and IRR can give different rankings. This can be seen by considering the four projects in Table 7-1. If the projects in Table 7-1 are ranked on the basis of IRR, the result is 1-3-2-4. If the same projects are ranked on the basis of NPV, the result is 3-2-4-1. These rankings are not the same and point out the ranking inconsistency that exists between the NPV and the IRR. In contrast to this result, it is sometimes stated in the literature that the IRR and NPV give a consistent choice of projects in capital budgeting problems. This is a correct statement *provided its full meaning is clearly understood.* The full meaning of this statement centers around a condition previously stated. That is, every additional requirement of capital must be justified. This condition can best be explained by considering a special case of the capital budgeting problem; namely, the case of mutually exclusive projects. Also by considering mutually exclusive projects, a ranking criterion for the capital budgeting problem can be established.

TABLE 7-1

Internal Rates of Return and Net Present Values

End of Year	Cash Flows			
	Project 1	Project 2	Project 3	Project 4
0	−$50,000	−$100,000	−$120,000	−$200,000
1	14,000	24,000	30,000	40,000
2	14,000	24,000	30,000	40,000
3	14,000	24,000	30,000	40,000
4	14,000	24,000	30,000	40,000
5	14,000	24,000	30,000	40,000
6	14,000	24,000	30,000	40,000
7	14,000	24,000	30,000	40,000
8	14,000	24,000	30,000	40,000
9	14,000	24,000	30,000	40,000
10	14,000	24,000	30,000	40,000
IRR	25.00%	20.21%	21.55%	15.11%
NPV (10%)	$36,024	$47,470	$64,338	$45,784

MUTUALLY EXCLUSIVE PROJECTS

Projects are mutually exclusive when the choice of one project precludes the choice of any other project. This implies that *only one* project is chosen from a group of acceptable projects. This is not an unusual situation. An example of mutually exclusive projects is the situation where there are several methods of making a new product. Each method has different initial costs, gross incomes, yearly costs, etc. The question is, Which method should be chosen? The answer to this question is, the method with the greatest economic advantage. Or, to be consistent with one of the basic conditions, the method that provides the greatest wealth to the stockholders.

The solution to the mutually exclusive capital budgeting problem involves a comparison of the return earned on an incremental amount of capital with the MARR value or a comparison of the NPV for each project. These two solution methods are discussed in the following example.

Example 7-1 _____

Determine which project should be chosen if the projects in Table 7-1 are mutually exclusive and MARR equals 10%.

The first step is to determine if all projects have an IRR that is equal or greater than MARR. This step has already been done and the results are given in Table 7-1. These results indicate that all projects are acceptable. If a project has an IRR that is less than MARR, it should be eliminated from further consideration.

The next step is to determine the rate of return earned on each additional increment of required capital. A comparison of Project 1 to doing nothing indicates a rate of return of 25% (Table 7-1) which is larger than MARR. Consequently, Project 1 is better than doing nothing. A comparison of Projects 1 and 2 (the yearly cash flows of Project 2 minus the yearly cash flows of Project 1) gives a rate of return, RR, of

$$0 = -100,000 + 50,000 + (24,000 - 14,000)(P/A \ i,10)$$

where

$$i = RR$$

$$= 15.11\%$$

Since this result is greater than MARR, it indicates that the additional capital required ($50,000) by Project 2 is justified by the yearly increase in cash flow ($10,000). Consequently, Project 2 is preferred over Project 1. A comparison of Projects 2 and 3 gives

$$0 = -120,000 + 100,000 + (30,000 - 24,000)(P/A \ i,10)$$

where

$$i = RR$$

$$= 27.50\%$$

This result is larger than MARR. Consequently, Project 3 is preferred over Project 2. A comparison of Projects 3 and 4 gives

$$0 = -200,000 + 120,000 + (40,000 - 30,000)(P/A \ i,10)$$

where

$$i = RR$$

$$= 4.28\%$$

which indicates Project 3 is preferred to Project 4 since the RR is smaller than MARR and consequently the final choice is Project 3. *Note that Project 3 is the choice if the decision were based on the largest NPV.*

Some Important Comments The results obtained in Example 7-1 can be generalized. The incremental RR approach will give the same choice of project as the project with the highest NPV. This is an important point because it serves as the basis for determining a solution to a more general form of the capital budgeting problem. The question sometimes arises, Why use the RR approach when the NPV is computationally easier? The answer to this question is, the RR in a practical situation is, in all probability, not used. The RR approach is presented here to show the basis of the statement given previously that the IRR and NPV give a consistent choice of projects in the capital budgeting problems. Example 7-1 shows that this statement is correct *provided* the internal rate of return approach is used in a correct manner. That is, an incremental approach is used. This statement *does not imply* that the project with the largest IRR should be chosen. It is sometimes erroneously argued that the project with the highest IRR should be chosen and money could be "saved" and used for "better investments" that might occur in the future. A problem with this statement is that "better investments" might *not* occur at that time. Also, if a better investment does occur in the future, then it should be undertaken (theoretically at least). Otherwise the wealth of the stockholders is not being maximized.

In Example 7-1, the cash flows are constant for each project. This is not a requirement. The cash flows can vary yearly (and often do). However, the basic procedure is the same for determining the RR on the increment but is computationally more involved. In cases of cash flows that vary yearly, the most direct way is to determine the NPV for each project. Sometimes, a present value of the incremental cash flows is calculated to determine if the incremental cash flows have an RR greater than MARR. This method has decided computational advantages over the incremental RR approach. For example, a comparison of Projects 1 and 2 in Example 7-1 on the basis of incremental present value, IPV, is

$$\text{IPV} = -100,000 + 50,000 + (24,000 - 14,000)(P/A\ 10,10)$$

$$= \$11,446$$

Since this value is positive, it implies that the RR is greater than MARR. As in Example 7-1, Project 2 is preferred over Project 1.

Different Lives   In Example 7-1, the cash flows for each project extend over the same period of time (ten years). This is not always the case. It is possible for the projects in capital budgeting problems to have cash flows that extend over different periods of time.

In general, any comparison of projects must be made over *the same period of time*. Otherwise, the comparison is questionable. In the comparison of projects with cash flows over different periods of time, certain assumptions are necessary in order to provide for a comparison that is over the same period of time. There are three basic assumptions that can be made. They are as follows:

1.   For a period of time equal to the longest project, make specific estimates about future investment alternatives that occur in

the period of time between the end of an alternative's life and the life of the longest project.

2. For a period of time equal to the longest project, assume that the cash flows for all projects will be invested at MARR.

3. Assume that each project's cash flows cycle for a period of time equal to the least common multiple (LCM) of all the projects' lives.

The meaning of these three assumptions is shown in the following example. Also, this example shows that these three assumptions can give different results (decisions).

Example 7-2

Using the cash flows given in Table 7-2 and the three assumptions for the comparison of projects with unequal lives, determine the net present values for each project if MARR equals 15%.

If Assumption 1 is used, this means that it is necessary to estimate specific investment opportunities that will be available at the end of the tenth year and their resulting cash flows through year twenty. From a practical standpoint, this is a rather difficult task. Obviously, the NPV of Project 1 will vary with the estimated investment opportunities. The NPV for Project 2 is

$$NPV_2 = -150,000 + 35,000(P/A\ 15,20)$$

$$= \$69,076$$

If Assumption 2 is used, the positive cash flows for each project are invested at MARR through year twenty. This means that the future worth, F, resulting from these positive cash flows at the end of year twenty is

$$F_1 = (32,000)\ (F/A\ 15,10)(F/P\ 15,10)$$

$$F_2 = (35,000)\ (F/A\ 15,20)$$

and the NPV for each project with this assumption is

$$NPV_1 = -100,000 + [32,000\ (F/A\ 15,10)(F/P\ 15,10)](P/F\ 15,20)$$

$$= \$60,602$$

TABLE 7-2

Projects with Different Lives

End of Year	Cash Flows	
	Project 1	*Project 2*
0	−$100,000	−$150,000
1	32,000	35,000
2	32,000	35,000
3	32,000	35,000
4	32,000	35,000
5	32,000	35,000
6	32,000	35,000
7	32,000	35,000
8	32,000	35,000
9	32,000	35,000
10	32,000	35,000
11	–	35,000
12	–	35,000
13	–	35,000
14	–	35,000
15	–	35,000
16	–	35,000
17	–	35,000
18	–	35,000
19	–	35,000
20	–	35,000

$$NPV_2 = -150,000 + [35,000(F/A\ 15,20)](P/F\ 15,20)$$

$$= \$69,076$$

The same net present values are obtained if the difference in project lives is *seemingly* disregarded. That is,

$$NPV_1 = -100,000 + 32,000\ (P/A\ 15,10)$$

$$= \$60,602$$

$$NPV_2 = -150,000 + 35,000\ (P/A\ 15,20)$$

$$= \$69,076$$

This is an important point since this result can be generalized. That is, with Assumption 2 the NPV for each project can be calculated without *explicit* consideration of the difference in project lives provided this assumption is considered applicable.

TABLE 7-3

Recycling Assumption

End of Year	Cash Flows		Project 2
	Project 1		Project 2
0	−$100,000		−$150,000
1	32,000		35,000
2	32,000		35,000
3	32,000		35,000
4	32,000		35,000
5	32,000		35,000
6	32,000		35,000
7	32,000		35,000
8	32,000		35,000
9	32,000		35,000
10	32,000	−100,000	35,000
11		32,000	35,000
12		32,000	35,000
13		32,000	35,000
14		32,000	35,000
15		32,000	35,000
16		32,000	35,000
17		32,000	35,000
18		32,000	35,000
19		32,000	35,000
20		32,000	35,000

If Assumption 3 is used, there is a second cycle of Project 1 as shown in Table 7-3. With this assumption, the net present values for the two projects are

$$\text{NPV}_1 = -100{,}000 - 100{,}000(P/F\ 15{,}10) + 32{,}000(P/A\ 15{,}20)$$
$$= \$75{,}578$$

$$\text{NPV}_2 = -150,000 + 35,000(P/A \ 15,20)$$

$$= \$69,076$$

Note that the net present values for Project 1 are different from Assumptions 2 and 3. In fact, a different choice of project is indicated if the projects are mutually exclusive. If Assumption 1 is used, this could also give an NPV that is different from either Assumption 2 or 3 depending on what estimate is made regarding future investment opportunities for Project 1.

Assumption for Unequal Lives   Example 7-2 shows that the three different assumptions for comparing projects with different lives can give different results. The question is, What assumption should be used? This text uses Assumption 2. The use of Assumption 2 is based on the combined consideration of plausibility, computational advantage, practicality, and theoretical correctness for the comparison of projects *with different earnings (gross incomes)*. A different assumption is used later in the comparison of projects *with equal earnings* (cost comparisons and replacement analysis). Assumption 1 has decided theoretical merit. However, it is not used in this text because of the difficulty (practicality) of estimating investment opportunities far into the future.

Assumption 3 is a popular assumption (especially in cost comparisons and replacement analysis). However, there are problems in regard to its plausibility and computational requirements. The idea that projects with identical cash flows are available in later years (the cycling requirement) is not very plausible, especially in the case of projects with different earnings. Consider two projects with lives of 15 and 25 years. The least common multiple of their lives is 75 years and implies a total of five cycles for the project with a life of 15 years and a total of three cycles for the project with a life of 25 years. This idea of project cycles is very difficult to justify on grounds of practicality and plausibility. Although the computational disadvantages with Assumption 3 are not insurmountable, they do increase as the number of cycles increases.

Assumption 2 has some merit since it does not suffer from plausibility or practicality considerations nor does it have computational disadvantages. If a broad view is taken in regard to the assumption that the cash flows are invested at MARR, Assumption 2 has theoretical merit. That is, the cash flows can be "invested" (theoretically at least) in retiring debt obligations and paying dividends to stockholders. These considerations make Assumption 2 a good choice for capital budgeting problems.

THE CAPITAL BUDGETING PROBLEM

One solution to the capital budgeting problem can be obtained by applying the procedures used to solve the mutually exclusive problem. This solution involves arranging all the possible combinations of projects into mutually exclusive "bundles" and then choosing the bundle that maximizes the NPV and does not violate any restrictions (constraints) placed on the solution. For example, if the projects in Table 7-1 are assumed to be independent and arranged in mutually exclusive "bundles" the results shown in Table 7-4 are obtained. If a restriction is imposed that only a certain amount of money can be spent for new projects (a capital expenditure budget), then those bundles with total capital expenditures exceeding this amount are eliminated from further consideration. For example, a capital expenditure budget of $450,000 means that bundle 14 (Projects 2, 3, 4) is chosen since it maximizes the NPV and does not exceed the limitation of $450,000. As two further examples, a budget restriction of $300,000 gives bundle 11 (Projects 1, 2, 3) as the choice, and a budget restriction of $250,000 gives bundle 8 (Projects 2, 3) as the choice. This approach to the capital budgeting problem has a computational disadvantage since the number of possible combinations (bundles) is $2^n - 1$, where n is the number of projects. For example if there are ten projects, there are 1,023 possible combinations (bundles). One way to avoid this computational disadvantage is to formulate the capital budgeting problem in a mathematical programming format. That is,

$$\text{maximize: } z = \sum_{i=1}^{n} (\text{NPV})_i x_i$$

$$\tag{7-1}$$

subject to:

$$\sum_{i=1}^{n} K_i x_i \leq B$$

$$\tag{7-2}$$

$$x_i = 0 \text{ or } 1 \text{ for all } i$$

$$\tag{7-3}$$

TABLE 7-4

Projects Arranged in Mutually Exclusive Bundles

Bundle	Projects	Capital Expenditure	Annual Cash Flow	NPV (10%)	IRR (%)
1	1	$ 50,000	$ 14,000	$ 36,204	25.00
2	2	100,000	24,000	47,470	20.21
3	3	120,000	30,000	64,338	21.55
4	4	200,000	40,000	45,784	15.11
5	1,2	150,000	38,000	83,494	23.25
6	1,3	170,000	44,000	100,362	24.36
7	1,4	250,000	54,000	81,808	19.29
8	2,3	220,000	54,000	111,808	21.57
9	2,4	300,000	64,000	93,254	17.00
10	3,4	320,000	70,000	110,122	17.71
11	1,2,3	270,000	68,000	147,832	22.94
12	1,2,4	350,000	78,000	129,278	18.22
13	1,3,4	370,000	84,000	146,146	18.72
14	2,3,4	420,000	94,000	157,592	18.33
15	1,2,3,4	470,000	108,000	193,616	19.04

where

$(NPV)_i$ = net present value for Project i

K_i = capital expenditure (investment) required by Project i

n = number of projects

x_i = decision variable for Project i

B = budget (capital expenditure) restriction

In mathematical programming vocabulary, Eq. (7-1) is referred to as the *objective* equation and Eqs. (7-2) and (7-3) are referred to as the *restrictions* (constraints). Equation (7-3) is a mathematical expression of the fact that a project is either accepted ($x_i = 1$) or rejected ($x_i = 0$). That is, the projects are not divisible.

The use of Eqs. (7-1), (7-2), and (7-3) is demonstrated in the following formulation using the data in Table 7-1 and a budget restriction of $250,000.

$$\text{maximize: } z = 36{,}204x_1 + 47{,}470x_2 + 64{,}338x_3 + 45{,}784x_4 \quad (7\text{-}4)$$

subject to:

$$50{,}000x_1 + 100{,}000x_2 + 120{,}000x_3 + 200{,}000x_4 \leq 250{,}000 \quad (7\text{-}5)$$

$$X_{1,2,3,4} = 0 \text{ or } 1 \quad (7\text{-}6)$$

Because of the small number of projects involved in this formulation, Eqs. (7-4), (7-5), and (7-6) can be solved by inspection. The solution is $x_1 = 0$, $x_2 = x_3 = 1$, and $x_4 = 0$. This is the same solution obtained using the bundle approach shown earlier. When there is a large number of projects, specialized algorithms are necessary. These algorithms are beyond the scope of this text and will not be discussed further. The formulation of the capital budgeting problem expressed by Eqs. (7-1), (7-2), and (7-3) can be extended to include certain other considerations that may be applicable to capital budgeting problems.

Mutually Exclusive Projects

A subset, m, of mutually exclusive projects in a capital budgeting problem can be accommodated by adding the restriction

$$\sum_m x_m \leq 1 \quad (7\text{-}7)$$

to the mathematical formulation. As an example suppose that in some particular capital budgeting problem, Projects 2, 6, 8, and 9 are mutually exclusive. Using Eq. (7-7), the restriction

$$X_2 + X_6 + X_8 + X_9 \leq 1 \quad (7\text{-}8)$$

is added to the mathematical formulation of the problem. Sometimes there is a tendency to choose the project with the highest NPV from a subset of mutually exclusive projects and include only this chosen project in the overall formulation of a capital budgeting problem. This is incorrect. It is possible to have some other mutually exclusive project with a lower net present value and lower capital investment that, when combined with some other project not in the mutually exclusive set, can give a higher total net present value.

Interdependent Projects   It is possible in the capital budgeting problem to have projects that are interdependent. In this case, the equation

$$x_r - x_s \leq 0 \qquad (7\text{-}9)$$

is added to mathematical programming formulation. Equation (7-9) expresses the situation that if Project r is done then Project s must be done. However, Project s can be done without Project r. Also, neither Project r or s need be done.

Labor and Material Restrictions   There are situations where the total available labor and/or materials are limited. These situations can be included in the formulation of the capital budgeting problem by adding a set of restrictions, m, of the form

$$\sum_m m_{ij} x_i \leq M_j \qquad (7\text{-}10)$$

where

$$m_{ij} = \text{materials (labor) required by Project } i \text{ in year } j$$
$$x_i = \text{decision variable for Project } i$$
$$M_j = \text{total materials (labor) available in year } j$$

Multiperiod Budgets   It is shown in Chapter 5 that the total expenditure required by a project can be expended over a several year period. Consequently, it is not unusual to have budget restrictions established for future years. In this case, a set of budget restrictions, m, replaces the single budget restriction. That is, the budget set

$$\sum_m K_{ij} x_i \leq B_j \qquad (7\text{-}11)$$

replaces the single budget restriction defined by Eq. (7-2) where K_{ij} is the capital expenditure required by Project i in year j.

Example 7-3

Using the data given in Table 7-5 and the following conditions, formulate the capital budgeting problem in a mathematical programming format and solve it by inspection.

1. The budget restriction for $j = 0$ is \$100,000.
2. The budget restriction for $j = 1$ is \$80,000.
3. The budget restriction for $j = 2$ is \$50,000.
4. Projects 2, 6, and 7 are mutually exclusive.
5. Projects 1 and 3 are interdependent: if Project 1 is done, Project 3 must be done; but Project 3 can be done without Project 1.

TABLE 7-5

Capital Budgeting Problem

Project Number	Capital Expenditure $j = 0$	Capital Expenditure $j = 1$	Capital Expenditure $j = 2$	Net Present Value
1	\$30,000	\$20,000	\$ 5,000	\$10,000
2	15,000	10,000	8,000	7,000
3	10,000	–	5,000	2,000
4	20,000	10,000	–	6,000
5	18,000	15,000	–	8,000
6	30,000	–	15,000	9,000
7	10,000	10,000	10,000	8,000
8	28,000	20,000	15,000	12,000
9	12,000	–	20,000	5,000
10	9,000	15,000	9,000	8,000

The mathematical programming format is to maximize:

$$z = 10,000x_1 + 7,000x_2 + 2,000x_3 + 6,000x_4 + 8,000x_5$$
$$+ 9,000x_6 + 8,000x_7 + 12,000x_8 + 5,000x_9 + 8,000x_{10}$$

subject to:

$$30{,}000x_1 + 15{,}000x_2 + 10{,}000x_3 + 20{,}000x_4 + 18{,}000x_5 + 30{,}000x_6$$
$$+ 10{,}000x_7 + 28{,}000x_8 + 12{,}000x_9 + 9{,}000x_{10} \leq 100{,}000$$

$$20{,}000x_1 + 10{,}000x_2 + 10{,}000x_4 + 15{,}000x_5 + 10{,}000x_7 + 20{,}000x_8$$
$$+ 15{,}000x_{10} \leq 80{,}000$$

$$5{,}000x_1 + 8{,}000x_2 + 5{,}000x_3 + 15{,}000x_6 + 10{,}000x_7 + 15{,}000x_8$$
$$+ 20{,}000x_9 + 9{,}000x_{10} \leq 50{,}000$$

$$x_2 + x_6 + x_7 \leq 1$$
$$x_1 - x_3 \leq 0$$
$$x_i = 0 \text{ or } 1 \text{ for } i = 1, 2, \ldots, 10$$

The solution to this problem is

x_1	=	0		
x_2	=	0		
x_3	=	1		
x_4	=	1		
x_5	=	1		

x_6	=	0
x_7	=	1
x_8	=	1
x_9	=	0
x_{10}	=	1

$$z = \$44{,}000$$

Some Incorrect Proposals   Certain incorrect methods are sometimes proposed to solve the capital budgeting problem. There are two particular incorrect methods that seem to be persistently proposed. The first method involves listing the project on the basis of highest rates of return and keeping a cumulative total of the capital expenditures. Once the cumulative total of the capital expenditures exceeds a given budget, the projects included in this listing are the ones selected. An example of this method using the projects in Table 7-1 is shown in Table 7-6. The results in Table 7-6 indicate that for a budget of $250,000, Projects 1 and 3 are selected. This selection gives a total NPV of $100,362. However if the NPV is maximized, the selected projects are 2 and 3 with a total NPV of $111,808. The latter answer (Projects 2 and 3) is the *correct solution* since it maximizes the NPV. It is true that this method can give correct answers to the capital budgeting problem. However, as shown in this example, it is not possible to determine if the answers given by this method do, in fact, maximize the NPV. Consequently, this method is not recommended.

TABLE 7-6

Project Ranking by Rate of Return

Project	Rate of Return (%)	Cumulative Capital Required ($)
1	25.00	50,000
3	21.55	170,000
2	20.21	270,000
4	15.11	470,000

A second method sometimes proposed to solve the capital budgeting problem is similar to the first method. Except in this second method, the projects are listed on the basis of NPV. This method is shown in Table 7-7 using the data given in Table 7-1. The results in Table 7-7 indicate Projects 2 and 3 should be selected for a budget restriction of $400,000 which gives a total NPV of $111,808. However, the correct solution is to choose Projects 1, 2, and 3 which give a total NPV of $147,832. This second method is not recommended since it too does not guarantee that the NPV is maximized.

The only two methods that guarantee that the NPV is maximized are the bundling approach and the mathematical programming approach. They are the methods recommended here.

TABLE 7-7

Projects Ranking by Net Present Value

Project	NPV $	Cumulative Capital Required ($)
3	64,338	120,000
2	47,470	220,000
4	45,784	420,000
1	36,024	470,000

PROBLEMS

7-1. The four projects listed below are mutually exclusive. Determine the following using an incremental rate of return approach:
(a)   Which project should be selected if MARR equals 12%?
(b)   Which project should be selected if MARR equals 20%?

	Project			
	1	2	3	4
Capital investment, $	40,000	50,000	70,000	100,000
Annual cash flow, $	8,000	10,000	13,000	18,000
Life, years $	10	10	10	10

7-2. Using the data in Problem 7-1, which project should be selected using the maximization of NPV as the criterion?

7-3. If the four projects listed below are mutually exclusive, determine the following using an incremental rate of return approach:
(a)   Which project should be selected if MARR equals 15%?
(b)   Which project should be selected if MARR equals 25%?

	Project			
	1	2	3	4
Capital investment, $	20,000	35,000	40,000	50,000
Annual cash flow, $	3,600	5,800	7,200	8,600
Life, years	15	15	15	15

7-4. Using the data in Problem 7-3, which project should be selected using the maximization of NPV as the criterion?

7-5. If the four projects listed below are mutually exclusive, determine the following:
(a)   Which project should be selected if MARR equals 15% and a rate of return approach is used?
(b)   Which project should be selected if MARR equals 15% and the NPV criterion is used?

HINT It is first necessary to determine how to calculate rate of return and NPV with an infinite life.

	Project			
	1	2	3	4
Capital investment, $	40,000	75,000	80,000	90,000
Annual cash flow, $	10,000	12,000	14,000	15,000
Life, years	∞	∞	∞	∞

7-6. If the projects listed below are mutually exclusive, determine which project should be selected using an incremental approach and MARR equal to 12%.

	Cash Flows			
End of Year	Project 1	Project 2	Project 3	Project 4
0	−$40,000	−$48,000	−$59,000	−$75,000
1	8,000	9,000	14,000	16,000
2	8,000	9,000	14,000	16,000
3	8,000	9,000	14,000	16,000
4	8,000	9,000	14,000	16,000
5	8,000	9,000	10,000	16,000
6	8,000	10,000	10,000	12,000
7	6,000	10,000	10,000	12,000
8	6,000	10,000	10,000	12,000
9	6,000	10,000	10,000	12,000
10	6,000	10,000	10,000	12,000

7-7. Repeat Problem 7-6, only use the NPV criterion.

7-8. Assuming the projects in Problem 7-7 are independent and not mutually exclusive, which projects should be selected if:
   (a) A capital expenditure restriction of $200,000 is imposed?
   (b) A capital expenditure restriction of $150,000 is imposed?

7-9. The four projects listed below are mutually exclusive. Determine which project should be selected using an incremental approach and MARR equal to 15%. Also what assumption(s) are implied in your answer?

	Project			
	1	2	3	4
Capital investment,$	100,000	130,000	150,000	190,000
Annual cash flow, $	24,000	26,000	42,000	43,000
Life, years	8	10	6	8

7-10. Repeat Problem 7-9, only use NPV as the basis of selecting a project.

7-11. Determine which project(s) should be accepted using the data given below and a MARR equal to 15% if:
(a) The projects are mutually exclusive.
(b) The projects are independent, and there is a budget restriction of $400,000.

Assume that the cash flows in year zero are the capital expenditures.

End of	Project Cash Flows				
Year	1	2	3	4	5
0	−80,000	−100,000	−150,000	−170,000	−200,000
1	19,000	24,000	36,000	40,000	46,000
2	19,000	24,000	36,000	40,000	46,000
3	19,000	24,000	36,000	40,000	46,000
4	19,000	24,000	36,000	40,000	46,000
5	19,000	24,000	36,000	40,000	46,000
6	19,000	24,000	36,000	40,000	46,000
7	19,000	24,000	36,000	40,000	46,000
8	19,000	24,000	36,000	40,000	46,000

7-12. Using the data and conditions given below, write the mathematical programming format needed to determine which project should be done.

Project	Capital Expenditure $j=0$	Capital Expenditure $j=1$	Capital Expenditure $j=2$	Net Present Value
1	$20,000	$7,000	$8,000	$6,000
2	3,000	—	2,000	2,000
3	4,000	4,000	—	4,000
4	10,000	6,000	—	7,000
5	8,000	5,000	4,000	5,000
6	6,000	—	3,000	2,000
7	9,000	8,000	7,000	3,000
8	7,000	5,000	—	8,000
9	10,000	7,000	5,000	6,000

Conditions

1. Budget restriction for $j = 0$ is $70,000.
2. Budget restriction for $j = 1$ is $40,000.
3. Budget restriction for $j = 2$ is $20,000.
4. Projects 6 and 8 are mutually exclusive.
5. Projects 2 and 3 are interdependent: Project 3 can be done without Project 2, but Project 2 must accompany Project 3.

7-13. For the data and conditions given below, determine the following:
  (a) The project that should be chosen if the projects are mutually exclusive.
  (b) The project(s) that should be chosen if the projects are independent and the budget for total capital expenditures in year $j = 0$ is $250,000 and in year $j = 1$ $200,000.

Conditions

1. The debt ratio is 30%.
2. The debt obligation is paid on the basis of constant interest over the life of the project at a cost of 10%.

3. Depreciation begins after the total capital expenditure is made, and for tax purposes a straight-line model is used with a life of ten years and a zero salvage value.
4. The MARR for equity is 20%.
5. The tax rate is 40%.

End of Year	Project 1			Project 2			Project 3		
	Capital Investment	Gross Income	Costs	Capital Investment	Gross Income	Costs	Capital Investment	Gross Income	Costs
0	100,000	–	–	120,000	–	–	150,000	–	–
1	70,000	–	–	80,000	–	–	100,000	–	–
2		100,000	40,000		130,000	50,000		150,000	60,000
•		•	•		•	•		•	•
•		•	•		•	•		•	•
•		•	•		•	•		•	•
15		100,000	40,000		130,000	50,000		150,000	60,000

8

BREAK-EVEN MODELS

Break-even models provide a method for understanding the basic relationships between profit and costs. Break-even models can also provide an understanding of the relationship between profit and net cash flow.

LINEAR BREAK-EVEN MODELS

In break-even models, the relationship between profit and costs can be either linear or nonlinear. For the linear case, the relationship between profit and costs is

$$P = (sV - cV - F - D_b - I) - (sV - cV - F - D - I)T \qquad (8\text{-}1)$$

where

P = after-tax profit per unit of time

V = volume of sales per unit of time

s = selling price per unit

c = variable cost per unit

F = fixed costs per unit of time, *excluding* book depreciation and debt interest expense

D_b = book depreciation (capital recovery) per unit of time. This is sometimes referred to as the company's depreciation

I = debt interest expense per unit of time

D = tax depreciation per unit of time. In general, D_b does not equal D

T = tax rate

sV = gross income (revenues) per unit of time

cV = variable costs per unit of time

Sometimes in break-even models, an overall fixed cost, F', is defined in the following manner

$$F' = F + D_b + I \tag{8-2}$$

and if it is assumed that $D_b = D$, Eq. (8-1) can be written as

$$P = (sV - cV - F')(1 - T) \tag{8-3}$$

Or, if $D_b \neq D$, Eq. (8-1) can be written as

$$P = (sV - cV - F')(1 - T) + (D - D_b)T \tag{8-4}$$

Although Eqs. (8-3) and (8-4) are more concise than Eq. (8-1), they are not used to any extent in this chapter. Equation (8-1) provides greater insights into the relationships between profits, costs, and net cash flows. Equation (8-1) implies certain assumptions. First, sales and production volumes (V) are the same. Second, fixed costs are independent of the production volume. Third, variable costs and gross income are both linear functions of the production (sales) volume. In practice the usual time unit in Eq. (8-1) is one year. That is, profit and other time dependent variables are often defined on an annual basis.

Variable Costs   These costs over a period of time (cV) are proportional to the volume of production. The variable cost per unit (c) comprises such costs as: raw material, direct labor, direct supplies, direct supervision and direct maintenance.

Fixed Costs   These costs are independent of the volume of production. In actuality, this is only true over a range of production. If the production volume continues beyond this range, fixed expenses will increase because additional equipment must be purchased, new buildings built, etc. However, for most break-even models, the assumption that the fixed costs are constant is adequate since the time period over which the profits and costs are usually considered is short (one year). Fixed costs include such items as depreciation, debt interest, property taxes, rent, insurance, and executive salaries.

Break-even models obtain their name from the determination of the point at which the profit and, consequently, the income taxes are zero. Two break-even points usually are of particular interest. The first break-even point is the volume of production (sales) at which the profit is zero. This point, V_b, can be determined by substituting zero for the profit and tax term in Eq. (8-1) which gives

$$V_b = \frac{F + D_b + I}{s - c} \tag{8-5}$$

The second point is the unit sales price at which the profit is zero, s_b, which, for a given volume of sales (V), is

$$s_b = c + \frac{F + D_b + I}{V} \tag{8-6}$$

Note in Eq. (8-6) that as the volume of sales (V) increases, the break-even selling price decreases.

Break-even models can be portrayed graphically. A generalized model is shown in Figure 8-1. The slope of the gross income line in Figure 8-1 is s, and the slope of the total cost line is c. Note that the total cost line begins at the fixed costs. In this way, the total costs are portrayed. The profit after tax is obtained using

Eq. (8-1), and the profit before tax, P_b, is obtained using the equation

$$P_b = (sV - cV - F - D_b - I) \qquad (8\text{-}7)$$

Example 8-1

A product sells for $70 per unit. Labor, material, and direct overhead costs are $15, $10, and $15 per unit respectively. The company's book depreciation is $50,000 per year, and debt interest is $10,000 per year. Other fixed expenses amount to $100,000 per year. Determine the following if the company's volume of sales is 10,000 units per year and tax rate is 40%.

  a.   The annual before-tax profit.
  b.   The annual after-tax profit if the tax depreciation is $60,000 per year.
  c.   The break-even volume of sales.
  d.   The break-even selling price per unit.
  e.   Plot a break-even chart for the data in this example.

For this example the variable cost per unit is

$$c \;=\; 15 + 10 + 15$$
$$=\; \$40$$

Using Eq. (8-7), the profit before tax for Part a is

$$P_b \;=\; 70(10{,}000) - 40(10{,}000) - 100{,}000 - 50{,}000 - 10{,}000$$
$$=\; \$140{,}000 \text{ per year}$$

For Part b, the after-tax profit using Eq. (8-1) is

$$P \;=\; [70(10{,}000) - 40(10{,}000) - 100{,}000 - 50{,}000 - 10{,}000]$$
$$-\, [70(10{,}000) - 40(10{,}000) - 100{,}000 - 60{,}000$$
$$-\, 10{,}000](0.40)$$
$$=\; \$88{,}000 \text{ per year}$$

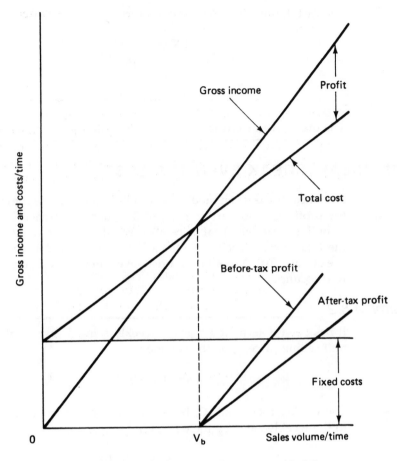

FIGURE 8-1 A Linear Break-even Model

For Part c, the break-even volume of sales using Eq. (8-5) is

$$V_b = \frac{100,000 + 50,000 + 10,000}{70 - 40}$$

$$= 5,333 \text{ units per year}$$

For Part d, the break-even selling price using Eq. (8-6) is

$$s_b = 40 + \frac{100,000 + 50,000 + 10,000}{10,000}$$

$$= \$56 \text{ per unit}$$

The break-even chart for this example is shown in Figure 8-2.

NONLINEAR BREAK-EVEN MODELS

Nonlinear break-even models occur when one or more components in the profit equation are not linear. The basic approach is the same as in linear models. That is, profit is equal to the gross income minus the total costs. Usually, nonlinear break-even models require some use of calculus. A nonlinear break-even model is discussed in the next example.

Example 8-2

It has been determined that the weekly sales, V, are related to the unit selling price, s, by the equation

$$s = (180 - 0.5V) \tag{8-8}$$

The weekly total costs, C, have also been determined to be related to the weekly sales by the equation

$$C = -0.25V^2 + 120V + 200 \tag{8-9}$$

The following information is required:

    a.   The volume of weekly sales for maximum profit.
    b.   The maximum weekly profit.
    c.   The break-even point.

For Part a, the profit equation, using Eqs. (8-8) and (8-9), is

$$P = (180 - 0.5V)V - (-0.25V^2 + 120V + 200) \tag{8-10}$$

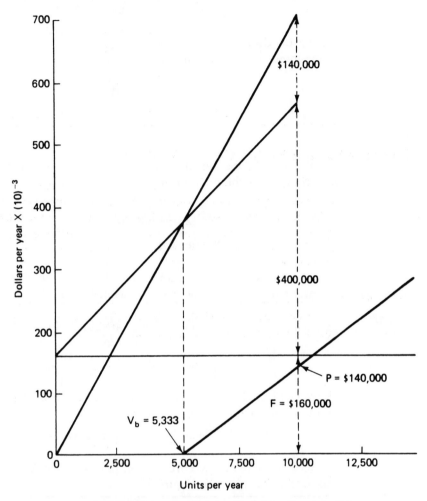

FIGURE 8-2 Break-even Model for Example 8-1

which simplifies to

$$P = -0.25V^2 + 60V - 200 \qquad (8\text{-}11)$$

Taking the derivative of Eq. (8-11) and setting it equal to zero gives the volume of sales for maximum profit.

$$\frac{dP}{dV} = 0 = -0.5V + 60$$

$$V = 120 \text{ units per week}$$

For Part b, the result of Part a is substituted into Eq. (8-11) which gives for the maximum profit

$$P = -0.25\,(120)^2 + 60(120) - 200$$

$$= \$3,400 \text{ per week}$$

The break-even point required in Part c is obtained using the quadratic formula and the coefficients in Eq. (8-11).

$$V_b = \frac{-60 \pm \sqrt{3600 - 4(-.25)(-200)}}{2(-.25)}$$

$$= \frac{-60 \pm 58.31}{-0.5}$$

$$= 3.38 \text{ and } 236.62 \text{ units per week}$$

In this case there are two break-even points. A break-even chart for this example is given in Figure 8-3.

An Additional Note   Economic theory states that maximum profit occurs when marginal income (revenue) equals marginal cost. In the context of Example 8-2, the marginal income is

$$\frac{dI}{dV} = \frac{d\,[180V - 0.5V^2]}{dV} \qquad (8\text{-}12)$$

$$= 180 - V$$

The marginal cost is

$$\frac{dC}{dV} = \frac{d\,[-0.25V^2 + 120V + 200]}{dV} \tag{8-13}$$

$$= -0.5V + 120$$

Setting Eq. (8-12) equal to Eq. (8-13) gives

$$180 - V = -0.5V + 120$$

$$V = 120 \text{ units per week}$$

which is the same result obtained in Example 8-2.

PROFIT AND NET CASH FLOW

In general, profit and net cash flow are not equal but they are related. The basic difference between profit and net cash flow is due to book (the company's) depreciation. In determining profit, the book depreciation is deducted as part of the fixed costs. It is a provision for recovering the capital investment. However, in determining net cash flows, the book depreciation is not deducted. Depreciation amounts stay within the company (actually, depreciation amounts become a source of investment funds; i.e., they are not "paid" to anyone). Consequently, depreciation is not a cash flow.

The relationship between yearly profits and net cash flows can be seen by considering the equity cash flow equation given in Chapter 5 and the profit equation, Eq. (8-1). For comparison purposes, the equation for net equity cash flows, Eq. (5-7), is repeated here as Eq. (8-14):

$$X_e = (G - C - I) - (G - C - I - D)\,T$$

$$- K + L + B - P \pm W + V \tag{8-14}$$

For convenience, the subscript, j, used in Eq. (5-7) has been omitted in Eq. (8-14). In order to make Eq. (8-1) more clearly resemble Eq. (8-14), the substitution $G = sV$ is made since the selling price multiplied by the volume of sales is the gross income. In Eq. (8-14),

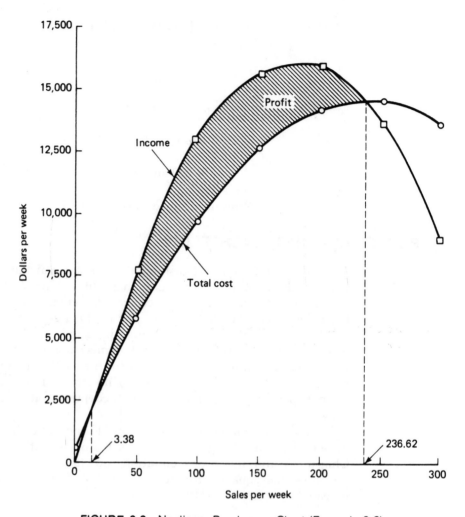

FIGURE 8-3   Nonlinear Break-even Chart (Example 8-2)

C is the *total costs excluding depreciation*. Consequently, the C in Eq. (8-14) is equal to $cV + F$ in Eq. (8-1). Making these substitutions, Eq. (8-1) can be written as

$$P = (G - C - D_b - I) - (G - C - D - I)T + V \qquad (8\text{-}15)$$

and some of the similarities between Eq. (8-14) and (8-15) are discernible. Some of the variables included in Eq. (8-14) are not included in the profit equation. The reasons for not including these variables in Eq. (8-15) are given in the following explanations:

1. Capital expenditures, K, are not considered in determining profits. They are an increase in the company's assets.
2. Salvage values, L, do not contribute to profit as long as the actual realizable salvage equals the book salvage value.
3. The borrowed money, B, is not a part of profit. It is a liability and is offset by the increase in capital assets purchased with the borrowed money.
4. Principal payments, P, are not a part of profits. The book depreciation, D_b, is based on the *total capital expenditure*. Consequently, the recovery of the debt capital (principal) is implied in the book depreciation.
5. Increases or decreases in working capital do not change profits. They are changes in a company's assets.

If the last five variables (K, L, B, P, and W) in Eq. (8-14) are zero, then the following relationship between profit and net cash flow is true

$$P = X_e - D_b \qquad (8\text{-}16)$$

Eq. (8-16) supports the statement made earlier that the *basic* difference between profit and net cash flow is the book depreciation.

Example 8-3

In this example, the data in Example 5-3 is used to determine the incremental yearly changes in after-tax profit that are expected to result from the project under consideration in Example 5-3. It is assumed that the tax and book depreciation are equal. However, this is not generally necessary. In practice the book and tax depreciation schedules usually are different.

Most of the data needed to determine the yearly incremental profits are available in Table 5-3. Using Eq. (8-15), some selected yearly profits are

$$P_0 = 0$$

$$P_1 = (40,000 - 10,000 - 9,000 - 4,000)$$
$$- (40,000 - 10,000 - 9,000 - 4,000)(0.40)$$

$$= \$10,200$$

$$P_5 = (40,000 - 10,000 - 9,000 - 2,400) - (40,000 - 10,000$$
$$- 9,000 - 2,400)(0.40)$$

$$= \$11,160$$

$$P_{10} = (40,000 - 10,000 - 9,000 - 400) - (40,000 - 10,000$$
$$- 9,000 - 400)(0.40)$$

$$= \$12,360$$

The remaining yearly profits are given in Table 8-1.

TABLE 8-1
Yearly Incremental Profits

End of Year	Incremental Profit
0	0
1	$10,200
2	10,440
3	10,680
4	10,920
5	11,160
6	11,400
7	11,640
8	11,880
9	12,120
10	12,360

PROBLEMS

8-1. A company is producing a particular unit that has the following data:

$$
\begin{aligned}
\text{volume of sales per year} &= 80{,}000 \text{ units} \\
\text{selling price per unit} &= \$50 \\
\text{variable cost per unit} &= \$30 \\
\text{fixed costs per year} &= \$900{,}000 \\
\text{tax rate} &= 40\%
\end{aligned}
$$

Using this data, determine the following:
(a) The before-tax profit.
(b) The after-tax profit assuming the tax and book depreciation are equal.
(c) The yearly sales volume in order to break even.
(d) The unit selling price in order to break even.
(e) Plot a break-even chart for this problem.

8-2. A company sells a product for $25 per unit. Material, labor, and direct overhead costs are respectively $4, $6, and $5 per unit. The company's book depreciation is $1,000,000 per year and debt interest is $200,000 per year. Other fixed expenses are $4,800,000 per year. The volume of sales per year is 1,000,000 units. If the company's tax rate is 40%, determine the following:
(a) The company's before-tax profit.
(b) The company's after-tax profit.
(c) The break-even yearly volume of sales.
(d) The break-even unit selling price.

8-3. A company is currently producing three products, X, Y, and Z, having the data shown in the following tables.

Product	Selling Price Per Unit	Variable Cost Per Unit	Volume of Sales Per Year
X	$50	$28	40,000
Y	20	11	70,000
Z	30	16	60,000

Product	Fixed Costs Per Year	Book Depreciation Per Year	Debt Interest Per Year
X	$100,000	$100,000	$ 50,000
Y	300,000	100,000	150,000
Z	100,000	200,000	100,000

The company is considering eliminating product Y and replacing it with product Q having the following data:

Product	Selling Price Per Unit	Variable Cost Per Unit	Volume of Sales Per Year
Q	$35	$20	50,000

If the company's tax rate is 40% and the tax and book depreciation are equal, should the company make this change?
(a)   Assume the fixed costs do not change.
(b)   Assume the current fixed costs increase by $500,000.
(c)   In Parts (a) and (b) what is the increase (decrease) in after-tax profits if product Q replaces product Y?

8-4.   A company is considering two methods for manufacturing a particular product. Both methods provide the same gross income. Using the data given in the following table, determine the range of yearly sales needed to choose (a) method X and (b) method Y.

Method	Variable Cost Per Unit	Fixed Costs Per Year
X	$40	$900,000
Y	80	500,000

8-5.   A company has a product that sells for $400 per unit. The total yearly before-tax cost of producing this product is given by the equation

$$C = n^2 - 2,000n + 1,000,000$$

where n is the number of units sold yearly. Determine the following:
(a)   The yearly fixed costs.
(b)   The number of units per year for maximum profit.
(c)   The maximum profit per year after tax assuming the tax rate is 40% and the tax and book depreciation are the same.
(d)   The break-even point.
(e)   Plot a break-even chart.

8-6.   Using the economic concept mentioned in this chapter that maximum profit occurs when marginal revenue equals marginal costs and the data in Problem 8-5, show that the volume of production for maximum profit is the same as that obtained in the solution to Problem 8-5.

8-7.   The weekly volume of sales of a particular unit is related to the unit selling price, S, by the function $(200-S)$. The total weekly costs are given by

$$500 + 100n + \frac{0.5n^2}{2}$$

where n is the weekly volume of sales. Determine the following:
(a)   The unit selling price for weekly maximum profit.
(b)   The maximum weekly profit.
(c)   The weekly volume of sales for maximum profit.
(d)   The break-even unit selling prices.

8-8.   Repeat Problem 8-6, only use the data in Problem 8-7.

8-9.   Determine the yearly incremental changes in after-tax profit resulting from the project described in Example 5-4. Assume the tax and book depreciation are equal.

8-10. Determine the yearly incremental changes in after-tax profit using the data in Example 6-1 assuming the minimum annual revenue requirements are the gross incomes. It should be noted that the tax and book depreciation are not equal.

9

COST COMPARISONS

Basically, cost comparisons are mutually exclusive capital budgeting problems with certain modifications. In cost comparisons, the gross incomes (revenues) are considered to be the same for all alternatives. Or stated another way, the alternatives are considered to provide equal service. Consequently, a comparison of the alternatives is based on their costs and the alternative with the least total cost is selected. The alternative of "doing nothing" is not a feasible alternative in cost comparisons since there is an implied need for service (use) that must be satisfied by one of the alternatives.

This text considers two approaches for making cost comparisons. One approach, called the conventional approach in this text, is only concerned with determining an equivalent annual amount of the costs and then making a comparison. A second approach involves the use of annual cash flows and their equivalent annual amounts in cost comparisons.

CONVENTIONAL METHODS

Conventional methods for making cost comparisons center around the determination of a single amount for each alternative. This single amount usually takes the form of an equivalent annual amount, a single present amount, or what is referred to as a capitalized amount. The equivalent annual amount appears to be the most popular. However, for the sake of completeness, all three methods are considered.

Equivalent Annual Cost Comparisons   An equivalent annual cost comparison involves the determination of an equivalent annual amount of the cash flows for each alternative. In making cost comparisons, the sign convention for the cash flows is usually reversed from that used in Chapter 5. That is, cash outflows are positive and cash inflows are negative. This sign convention minimizes the use of the negative sign.

Example 9-1 _____

For the two alternatives in Table 9-1, make an equivalent annual cost comparison. The implied timing of the cash flows given in Table 9-1 is shown in Table 9-2. Consequently, the equivalent annual amounts for the two alternatives are

$$E_1 = (100{,}000 - 10{,}000 \ (P/F \ 20{,}8) + 8{,}000 \ (P/A \ 20{,}8)) \ (A/P \ 20{,}8)$$

$$= (128{,}372)(.2606) = \$33{,}454$$

$$E_2 = (150{,}000 - 20{,}000(P/F \ 20{,}8) + 3{,}000(P/A \ 20{,}8)) \ (A/P \ 20{,}8)$$

$$= (156{,}860)(.2606) = \$40{,}878$$

and the choice is alternative one.

TABLE 9-1
Data for Example 9-1

	Alternative	
	1	2
Initial cost	$100,000	$150,000
Salvage value	$10,000	$20,000
Life, years	8	8
Required return	20%	20%
Annual cost of operation, and maintenance	$8,000	$3,000

TABLE 9-2
Timing of Cash Flows for Example 9-1

End of Year	Alternatives			
	1		2	
0	$100,000		$150,000	
1		$8,000		$3,000
2		8,000		3,000
3		8,000		3,000
4		8,000		3,000
5		8,000		3,000
6		8,000		3,000
7		8,000		3,000
8	$L = 10,000$	8,000	$L = 20,000$	3,000

It is also possible to obtain the equivalent annual amounts using Eq. (3-18). This simplifies the calculations. If Eq. (3-18) is used, the results are

$$E_1 = (100,000 - 10,000)(A/P\ 20,8) + 10,000\ (.20) + 8,000$$

$$= \$33,454$$

$$E_2 = (150,000 - 20,000) \, (A/P \ 20,8) + 20,000(.20) + 3,000$$

$$= \$40,878$$

which are the same values obtained earlier. In future discussions Eq. (3-18) is used extensively.

The Required Return   In Example 9-1, the required return is simply stated to be 20%. In conventional methods for making cost comparisons, a value for taxes (t) is not explicitly included in the calculations to determine an equivalent annual cost. The implication is that the required return used in conventional methods has been adjusted, in some manner, to approximate the tax effects of operating costs, depreciation, and debt interest. This approach is sometimes referred to as an implicit method for including tax effects. An explicit method is presented later in this chapter. An approximation that is sometimes suggested is to divide k_a by the term $(1 - T)$ to obtain

$$k'_a = ck_d + \frac{(1-c)k_e}{(1-T)} \tag{9-1}$$

where k'_a is the required return for conventional approaches to cost comparisons.

COST COMPARISONS WITH DIFFERENT LIVES

In Example 9-1, the cost comparison is based on a period of eight years which is also the life of each alternative. This cost comparison implies the assumption that the need for the service provided by the alternatives is at least eight years. In actuality, there is no requirement that the lives of the alternatives equal the period of service (need). Therefore, it is the purpose of this section to consider cost comparisons of alternatives with different lives.

In making cost comparisons, there are two basic conditions that must be satisfied. These two conditions are (1) the alternatives must be compared over an *equal period of time* and (2) this period of time must equal the service life. The basic assumption made in comparing *cost alternatives* (not projects with explicit gross incomes as in Chapter 5) is that the cost data for each alternative cycles over a period of time equal to the service life, or, in some cases, over a period of time equal to the least common multiple (LCM) of the lives of the alternatives. This assumption is reasonable once it is understood that *it does not imply that a selected alternative must be kept until the end of its life. Theoretically, a selected alternative can be replaced at any point in time* by another alternative that provides an economic advantage. The service life can be either infinite or finite.

Infinite Service Life   With an infinite service life, the annual costs and the equivalent annual cost for each alternative are determined using the life of the particular alternative. With the cycling assumption, these annual costs cycle to infinity and a comparison of the alternatives is possible over the same service life (infinity).

Example 9-2

Make a cost comparison for the two alternatives given in Table 9-3 using an equivalent annual cost approach and assuming an infinite need. The equivalent annual costs for each alternative are

$$E_1 = (40,000 - 2,000)\,(A/P\ 20,4) + 2,000(.20) + 4,000$$

$$= \$19,079$$

$$E_2 = (60,000 - 4,000)\,(A/P\ 20,7) + 4,000(.20) + 3,000$$

$$= \$19,334$$

TABLE 9-3
Cost Data for Example 9-2

| | *Alternative* | |
	1	2
Initial cost	$40,000	$60,000
Salvage values	$2,000	4,000
Life, years	4	7
Required return	20%	20%
Annual operation and maintenance	$4,000	$3,000

It may appear that the calculations in Example 9-2 ignore the difference in the lives of the two alternatives. This is not the case. The actual comparison that is implied is shown in Table 9-4. This table shows the result of the cycling assumption previously mentioned. That is, since the cost data for each alternative cycle, the annual costs cycle for each alternative and consequently, the equivalent annual cost is the same each year.

TABLE 9-4
Cost Comparison for an Infinite Need

End of Year	Equivalent Annual Cost	
	Alternative 1	Alternative 2
1	$19,079	$19,334
2	19,079	19,334
3	19,079	19,334
4	19,079	19,334
•	•	•
•	•	•
•	•	•
∞	19,079	19,334

Capitalized Cost Comparisons If the service life is considered to be infinite, another method for making cost comparisons is sometimes used. This method is called a capitalized cost comparison and is defined as a single amount at the present that is equivalent to a series of cash flows that are repeated forever. In part, this definition requires the same cycling assumption made for an infinite service life. In Example 9-2, it is shown that this cycling assumption results in an equivalent annual cost that extends from year one through infinity. Consequently by its definition, the capitalized cost (CC) is

$$(CC) = E \, (P/A \, k,n) \qquad (9\text{-}2)$$

where n is infinity. The limit of the P/A factor in Eq. 9-2 as n approaches infinity is

$$\lim_{n \to \infty} \left[(P/A \ k,n)\right] = \lim_{n \to \infty} \left[\frac{1}{k} - \frac{1}{k\,(1+k)^n}\right] = \frac{1}{k} \qquad (9\text{-}3)$$

Consequently, a capitalized amount, in general is

$$(CC) = \frac{E}{k} \qquad (9\text{-}4)$$

A capitalized cost comparison for the data in Example 9-2 is

$$(CC)_1 = \frac{19{,}079}{.20}$$

$$= \$95{,}395$$

$$(CC)_2 = \frac{19{,}334}{.20}$$

$$= \$96{,}670$$

Based on these results, Alternative 1 is the choice, which is the same result given by a comparison of the equivalent annual costs. This is always the case. A capitalized cost comparison should always give the same decision as an equivalent annual cost comparison. It should be noted that by its definition, *a capitalized cost comparison is only applicable for an infinite service life.* Consequently, it is not discussed later when the service life is finite.

Present Worth Comparisons Previous discussions considered equivalent annual and capitalized cost comparisons for an infinite need. Another procedure is to make a present worth comparison. A present worth cost comparison is made by discounting all the cash flows for each alternative to the present and then comparing these amounts. *For an infinite need, the period of the comparison is the least common multiple (LCM) of the lives of the assets.*

Example 9-3

Make a present worth comparison for the alternatives described in
Example 9-2. Since the LCM of the lives of the two alternatives in
Table 9-3 is 28, the costs shown in Table 9-5 are implied.

TABLE 9-5

An Example of the Cycling Assumption for a Present Worth Cost Comparison

End of Year	Alternative 1		Alternative 2	
0	$40,000		$60,000	
1		$4,000		$3,000
2		4,000		3,000
3		4,000		3,000
4	40,000; $L = 2,000$	4,000		3,000
5		4,000		3,000
6		4,000		3,000
7		4,000	60,000; $L = 4,000$	3,000
8	40,000; $L = 2,000$	4,000		3,000
9		4,000		3,000
10		4,000		3,000
11		4,000		3,000
12	40,000; $L = 2,000$	4,000		3,000
13		4,000		3,000
14		4,000	60,000; $L = 4,000$	3,000
15		4,000		3,000
16	40,000; $L = 2,000$	4,000		3,000
17		4,000		3,000
18		4,000		3,000
19		4,000		3,000
20	40,000; $L = 2,000$	4,000		3,000
21		4,000	60,000; $L = 4,000$	3,000
22		4,000		3,000
23		4,000		3,000
24	40,000; $L = 2,000$	4,000		3,000
25		4,000		3,000
26		4,000		3,000
27		4,000		3,000
28	$L = 2,000$	4,000	$L = 4,000$	3,000

The present-worth of the costs for the two alternatives in Table 9-5 are

P_1 = 40,000(1 + P/F 20,4 + P/F 20,8 + P/F 20,12 + P/F 20,16

+ P/F 20,20 + P/F 20,24) – 2,000(P/F 20,4 + P/F 20,8

+ P/F 20,12 + P/F 20,16 + P/F 20,20 + P/F 20,24

+ P/F 20,28) + 4,000 P/A 20,28

= \$94,817

P_2 = 60,000(1 + P/F 20,7 + P/F 20,14 + P/F 20,21)

– 4,000(P/F 20,7 + P/F 20,14 + P/F 20,21 + P/F 20,28)

+ 3,000 P/A 20,28

= \$96,084

Another and much simpler method for obtaining the present worth of the costs is to use the equation

$$P = E (P/A \ k,LCM) \qquad (9\text{-}5)$$

For example, using the solution given in Example 9-2, the present worth of the costs are

P_1 = 19,079 (P/A 20,28)

= \$94,817

P_2 = 19,334 (P/A 20,28)

= \$96,084

which are the same results obtained in Example 9-3.

It should be noted that all three cost comparison methods give the same decision (alternative one). Further, Example 9-3 shows that a present worth comparison does have a computational disadvantage. Basically, the capitalized and present worth cost comparisons offer no advantages over an equivalent annual cost comparison. Consequently, further discussions of cost comparisons (and replacement analysis) are limited to only equivalent annual cost comparisons.

Finite Service Life   When the service life is determined (estimated) to be some finite period of time, any cost comparison should be based on this same period of time. *A finite service life implies, in this text, that there is no need for an asset after the service life and the involved equipment could be sold, used for some other service, or discarded (scrapped).* Relative to an infinite service life, a finite service life is unusual. By far, in practice, most cost comparisons are based on an infinite service life because of its computational convenience and the difficulties in estimating a finite service life. The assumption of a very long (infinite) service life is the usual approach. However, on occasion, a finite service life can occur. Therefore, it is considered in this section.

The approach for making a cost comparison with a finite service life is dependent upon the LCM of the lives of the alternatives and the service life. There are three possibilities. They are

(1)   LCM = service life

(2)   LCM < service life

(3)   LCM > service life

When the LCM equals the service life, the cost comparison is numerically the same as the case of an infinite service life because of the cycling assumption. For example, if the service life in Example 9-2 is 28 years, the equivalent annual costs for Alternative 1 and Alternative 2, respectively, are $19,079 and $19,334.

When the LCM is less than the service life, the cost comparison is again numerically the same as the case of an infinite service. This is based on the cycling assumption for the period of time from the present to the LCM and on an additional assumption regarding the period of time from the LCM to the service life. This additional assumption is that the most economical (least cost) choice of an alternative is made for the period of time between the LCM and the service life. This merely implies that the decision-maker is rational and will choose the least cost alternative. This is considered to be a reasonable assumption. As an example, suppose the service life for Example 9-2 is 35 years. This implies, from the standpoint of equivalent annual costs, the cost comparison shown in Table 9-6 where E_s represents the equivalent annual cost of the best (least cost) alternative that is available for the period of years 29 through 35. This alternative may or may not be related to Alternatives 1 and 2 in Table 9-3. Also, specific numerical values are not required for E_s; all that is required is the assumption that it is the best (cheapest) alternative for the years remaining after the LCM (years 29 through 35). With this assumption it can be seen that, by choosing the alternative with the least equivalent annual cost (using only equivalent annual costs as the decision criterion) over the LCM, the costs over the service period are minimized. From a computational standpoint, all that is required is an infinite service life cost comparison in order to choose an alternative.

TABLE 9-6
Cost Comparison with
LCM < Service Life

End of Year	Equivalent Annual Cost 1	2
1	$19,079	$19,334
2	19,079	19,334
•	•	•
•	•	•
•	•	•
28	19,079	19,334
29	E_s	
•	•	
•	•	
•	•	
35	E_s	

When the LCM is greater than the service life, it is necessary to estimate for each alternative the costs and salvage values that are expected to occur at particular points in time over the service life. The approach taken in this text, for cost comparison and this case, is to estimate these costs and salvage values on the basis that the cost data for each alternative cycles. For partial cycles that may occur just prior to the service life, salvage values are estimated for the implied period of use. With these salvage values, it is possible to determine the equivalent annual cost of the service life. For example if the service life is ten years in Example 9-2, this implies the cost comparison shown in Table 9-7.

TABLE 9-7
Cost Comparison with LCM > Service Life

End of Year	Equivalent Annual Costs Alternative 1	Alternative 2
1	$19,079	$19,334
2	19,079	19,334
3	19,079	19,334
4	19,079	19,334
5	19,079	19,334
6	19,079	19,334
7	19,079	19,334
8	19,079	E_y
9	E_x	E_y
10	E_x	E_y

The equivalent annual costs in years one through eight for alternative one are the same as determined in Example 9-2 due to the cycling assumption. The equivalent annual costs in years nine and ten (E_x) must be determined. Similarly, the equivalent annual costs in years one through seven are the same as determined in Example 9-2. The equivalent annual costs for years eight through ten (E_y) must be determined. E_x and E_y can be determined by estimating salvage values for alternative one after two years of use and after three years of use for alternative two. For example if these respective salvage values are $6,000 and $10,000, E_x and E_y are

$$E_x = (40,000 - 6,000)(AP\ 20,2) + 6,000(.20) + 4,000$$

$$= \$27,456$$

$$E_y = (60{,}000 - 10{,}000(AP\ 20{,}3) + 10{,}000(.20) + 3{,}000$$

$$= \$28{,}735$$

With these values for E_x and E_y the equivalent annual costs for the two alternatives can be determined for a ten-year service life in the following manner:

$$E_1 = (19{,}079\ PA\ 20{,}8 + 27{,}456\ (PA\ 20{,}2)(P/F\ 20{,}8))\ (AP\ 20{,}10)$$

$$= \$19{,}787$$

$$E_2 = (19{,}334\ (PA\ 20{,}7) + 28{,}735\ (PA\ 20{,}3)(P/F\ 20{,}7))\ (AP\ 20{,}10)$$

$$= \$20{,}651$$

A CASH FLOW APPROACH TO COST COMPARISONS

The use of cash flows provides a method for explicitly including taxes in cost comparisons and shows the yearly incremental changes in cash flow resulting from the alternatives.

The net cash flow approach to cost comparisons is based on the various definitions of cash flow given in Chapter 5. The cash flow definitions are modified for cost comparisons by omitting the gross income (G_j) term (the alternatives provide equal service) and, for convenience, reversing the sign convention (cash outflows are positive and cash inflows are negative). For example, with these changes, the operating cash flow definition for cost comparisons, X'_{oj}, is

$$X'_{oj} = C_j - (C_j + D_j + I_j)\ T + K_j - L_j - V_j \tag{9-6}$$

and, respectively, the total (X'_j) and equity cash flow (X'_{ej}) definitions for cost comparisons become

$$X'_j = C_j - (C_j + D_j)\ T + K_j - L_j - V_j \tag{9-7}$$

$$X'_{ej} = C_j + I_j - (C_j + D_j + I_j)\ T + K_j - L_j - V_j - B_j + P_j \tag{9-8}$$

In Eqs. (9-6), (9-7) and (9-8), the nomenclature is the same as in Chapter 5. Also, the working capital term has been omitted in

Eqs. (9-6), (9-7), and (9-8) because, in most instances, it is not a consideration in cost comparisons.

Example 9-4

In this example the use of cash flows in cost comparisons is demonstrated using Eqs. (9-6), (9-7), (9-8), an infinite need, and the data in Table 9-8. At this point some comments are necessary regarding the data in Table 9-8. The tax depreciation method, salvage value, and period (life) are based on tax regulations. They may or may not be related to the realizable (actual) salvage value or the life of the alternative. That is, the realizable salvage value represents the estimated value of the alternative at the end of its life. In this example, the life of the alternatives and the tax depreciation period are the same. *This should not be generalized.* In general, it would be expected that the life of an alternative would be greater than its tax depreciation period and *the cash flows should be generated over the life of the alternative not just the tax depreciation period.*

TABLE 9-8
Cost Data for Example 9-4

	Alternative	
	1	*2*
Initial cost	$40,000	$60,000
Annual cost of operation & maintenance	$4,000	$3,000
Realizable salvage value	$2,500	$3,500
Life of alternative, years	4	7
Tax depreciation	SYD	SYD
salvage value	$2,000	$4,000
depreciation period, years	4	7
Cost of debt capital	12.5%	12.5%
Cost of equity capital	25%	25%
Debt ratio	40%	40%
Tax rate	40%	40%
Investment tax credit	1981 Tax Code	

TABLE 9-9
Total Cash Flow for Example 9-4

Alternative 1

End of Year	Cap. Exp. & Salvage $K_j\ L_j$	Annual Costs C_j	Tax Depreciation D_j	Taxes t_j	Investment Tax Credit V_j	Total Cash Flow X'
0	$40,000	—	—	—	—	$40,000
1	—	$4,000	$15,200	$7,680	$1,333	−5,013
2	—	4,000	11,400	6,160	—	−2,160
3	—	4,000	7,600	4,640	—	−640
4	L = 2,500	4,000	3,800	3,120	—	−1,620

Alternative 2

End of Year	Cap. Exp. & Salvage $K_j\ L_j$	Annual Costs C_j	Tax Depreciation D_j	Taxes t_j	Investment Tax Credit V_j	Total Cash Flow X'
0	$60,000	—	—	—	—	$60,000
1	—	$3,000	$14,000	$6,800	$6,000	−9,800
2	—	3,000	12,000	6,000	—	−3,000
3	—	3,000	10,000	5,200	—	−2,200
4	—	3,000	8,000	4,400	—	−1,400
5	—	3,000	6,000	3,600	—	−600
6	—	3,000	4,000	2,800	—	200
7	L = 3,500	3,000	2,000	2,000	—	−2,500

Tables 9-9, 9-10, and 9-11 give, respectively, the total, equity, and operating cash flows for the two alternatives. Some sample calculations of these cash flows follow:

The total cash flows for years 0, 1, and 4 for alternative 1 are

$$X'_0 = \$40,000$$

$$X'_1 = 4,000 - (4,000 + 15,200)(.40) - \frac{1}{3}(.10)(40,000)$$

$$= -\$5,013$$

$$X'_4 = 4,000 - (4,000 + 3,800)(.40) - 2,500$$

$$= -\$1,620$$

TABLE 9-10
Equity Cash Flows for Example 9-4

End of Year	Cap. Exp. & Salvage K_j, L_j	Annual Costs C_j	Debt Interest I_j	Tax Depreciation D_j	Taxes t_j	Investment Tax Credit V_j	Borrowed Capital B_j	Recovery of Debt Capital P_j^*	Equity Cash Flow X'_e
				Alternative 1					
0	$40,000	—	—	—	—	—	$16,000	—	$24,000
1	—	$4,000	$2,000	$15,200	$8,480	$1,333	—	$4,000	187
2	—	4,000	1,500	11,400	6,760	—	—	4,000	2,740
3	—	4,000	1,000	7,600	5,040	—	—	4,000	3,960
4	L = 2,500	4,000	500	3,800	3,320	—	—	4,000	2,680
				Alternative 2					
0	$60,000	—	—	—	—	—	$24,000	—	$36,000
1	—	$3,000	$3,000	$14,000	$8,000	$6,000	—	$3,429	-4,571
2	—	3,000	2,571	12,000	7,028	—	—	3,429	1,972
3	—	3,000	2,142	10,000	6,057	—	—	3,429	2,514
4	—	3,000	1,713	8,000	5,085	—	—	3,429	3,057
5	—	3,000	1,284	6,000	4,114	—	—	3,429	3,599
6	—	3,000	855	4,000	3,142	—	—	3,429	4,142
7	L = 3,500	3,000	426	2,000	2,170	—	—	3,429	1,185

TABLE 9-11
Operating Cash Flows for Example 9-4

End of Year	Cap. Exp. & Salvage K_j, L_j	Annual Costs C_j	Debt Interest I_j	Tax Depreciation D_j	Taxes t_j	Investment Tax Credit V_j	Operating Cash Flows X_o
				Alternative 1			
0	$40,000	—	—	—	—	—	$40,000
1	—	$4,000	$2,000	$15,200	$8,480	$1,333	-5,813
2	—	4,000	1,500	11,400	6,760	—	-2,760
3	—	4,000	1,000	7,600	5,040	—	-1,040
4	L = 2,500	4,000	500	3,800	3,320	—	-1,820
				Alternative 2			
0	$60,000	—	—	—	—	—	$60,000
1	—	$3,000	$3,000	$14,000	$8,000	$6,000	-11,000
2	—	3,000	2,571	12,000	7,028	—	-4,028
3	—	3,000	2,142	10,000	6,057	—	-3,057
4	—	3,000	1,713	8,000	5,085	—	-2,085
5	—	3,000	1,284	6,000	4,114	—	-1,114
6	—	3,000	855	4,000	3,142	—	-142
7	L = 3,500	3,000	426	2,000	2,170	—	-2,670

For alternative 2, the total cash flows for years 0, 1, and 7 are

$$X'_0 = \$60,000$$
$$X'_1 = 3,000 - (3,000 + 14,000)(.40) - (.10)(60,000)$$
$$= -\$9,800$$
$$X'_7 = 3,000 - (3,000 + 2,000)(.40) - 3,500$$
$$= -\$2,500$$

The equity cash flows for years 0, 1, and 4 for alternative 1 are

$$X'_{e0} = 40,000 - (.40)(40,000)$$
$$= \$24,000$$
$$X'_{e1} = 4,000 + 2,000 - (4,000 + 2,000 + 15,200)(.40)$$
$$+ 4,000 - \frac{1}{3} (.10)(40,000)$$
$$= 187$$
$$X'_{e4} = 4,000 + 500 - (4,000 + 500 + 3,800)(.40)$$
$$+ 4,000 - 2,500$$
$$= \$2,680$$

For alternative 2, the equity cash flows for years 0, 1, and 7 are

$$X'_{e0} = 60,000 - (.40)(60,000)$$
$$= \$36,000$$
$$X'_{e1} = 3,000 + 3,000 - (3,000 + 3,000 + 14,000)(.40)$$
$$+ 3,429 - 6,000$$
$$= -\$4,571$$
$$X'_{e7} = 3,000 + 426 - (3,000 + 426 + 2,000)(.40) + 3,429 - 3,500$$
$$= \$1,185$$

It should be noted that the convention for the recovery of the debt capital (B_j) used in this example is based on an equal annual amount spread over the life of the alternative (not the depreciation period.) The interest amounts are on the unrecovered amounts. This convention is used throughout this chapter and in a later chapter (Replacement Analysis).

The operating cash flows for years 0, 1, and 4 for alternative 1 are

$$X'_{o0} = \$40,000$$

$$X'_{o1} = 4,000 - (4,000 + 2,000 + 15,200)(.4)$$

$$-\frac{1}{3}(.10)\,40,000$$

$$= -\$5,813$$

$$X'_{o4} = 4,000 - (4,000 + 500 + 3,800)(.40) - 2,500$$

$$= -\$1,820$$

For alternative 2, the operating cash flows for years 0, 1, and 7 are

$$X'_{o0} = \$60,000$$

$$X'_{o1} = 3,000 - (3,000 + 3,000 + 14,000)(.40) - (.10)(60,000)$$

$$= -\$11,000$$

$$X'_{o7} = 3,000 - (3,000 + 426 + 2,000)(.40) - 3,500$$

$$= -\$2,670$$

If the equivalent annual amounts of the cash flows are determined (remembering to use the correct discount rate), the results in Table 9-12 are obtained. For example, the equivalent annual amount of the total cash flows, E', for alternative one is

$$E'_1 = \left[40,000 - 5,013(P/F\ 18, 1) \ldots -1,620(P/F\ 18,4)\right]AP\ 18,4$$

$$= \$12,257$$

and the equivalent annual amounts of the equity, E_{e1}, and operating, E_{b1}, cash flows for alternative one are

$$E_{e1} = \left[24,000 + 187(P/F\ 25, 1) \ldots + 2,680(P/F\ 25,4)\right]AP\ 25,4$$

$$= \$12,294$$

TABLE 9-12
Equivalent Annual Cash Flows

| Cash Flow | Alternative | |
Definition	1	2
Total	$12,257	$12,202
Equity	$12,294	$12,231
Operating	$12,269	$12,211

$$E_{b1} = \left[40{,}000 - 5{,}813(P/F\ 20, 1)\ldots - 1{,}820(P/F\ 20{,}4)\right] AP\ 20{,}4$$

$$= \$12{,}269$$

It is pointed out that cost comparisons based on cash flows involve the same cycling assumptions mentioned earlier in the chapter. Therefore, the cost comparison implied for an infinite service life, using total cash flows as the example, is shown in Table 9-13 and indicates, from an equivalent amount standpoint, that alternative two is the choice. However, the decision process would also involve a comparison of the yearly cash flows (short-term effects).

Tax Effects   The tax effects resulting from differences in realizable and tax salvage values can be approximated in cost comparisons in a manner similar to that discussed in Chapter 5. For example if tax effects are included in Problem 9-4, the total cash flow for year four of alternative one (assuming Sec. 1245 property) is

$$X'_4 = -1{,}620 + (2{,}500 - 2{,}000)\ (.40) + 40{,}000$$

$$= -\$1{,}420 + 40{,}000$$

TABLE 9-13

Cost Comparison Using Cash Flows with an Infinite Need

End of Year	Alternative 1		Alternative 2	
	Cash Flow	Equivalent Cash Flow	Cash Flow	Equivalent Cash Flow
0	$40,000	—	$60,000	—
1	−5,013	$12,257	−9,800	$12,202
2	−2,160	12,257	−3,000	12,202
3	−640	12,257	−2,200	12,202
4	−1,620 + 40,000	12,257	−1,400	12,202
5	−5,013	12,257	−600	12,202
6	−2,160	12,257	200	12,202
7	−640	12,257	−2,500 + 60,000	12,202
8	−1,620 + 40,000	12,257	−9,800	12,202
9	−5,013	12,257	−3,000	12,202
10	•	•	•	•
11	•	•	•	•
12	−1,620 + 40,000	•	−600	•
13	−5,013	•	200	•
14	−2,160	•	−2,500 + 60,000	•
15	−640	•	−9,800	•
•	•	•	•	•
•	•	•	•	•
•	•	•	•	•
∞	−1,620	12,257	−2,500	12,202

and the total cash flow for year seven of alternative two is

$$X'_7 = -\$2{,}500 + \$60{,}000 - (4{,}000 - 3{,}500)(.40)$$

$$= -\$2{,}700 + 60{,}000$$

The $40,000 and $60,000 amounts added, respectively, to X'_4 and X'_7 are the capital expenditures for the alternatives and reflect the beginning of a new cycle. The term $(2,500 - 2,000)(.40)$ is added for alternative one because the realizable salvage value ($2,500) is larger than the tax salvage value ($2,000) and the gain ($500) would be taxed as ordinary income. The term $(4,000 - 3,500)(.40)$ is subtracted from X_7 because the realizable salvage (3,500) is less than the tax salvage ($4,000). The difference ($500) is a Sec. 1231 loss. Since there are no Sec. 1231 gains, this difference is deductible as ordinary income. If equity or operating cash flows are used, the same two tax adjustments, just discussed, would be included in the cash flows.

This discussion of tax effects makes the assumption that the inclusion of tax effects in the cost comparison is applicable. In all probability tax effects would not be included due to the recycling assumption implied in an infinite need. That is, the cost data cycles. It could be argued, and defended, that the replacements (cycles) constitute "like-kind" exchanges and, therefore, tax effects are not recognized. However, in the case of a finite need (discussed later), this may not be the case, particularly, in regard to partial cycles.

Example 9-4 is worked on the basis of an infinite service life. A cash flow approach can also be used for a finite service life. In this approach, the same assumptions made for a conventional approach with a finite life are still applicable. That is, if the LCM = service life, the cost comparison is numerically the same as the case of an infinite service life. This is also true for the case of LCM < service life. The case of LCM > service life is shown in the next example.

Example 9-5

In this example, Example 9-4 is repeated for a finite service life of ten years using equity cash flows. It assumes the salvage value for alternative one after two years of service is $20,000 and the salvage value for alternative two is $30,000 after three years of service. *This example includes tax effects resulting from the disposal of the assets at the end of partial cycles. However, tax effects are not included at the end of a full cycle.* This procedure is based on "like-kind" exchanges for full cycles and disposal of the assets at the end of the finite service life. The investment tax credit, for partial cycles, is based on the tax depreciation period and possible investment tax penalties are based on the partial cycle length.

With these assumptions and conditions, the equity cash flows must be calculated for each alternative over the service life (10 years). These cash flows are shown in Table 9-14. The cash flows for alternative one are the same as in Table 9-10 for years zero through four and then repeat for years five through eight (the cycling assumption). The cash flow components for years nine and ten are shown in Table 9-15 and the equity cash flows are calculated in the following manner:

$$X'_{e9} = 4{,}000 + 2{,}000 - (4{,}000 + 2{,}000 + 15{,}200)(.40)$$
$$- 1/3\,(.10)\,(40{,}000) + 8{,}000$$
$$= \$4{,}187$$

$$X'_{e10} = 4{,}000 + 1{,}000 - (4{,}000 + 1{,}000 + 11{,}400)(.40)$$
$$+ 1/3\,(.10)\,(40{,}000) + 8{,}000 - 20{,}000$$
$$+ (20{,}000 - 13{,}400)\,(.40)$$
$$= -\$9{,}587$$

TABLE 9-14
Cash Flows for Example 9-5

| End of | Alternative | |
Year	1	2
0	$24,000	$36,000
1	187	–4,571
2	2,740	1,972
3	3,960	2,514
4	2,680 + 24,000	3,057
5	187	3,599
6	2,740	4,142
7	3,960	1,185 + 36,000
8	2,680 + 24,000	0
9	4,187	6,200
10	–9,587	–17,200

TABLE 9-15
Equity Cash Flows for Example 9-5

End of Year	Cap. Exp. & Salvage $K_j L_j$	Annual Costs C_j	Debt Interest I_j	Tax Depreciation D_j	Taxes t_j	Investment Tax Credit V_j	Borrowed Capital B_j	Recovery of Debt Capital P_j^*	Equity Cash Flows X'_e
				Alternative 1					
8	$40,000	—	—	—	—	—	$16,000	—	$24,000
9	—	$4,000	$2,000	$15,200	$8,480	$1,333	—	$8,000	4,187
10 L = 20,000		4,000	1,000	11,400	6,560	(1,333)[a]	—	8,000	−9,587
						[a]investment tax penalty			
				Alternative 2					
7	$60,000	—	—	—	—	—	$24,000	—	$36,000
8	—	$3,000	$3,000	$14,000	$8,000	$6,000	—	$8,000	0
9	—	3,000	2,000	12,000	6,800	—	—	8,000	6,200
10 L = 30,000		3,000	1,000	10,000	5,600	(4,000)[a]	—	8,000	−17,200
						[a]investment tax penalty			

The investment tax credit (–$1,333) is included in year nine based on a tax depreciation period of four years and the investment tax penalty ($1,333) is included in year ten because the partial cycle is only two years. It should be noted that the tax depreciation amounts for years nine and ten do not change. They are the same as years one and two for a full cycle. The tax depreciation amounts are based on tax laws and they do not change simply because the life is only two years (nine and ten). However, the debt recovery ($8,000) is based on the partial cycle length. That is, the debt capital ($16,000) divided by partial cycle length (two years). Interest is based on the unrecovered debt capital. The $(20,000 - 13,400)$ $(.40)$ term is the tax effect based on a realizable salvage of ($20,000) and a tax book value at the end of two years. That is

$$\text{tax book value} = 40,000 - (15,200 + 11,400)$$
$$= \$13,400$$

For alternative two, the cash flows for the first seven years are the same as in Table 9-10. The cash flow components are shown in Table 9-15 for years 8, 9, and 10. The cash flows are

$$X'_{e8} = 3,000 + 3,000 - (3,000 + 3,000 + 14,000)(.40)$$
$$- (.10)(60,000) + 8,000$$
$$= \$0$$
$$X'_{e9} = 3,000 + 2,000 - (3,000 + 2,000 + 12,000)(.40) + 8,000$$
$$= \$6,200$$
$$X'_{e10} = 3,000 + 1,000 - (3,000 + 1,000 + 10,000)(.40) + 8,000$$
$$- 30,000 + 2/3 \, (.10)(60,000)$$
$$+ (30,000 - 24,000)(.40)$$
$$= - \$17,200$$

The full investment tax credit ($6,000) is deducted because the depreciation period is seven years. The investment tax penalty ($4,000) is added because the partial cycle length is three years.

The equivalent annual amounts for the two alternatives are

$$E_{e1} = [24,000 + 187 \, (P/F \, 25,1) + \ldots + 26,680 \, (P/F \, 25,4)$$

$$+ \ldots -9,587 \, (P/F \, 25,10)] \, AP \, 25,10$$

$$= \$12,455$$

$$E_{e2} = [36,000 - 4,571 \, (P/F \, 25,1) + \ldots + 37,185 \, (P/F \, 25,7)$$

$$+ \ldots -17,200 \, (P/F \, 25,10)] \, AP \, 25,10$$

$$= \$12,744$$

From an equivalent annual amount standpoint, the decision is alternative one.

PURCHASE VERSUS LEASE

Sometimes, leasing equipment is an alternative to purchasing equipment. In general, a lease involves a constant periodic (monthly, yearly, etc.) payment over some set period of time (the length of the lease). Leasing payments are, usually, made at the beginning of a period. In many leases, the purchaser of the lease must pay certain maintenance expenses and in almost all leases the purchaser must pay the operating costs. If a lease is discontinued (broken), penalties can be assessed.

Leasing equipment has an appeal because of possible tax advantages and because leasing can avoid long-term commitments of capital. In actuality, leasing may or may not provide a tax advantage. It depends on the depreciation amounts, operating costs, and possible investment tax credit of the purchase alternative. In any event, all purchase-lease decisions should be determined by an actual cost comparison. Basically, a cost comparison involving a leasing alternative is made in the same manner as any other cost comparison. That is, the costs of the leasing and purchase alternatives are compared over an infinite or finite service life using the same cycling assumptions discussed previously *for the purpose of making a comparison.* As mentioned earlier, the cycling assumption does not imply that the alternative selected must be kept until the end of its life. Theoretically, it is always possible to replace an alternative at any point in time if an economic evaluation indicates it is desirable.

Example 9-6

If alternative two in Example 9-4 is the purchase alternative, make a cost comparison under the following conditions:

(a) The service life is infinite and for a four year lease the cost is $15,000 per year with an estimated combined operating and maintenance cost of $5,000 per year.

(b) The service life is four years (finite) and the leasing costs are the same as in Part a. Assume the net realizable salvage at the end of four years is $4,500 for the purchase alternative.

For Part a, the cash flows and their equivalent annual amount must be determined for the purchase alternative. This has been done previously and the cash flows are given in Tables 9-9, 9-10, 9-11, and 9-12. For this example, equity cash flows (Table 9-10) are used for discussion purposes. The cash flows for the leasing alternative are the leasing, operating, and maintenance costs. A comparison of the cash flows and their equivalent annual amounts for the two alternatives is shown in Table 9-16. In Table 9-16, the cash flows under the leasing alternative are multiplied by the term $(1 - T)$, a value of 0.6, because they are tax deductible. Also, the leasing costs ($15,000) are shown as beginning of the year amounts and the combined operation and maintenance costs are shown as end of the year amounts. The equivalent annual amount for one cycle of the leasing alternative is

$$E = [.6(15,000) + .6(15,000)PA\ 25,3]\ AP\ 25,4 + .6\ (5,000)$$

$$= \$14,252$$

Based on equivalent annual amounts, the purchase alternative is the best choice.

For Part (b), the cash flows for the leasing alternative are the same as in Part (a). However, the cash flows for the purchase alternative must be changed because of the shorter life (four years) and a different salvage value ($4,500). These cash flows are shown in Table 9-17 and the comparison is shown in Table 9-18. It indicates that the leasing alternative is the best choice from the standpoint of equivalent annual amounts.

TABLE 9-16

A Purchase-Lease Comparison
with an Infinite Service Life

End of Year	Purchase Alternative		Lease Alternative	
	Cash Flow	Equivalent Amount	Cash Flow	Equivalent Amount
0	$36,000	—	$15,000(.6)	—
1	−4,571	$12,231	(15,000 + 5,000).6	$14,252
2	1,972	12,231	(15,000 + 5,000).6	14,252
3	—	12,231	(15,000 + 5,000).6	14,252
4	—	12,231	(15,000 + 5,000).6	14,252
5	—	12,231	•	•
6	—	12,231	•	•
7	36,000 + 1,185	12,231	•	•
8	−4,571	12,231	•	•
•	•	•	•	•
•	•	•	•	•
•	•	•	•	•
∞	1,185	12,231	5,000(.6)	14,252

TABLE 9-18

A Purchase-Lease Comparison
with a Finite Need

End of Year	Purchase Alternative		Lease Alternative	
	Cash Flow	Equivalent Amount	Cash Flow	Equivalent Amount
0	$36,000	—	$15,000(.6)	—
1	−2,000	$17,556	(15,000 + 5,000)(.6)	$14,252
2	4,350	17,556	(15,000 + 5,000)(.6)	14,252
3	4,700	17,556	(15,000 + 5,000)(.6)	14,252
4	4,550	17,556	(5,000)(.6)	14,252

TABLE 9-17
Equity Cash Flows for Example 9-6

End of Year	Cap. Exp. & Salvage $K_j L_j$	Annual Costs C_j	Debt Interest I_j	Tax Depreciation D_j	Taxes t_j	Investment Tax Credit V_j	Borrowed Capital B_j	Recovery of Debt Capital P_j^*	Equity Cash Flows X'_e
0	$60,000	—	—	—	—	—	$24,000	—	$36,000
1	—	$3,000	3,000	$14,000	$8,000	$6,000	—	$6,000	-2,000
2	—	3,000	2,250	12,000	6,900	—	—	6,000	4,350
3	—	3,000	1,500	10,000	5,800	—	—	6,000	4,700
4	L = 4,500	3,000	750	8,000	4,700	(4,000)[a]	—	6,000	4,550

[a]investment tax penalty

It should be noted that, in this example, tax effects are not included in either part (a) or (b). Also in part (b) , the maximum investment tax credit ($6,000) is taken and penalty ($4,000) is paid in the fourth year.

A RELATIONSHIP BETWEEN CASH FLOWS AND REVENUE REQUIREMENTS

It is possible to develop a relationship between the equivalent annual (levelized) amounts of the minimum annual revenue requirements and the cash flows used in cost comparisons.

It has been shown in Chapter 6 that

$$(1-T) \sum_{j=1}^{n} (G_j - R_j)(P/F\,k_{x},j) = NPV_x \tag{9-9}$$

By using the definition of equity cash flows for the NPV, Eq. (9-9) becomes

$$(1-T) \sum_{j=1}^{n} (G_j - R_j)(P/F\,k_e,j)$$

$$= \sum_{j=1}^{n} [G_j - C_j - I_j - (G_j - C_j - I_j - D_j)\,T$$

$$-K_j + B_j - P_j + L_j + V_j]\,(P/F\,k_e,j) \tag{9-10}$$

The working capital term ($\pm W$) is omitted in Eq. (9-10) because working capital changes are not usually involved in cost comparisons. The use of equity cash flows is not required. It is possible to use the definitions of total or operating cash flows, with the correct discount rate (k_a, or k_b), for the development of the following relationship.

With some algebraic manipulations, Eq. (9-10) can be written as

$$(1-T) \sum_{j=1}^{n} G_j(P/F\,k_e,j) - (1-T) \sum R_j(P/F\,k_e,j)$$

$$= \sum_{j=1}^{n} [G_j - C_j - I_j - (G_j - C_j - I_j - D_j)T - K_j - B_j - L_j + P_j - V_j](P/F\,k_e,j) \tag{9-11}$$

By eliminating like-terms, multiplying by minus one and the term $A/P\ k_e, n$, Eq. (9-11) becomes

$$(1-T)(A/P\,k_{ej}n)\sum_{j=1}^{n} R_j(P/F\,k_{e},j)$$

$$= (A/P\,k_{ej}n)\sum_{j=1}^{n} [C_j+I_j- (C_j+I_j+D_j)T$$

$$+ K_j- B_j- L_j+ P_j- V_j] (P/F\,k_{ej}) \tag{9-12}$$

Now, the left-hand side of Eq. (9-12) is the equivalent annual amount of the revenue requirements, E_R, and the right-hand side of Eq. (9-12) is the equivalent annual amount of the cash flows, E_C, for a cost comparison. Therefore,

$$(1-T)\,E_R = E_C \tag{9-13}$$

Equation (9-13) suggests that revenue requirements could be used for cost comparisons instead of cash flows by comparing equivalent annual amounts of the revenue requirements for each alternative. The use of revenue requirement or cash flows is a matter of preference. The basic difference is that revenue requirements are before-tax (gross) amounts while cash flows are after-tax amounts.

Example 9-7

The purpose of this example is to demonstrate, numerically, Eq. (9-13). For this purpose, alternative one in Table 9-8 is used. First, the revenue requirements are generated giving the results shown in Table 9-19.

In generating these results, the book depreciation is based on a four-year life, a straight-line model, and a salvage of $2,500. The next step is to generate the equity cash flows as shown in Table 9-20. In determining these cash flow values, the debt recovery (P_j) must be modified from that previously used in this chapter (the borrowed money divided by the life) to be consistent with the debt recovery implied in revenue requirements. That is, the use of Eqs. (6-2) and (6-3) to determine the debt recovery schedule.

TABLE 9-19
Minimum Annual Revenue Requirements for Example 9-7

End of Year	Book Depreciation D_b	Tax Depreciation D	Book Value B	Equity Return F_e	Debt Interest I	Tax t	Annual Costs C	Minimum Annual Revenue Requirement
0	—	—	$40,000	—	—	—	—	—
1	$9,375	$15,200	30,625	$6,000	$2,000	$117	$4,000	$19,270[a]
2	9,375	11,400	21,250	4,594	1,531	1,713	4,000	21,213
3	9,375	7,600	11,875	3,188	1,062	3,310	4,000	20,935
4	9,375	3,800	2,500	1,781	594	4,906	4,000	20,656

[a]Includes investments tax credit ($1,333).

TABLE 9-20
Equity Cash Flows for Example 9-7

End of Year	Cap. Exp. & Salvage $K_j; L_j$	Annual Costs C_j	Debt Interest I_j	Tax Depreciation D_j	Taxes t_j	Investment Tax Credit V_j	Borrowed Capital B_j	Recovery of Debt Capital P_j^*	Equity Cash Flow X'_e
0	$40,000	—	—	—	—	—	$16,000	—	$24,000
1	—	$4,000	$2,000	$15,200	$8,480	$1,333	—	$3,750	-63
2	—	4,000	1,531	11,400	6,772	—	—	3,750	2,509
3	—	4,000	1,062	7,600	5,065	—	—	3,750	3,747
4	L = 2,500	4,000	594	3,800	3,358	—	—	3,750 + 1,000	3,486

*Based on Eqs. (6-2) and (6-3)

The equivalent annual amount of the revenue requirements is

$$E_R = [19{,}270(P/F\ 25{,}1) + \ldots$$
$$+ 20{,}656(P/F\ 25{,}4)](A/P\ 25{,}4)$$
$$= \$20{,}401$$

and for the cash flows is

$$E_C = (24{,}000 - 63(P/F\ 25{,}1) + \ldots + 3{,}468(P/F\ 25{,}4)]\ AP\ 25{,}4$$
$$= \$12{,}241$$

Multiplying E_R by $(1 - T)$ gives the same value as E_C.

Some comments are needed in regard to the basic assumptions made in this chapter. The cycling assumption is a common assumption for cost comparisons. It is usually made by default. That is, there is no evidence or estimates to the contrary. Also, from the practical standpoint of numerical calculations, the cycling assumption is convenient. The assumption made in this text for partial cycles that may occur when the LCM is larger than the service life is not, of course, the only assumption. It is possible to assume (estimate) some completely independent alternatives for partial cycles. For that matter, in theory at least, it is possible to assume alternatives that have no relationship to the initial alternatives for any part of the service life that remains after the lives of the initial alternative. In the final analysis, a decision must be made between the difficulties of estimating and the convenience of the assumptions used in this chapter.

PROBLEMS

9-1 For the two alternatives shown in the following table and assuming an infinite service life, determine the following using the conventional approach
(a) an equivalent annual cost comparison
(b) a present worth cost comparison
(c) a capitalized cost comparison

| | Alternative | |
	1	2
Initial cost	$100,000	$150,000
Salvage value	$10,000	$20,000
Life, (capital recovery period) years)	8	12
Required before-tax return	20%	20%
Annual cost of operation, and maintenance	$8,000	$4,000

9-2 Using the data given in Problem 9-1, make an equivalent annual cost comparison for service lives of (a) 24 years, (b) 30 years, and (c) 15 years. Assume the salvage value of alternative one is $12,000 after seven years of use and the salvage value for alternative two is $90,000 after three years of use.

9-3 A company is considering the purchase of one of the two alternatives shown below:

| | Alternatives | |
	1	2
Initial cost	$60,000	$80,000
salvage value	6,000	8,000
life, years	8 years	8 years
Tax depreciation	MACRS:	5 years
Annual cost of operation and maintenance	$7,000	$4,000
Cost of debt capital	15%	15%
Cost of equity capital	25%	25%
Debt ratio	40%	40%
Tax rate	40%	40%
Investment tax credit	1981 tax code	

Assuming the service life is infinite and there are no tax effects, make a cost comparison using equity cash flows.

9-4 Repeat Problem 9-3 using total cash flows.

9-5 If the alternatives in Problem 9-3 are needed for only 4 years and the net realizable salvage values after four years of use for alternatives one and two are, respectively, $18,000 and $30,000, make a cost comparison using equity cash flows under the following conditions. Assume the alternatives are Sec. 1245 property and the 1981 investment tax code is applicable.
   (a)   There are no tax effects and the investment tax credit is taken so that there is no investment tax penalty.
   (b)   There are tax effects and the maximum investment tax credit is taken with penalties paid at the end of the needed life.

9-6 Using equity cash flows, make a cost comparison of the two assets shown in the following table under the following conditions.
   (a)   an infinite service need and no tax effects
   (b)   a need that is greater than eight years and no tax effects
   (c)   repeat Part (a) with tax effects

	Asset	
	1	2
Initial Cost	$60,000	$75,000
life, years	8	8
salvage, value	$0	$3,000
Annual Cost of operation and maintenance	$8,000	$5,000
Tax depreciation	MACRS:	5 years
Tax rate	40%	40%
Debt ratio	40%	40%
Return on equity	25%	25%
Cost of debt	15%	15%
Investment tax credit	1981 tax code	

9-7 Using the data in Problem 9-6, make a cost comparison for a service life of four years under the following conditions:
  (a) the net realizable salvage value for asset one after four years of use is $6,000
  (b) the net realizable salvage value for asset two after four years of use is $3,000
  (c) all possible tax effects are to be included and the assets are Sec. 1245 property
  (d) the maximum allowable investment tax credit (1981 Code) is taken and any possible penalty is paid at the end of the service life

9-8 A company is considering the purchase of an alternative shown below:

	Alternative	
	1	2
Initial Cost	$60,000	$75,000
Annual Cost of operation and maintenance	$7,000	$4,000
Life of alternatives, years	4	6
Salvage, value	$6,000	$1,500
Tax depreciation	SYD	SYD
life	4	6
salvage	$4,000	$1,500
Cost of debt capital	15%	15%
Cost of equity capital	25%	25%
Debt ratio	40%	40%
Tax rate	40%	40%
Investment tax credit	1981 Code	

Assume the maximum allowable investment tax credit is taken and penalties paid where required. Also assume, there are no tax effects resulting from the disposal of assets. Determine the following using equity cash flows:
(a) A cost comparison for an infinite need
(b) A cost comparison for a need of 12 years

(c)   A cost comparison for a need of 20 years
(d)   A cost comparison for a need of 10 years
If salvage values are needed, use the following table.

EOY	Salvage Value for Alternatives	
	1	2
1	50,000	60,000
2	30,000	35,000
3	10,000	30,000
4	6,000	15,000
5	—	7.000
6	—	1,500

9-9   Repeat Problem 9-8 recognizing all tax effects where applicable.

9-10   Repeat Problem 9-8 parts (a) and (d) using total cash flows.

9-11   Make a cost comparison of the two alternatives given in the following table using equity cash flows.

	Alternative	
	1	2
Initial cost	$75,000	$90,000
Life, years	8	12
Salvage values	$3,000	$6,000
Annual cost of operation and maintenance	$5,000	$3,000
Tax depreciation	MACRS: 5 years	
Tax rate	40%	40%
Debt ratio	40%	40%
Return to equity	20%	20%
Cost of debt	10%	10%
Investment tax credit	1981 Code	

Assume that the maximum allowable investment tax credit
indicated by the tax depreciation life is taken for any partial cost
cycles and any investment tax penalties are taken in the last year
of a partial cost cycle. Also assume that there are no tax effects
resulting from the disposal of the alternatives and the salvage
values of the two alternatives at any point are given by the
following table.

| | Salvage Values for Alternative | |
EOY	1	2
1	50,000	80,000
2	40,000	60,000
3	30,000	40,000
4	20,000	30,000
5	15,000	25,000
6	10,000	20,000
7	7,000	15,000
8	3,000	10,000
9	—	9,000
10	—	8,000
11	—	7,000
12	—	6,000

Make the cost comparison on the basis of the following needs:
  (a)   infinite
  (b)   thirty years
  (c)   twenty years

9-12   Repeat Problem 9-11 recognizing all possible tax effects.

9-13   A company can lease or purchase certain needed equipment.
    The cost data for the purchase alternative is shown below:

Initial cost	$2,000,000
Annual cost of operation and maintenance	$50,000

Life, years	10
Salvage value	$200,000
Tax depreciation	MACRS: 5 years
Required debt return	10%
Required equity return	25%
Tax rate	40%
Debt ratio	30%
Investment tax credit	8%

If the annual cost of leasing the equipment is (a) $ 520,000 and (b) $900,000 per year for five years, should the equipment be purchased or leased for an infinite need? For a need of five years? Assume the salvage value at the end of five years for the purchase alternative is $800,000 and there are no tax effects. Use equity cash flows.

9-14 Using Alternative 2 in Problem 9-8 show, numerically, that Eq. (9-13) is correct for
   (a)   equity cash flows
   (b)   total cash flows

Use straight-line for the book depreciation when determining the revenue requirements.

10

REPLACEMENT ANALYSIS

Basically, replacement analysis involves the economic evaluation of two alternatives. One alternative is to keep some existing asset (sometimes referred to as the defender). The second alternative is to replace the existing asset with some new asset (sometimes referred to as the challenger). This situation usually occurs as a result of some inadequate performance on the part of the existing asset. In this chapter, the economic evaluation is based on the costs of the alternatives. Consequently, the economic evaluations assume *the assets provide equal service*. Two approaches are presented in this chapter for the economic evaluation of replacement alternatives. The first approach is called the conventional approach and the second approach involves the use of cash flows.

THE CONVENTIONAL APPROACH

In this text, the conventional approach to replacement analysis involves the determination of an equivalent annual cost for each alternative. This approach is further explained in the following example.

Example 10-1 _____

Seven years ago, an asset was purchased and installed to provide some needed service. At that time, the data given in Table 10-1 was estimated and determined to be applicable for this existing asset. However, experience with this asset indicates that some of the original estimates were incorrect. Consequently, the replacement of the existing asset with a new asset is now being considered.

TABLE 10-1
*Original Data for Existing Asset
(Example 10-1)*

Initial cost	$90,000
Annual cost of operation and maintenance	$3,000
Life, years	12
Required return	25%
Salvage value	$6,000

As a result of past experience, it is estimated that the annual cost of operation and maintenance is $7,000 for the remaining life of the existing asset which is estimated to be five years. The salvage value at the end of five years is now estimated to be $5,000. The present realizable salvage value for the existing asset is $30,000. Further, the required return is now 30%.

A new asset is now available that provides equal service and has the estimated cost data given in Table 10-2. It is desired to compare the existing and new assets on the basis of a conventional comparison assuming the need for the service is infinite (a finite service life is considered later).

TABLE 10-2
Cost Data for New Asset
(Example 10-1)

Initial cost	$60,000
Annual cost of operation and maintenance	$4,000
Life, years	10
Required return	30%
Salvage value	$6,000

TABLE 10-3
Cost Data for Example 10-1

End of Year	Existing Asset		End of Year	New Asset	
-7	$K = \$90,000; n = 12; L = \$6,000$		-7	—	
-6	—		-6	—	
•	—		•	—	
•	—		•	—	
•	—		•	—	
0	$30,000		0	$60,000	
1		$7,000	1		4,000
2		•	2		4,000
3		•	3		4,000
4		•	•		•
5	$L = 5,000$	7,000	•		•
			•		•
			10	$L = 6,000$	4,000

It is desirable in replacement analysis to portray the applicable data as shown in Table 10-3. The equivalent annual cost for the existing asset, E'_d, using Eq. (3-18) is

$$E'_d = (30,000 - 5,000) (A/P \ 30,5) + 5,000(.3) + 7,000$$

$$= \$18,765$$

and the equivalent annual cost for the new asset, E'_n is

$$E'_n = (60,000 - 6,000) \ (A/P \ 30,10) + 6,000 \ (.3) + 4,000$$

$$= \$23,269$$

A comparison of these values indicates that the existing asset should be kept. This decision implies an assumption since the lives of the two alternatives are different. This assumption is discussed in the following comments.

Comments   In Example 10-1, it may appear that the solution ignores the difference in the lives of the alternatives. This is not the case. A certain assumption is being made in the solution. Specifically, this assumption is that the new asset is the best (least cost) possible replacement available at the present time. Consequently, the new asset replaces the existing asset at the end of its life and the cost data for the new asset then cycles out to the service life (infinity in Example 10-1) for the alternative of keeping the existing asset. The alternative of purchasing the new asset involves the assumption that its cost data cycles out to the service life. As in cost comparisons (Chapter 9), the comparison of replacement alternatives must be over the same period of time. This time period is the service life, which can be either finite on infinite. Using the equivalent annual cost values obtained in Example 10-1 and an infinite service life, these assumptions imply the cost comparison shown in Table 10-4. This table shows that, with these assumptions, the equivalent annual costs are the same after the fifth year for the two alternatives. As a result, *if the service life is infinite,* all that is needed from a computational standpoint for a conventional comparison of the alternatives are the equivalent annual costs of the existing and new assets. Where, the equivalent annual costs are computed on the basis of their respective lives. Another assumption that is sometimes made in replacement studies is to assume that the cost data for existing and new assets both cycle out to the service life. For example, using the data in Example 10-1, this latter assumption implies the cost comparison shown in Table 10-5. This table shows that for *an infinite service life* both assumptions lead to a comparison of the same numerical values ($18,765 and $23,269) and, consequently, the

TABLE 10-4
Cycling Assumption
(Example 10-1)

End of Year	Alternatives Keep Existing Asset	Purchase New Asset
0	—	—
1	$18,765	$23,269
2	•	•
3	•	•
4	•	•
5	18,765	23,269
6	23,269	23,269
7	23,269	23,269
•	•	•
•	•	•
•	•	•
∞	23,269	23,269

TABLE 10-5
Another Cycling Assumption

End of Year	Alternatives Keep Existing Asset	Purchase New Asset
0	—	—
1	$18,765	$23,269
2	18,765	23,269
•	•	•
•	•	•
•	•	•
∞	18,765	23,269

same choice of an alternative. However, when the service life is finite, the cycling assumption used can make a difference in the choice of an alternative. This text takes the point of view that the first assumption is more plausible than this latter assumption and is the one used in future discussions in this chapter. At this point, the discussions in Chapter 9 of the assumptions regarding the cycling of cost data should be remembered. That is, once a comparison of alternatives indicates a particular choice of asset, there is no requirement that the chosen asset must be kept until the end of its cycle. Theoretically, at least, it is possible to replace the asset at any point in time that an economic evaluation indicates a replacement is desirable.

Another point should be understood when making replacement comparisons. There is no requirement that past estimates or values associated with the existing asset must be maintained in the evaluation of replacement alternatives. There are some exceptions (for example, tax depreciation) to this point when taxes are explicitly included (discussed later). The conventional evaluation of replacement alternatives should be based on what is *presently* considered to be correct estimates and values. That is, the original estimates and values used for the existing asset can be revised for the evaluation of the alternative of keeping the existing asset. Further, any differences between original estimates made for the existing asset and actual values are *sunk costs*. These sunk costs are a result of *past errors* in estimating and, consequently, should not be used in the comparison of replacement alternatives. For example, the difference between the book value of the existing asset and the present realizable salvage value is a sunk cost. Using the data in Example 10-1, the book value, based on straight-line depreciation, after seven years is

$$B_7 = 90,000 - 7/12(90,000 - 6,000)$$

$$= \$41,000$$

and the sunk cost is

$$\text{sunk cost} = 41,000 - 30,000$$

$$= \$11,000$$

$$150,000 - 7/25\,(150000 - 10000)$$

Since this sunk cost, is a result of past estimates, it is not included in a conventional comparison of replacement alternatives. However, it *may* have an effect in a comparison of the replacement alternatives when taxes are explicitly included.

Finite Service Life   In Example 10-1 an infinite service life is used. If a finite service life is used, it is necessary to estimate the salvage value of the new *asset* at the end of a period of use. The length of this use period is dependent upon the period of time from the end of a cycle of an asset to the service life. It should be noted that the concept of a least common multiple (LCM) of the lives of the alternatives introduced in Chapter 9 is not applicable for replacement studies. This is because of the assumption that the new asset replaces the existing asset and, consequently, an LCM cannot be defined for the alternatives.

Example 10-2

Repeat Example 10-1 for a finite service life of (a) ten years and (b) fifteen years. Assume that the salvage value of the new asset, after five years of use, is $20,000.

TABLE 10-6
Cost Data Cycles for Example 10-2
(Part a)

End of Year	Existing Asset		New Asset	
0	$K = \$30,000$		$K = \$60,000$	
1		$7,000		$4,000
2		7,000		4,000
3		7,000		4,000
4		7,000		4,000
5	$L = \$5,000; K = \$60,000$	7,000		4,000
6		4,000		4,000
7		4,000		4,000
8		4,000		4,000
9		4,000		4,000
10	$L = 20,000$	4,000	$L = 6,000$	4,000

For Part (a), the cost data cycles are shown in Table 10-6. In order to make a conventional comparison of the cost data in Table 10-6, the equivalent annual cost for the two alternatives must be calculated. The equivalent annual cost of the new asset is calculated in Example 10-1 and is $23,269. The calculation of the equivalent annual cost of the existing asset can be accomplished in two ways. The first way is to discount all values back to the present (remember salvage values are negative) and then spread this result over the ten year period using an appropriate A/P factor. The second way is to use Eq. (3-18) for each cycle and then combine these results using the appropriate interest factors. Using this second way, the equivalent annual cost for the first five years (cycle) is

$$(30,000 - 5,000) \, (A/P \; 30,5) + 5,000(.3) + 7,000 = \$18,765$$

which could have been obtained from the solution to Example 10-1. The equivalent annual cost for the second five years is

$$(60,000 - 20,000)(A/P \; 30,5) + 20,000(.3) + 4,000 = \$26,424$$

TABLE 10-7

Equivalent Annual Cost Cycles for Examples 10-2 (Part a)

| End of Year | Alternatives | |
	Keep Existing Asset	Purchase New Asset
0	—	—
1	$18,765	$23,269
2	18,765	23,269
3	18,765	23,269
4	18,765	23,269
5	18,765	23,269
6	26,424	23,269
7	26,424	23,269
8	26,424	23,269
9	26,424	23,269
10	26,424	23,269

The equivalent annual costs for these two cycles and for one cycle of the new asset are shown in Table 10-7. Combining the equivalent annual costs of the two cycles, the equivalent annual cost for the alternative of keeping the existing asset (E'_d) is

$$
\begin{aligned}
E'_d \ &= \ [18{,}765(P/A \ 30{,}5) \\
&\quad + \ 26{,}424(P/A \ 30{,}5)(P/F \ 30{,}5)] \ (A/P \ 30{,}10) \\
&= \ [63{,}036] \ (0.3235) \\
&= \ \$20{,}392
\end{aligned}
$$

Comparing this result ($20,392) with the equivalent annual cost of new asset alternative ($23,269), indicates that keeping the existing asset is the better choice.

For Part b, the cost data cycles are shown in Table 10-8.

TABLE 10-8
Equivalent Annual Cost Cycles for Examples 10-2 (Part b)

End of Year	Existing Asset		New Asset	
0	$K = \$30{,}000$	—	$K = \$60{,}000$	—
1		$7{,}000		$4{,}000
2		7{,}000		4{,}000
3		7{,}000		4{,}000
4		7{,}000		4{,}000
5	$L = \$5{,}000; K = \$60{,}000;$	7{,}000		4{,}000
6		4{,}000		4{,}000
7		4{,}000		4{,}000
8		4{,}000		4{,}000
9		4{,}000		4{,}000
10		4{,}000	$L = \$6{,}000; K = \$60{,}000$	4{,}000
11		4{,}000		4{,}000
12		4{,}000		4{,}000
13		4{,}000		4{,}000
14		4{,}000		4{,}000
15	$L = 6{,}000$	4{,}000	$L = 20{,}000$	4{,}000

The equivalent annual costs for the two alternatives are calculated using the procedure mentioned in Part (a). The equivalent annual cost for the first five years for the alternative of keeping the existing asset has been calculated previously and is $18,765. The equivalent annual cost for years six through fifteen has also been calculated in Example 10-1 and is $23,269. Combining these values, the equivalent annual cost of the alternative of keeping the existing asset, E'_d is

$$E'_d = [18,765(P/A\ 30,5)$$
$$+ 23,269(P/A\ 30,10)\ (P/F\ 30,5)]\ (A/P\ 30,15)$$
$$[65,076]\ (0.3060)$$
$$= \$19,913$$

In a similar manner, the equivalent annual cost for the first ten years for the alternative of purchasing a new asset is $23,269 (calculated previously). The equivalent annual cost for years ten through fifteen is $26,424 which is calculated in Part (a). Combining these values, the equivalent annual cost of the alternative of purchasing a new asset, E'_n is

$$E'_n = [23,269(P/A\ 30,10)$$
$$+26,424(P/A\ 30,5)\ (P/F\ 30,10)](A/P\ 30,15)$$
$$= [76,602](0.3060)$$
$$= \$23,440$$

A comparison of the two equivalent annual costs indicates that keeping the existing asset is the better choice.

THE OVERHAUL ALTERNATIVE

In replacement analysis, there often occurs a third alternative in addition to the two basic alternatives of keeping the existing asset or replacing it with a new asset. This third alternative is to overhaul the existing asset and is an especially viable alternative when production-type equipment is involved in a replacement study. If the overhaul alternative is an alternative, the approach, for a conventional comparison, is to determine the equivalent annual cost for the overhaul and compare this cost with the equivalent annual costs for the alternatives of keeping the existing asset and purchasing a new asset. The same cycling assumption, mentioned previously, is applicable to the overhaul alternative. That is, at the end of the overhaul cost cycle, the cost data for the new asset begins to cycle out to the service life.

Example 10-3

In Examples 10-1 and 10-2, it is possible to overhaul the existing asset at a cost of $18,000 and this overhaul decreases annual operation and maintenance costs to $5,000. Further, this overhaul will increase the life of the existing asset to eight years and the total salvage (existing and overhaul portions) is estimated to be $4,000 at that time. Determine a conventional cost comparison for the three alternatives in Examples 10-1 and 10-2.

The equivalent annual cost for the overhaul of the existing asset is

$$E'_o = (30,000 + 18,000 - 4,000)(A/P\ 30,8)$$
$$+ (4,000)\ (.3) + 5,000$$
$$= \$21,244$$

Since in Example 10-1 the service life is infinity, the cost cycles shown in Table 10-9 are implied. A comparison of the values in Table 10-9 indicates that a choice of an alternative is not as clear as in the case of only two alternatives (keep the existing asset versus purchasing a new asset). Since the equivalent annual cost of the new asset is larger than both alternatives of keeping the existing asset and the overhaul, the new asset can immediately be eliminated as a possible choice. However, the choice between the remaining two alternatives is not clear without further analysis. Because in years one through five, the equivalent annual cost of the existing asset alternative is less than the overhaul alternative but larger in years six through eight. From year nine to infinity, the equivalent annual costs are the same for these two alternatives. The approach taken, in this text, for this situation is to compare the equivalent annual costs over a period of time beginning with year one and ending at the point where the equivalent annual costs become the same for the alternatives. This period of time is the first eight years in this example. The equivalent annual cost over this eight year period for the alternative of keeping the existing asset equals

$$E'_o = [18,765(P/A\ 30,5)$$
$$+ 23,269(P/A\ 30,3)(P/F\ 30,5)]\ (A/P\ 30,8)$$

which gives a value of $19,517. Since this value ($19,517) is less than the overhaul alternative ($21,244), the choice is to keep the existing asset. It is noted that this type of additional analysis is only required in situations where $E'_d < E'_o < E'_n$. This situation is discussed in greater detail after this example.

TABLE 10-9
Equivalent Annual Cost Cycles for Example 10-3
(Infinite Service Life)

End of Year	Keep Existing Asset	Alternatives Purchase New Asset	Overhaul Asset
0	—	—	—
1	$18,765	$23,269	$21,244
2	18,765	23,269	21,244
3	18,765	23,269	21,244
4	18,765	23,269	21,244
5	18,765	23,269	21,244
6	23,269	23,269	21,244
7	23,269	23,269	21,244
8	23,269	23,269	21,244
9	23,269	23,269	23,269
•	•	•	•
•	•	•	•
•	•	•	•
∞	23,269	23,269	$23,269

In Example 10-2 two finite service lives are specified. The first service life is ten years. For this case it is necessary to estimate the salvage value of the new asset after two years of use; since, it is assumed that the new asset replaces the overhaul at the end of the cost data for the overhaul (eight years). Consequently, for a ten year service life, the equivalent annual costs are needed for years nine and ten. Assuming the salvage value is $40,000, the equivalent annual cost for years nine and ten is

$$(60,000 - 40,000)(A/P\ 30,2) + 40,000(.3) + 4,000$$

TABLE 10-10

Equivalent Annual Cost Cycles for Example 10-3
(A Finite Service Life of 10 Years)

End of Year	Keep Existing Asset	Alternatives Purchase New Asset	Overhaul Asset
0	—	—	—
1	$18,765	$23,269	$21,244
2	18,765	23,269	21,244
3	18,765	23,269	21,244
4	18,765	23,269	21,244
5	18,765	23,269	21,244
6	26,424	23,269	21,244
7	26,424	23,269	21,244
8	26,424	23,269	21,244
9	26,424	23,269	30,696
10	26,424	23,269	30,696

which gives a value of $30,696. The equivalent annual cost cycles are shown in Table 10-10 and are the same as Table 10-7 with the addition of the overhaul alternative. Combining the equivalent annual cost cycles, the equivalent annual cost for the overhaul alternative is

$$E'_o = [21,244\ (P/A\ 30,8)$$
$$+ (30,696)(P/A\ 30,2)(P/F\ 30,8)]\ (A/P\ 30,10)$$

$$= [67,254] (0.3235)$$

$$= \$21,757$$

A comparison of this value ($21,757) with the values obtained in Example 10-2 ($20,392 and $23,269) indicates that keeping the existing asset is the best alternative.

For the second part of Example 10-2, where a finite service life of fifteen years is specified, it is necessary to estimate the salvage value of the new asset after seven years of use. Assuming this salvage value is $18,000, the equivalent annual cost for seven years of use of the new asset is

$$(60,000 - 18,000) \; (A/P \; 30,7) + 18,000(.3) + 4,000$$

TABLE 10-11

Equivalent Annual Cost Cycles for Examples 10-3 (A Finite Service Life of 15 Years)

End of Year	Keep Existing Asset	Alternatives Purchase New Asset	Overhaul Existing Asset
0	—	—	—
1	$18,765	$23,269	$21,244
2	18,765	23,269	21,244
3	18,765	23,269	21,244
4	18,765	23,269	21,244
5	18,765	23,269	21,244
6	23,269	23,269	21,244
7	23,269	23,269	21,244
8	23,269	23,269	21,244
9	23,269	23,269	24,390
10	23,269	23,269	24,390
11	23,269	26,424	24,390
12	23,269	26,424	24,390
13	23,269	26,424	24,390
14	23,269	26,424	24,390
15	23,269	26,424	24,390

which gives a value of $24,390. The equivalent annual cost cycles are shown in Table 10-11. Many of the values shown in Table 10-11 are determined in Examples 10-1 and 10-2. The combined equivalent annual cost cycles for the alternatives of keeping the existing asset and purchasing a new asset are, respectively, $19,913 and $23,440 (determined in Example 10-2). The combined equivalent annual cost cycles for the overhaul alternative gives

$$E'_o = [21,244 \ (P/A \ 30,8)$$
$$+ \ 24,390(P/A \ 30,7)(P/F \ 30,8)] \ (A/P \ 30,15)$$
$$= \ [70,511] \ (0.3060)$$
$$= \ \$21,576$$

A comparison of these three values indicates that keeping the existing asset is the best alternative.

Some Comments   In the case of an infinite service life, the choice of an alternative is very direct when keeping the existing asset and purchasing a new asset are the only alternatives. For, in this case, it is only necessary to determine the equivalent annual costs for the two alternatives over their respective lives in order to choose an alternative. This is because of the cycling assumption previously discussed and shown in Table 10-4. However, when an overhaul alternative is included with the alternatives of keeping the existing asset and purchasing a new asset, there is a special situation where an additional computation is necessary before a choice of an alternative is possible. This special situation is discussed in the first part of Example 10-3 and shown in Table 10-9. It occurs when all of the following three conditions are satisfied

$$E'_d < E'_o < E_n \qquad\qquad (10\text{-}1)$$
$$\text{service life} = \text{infinity} \qquad\qquad (10\text{-}2)$$
$$n_d < n_o < n_n \qquad\qquad (10\text{-}3)$$

where n_d, n_o, and n_n are the lives, respectively, of the existing asset, the overhaul, and the new asset. Equation (10-3) is, by far, the usual case with the possible exception of

$$n_d = n_o < n_n \qquad\qquad (10\text{-}4)$$

In general, it is not realistic in replacement studies to consider the case of n_n being less than either n_d or n_o or the case of n_o being less than either n_d or n_n. If Eq. (10-4) is the case and both Eqs. (10-1) and (10-2) are satisfied, a direct solution is possible. That is, the choice is E'_d. However, if Eq. (10-1) through (10-3) are satisfied, it is necessary to use the relationship

$$[E'_d(P/A \ k,n_d) + E'_n(P/A \ k,(n_o - n_d))(P/F \ k,n_d)] \ (A/P \ k, n_o) \qquad (10\text{-}5)$$

to determine a value for a comparison with E'_o and E'_n. The use of Eq. (10-5) has been shown in Example 10-3 in obtaining the value of $19,517.

In the past discussion of the conventional approach to replacement analysis, the required return is simply specified to be a value (30% in Examples 10-1, 10-2, 10-3). The implication in conventional approaches to replacement analysis is the same as in cost comparisons regarding the required return. That is, the required return has been adjusted, in some manner, to approximate tax effects of operating costs, depreciation and debt interest. As mentioned in Chapter 9, this adjustment is sometimes made in accordance with Eq. (9-1).

A CASH FLOW APPROACH

Cash flows can be used in replacement analysis. They provide the advantages of explicit tax considerations and the yearly effect of investment decisions. As in cost comparisons, the cash flow definitions are based on Eqs. (9-7), (9-8), and (9-9). The cash flow approach is explained in the following examples for infinite and finite service periods.

Example 10-4 _____

Five years ago, an asset was purchased and installed to provide some needed service. At that time, the data given in Table 10-12 was estimated and determined to be applicable for this existing asset. However, experience with this asset indicates that some of the original estimates were incorrect. Consequently, the replacement of the existing asset with a new asset is now being considered.

As a result of past experience, it is estimated that the annual cost of operation and maintenance is $7,000 for the remaining life of the existing asset which is estimated to be five years. The salvage value at the end of five years is now estimated to be $5,000. The present realizable salvage value for the existing asset is $30,000. Further, the future debt ratio is considered to be the same as the one originally used (40%). However, the cost of debt capital is now considered to be 10%, the required return on equity is 20%, and the tax rate is 40%.

TABLE 10-12
Original Data for Existing Asset
(Example 10-4)

Initial cost	$90,000
salvage value	$8,000
life, years	12
Annual cost of operation and	
maintenance	$3,000
Tax depreciation	SYD
salvage value	$6,000
life, years	7
Tax rate	52%
Debt ratio	40%
Return on equity	25%
Cost of debt	15%
Investment tax credit	1981 Code

A new asset is now available that provides equal service and has the estimated cost data given in Table 10-13. It is desired to compare the existing and new assets on the basis of equity cash flows assuming the need for the service is infinite (a finite service life is considered later).

The applicable data for this example is shown in Table 10-14. The first step is to generate the equity cash flows for the existing asset. These values are shown in Table 10-15 and are explained in the following discussion. First, the capital expenditure is the present realizable salvage value. The rationale here is, the existing asset

TABLE 10-13
Cost Data for New Asset
(Example 10-4)

Initial cost	$60,000
salvage value	$6,000
life, years	10
Annual cost of operation and	
maintenance	$4,000
Tax depreciation	MACRS: 5 yrs
Tax rate	40%
Debt ratio	40%
Return on equity	20%
Cost of debt	10%
Investment tax credit	8%

could return to the company's "pool of capital" this amount of money ($30,000 in this example). Consequently, by continuing with the existing asset, the capital expenditure, in effect, is the present realizable salvage value. Any difference between the present realizable salvage value and the value given by the company's depreciation schedule is a sunk cost. A difference between the present realizable salvage value and the tax book value may have tax implications. These tax implications are discussed later.

The tax depreciation amounts in Table 10-15 are based on the originally established tax depreciation schedule (see Table 10-12). Since five years have elapsed, there are only two remaining years of depreciation until the existing asset is fully depreciated from the standpoint of the tax depreciation schedule.

The borrowed capital ($12,000) in Table 10-15 is based on the current debt ratio (40%) and its recovery is provided for by equal annual amounts ($2,400) over the remaining life of the existing asset (5 years). The debt interest is 10% of the unrecovered debt capital.

As examples, the cash flows for years 0, 1, and 5 are

$$X_{e0} = 30,000 - 12,000$$

$$= \$18,000$$

TABLE 10-14
Cost Data for Example 10-4

End of Year	Existing Asset		End of Year	New Asset	
−5	$K = \$90,000$; $n=12$; $L = \$8,000$		−5	—	
−4	—		−4	—	
•	—		•	—	
•	—		•	—	
•	—		•	—	
0	$30,000		0	$60,000	
1		$7,000	1		$4,000
2		•	2		4,000
3		•	3		4,000
4		•	•		•
5	$L = 5,000$	7,000	•		•
			10	$L = \$6,000$	4,000

$$X_{e1} = 7,000 + 1,200 - (7,000 + 1,200 + 6,000)(0.40)$$

$$+ 2,400$$

$$= \$4,920$$

$$X_{e5} = 7,000 + 240 - (7,000 + 240)(0.40) + 2,400 - 5,000$$

$$= \$1,744$$

The next step is to calculate the equity cash flows for the new asset. These values are given in Table 10-16. In Table 10-16, there are two values in year one under the investment tax column. The $4,800 value is the investment tax credit (8%) realized if the new asset is purchased. The second value ($3,000), is an investment tax penalty. This penalty occurs only if the new asset is purchased and the existing asset is retired. It occurs only once (year one) under the alternative of buying a new asset. The penalty is due to the existing asset originally taking an investment tax credit of $(0.10)(90,000) = \$9,000$ since the tax depreciation life is seven years and the 1981

TABLE 10-15
Equity Cash Flows for Existing Asset
(Example 10-4)

End of Year	Cap. Exp & Salvage Value $K_j L_j$	Annual Costs C_j	Debt Interest I_j	Tax Depreciation D_j	Taxes t_j	Borrowed Capital B_j	Debt Recovery P_j	Investment Tax V_j	Equity Cash Flow X'_e
0	$30,000	—	—	—	—	$12,000	—	—	$18,000
1	—	$7,000	$1,200	$6,000	$5,680	—	$2,400	—	4,920
2	—	7,000	960	3,000	4,384	—	2,400	—	5,976
3	—	7,000	720	—	3,088	—	2,400	—	7,032
4	—	7,000	480	—	2,992	—	2,400	—	6,888
5	L = 5,000	7,000	240	—	2,896	—	2,400	—	1,744

TABLE 10-16
Equity Cash Flows for New Asset
(Example 10-4)

End of Year	Cap. Exp. & Salvage Value K_j, L_j	Annual Costs C_j	Debt Interest I_j	Tax Depreciation D_j	Taxes t_j	Borrowed Capital B_j	Debt Recovery P_j	Investment Tax V_j	Equity Cash Flow X'_e
0	$60,000	—	—	—	—	$24,000	—	—	$36,000
1	—	$4,000	$2,400	$12,000	$7,360	—	$2,400	$4,800 (3,000)[a]	-360
2	—	4,000	2,160	19,200	10,144	—	2,400	—	-1,584
3	—	4,000	1,920	11,520	6,976	—	2,400	—	1,344
4	—	4,000	1,680	6,912	5,037	—	2,400	—	3,043
5	—	4,000	1,440	6,912	4,941	—	2,400	—	2,899
6	—	4,000	1,200	3,456	3,462	—	2,400	—	4,138
7	—	4,000	960	—	1,984	—	2,400	—	5,376
8	—	4,000	720	—	1,888	—	2,400	—	5,232
9	—	4,000	480	—	1,792	—	2,400	—	5,088
10	L=6,000	4,000	240	—	1,696	—	2,400	—	-1,056

[a]investment tax penalty

Code is used. Because only five years have elapsed since its purchase, the penalty is $1/3$ (9,000) = $3,000 under the 1981 Code.

As sample calculations, the cash flows for years 0, 1, and 10 are

$$X_{e0} = 60,000 - 24,000$$

$$= \$36,000$$

$$X_{e1} = 4,000 + 2,400 - (4,000 + 2,400 + 12,000)(0.40)$$

$$+ 2,400 - 4,800 + 3,000$$

$$= -\$360$$

$$X_{e10} = \qquad\qquad\qquad\qquad 4,000 + 240 - (4,000 + 240)(0.40)$$

$$+ 2,400 - 6,000$$

$$= -\$1,056$$

The equivalent annual amount of the cash flows in Table 10-15, using the required return for equity, is

$$E_d = [18,000 + 4,920(P/F\ 20,1)+ \ldots +1,744(P/F\ 20,5)]\ A/P\ 20,5$$

$$= \$11,492$$

and the equivalent annual amount of the cash flows in Table 10-16 is

$$E_n = [36,000 - 360(P/F\ 20,1)+ \ldots -(1,056)(P/F\ 20,10)]\ A/P\ 20,10$$

$$= \$10,239$$

A comparison of the equivalent annual amounts and cash flows is given in Table 10-17 which implies the same cycling assumption made in the conventional approach. However, it should be noted that the cash flow in year one under the new alternative is different than year eleven under the new alternative (the first year of the second cycle) and different than the cash flow in year six under the existing asset (the first cycle of the new asset replacing the existing asset). This is because the investment tax penalty ($3,000) only occurs once and, therefore, is only included in year one under the alternative of buying a new asset. The omission of the investment tax penalty, of course, reduces the equivalent annual amount of the corresponding cash flows to $9,643.

TABLE 10-17
A Cost Comparison for Example 10-4

End of Year	Alternative 1 Cash Flow	Alternative 1 Equivalent Amount	Alternative 2 Cash Flow	Alternative 2 Equivalent Amount
0	$18,000	—	$36,000	—
1	4,920	$11,492	−360	$10,239
2	5,976	•	−1,584	•
3	7,032	•	1,344	•
4	6,888	•	3,043	•
5	1,744 + 36,000	11,492	2,899	•
6	−3,360	9,643	4,138	•
7	−1,584	•	5,376	•
8	1,344	•	5,232	•
9	3,043	•	5,088	•
10	2,899	•	−1,056 + 36,000	10,239
11	4,138	•	−3,360	9,643
•	•	•	•	•
•	•	•	•	•
•	•	•	•	•
15	−1,056 + 36,000	9,643	2,889	•
16	−3,360	•	•	•
•	•	•	•	•
•	•	•	•	•
•	•	•	•	•
∞	−1,056	9,643	−1,056	9,643

If equivalent annual amounts are used as the basis of making a choice of alternative, another calculation is necessary. This is because of a conflict in the equivalent annual amounts for the first ten years (from year eleven to infinity they are the same). For the first five years the equivalent annual amount for the existing asset is larger ($11,492) than for the new asset ($10,239). However, for years six through ten, the equivalent annual amount under the alternative of keeping the existing asset is smaller ($9,643) than under the alternative of buying a new asset ($10,239). Therefore in order to make a choice, the equivalent annual amount of the values $11,492 and $9,643 must be determined over a ten-year period as shown below:

$$E = [11,492 \, P/A \, 20,5 + 9,643 \, P/A \, 20,5 \, (P/F \, 20,5) \,] \, A/P \, 20,10 = \$10,962$$

Since this value ($10,962) is larger than $10,239, the choice of alternative, from the standpoint of equivalent amounts, is the new alternative.

Tax Effects   In Example 10-4 the only tax effects included, aside from the $(C + D + I) \, T$ term, are the investment tax credit and penalty. There are other possible tax effects that can be included. Basically, these are tax effects that can result from differences in realizable (actual) salvage values and the tax book value at the point in time when an asset is retired. They are similar to the tax effects discussed in Chapter 9. As mentioned in Chapter 9, these tax effects may or may not be applicable due to tax regulations regarding like-kind exchanges. It is highly likely they would not be applicable in replacement analysis because in all probability a replacement would constitute a like-kind exchange. The most likely situation where tax effects are applicable is when there is an implied cessation of use and there is no implied replacement, such as in partial cycles (a finite need). However, for the sake of completeness, a procedure for including tax effects is presented in this section. The procedures presented in this section assume the property is classified as Sec. 1245 property and are approximate procedures since they only consider the gains and losses occurring from the disposal of the assets involved in the particular replacement analysis under consideration. The procedures do not consider the combined effect of disposals of other assets and the assets involved in a particular replacement analysis. The consideration of a combined effect would require an impossible estimating task.

In replacement studies, there are two possible places for tax effects. The first one is a tax effect resulting from the present realizable salvage value. The second effect occurs at the end of cycles or partial cycles. As an example, the present realizable salvage of the existing asset is $30,000 in Example 10-4. The tax book value of the existing asset after five years of use is

$$B = (90,000 - 6,000)\left(\frac{7-5}{7}\right)\left(\frac{7-5+1}{8}\right) + 6,000$$

$$= \$15,000$$

The difference between the present realization salvage ($30,000) and the present tax book value ($15,000) is taxable as ordinary income (Sec. 1245) and there is a tax of $(0.40)(15,000) = \$6,000$ that could possibly occur if the existing asset is retired (assuming the retirement is not classified as a like-kind exchange). This value ($6,000) occurs once and only if the new asset is purchased. Consequently, this text takes the point-of-view that it should be added to the cash flow for year one under the alternative of buying a new asset. That is, the cash flow for year one is

$$X_{e1} = -360 + 6,000$$

$$= \$5,640$$

if this tax effect is recognized. If the present realizable salvage value is less than the tax book value, there is a Sec. 1231 loss. This loss, in absence of any Sec. 1231 gains, would be subtracted from the cash flow of year one under the alternative of buying a new asset.

As an example of the tax effects at the end of cycle, the tax book value for the existing asset at the end of the fifth year is $6,000 since it is fully depreciated. The actual salvage value at this time is $5,000. Since the tax salvage is more, the tax effect, $1000 (.40) = \$400$, would be subtracted from the cash flow in year five giving a value of $1,344. This tax effect would also change the equivalent annual amount of the existing assets to $11,438.

The new asset uses MACRS depreciation which means a tax salvage of zero at the end of a cycle (10 years). The realizable salvage at the end of a cycle is $6,000. Therefore, the gain is $6,000 and there is a tax of $(0.40)(6,000) = \$2,400$ that would be added to the cash flow at the end of each new asset's complete cycle. Of course, if these tax effects are included in the analysis (cash flows), the equivalent annual amounts would change. In Example 10-4, the equivalent annual amount of $10,239, with the tax effects, is

$$E = 10{,}239 + [6{,}000 \ (P/F \ 20{,}1) + 2{,}400 \ (P/F \ 20{,}10)](A/P \ 20{,}10)$$
$$= \$11{,}524$$

The equivalent annual amount of $9,643 becomes

$$E = 9{,}643 + 2{,}400 \ (P/F \ 20{,}10) \ A/P \ 20{,}10$$
$$= \$9{,}735$$

There is no change for the equivalent annual amount of $11,492 for this example since there are no tax effects.

Example 10-5 _____

In this example, the case of a finite period of service (need) is discussed using the data in Example 10-4 and the following conditions:

(a)   a need of five years recognizing all tax effects. Assume the salvage value of the new asset is $20,000 after five years of service.

(b)   a need of fifteen years recognizing all tax effects.

For Part (a) the equity cash flows must be determined for the existing and new asset over the service period. In the case of the existing asset, this has been done (Table 10-15) except for consideration of possible tax effects in year five. In the discussion of tax effects, it is pointed out that the tax effect is $400. Therefore since it is a loss, the cash flow in year five in Table 10-15 would change to $1,344.

The cash flows for the new asset over the service period are given in Table 10-18 and include all possible tax effects. For example, the cash flow for year one is

$$X_{e1} = 4{,}000 + 2{,}400 - 7{,}360 + 4{,}800 - 4{,}800 + 3{,}000 + 6{,}000$$
$$= \$8{,}040$$

where, the $3,000 is the investment tax penalty and the $6,000 is the tax effect resulting from the disposal of the existing asset

TABLE 10-18
Equity Cash Flows for New Asset
(Example 10-5)

End of Year	Cap. Exp. & Salvage Value $K_j L_j$	Annual Costs C_j	Debt Interest I_j	Tax Depreciation D_j	Taxes t_j	Borrowed Capital B_j	Debt Recovery P_j	Investment Tax V_j	Equity Cash Flow X'_e
0	$60,000	—	—	—	—	$24,000	—	—	36,000
1	—	$4,000	$2,400	$12,000	$7,360	—	4,800	4,800 (3,000)[a]	8,040
2	—	4,000	1,920	19,200	10,048	—	4,800	—	672
3	—	4,000	1,440	11,520	6,784	—	4,800	—	3,456
4	—	4,000	960	6,912	4,745	—	4,800	—	5,015
5	L = 20,000	4,000	480	6,912	4,557	—	4,800	—	-8,659[b]

[a] investment tax penalty
[b] include tax effect of $(20,000 - 3,456)(0.40)$

which has been previously discussed. The cash flow in year five is

$$X_{e5} = 4,000 + 480 - 4,557 + 4,800 - 20,000$$

$$+ (20,000 - 3,456)(0.40)$$

$$= -\$8,659$$

Where, the $20,000 is the realizable salvage and $3,456 is the tax book value at the end of five years. That is,

$$B_5 = 60,000 - (12,000 + 19,200 + 11,520 + 6,912 + 6,912)$$

$$= \$3,456$$

It should be remembered, a finite service implies, in this text, that the equipment is removed at the end of the service period.

The equivalent annual amount has been determined in Example 10-4 and is $11,438. The equivalent annual amount for the new asset is

$$E_n = [36,000 + 8,040(P/F\ 20,1) + \ldots$$

$$-(8,659)(P/F\ 20,5)]\ AP\ 20,5$$

$$= \$14,749$$

TABLE 10-19

A Cost Comparison for Example 10-5
(Service Life = 5 years)

End of Year	Alternative 1 Cash Flow	Alternative 1 Equivalent Amount	Alternative 2 Cash Flow	Alternative 2 Equivalent Amount
0	$18,000	—	$36,000	—
1	4,920	$11,438	8,040	$14,749
2	5,976	11,438	672	14,749
3	7,032	11,438	3,456	14,749
4	6,888	11,438	5,015	14,749
5	1,344	11,438	-8,659	14,749

A comparison of the cash flows and equivalent annual amounts is given in Table 10-19 and indicates that keeping the existing alternative is the best choice from the standpoint of equivalent amounts.

For Part (b), the cash flows over a service period of fifteen years are needed. Fortunately, these cash flows have already been determined in Examples 10-4 and 10-5. They can be used as a result of the cycling assumption with some changes due to tax effects. A comparison of the cash flows and equivalent annual amounts is given in Table 10-20.

TABLE 10-20

A Cost Comparison for Example 10-5
(Service Life = 15 years)

| | Alternative | | | |
| | 1 | | 2 | |
End of Year	Cash Flow	Equivalent Amount	Cash Flow	Equivalent Amount
0	18,000	—	36,000	—
1	4,920	11,438	5,640	11,524
2	5,976	11,438	−1,584	•
3	7,032	11,438	1,344	•
4	6,888	11,438	3,043	•
5	1,344 + 36,000	11,438	2,899	•
6	−3,360	9,735	4,138	•
7	−1,584	9,735	5,376	•
8	1,344	•	5,232	•
9	3,043	•	5,088	•
10	2,899	•	1,344 + 36,000	11,524
11	4,138	•	−960	12,241
12	5,376	•	672	12,241
13	5,232	•	3,456	12,241
14	5,088	9,735	5,015	12,241
15	1,344	9,735	−8,659	12,241

From the standpoint of equivalent amounts, the existing asset is the best alternative. This choice of alternative is evident because the equivalent annual amounts for the various cycles of the existing asset are all less than the equivalent annual amounts for the new asset. In some cases, the choice is not as evident and it is necessary to combine the cycle equivalent amounts into a single value. For this example, these single values are

$$E_d \; = \; [11{,}438 \; PA \; 20{,}5 + 9{,}735 \; PA \; 20{,}10 \; (P/F \; 20{,}5)] \; AP \; 20{,}15$$

$$= \; \$10{,}825$$

$$E_n \; = \; [11{,}524 \; PA \; 20{,}10 + 12{,}241 \; PA \; 20{,}5 \; (P/F \; 20{,}10] \; AP \; 20{,}15$$

$$= \; \$11{,}598$$

THE OVERHAUL ALTERNATIVE

If an overhaul alternative is possible, cash flows can be used in the evaluation of this alternative. The following example describes the methodology for an overhaul alternative.

Example 10-6

Suppose in Example 10-4 it is possible to overhaul the existing asset at a cost of $8,500. If this overhaul is made, it is estimated that the life of the existing asset will be extended to seven years and the total (existing and overhaul) salvage value will be $7,000. The operating and maintenance costs are estimated to be $5,000 per year as a result of the overhaul.

The overhaul is considered to be depreciable on the basis of MACRS (five years) and qualifies for an 8% investment tax credit. It is desired to include this overhaul as a third alternative in

    (a)   Example 10-4
    (b)   Example 10-5 (Part b)

For Part a, the cash flows for the overhaul alternative must be determined. These are shown in Table 10-21. The basic procedure in generating the cash flows in Table 10-21 is the same as in Examples 10-4 and 10-5. One point, the investment tax credit (8%) in Table 10-21 is only applicable for the overhaul cost ($8,500). The equivalent annual amount of the cash flows in Table 10-21 is

$$E_0 \; = \; [23{,}100 + 2{,}366(P/F \; 20{,}1) + \ldots -1{,}668 \; (P/F \; 20{,}7)] \; A/P20{,}7$$

$$= \; \$10{,}158$$

TABLE 10-21
Cash Flows for Overhaul
(Example 10-6)

End of Year	Cap. Exp. & Salvage Value K_j, L_j	Annual Costs C_j	Debt Interest I_j	Tax Depreciation D_j	Taxes t_j	Borrowed Capital B_j	Debt Recovery P_j	Investment Tax V_j	Equity Cash Flow X'_e
0	$30,000 + 8,500	—	—	—	—	$15,400	—	—	$23,100
1	—	$5,000	$1,540	$6,000 + 1,700	$5,696	—	$2,200	$680	2,364
2	—	5,000	1,320	3,000 + 2,720	4,816	—	2,200	—	3,704
3	—	5,000	1,100	1,632	3,093	—	2,200	—	5,207
4	—	5,000	880	979	2,744	—	2,200	—	5,336
5	—	5,000	660	979	2,656	—	2,200	—	5,204
6	—	5,000	440	490	2,372	—	2,200	—	5,268
7	L = 7,000	5,000	220	—	2,088	—	2,200	—	-1,668

The cash flows and equivalent amounts for an infinite service life without tax effects are shown in Table 10-22. This table shows the basic cycling assumption. That is, the new asset replaces the overhaul alternative. Consequently, the cash flows after the overhaul are the same as in Table 10-16 without the investment tax penalty ($3,000). This table (10-16) is then included as a third

TABLE 10-22
Cost Cycles for Overhaul Alternative with an Infinite Service
(Example 10-6)

End of Year	Cash Flows	Equivalent Amounts
0	23,100	—
1	2,364	10,158
2	3,704	10,158
3	5,207	10,158
4	5,336	10,158
5	5,204	10,158
6	5,268	10,158
7	−1,668+36,000	10,158
8	−3,360	9,643
9	−1,584	9,643
10	1,344	9,643
•	•	•
•	•	•
•	•	•
17	−1,056+36,000	9,643
18	−3,360	9,643
19	−1,584	9,643
•	•	•
•	•	•
•	•	•
∞	−1,056	9,643

alternative and compared with the data in Table 10-17. A comparison of the equivalent annual amounts indicates the special situation described earlier in this chapter ($E_d < E_o < E_n$). First, the new asset is eliminated as an alternative since its equivalent amount is larger than the overhaul's amounts for the first ten years. Next, Eq. (10-5) is used to make a decision between the existing and overhaul alternatives.

$$E = [11{,}492 \, PA \, 20{,}5 + 9{,}643 \, PA \, 20{,}2 \, (P/F \, 20{,}5)] \, AP \, 20{,}7$$

$$= \$11{,}178$$

This value is larger than the overhaul alternative ($10,158). Therefore, the choice is the overhaul. Part (b) of Example 10-6 requires a service life of fifteen years and the recognition of tax effects (as specified in Example 10-5). The cash flows for the overhaul portion (the first seven years) of the service life (15 years) are the same as those given in Table 10-21 with the exception of year seven. At the end of year seven, the salvage value is $7,000 (see Table 10-21). The tax book value at this same point in time is $6,000. This value ($6,000) is the sum of the tax book values from the original asset ($6,000), given in Table 10-12, and the overhead portion (a value of zero since MACRS is used). Therefore, the tax effect of

$$(7{,}000 - 6{,}000)(.4) = \$400$$

must be added to the cash flow in year seven, which gives the result

$$X_7 = -1{,}668 + 400$$

$$= \$-1{,}268$$

Including this tax effect ($400) in the equivalent annual amount for the first seven years gives

$$\$10{,}158 + 400AF \, 20{,}7 = \$10{,}189$$

It is now necessary to generate the cash flows over an eight year period (the remaining portion of the service life) including any tax effects. It is estimated for this purpose that the salvage value of the new assets is $8,000 at the end of eight years. The cash flows for the new asset over a period of eight years are given in Table 10-23 and their equivalent annual amount is

$$E_n = [36{,}000 - 2{,}760(P/F \, 20{,}1) + \ldots + 780(P/F \, 20{,}8)] \, A/P \, 20{,}8$$

$$= \$10{,}540$$

TABLE 10-23
Equity Cash Flow for New Asset Over Eight Years
(Example 10-6)

End of Year	Cap. Exp. & Salvage Value $K_j L_j$	Annual Costs C_j	Debt Interest I_j	Tax Depreciation D_j	Taxes t_j	Borrowed Capital B_j	Debt Recovery P_j	Investment Tax V_j	Equity Cash Flow X_e
0	$60,000	—	—	—	—	$24,000	—	—	$36,000
1	—	$4,000	$2,400	$12,000	$7,360	—	$3,000	$4,800	-2,760
2	—	4,000	2,100	19,200	10,120	—	3,000	—	-1,020
3	—	4,000	1,800	11,520	6,928	—	3,000	—	1,872
4	—	4,000	1,500	6,912	4,965	—	3,000	—	3,535
5	—	4,000	1,200	6,912	4,845	—	3,000	—	3,355
6	—	4,000	900	3,456	3,342	—	3,000	—	4,558
7	—	4,000	600	—	1,840	—	3,000	—	5,760
8	L = 8,000	4,000	300	—	1,720	—	3,000	—	780[a]

[a]includes a tax effect of (8,000–0) (.4) = $3,200

The cash flow sequence and equivalent annual amounts for this part of the example are shown in Table 10-24. The $10,270 amount given in Table 10-24 is the combined equivalent amount. That is,

$$E_o = [10,189(P/A\ 20,7) + 10,540(P/A\ 20,8)(P/F\ 20,7)]\ (A/P\ 20,15)$$

$$= \$10,270$$

A comparison of this value ($10,270) with the combined amounts given in Example 10-5 ($10,566 and $11,598) indicates that the overhaul alternative is the choice from the standpoint of equivalent annual amounts.

COMMENTS

Some comments are in order regarding the decision criterion used in the previous cash flow examples. In these examples, the choice of an alternative is based on the equivalent annual amounts. Using equivalent annual amounts as the decision criterion is the

TABLE 10-24

*Cost Cycles for Overhaul Alternative
with a Finite Service (Example 10-6)*

End of Year	Cash Flows	Equivalent Amounts	
0	$23,100	—	—
1	2,364	$10,189	$10,270
2	3,704	10,189	10,270
3	5,207	10,189	10,270
4	5,336	10,189	10,270
5	5,204	10,189	10,270
6	5,268	10,189	10,270
7	−1,268+36,000	10,189	10,270
8	−2,760	10,540	10,270
9	−1,020	10,540	10,270
10	1,872	10,540	10,270
11	3,535	10,540	10,270
12	3,355	10,540	10,270
13	4,758	10,540	10,270
14	5,760	10,540	10,270
15	780	10,540	10,270

best procedure from a theoretical standpoint. However, annual cash flows do provide for a yearly evaluation of the alternatives. Thus, it is possible to base decisions on a comparison of the short-term effects (yearly cash flows) as well as on the long-term effects (equivalent annual amounts). This is a major advantage of cash flows. It is not unusual, in practical situations, to have the short-term effects outweigh the long-term effects, especially when the magnitude of differences is small.

In the discussions of an overhaul alternative, it is assumed the total overhaul cost is depreciable. It is possible to have a portion of the overhaul cost classified as an expense. In this case, the expensed amount becomes a part of the cost for year one and the remaining part of the overhaul is depreciated for tax purposes and may be applicable for the investment tax credit. After these modifications, the procedure for generating the cash flows is the same as discussed in previous examples.

ECONOMIC LIFE OF AN ASSET

In all of the previous examples, the annual cost of operation and maintenance is a constant. However, when the annual cost of operation and maintenance increases yearly for an asset, it is possible to define an economic life for the asset. The economic life is the number of years of use that minimizes an asset's equivalent annual cost. Theoretically, at the end of an asset's economic life, it is replaced with another asset having the same cost data as the initial asset. This replacement is repeated over and over again. In this way, the costs over a period of time are minimized. Also, in comparing assets on the basis of costs, the cost used in the comparison should be based on each asset's respective economic life.

The economic life occurs, with yearly increasing operation and maintenance costs, because the total equivalent annual cost consists of an increasing and a decreasing cost component. That is, the equivalent annual amounts of the yearly operations and maintenance costs increase as the years of use increase. While, the equivalent annual cost of the capital recovery and return decreases as the number of years of use increases. The economic life can be determined using either a conventional or cash flow approach. These two approaches are presented in the following examples.

Example 10-7

In this example, a conventional approach is used to determine the economic life of an asset having the cost data in Table 10-25.

Basically, the conventional approach involves the determination of the asset's equivalent annual costs for various use periods. These equivalent annual costs are calculated using the equation

$$E'_u = (K - L_u) (A/P\ k, u) + L_u(k)$$

$$+ (A/P\ k,u) \left[\sum_{j=1}^{u} C_j(P/F\ k,j) \right] \qquad (10\text{-}6)$$

where

E'_u = the equivalent annual cost for a period of u years

C_j = operation and maintenance cost for the year j.

L_u = salvage value at the end of u years.

k = the required return.

TABLE 10-25
Cost Data for Example 10-7

Initial cost		$30,000
Required return		25%

End of Year	Salvage Value	Operation & Maintenance
1	15,000	4,000
2	10,000	5,000
3	7,000	6,000
4	4,000	8,000
5	2,000	11,000
6	1,000	15,000
7	500	20,000

The remaining nomenclature in Eq. (10-6), is defined previously. With the required return and Eq. (10-6), the equivalent annual costs for the various periods of use given in Table 10-26 can be determined. For example,

$$E'_1 = (30,000 - 15,000)(A/P\ 25,1) + 15,000(0.25)$$
$$+ (A/P\ 25,1)\ [4,000(P/F\ 25,1)]$$
$$= \$26,500$$

TABLE 10-26
Equivalent Annual Costs for Various Periods of Use (Example 10-7)

Period of Use	Equivalent Annual Cost E'_u
1	$26,500
2	20,835
3	18,385
4	17,410
5	16,995
6	16,948
7	17,204

$$E'_4 = (30,000 - 4,000)(A/P\ 25,4) + 4,000(0.25)$$
$$+ (A/P\ 25,4)\ [4,000(P/F\ 25,1) + 5,000(P/F\ 25,2)$$
$$6,000(P/F\ 25,3) + 8,000(P/F\ 25,4)]$$
$$= \$17,410$$

$$E'_6 = (30,000 - 1,000)(A/P\ 25,6) + 1,000(0.25)$$
$$+ (A/P\ 25,6)\ [4,000(P/F\ 25,1) + 5,000(P/F\ 25,2)$$
$$+ 6,000(P/F\ 25,3) + 8,000(P/F\ 25,4)$$
$$+ 11,000(P/F\ 25,5) + 15,000(P/F\ 25,6)]$$
$$= \$16,948$$

A comparison of the equivalent annual costs in Table 10-26 indicates that the smallest value occurs after six years of use. Consequently, the economic life is six years. This implies that after six years of use the asset is replaced with another asset having the same cost data given in Table 10-25.

The economic life is sometimes approximated on the basis of a zero return ($k = 0$). When this is done, the terminology is changed from equivalent annual costs to *average annual costs*. The average annual costs for u years, A_u, are determined using the equation

$$A_u = \frac{P - L_u}{u} + \frac{\sum_{j=1}^{u} C_j}{u} \tag{10-7}$$

For example, some selected average annual costs, using the data in Table 10-25 and Eq. (10-7), are

$$A_1 = \frac{30,000 - 15,000}{1} + \frac{4,000}{1}$$

$$= \$19,000$$

$$A_4 = \frac{30,000 - 4,000}{4} + \frac{23,000}{4}$$

$$= \$12,250$$

$$A_6 = \frac{30,000 - 1,000}{6} + \frac{49,000}{6}$$

$$= \$13,000$$

The remaining average annual costs are given in Table 10-27.

A comparison of the average annual costs in Table 10-27 indicates that the economic life is four years which is less than the economic life indicated by the equivalent annual costs (six years). This result can be generalized. That is, for the same cost data, the economic life indicated by the average annual costs is always less than the economic life indicated by the equivalent annual costs. However, the difference between these two economic lives is small; usually, only a difference of one or two years. Consequently, because of their computational advantage, average annual costs are often used as a beginning point to narrow the range in which the equivalent annual costs must be calculated to determine the economic life of an asset.

TABLE 10-27
Average Annual Costs for Various Periods of Use (Example 10-7)

Period of Use	Average Annual Cost A_u
1	$19,000
2	14,500
3	12,666
4	12,250
5	12,400
6	13,000
7	14,071

Economic Life In Cost Comparisons   In addition to the use of the economic life to determine the time at which a particular asset should be replaced, the economic life is an important consideration in the comparison of assets. That is, all cost comparisons should be based on a comparison of the equivalent annual costs associated with the economic life of the assets.

Example 10-8 _____

In this example, the use of the economic life and associated equivalent annual costs in cost comparisons is explained.

Two assets, X and Y, have increasing operation and maintenance costs. The equivalent annual costs for various periods of use are determined using Eq. (10-6) and the results shown in Table 10-28 are obtained.

Table 10-28 indicates that the economic lives for assets X and Y are, respectively, four and six years. Therefore, for an infinite service life, the comparison is between the equivalent annual costs for the economic lives. In this example, these equivalent annual costs are $16,000 and $18,000. A comparison of these equivalent annual costs indicates that asset X should be chosen since it has the smaller cost. This comparison implies the assumption that the cost

TABLE 10-28
Equivalent Annual Costs for Assets X & Y
(Example 10-8)

Period of Use	Equivalent Annual Costs Asset X	Asset Y
1	$19,000	$24,000
2	17,000	21,000
3	16,500	19,000
4	16,000	18,700
5	16,400	18,500
6	17,300	18,000
7	—	18,300
8	—	18,900

data cycles for each alternative and, consequently, the alternatives are replaced at the end of their respective economic lives.

CASH FLOWS AND THE ECONOMIC LIFE

Cash flows (total, equity, or operating) can be used to determine the economic life. This is demonstrated in the following example.

Example 10-9

This example uses an equity cash flow approach to Example 10-7 with the additional following data:

tax depreciation	MACRS, five years
tax rate	40%
debt ratio	40%
required return for equity	20%
debt interest rate	10%

The cash flows are based on Eq. (9-8). The cash flows include possible tax effects resulting from differences in salvage values and the tax book values. They also include the investment tax credit and possible investment tax penalties. The investment tax credit and penalties are based on the following schedule:

Tax Depreciation Life	Investment Tax Credit
Less than 3 years	0%
three or four years	4%
five or more years	8%

The tax effects are based on the assumption of Sec. 1245 property and are included when the salvage value is larger than the tax book value.

The cash flow approach requires that the yearly cash flows be determined for each period of use and then determine the equivalent annual amount of these cash flows. In order to determine these equity cash flows, the debt recovery and interest schedules must be determined for each period of use based on a debt capital value of $(0.40)(30,000) = \$12,000$. These schedules are given in Tables 10-29 and 10-30. The debt recovery table is determined by

TABLE 10-29
Debt Recovery Schedule for Example 10-9

				Years of Use			
j	1	2	3	4	5	6	7
0	–	–	–	–	–	–	–
1	12,000	6,000	4,000	3,000	2,400	2,000	1,714
2	—	6,000	4,000	3,000	2,400	2,000	1,714
3	—	—	4,000	3,000	2,400	2,000	1,714
4	—	—	—	3,000	2,400	2,000	1,714
5	—	—	—	—	2,400	2,000	1,714
6	—	—	—	—	—	2,000	1,714
7	—	—	—	—	—	—	1,714

dividing the debt capital ($12,000) by the period of use. The debt interest table is determined by the assessment of the debt interest rate (10% in this example) on the unrecovered balance. It is also desirable to generate the tax depreciation schedule (MACRS, five years for this example) as shown in Table 10-31. These values do not change in determining the cash flows since the tax depreciation schedule is fixed as a result of tax regulations (tax depreciation life). With these tables, the yearly equity cash flows for each year of use and their equivalent annual amount can be determined. These cash flows are given in Table 10-32. The calculations necessary to obtain the values in Table 10-32 are explained in the following discussion. For one year of use, the cash flows are

$$X_0 = 30,000 - 30,000(0.40)$$
$$= \$18,000$$
$$X_1 = 4,000 + 1,200 - (4,000 + 1,200 + 6,000)(0.40)$$
$$+ 12,000 - 15,000 - (24,000 - 15,000)(0.40)$$
$$= -\$5,880$$

TABLE 10-30
Debt Interest Schedule for Example 10-9

				Years of Use			
j	1	2	3	4	5	6	7
0	–	–	–	–	–	–	–
1	1,200	1,200	1,200	1,200	1,200	1,200	1,200
2	—	600	800	900	960	1,000	1,029
3	—	—	400	600	720	800	858
4	—	—	—	300	480	600	687
5	—	—	—	—	240	400	516
6	—	—	—	—	—	200	345
7	—	—	—	—	—	—	174

TABLE 10-31
Tax Depreciation Schedule for Example 10-9

End of Year	Tax Depreciation	Tax Book Value
0	—	30,000
1	6,000	24,000
2	9,600	14,400
3	5,760	8,640
4	3,456	5,184
5	3,456	1,728
6	1,728	0

TABLE 10-32
Equity Cash Flows and Equivalent Annual Amounts (Example 10-9)

			Years of Use				
j	1	2	3	4	5	6	7
0	18,000	18,000	18,000	18,000	18,000	18,000	18,000
1	−5,580	4,320	2,320	1,320	720	320	34
2	—	−3,840	3,640	2,700	2,136	1,760	1,491
3	—	—	−920	4,656	4,128	3,776	3,525
4	—	—	—	3,324	6,106	5,778	5,544
5	—	—	—	—	5,871	7,458	7,241
6	—	—	—	—	—	9,829	10,230
7	—	—	—	—	—	—	13,518
Equiv. Amount	16,020	12,392	10,410	9,763	9,288	9,247	9,386

There is no investment tax credit (or penalty) because there is only one year. The tax effect of $(24,000 - 15,000)(0.40)$ is subtracted because the tax book value ($24,000) is more than the actual salvage ($15,000), implying a reduction in taxes. The other values used in these calculations are given in Example 10-7 or Tables 10-29 or 10-30. The equivalent annual amount for one year of use is

$$E = [18,000 - 2,280 \ (P/F \ 20,1) \ ] \ A/P \ 20,1$$
$$= \$19,320$$

The cash flows for three years of use are

$$X_0 = \$18,000$$
$$X_1 = 4,000 + 1,200 - (4,000 + 1,200 + 6,000)(0.40)$$
$$\qquad + 4,000 - 2,400$$
$$\quad = \$2,320$$
$$X_2 = 5,000 + 800 - (5,000 + 800 + 9,600) \ (0.40) + 4,000$$
$$\quad = \$3,640$$
$$X_3 = 6,000 + 400 - (6,000 + 400 + 5,760)(0.40) + 4,000$$
$$\qquad + 1,200 - 7,000 - (8,640 - 7,000)(0.40)$$
$$\quad = -\$920$$

and the equivalent annual amount is

$$E = [18,000 + 2,320 \ (P/F \ 20,1) + 3,640 \ (P/F \ 20,2)$$
$$\qquad + (-264) \ (P/F \ 20,3)] \ A/P \ 20,3$$
$$= \$10,410$$

In year one, the $2,400 value is the investment tax credit. The $1,200 value in year three is the investment tax penalty. The term $(8,640 - 7,000)(0.40)$ is the tax effect.

The cash flows for five years of use are

$$X_0 = \$18,000$$

$$X_1 = 4,000 + 1,200 - (4,000 + 1,200 + 6,000)(0.40)$$
$$\qquad + 2,400 - 2,400$$
$$\quad = \$720$$

$$X_2 = 5,000 + 960 - (5,000 + 960 + 9,600)(0.40) + 2,400$$
$$\quad = \$2,136$$

$$X_3 = 6,000 + 720 - (6,000 + 720 + 5,760)(0.40) + 2,400$$
$$\quad = \$4,128$$

$$X_4 = 8,000 + 480 - (8,000 + 480 + 3,456)(0.40) + 2,400$$
$$\quad = \$6,106$$

$$X_5 = 11,000 + 240 - (11,000 + 240 + 3,456)(0.40) + 2,400$$
$$\qquad - 2,000 + (2,000 - 1,728)(0.40)$$
$$\quad = \$5,871$$

The last term in the cash flow for year five is the tax effect since the salvage value ($2,000) is greater than the tax book value ($1,728). There is no investment tax penalty since the period of use is five years. The equivalent annual amount for the five years of use is

$$E = [18,000 + 720 \, (P/F \; 20,1) + \ldots + 5,871 \, (P/F \; 20,5)] \, A/P \; 20,5$$
$$\quad = \$9,288$$

A comparison of the equivalent annual amounts in Table 10-32 indicates the economic life is six years.

A comment In theory, the concept of an economic life is sound. However, its use in practice is limited. This is a result of several considerations: (1) the difficulty in estimating yearly salvage values and increasing operation and maintenance costs and (2) assets are usually replaced on the basis of current costs rather than on cost at the time of original purchase.

PROBLEMS

10-1 A company is considering replacing certain equipment that has been in use for seven years. This equipment originally cost $150,000 and had an estimated salvage value of $10,000 at the end of twenty-five years. Operations and maintenance costs have amounted to $15,000 per year. If this existing equipment is continued, it is believed this annual cost of operation and maintenance will be the same. However, it is now estimated that the existing equipment will only last eight more years and have a salvage value of $8,000 at that time. The present realizable salvage value for the existing equipment is $80,000.

Present available equipment that provides equal service indicates that there may be an economic advantage to replacing the existing equipment. There is now equipment available that will reduce the annual cost of operation and maintenance to $5,000 per year. This new equipment initially costs $120,000, lasts fifteen years, and has a salvage value of $10,000.

Assuming the required MARR value is 20%, make an equivalent annual cost comparison for the following service lives.

(a) infinity

(b) eight years assuming the salvage value of the new equipment is $40,000 after eight years of use

(c) twenty years assuming the salvage values of the new equipment after twelve and five years of use respectively, are $15,000 and $45,000

10-2 What is the sunk cost in Problem 10-1 assuming straight-line depreciation?

10-3 Determine the present realizable salvage value in Part (a) of Problem 10-1 that makes the equivalent annual costs equal. How, in general, could such a value be used for decision purposes?

10-4 Repeat Parts (a) and (c) of Problem 10-1 assuming there is an overhaul alternative that costs an additional $25,000, extends the life of the existing asset to ten years with a total salvage of $4,000, and reduces operation and maintenance costs to $8,000 per year. Also assume that the salvage value of the new equipment after ten years of use is $18,000.

10-5 Repeat Problem 10-4 on the basis that $5,000 of the overhaul cost can be expensed and the remaining amount ($20,000) is depreciable.

10-6 Five years ago, an asset with the data shown below was purchased and put in service. The original estimate of the operation and maintenance costs ($6,000) has been low. The cost of operation and maintenance has amounted to $12,000 per year and is expected to continue at this amount if the asset is not replaced. Consequently, a replacement is being considered for the existing asset. The data for the replacement asset is given below. It is now estimated that the existing asset will last six more years and have a salvage value of $10,000 at that time. The realizable salvage value for the existing asset, at the present time, is $90,000. Under the following conditions, determine if the existing asset should be replaced using equity cash flows.
(a)   infinite service life
(b)   there are no tax effects on the gains and losses resulting from the disposal of assets.

ORIGINAL DATA FOR EXISTING ASSET

Initial cost	$150,000
life	15
salvage	$ 30,000
Annual cost of operation and	
maintenance	$6,000
Tax depreciation	SYD
life, years	10
salvage value	$18,000
Debt ratio	40%
Required debt return	15%
Required equity return	25%
Investment tax rate	1981 Code
Tax rate	52%

DATA FOR REPLACEMENT ASSET

Initial cost	$140,000
life	10
salvage	$20,000
Annual cost of operation and maintenance	$5,000
Tax depreciation	MACRS: 5 years
Debt ratio	40%
Required debt return	10%
Required equity return	20%
Investment tax rate	8%
Tax rate	40%

10-7 Repeat Problem 10-6 only the service lives are
(a) 6 years and (b) 10 years. Assume that the realizable salvage at any point in time (j) for the new asset is given by $L = (0.823)^j \ (140,000)$

10-8 Repeat Problem 10-6 recognizing all tax effects.

10-9 Repeat Part (a) of Problem 10-7 recognizing all tax effects.

10-10 It has been decided that it is possible to overhaul the existing asset in Problem 10-6. Using the data given below, determine the equity cash flows for the overhaul alternative and include them in the comparison of alternatives in Problem 10-6.

OVERHAUL DATA

Cost of overhaul	$40,000
life, years	8
Annual operation and maintenance	$ 8,000
Tax depreciation for overhaul	MACRS: 5 years
Total salvage (overhaul & existing asset)	$ 8,000
Investment tax credit	8%

10-11   Repeat Problem 10-10 on the basis that $10,000 of the overhaul can be expensed and the remaining amount ($30,000) is depreciable.

10-12   Repeat *Example* 10-5 for a service life of 10 years and recognize all tax effects.

10-13   Repeat Problem 10-6 using total cash flows.

10-14   Repeat Problem 10-6 recognizing all tax effects and using total cash flows.

10-15   If the initial cost of an asset is $50,000 and has the additional data given in the following table, determine the economic life if (a) MARR = 0% and (b) MARR = 15%. Use a conventional approach.

Years of Use	Salvage Value	Operation & Maintenance
1	$34,000	$ 5,000
2	26,000	6,000
3	20,000	7,000
4	16,000	8,000
5	14,000	9,000
6	12,000	10,000
7	10,000	12,000
8	8,000	14,000
9	6,000	18,000
10	4,000	20,000

10-16   Using the data given in Problem 10-15, determine the economic life of the asset using total cash flows and assuming (1) the correct discount rate (k_a) is 20%, (2) there is no investment tax credit, (3) there are no tax effects, and (4) the tax depreciation is MACRS (five years) with a tax rate of 40%.

10-17   In *Example* 10-9, make the necessary calculations to check the cash flows given in Table 10-32 for periods of use where there are no sample calculations.

10-18 Repeat *Problem* 10-9 using total cash flows.

10-19 For two assets *A* and *B*, the equivalent annual costs for various periods of use have been determined with the results shown below. Make a cost comparison if the need is infinite.

ASSET A		ASSET B	
Years of Use	Equivalent Annual Cost	Years of Use	Equivalent Annual Cost
0	—	0	—
1	$50,000	1	$45,000
2	40,000	2	38,000
3	35,000	3	33,000
4	33,000	4	30,000
5	31,000	5	28,000
6	28,000	6	26,000
7	25,000	7	26,500
8	24,000	8	25,000
9	25,500	9	24,000
10	26,500	10	23,500
		11	22,000
		12	20,000
		13	21,500
		14	22,000
		15	23,000

11

MINIMUM ANNUAL REVENUE REQUIREMENT EXTENSIONS

In Chapter 6, the determination and use of revenue requirements are presented. This chapter includes some extensions to minimum annual revenue requirements.

WORKING CAPITAL AND REVENUE REQUIREMENTS

As discussed in Chapter 5, working capital changes are an important consideration in the determination of the acceptability of a capital investment. Consequently, it is the purpose of this section to provide a method for including working capital changes in the analysis of capital expenditures when revenue requirements are used.

A Review of Revenue Requirements   The method for determining minimum annual revenue requirements without working capital changes is provided in Chapter 6. Consequently, they are not discussed in any great depth in this chapter. However, it is desirable, at this point, to provide a brief review of the method for determining minimum annual revenue requirements for the purpose of serving as a foundation for the development of a method for including working capital changes in the revenue requirement approach to capital investment analysis. This review is presented in Example 11-1.

Example 11-1 _____

A capital investment is being considered with the data given in Table 11-1. This capital investment is expected to provide a yearly gross income of $40,000 over the life of the project (7 years). The question is, Is the project acceptable? If a revenue requirement approach is used to answer this question, it is necessary to determine the revenue requirements given in Table 11-2. The values in Table 11-2 are calculated using the relationships given in Chapter 6. The acceptability of the investment can be determined using Eq. (11-1) (the same as Eq. 6-13). Eq. (11-1) determines the net

TABLE 11-1
Capital Investment Data for Example 11-1

Capital investment = $100,000
Book depreciation = straight line
   salvage = $16,000
   life= 7 years
Tax depreciation= MACRS (5 years)
Required return on equity = 25%
Cost of debt capital = 10%
Debt ratio = 30%
Investment tax credit = 8%
Operation and maintenance = $5,000 per year
Tax rate = 40%

TABLE 11-2
Minimum Annual Revenue Requirements
(Example 11-1)

End of Year	Book Depr. D_h	Tax Depr. D	Book Value B	Equity Return F_e	Debt Interest I	Tax t	Oper. & Maint. C	Revenue Reqm't. R
0	-	-	100,000	-	-	-	-	-
1	12,000	20,000	88,000	17,500	3,000	6,333	5,000	30,500[a]
2	12,000	32,000	76,000	15,400	2,640	-3,067	5,000	31,973
3	12,000	19,200	64,000	13,300	2,280	4,067	5,000	36,647
4	12,000	11,520	52,000	11,200	1,920	7,787	5,000	37,907
5	12,000	11,520	40,000	9,100	1,560	6,387	5,000	34,047
6	12,000	5,760	28,000	7,000	1,200	8,827	5,000	34,027
7	12,000	-	16,000	4,900	840	11,267	5,000	34,007

[a]includes investment tax credit ($8,000)

present value of the

$$NPV_e = (1-T)\sum_{j=1}^{n} (G_j - R_j)(P/F\,k_e, j)$$

$(11-1)$

equity cash flows since k_e is used as the discount rate. For this example Eq. (11-1) gives

$$NPV_e = (1-.40)\ [(40{,}000-30{,}500)\ P/F\ 25{,}1$$
$$+ (40{,}000-31{,}973)\ P/F\ 25{,}2$$

$$\vdots$$

$$+ (40{,}000-34{,}007)\ P/F\ 25{,}7$$
$$= (.60)(20{,}085)$$
$$= \$12{,}051$$

which indicates the investment is acceptable since the net present value (NPV$_e$) is positive.

Working Capital Changes

In developing a method for including working capital changes in revenue requirements, the same implication involved in revenue requirements is made. That is, investments are financed from a company's pool of capital that is obtained from debt and equity sources. Consequently, since working capital is an investment, a portion of the working capital is supported by debt obligations and the remaining portion by equity sources. These portions are directly related to the debt ratio, c, of the pool of capital available for investments.

In order to include working capital changes (increases or decreases), it is first necessary to estimate the amount (Wj) and timing (j) of the working capital changes. Once these values have been estimated, it is possible to determine the yearly changes in revenue requirements resulting from the working capital.

For increases in working capital, the same convention given in Chapter 5 is used. That is, working capital increases that occur in the early years of a project's life are recovered at the end of a project's life. This convention is, of course, not mandatory. It is possible to assume the recovery of the working capital occurs over a longer period of time.

Once the amount and timing of the working capital increases, Wj, have been estimated, the yearly increase in revenue requirements, R'j, resulting from the increased working capital requirement can be determined by the following equations

$$R'_j = F'_{ej} + I'_j + t'_j + C'_j \tag{11-2}$$

where

$$F'_{ej} = k_e \, (1\text{-}c) \sum_{x=0}^{j-1} W_x \tag{11-3}$$

$$I'_j = k_d \, (c) \sum_{x=0}^{j-1} W_x \tag{11-4}$$

$$t'_j = \frac{T}{1\text{-}T} \, (F'_{ej}) \tag{11-5}$$

and C'j is any operation and maintenance costs that are directly attributed to the increase in working capital. In this example C'j is assumed to be a constant. However, this assumption is not required.

The inclusion of the working capital increases and their resulting revenue requirements into Eq. (11-1) is shown in Eq. (11-6).

$$NPV_e = (1\text{-}T) \sum_{j=0}^{n} (G_j - R_j - R'_j) \, (P/F \, k_{e,j}) \tag{11-6}$$

Eqs. (11-2) through (11-5) are adaptations of the equations given in Chapter 6 for determining revenue requirements and are based on the following considerations. Since working capital is a non-depreciable asset from the standpoint of tax regulations, there is no tax depreciation (D_j). There are no capital recovery (D_{tj}) terms included in Eqs. (11-2) and (11-15). This is because the recovery of working capital has no tax or revenue requirement effect. Its effect is a release of capital (a cash inflow) that is similar to a salvage value associated with the termination of a capital investment.

Example 11-2

Suppose in Example 11-1, the investment required a working capital increase in year one of $10,000 and an additional increase in working capital of $20,000 in year two. Also, these working capital changes require an additional $500 per year for maintenance and operations beginning in year two. With these changes, is the investment justified?

Since the revenue requirements for the capital investment have been determined in Example 11-1 (Table 11-2), only the revenue requirements for the working capital changes are needed to use Eq. (11-6). These are shown in Table 11-3.

TABLE 11-3
Revenue Requirements for Working Capital Changes
(Example 11-2)

End of Year	Working Capital Reqm't. W	Cumulative Working Capital Σ_W	Equity Return F'_e	Debt Return I'	Taxes t'	Oper. & Maint. C'	Revenue Reqm't. R'
0	-	-	-	-	-	-	-
1	10,000	10,000	-	-	-	-	-
2	20,000	30,000	1,750	300	1,167	500	3,717
3	-	30,000	5,250	900	3,500	500	10,150
4	-	30,000	5,250	900	3,500	500	10,150
5	-	30,000	5,250	900	3,500	500	10,150
6	-	30,000	5,250	900	3,500	500	10,150
7	-	0	5,250	900	3,500	500	10,150

Substituting the results in Tables 11-2 and 11-3 into Eq. (11-6) gives

$$NPV_e = (1-.40) \, [(40{,}000\text{-}30{,}500) \, (P/F \ 25, \ 1)$$
$$+(40{,}000\text{-}31{,}973\text{-}3{,}717)(P/F \ 25{,}2)$$
$$+(40{,}000\text{-}36{,}647\text{-}10{,}150) \, (P/F \ 25{,}2)$$

$$\vdots$$

$$+(40{,}000\text{-}34{,}007\text{-}10{,}150)(P/F \ 25{,}7)]$$
$$= \$142$$

which indicates there is a significant reduction in the net present value due to the working capital requirement.

A Comment   In Eqs. (11-1) and (11-2) and Examples 11-1 and 11-2, the discount rate used to determine the net present value is the required return on equity (k_e).

Decreases in working capital requirements can be included in revenue requirements with some slight modifications to the method for increases in working capital. First, Eqs. (11-2) through (11-5) can be used to determine the yearly revenue requirement effect resulting from a decrease in working capital except the results from Eq. (11-2) gives a decrease in revenue requirements (a savings). The W_j term in Eqs. (11-3) and (11-4) is the estimated decrease in working capital. Incorporating these changes into Eq. (11-6), gives Eq. (11-7) for the evaluation of capital investments that involve decreases in working capital.

$$NPV_e = (1\text{-}T) \sum_{j=1}^{n} (G_j - R_j + R'_j)(P/F \ k_e, j) \tag{11-7}$$

Example 11-3 _____

Suppose in Example 11-1, it is estimated that the capital investment will also reduce the working capital requirements by $30,000 and the timing of this recovery is $W_1 = \$10{,}000$ and $W_2 = \$20{,}000$. Further as a result of the decrease in working capital, certain operations and maintenance costs are reduced by $500 per year. Since these decreases in working capital and timing are numerically the same as in the previous example, it is possible to use the data in Table 11-3 with the appropriate sign changes. Using Eq. (11-7), the net present value is

$$NPV_e = (1-.40)[(40,000-30,500)(P/F\ 25,1)$$
$$+(40,000-31,973+3,717)(P/F\ 25,2)$$
$$+(40,000-36,647+10,150)\ (P/F\ 25,3)$$

$$\vdots$$

$$+\ (40,000-34,007+10,150)\ (P/F\ 25,\ 7)]$$
$$=\$23,\ 960$$

which indicates the project is acceptable and the NPV is significantly greater than the NPV of the project without decreases in working capital ($12,051).

A Comment   Examples 11-1, 11-2, and 11-3 show the effects of working capital on the net present value. Many capital expenditure projects involve changes in working capital requirements. Increases in working capital requirements have the effect of increasing investment outflows and minimum annual revenue requirements. Decreases in working capital requirements have the opposite effect. Therefore, it is important that working capital changes be included, when applicable, in the economic evaluations of capital expenditures. otherwise, incorrect evaluations are possible.

THE NORMALIZING METHOD

Minimum annual revenue requirements can be generated using either the flow-through or normalizing methods. Up to this point, all discussions of revenue requirements have been based on the flow-through method. The normalizing method is most often used by public utilities because it includes many of the accounting conventions and procedures required by regulatory agencies in establishing utility rates. This method is presented in this section.

The minimum annual revenue requirements, R, using the normalizing method, include the following components.

$$R = \begin{cases} + & \text{book depreciation} \\ + & \text{deferred taxes} \\ + & \text{investment tax credit} \\ - & \text{amortized investment tax credit} \\ + & \text{debt interest excluding capitalized interest} \\ + & \text{return on equity} \\ + & \text{taxes} \\ + & \text{operation and maintenance costs} \end{cases} \quad (11\text{-}8)$$

The evaluation of the components in Eq. (11-8) is demonstrated in the following example.

Example 11-4

In this example the minimum annual revenue requirements are generated using the normalizing method and the data given in Table 11-4. The revenue requirements are shown in Table 11-5.

TABLE 11-4
Data for Example 11-4

Initial (construction) cost = $120,000
Book depreciation = SL
    salvage $ 20,000
    life, years = 8
Tax depreciation = MACRS (5 years)
Required return on equity = 25%
Required return on debt = 10%
Debt ratio = 40%
Capitalized interest = 2%
Investment tax credit = 8%
Tax rate = 40%
Operation and maintenance per year = $ 15,000

The method for determining the components in Table 11-5 is given in the following discussion.

The capitalized investment, K, must be determined. This is given by Eq. (11-9).

$$K = P + bP \qquad (11-9)$$

where P is the actual (construction) cost of the project and b is the capitalized interest rate. For this example, Eq. (11-9) gives

$$K = 120,000 + (.02)(120,000)$$
$$= \$122,400$$

Capitalized interest ($2,400) is the interest paid on money during the construction phase of the project. The usual convention in generating minimum annual revenue requirements is to take this interest as a tax deduction in the first year of the project since this is when it is actually paid, and recover the interest over the life of the project beginning in the first year. The argument is that, in this way, present customers are not "penalized" for the interest cost of

TABLE 11-5
Minimum Annual Revenue Requirements using Normalizing methods
(Example 11-4)

End of Year	Book Dep.	SL for Tax	Tax Dep.	Def. Taxes	Inv. Tax Credit	Amort. Tax Credit	Charg. Inv.	Return on Equity	Debt Int.	Cap. Int.	Tax	Costs	Rev. Reqm't
0	-	-	-	-	-	-	122,400	-	-	-	-	-	-
1	12,800	20,000	24,000	1,600	9,600	1,200	99,600	18,360	4,896	2,400	-6,160[a]	15,000	54,896
2	12,800	20,000	38,400	7,360	-	1,200	80,640	14,940	3,984	-	-3,000	15,000	49,884
3	12,800	20,000	23,040	1,216	-	1,200	67,824	12,096	3,226	-	1,248	15,000	44,386
4	12,800	20,000	13,824	-2,470	-	1,200	58,694	10,174	2,713	-	3,653	15,000	40,670
5	12,800	20,000	13,824	-2,470	-	1,200	49,564	8,804	2,348	-	2,470	15,000	37,752
6	12,800	20,000	6,912	-5,236	-	1,200	43,200	7,435	1,983	-	4,591	15,000	35,373
7	12,800	-	-	-	-	1,200	31,600	6,480	1,728	-	12,053	15,000	46,861
8	12,800	-	-	-	-	1,200	20,000	4,740	1,264	-	10,893	15,000	43,497

[a]includes investment tax credit

new construction. Instead, by spreading it over the life of the project, this interest is assessed to both present and future customers. Usually, the capitalized interest rate is established by regulatory agencies.

Three depreciation schedules must be determined for the normalizing method. These three schedules are (1) depreciation for book (capital recovery) purposes (D_b), (2) straight-line for tax purposes (D_s) and (3) the tax depreciation (D_t). These three depreciation schedules use different initial costs, lives, and salvage values. For D_b, the initial cost is K, the life is the book depreciation life and the salvage value is the book salvage value. For the tax depreciation, the MACRS (five years) is specified and the percentages given in the tax regulations are used. Also, the depreciation amounts are based on using the actual construction cost (P) . The straight-line for tax purposes is based on the construction cost, the tax salvage and tax depreciation period. Since the MACRS is specified in this example, this means D_s is over six years and the salvage value is zero. The three depreciation schedules are given in Table 11-6. These are the first three columns in Table 11-5.

TABLE 11-6
Depreciation Schedules
(Example 11-4)

EOY	D_b	D_s	D_t
0	-	-	-
1	12,800	20,000	24,000
2	12,800	20,000	38,400
3	12,800	20,000	23,040
4	12,800	20,000	13,824
5	12,800	20,000	13,824
6	12,800	20,000	6,912
7	12,800	-	-
8	12,800	-	-

The next step is to calculate the deferred taxes. Mathematically, the deferred taxes in year j are determined using Eq. (11-10).

$$d_j = (D_{tj} - D_{sj})T \qquad (11\text{-}10)$$

where T is the tax rate. For example, the deferred taxes for years one and two are

$$d_1 = (24{,}000 - 20{,}000)(.4)$$
$$= \$1{,}600$$
$$d_2 = (38{,}400 - 20{,}000)(.4)$$
$$= \$7{,}360$$

The remaining values are given in Table 11-5. It should be noted that the deferred taxes become negative at some point in time (year four in this example). Basically, deferred taxes are the difference in taxes that result from the use of an accelerated depreciation model (MACRS). There is a reluctance to pass these "savings" on to customers due to the fact that tax rates and laws may change in the future. Consequently, deferred taxes are *normalized* by most public utilities. This means that deferred taxes are included as an expense in the early years and given as a credit in later years. Some credit is given for deferred taxes in the early years due to the manner in which the chargeable investment is calculated and used. These later two statements become evident in subsequent steps.

The investment tax credit, V, is given by Eq. (11-11)

$$V = k_c P \qquad (11\text{-}11)$$

and the amortized investment tax credit, A, is given by Eq. (11-12)

$$A = V / n \qquad (11\text{-}12)$$

where n is the book depreciation life. For this example, Eqs. (11-11) and (11-12) give

$$V = (.08)(120{,}000)$$
$$= \$9{,}600$$
$$A = 9{,}600 / 8$$
$$= \$1{,}200$$

The chargeable investment for year j, K_j is determined using Eq. (11-13) and for years one and two are

$$K_j = K_{j-1} - D_{bj} - V - d_j + A_j \qquad (11\text{-}13)$$
$$K_1 = 122{,}400 - 12{,}800 - 9{,}600 - 1{,}600 + 1{,}200$$
$$= \$99{,}600$$
$$K_2 = 99{,}600 - 12{,}800 - 7{,}360 + 1{,}200$$
$$= \$80{,}640$$

The remaining values are given in Table 11-5. It should be noted that the last (year eight) chargeable investment is the book salvage value ($20,000).

The next step is to calculate the required return an equity, Fe, for the year j. These values are determined using Eq. (11-14) where c is the debt ratio

$$F_{ej} = (1-c)\, k_e\, K_{j-1} \qquad (11\text{-}14)$$

and k_e is the required rate of return for equity. For years one and two these values are

$$
\begin{aligned}
F_{e1} &= (1\text{-}.4)(.25)(122{,}400) \\
&= \$18{,}360 \\
F_{e2} &= (1\text{-}.4)(.25)(99{,}600) \\
&= \$14{,}940
\end{aligned}
$$

The debt interest, I, for year j is determined using Eq. (11-15) where k_d is the required rate

$$I_j = ck_d\, K_{j-1} \qquad (11\text{-}15)$$

of debt interest. For this example, Eq. (11-15) gives the following for years one and two

$$
\begin{aligned}
I_1 &= (.4)(.10)(122{,}400) \\
&= \$4{,}896 \\
I_2 &= (.4)(.10)(99{,}600) \\
&= \$3{,}984
\end{aligned}
$$

The taxes are calculated using Eq. (11-16)

$$t_j = \frac{T}{1\text{-}T} (F_{ej} - D_{tj} + d_j + V - A - D_j - bP) - \frac{V}{1\text{-}T} \qquad (11\text{-}16)$$

and for years one and two are

$$t_1 = \frac{.4}{.6}(18{,}360 + 12{,}800 + 1{,}600 + 9{,}600\ \text{-}1{,}200 - 24{,}000 - 2{,}400) - \frac{9600}{.6}$$
$$= \text{-}\$6{,}160$$
$$t_2 = (.4/.6)(14{,}940 + 12{,}800 + 7{,}360 - 1{,}200 - 38{,}400)$$
$$= \text{-}\$3{,}000$$

The minimum annual revenue requirements are determined using Eq. (11-17) where C_j is the

$$R_j = D_{bj} + d_j + V - A + F_{ej} + I_j + t_j + C_j \qquad (11\text{-}17)$$

yearly operation and maintenance costs and for this example are $15,000. For years one and two, Eq. (11-17) gives

$$R_1 = 12,800 + 1,600 + 9,600 - 1,200 + 18,360 + 4,896 - 6,160 + 15,000$$
$$= \$54,896$$
$$R_2 = 12,800 + 7,360 - 1,200 + 14,940 + 3,984 - 3,000 + 15,000$$
$$= \$49,884$$

The remaining values are given in Table 11-5.

At this point, it is instructive to determine the taxes using Eq. (11-18) and assuming $G_j = R_j$.

$$t_j = (G_j - C_j - I_j - D_j)(T) - V \qquad (11\text{-}18)$$
$$t_1 = (54,896\ 15,000 - 4,896 - 2,400 - 24,000)(.4) - 9,600$$
$$= -\$6,160$$
$$t_2 = (49,884 - 115,000 - 3,984 - 38,400)(.4)$$
$$= -\$3,000$$

These are the same values obtained using Eq. (11-16) .

Comments   The basic use of revenue requirements generated using the normalizing method is the same as the use of revenue requirements generated using the flow-through method. That is, if the expected gross revenues (incomes) for a particular project are greater than the revenue requirements, the project is acceptable. From a utility company standpoint, the minimum revenue requirements are often referred to as annual costs and form a basis of establishing utility rates.

PROBLEMS

11-1   Generate the minimum annual revenue requirements using the data given below:

Initial cost = \$200,000
   book depreciation = SL
   life, years = 8
   salvage value = \$20,000
   tax depreciation = MACRS (five years)
Required return on equity = 20%
Required return for debt = 10%
Debt ratio = 30%
Investment tax credit = 8%
Tax rate = 40%
Annual operation and maintenance = \$10,000
Working capital increases:
   for year one = \$20,000

for year two = $40,000

additional costs beginning in year two = $3,000

11-2 What are the revenue requirements in Problem 11-1 if the working capital increases are decreases?

11-3 If the expected gross incomes are those shown below, determine the net present value of the project in Problem 11-1. Is the project acceptable? Why?

$G_1 = \$50,000, G_2 = \$60,000, G_3 = \$70,000, G_4 = \$80,000,$
$G_5 = \$90,000, G_6 = \$90,000, G_7 = \$90,000, G_8 = \$80,000$

11-4 For the conditions given in Problem 11-2 and the gross incomes given below, determine the net present value. Is the project acceptable? Why?

$G_1 = \$44,000, G_2 = \$45,000, G_3 = \$45,000, G_4 = \$45,000,$
$G_5 = \$45,000, G_6 = \$45,000, G_7 = \$45,000, G_8 = \$43,000.$

11-5 A computer system is being considered that is expected to reduce in-process inventories (working capital). The cost data for the computer system is given below:

Computer System

Initial cost	= $80,000
Book depreciation	= SL
life, years	= 5
salvage value	= $5,000
Tax depreciation	= MACRS (3 years)
the proportions for MACRS	= 33.33%, 44.45%
	14.81%, 7.41%
Required return on equity	= 20%
Required return for debt	= 10%
Debt ratio	= 30%
Tax rate	= 40%
Investment tax credit	= 4%
Annual operation and maintenance	= $2,000

The timing and amounts of the reduction of in-process inventories are estimated to be those shown below:

End of Year	Inventory Reductions
0	$10,000
1	20,000
2	30,000

In addition, it is estimated that existing operations and maintenance costs associated with the in-process inventories can be reduced by $5,000 per year. Is the computer system justified on the basis of an implied equity cash flow definition?

11-6 Generate the minimum annual revenue requirements using the normalizing method and the data given in the following table.

Data

Initial (construction) cost	$240,000
Book depreciation	SL
salvage value	$ 20,000
life, years	10
Annual operation & maintenance	$ 15,000
Tax depreciation	MACRS (5 years)
Debt ratio	40%
Required equity return	20%
Required debt return	10%
Tax rate	40%
Capitalized interest rate	2%
Investment tax credit schedule	
five or more years	8%
three or four years	4%
less than three years	0%

12

THE COST OF CAPITAL AND THE MINIMUM ACCEPTABLE RETURN

The minimum acceptable (attractive) rate of return (MARR) is an important factor in determining the desirability of an investment; that is, the internal rate of return is compared to MARR and the interest rate used in calculating net present value is also MARR. Consequently, establishing a value for MARR is an important aspect in the evaluation of projects. Hence, this chapter considers a basis on which a value for MARR may be established.

Basically, the MARR is related to a well-discussed financial concept; namely, the weighted average cost of capital which is briefly discussed in Chapter 5. In general, the cost of capital is the weighted average of the cost of capital from specific sources. Or, expressed mathematically, the cost of capital, k, is

$$k = \sum_{j=1}^{n} w_i k_i$$

$$(12-1)$$

where

w_i = proportion of capital from source i

k_i = cost of capital from source i

Although there is general agreement on Eq. (12-1), there still exists some controversy about the evaluation of some of the components included in Eq. (12-1). As a result of this controversy, the determination of the cost of capital still requires some degree of judgment and estimation. This chapter presents some of the more basic considerations in determining the cost of capital in an attempt to narrow the range in which judgment and estimates are required. For those who wish to make an in-depth study of the cost of capital, references are provided at the end of this chapter. The two major sources of capital are (1) debt and (2) equity.

COST OF DEBT CAPITAL

Debt capital is money that is obtained from external sources. Some of the principal sources of debt capital are mortgages, loans, and company bonds.

Mortgages and Loans

The cost of capital for these two sources of capital is the *actual* interest rate being paid on the mortgage or loan. Many times, the stated interest rate on a mortgage or loan is not the same as the actual effective interest rate being paid due to discounting practices or the manner in which the loan is paid back. Consequently, it is most important to convert the stated interest rate on a mortgage or loan to an effective yearly compound rate, for it is in this context that is it most often used as the cost of capital in economic studies.

In general, the after tax cost of capital from debt sources can be determined by the following relationship

$$B - \sum_{j=1}^{n} \frac{I_j(1-T) + P_j}{(1 + k_d)^j} = 0$$

(12-2)

where

B = actual borrowed money received

I_j = interest payment in year j

P_j = principal payment in year j

n = number of years of debt payment

k_d = after-tax cost of debt capital

T = effective tax rate

Eq. (12-2) implies that the after-tax cost of debt capital, k_d, is the interest rate that makes the present value of the interest and principal payments equal the actual money received. If the before tax cost of debt capital is desired, then the tax rate (T) in Eq. (12-2) becomes zero.

Example 12-1 _____

Suppose a loan of $10,000 is desired for five years and the stated interest rate is 10%. However, the loaning agency has a practice of discounting loans by 5%. This rate (5%) should not be considered representative of discount rates.

The discounting of the loan implies that if $10,000 is borrowed, the actual amount received is

$$B = 10,000 - 10,000 \,(.05) = \$9,500$$

or in order to receive $10,000, the amount of the loan must be

$$10,000 = P - .050(P)$$
$$P = 10,000/0.95 = \$10,526.32$$

TABLE 12-1
Debt Payment Methods
(Actually Received = $9,500)

(a) Constant Principal			(b) Constant Interest		
EOY	Principal	Interest	EOY	Principal	Interest
0	-	-	0	-	-
1	$2,000	$1,000	1	-	$1,000
2	2,000	800	2	-	1,000
3	2,000	600	3	-	1,000
4	2,000	400	4	-	1,000
5	2,000	200	5	10,000	1,000

(c) Constant Annual Payment			
EOY	Payment	Unpaid Principal	Interest	Principal Paid
0	-	$10,000	-	-
1	$2,638	8,362	1,000	1,638
2	2,638	6,650	836	1,802
3	2,638	4,578	656	1,982
4	2,638	2,398	458	2,180
5	2,638	0	240	2,398

In order to use Eq. (12-2), it is necessary to know the manner in which the loan (both principal and interest) is paid back. The four common methods for paying loans are shown in Chapter 5. Three of these methods are shown in Table 12-1 for the case of receiving $9,500. The values in Table 12-1(a) are based on paying the principal ($10,000) in equal yearly installments with interest assessed on the unpaid balance (principal). In Table 12-1(b), the principal is paid back at the end of the loan (5 years) and the interest is assessed on the principal, which results in a constant interest payment. The principal and interest payments in Table 12-1(c) are based on a constant yearly payment (interest and principal) of

$$A = 10,000 \ (A/P \ 10,5) = \$2,638$$

If the before-tax interest rate is calculated for these three cases, the results are

$$9,500 = 2,000(P/A \ i,5) + [1,000-200(A/G \ i,5)] \ P/A \ i,5$$
$$i = 12.16\%$$
$$9,500 = 1,000(P/A \ i,5) + 10,000(P/F \ i,5)$$
$$i = 11.37\%$$
$$9,500 = 2,638(P/A \ i,5)$$
$$i = 12.04\%$$

It is not unusual to approximate the after-tax rate of loans by multiplying the before-tax rate by the term (1-T). Using a tax rate of 40%, the after-tax rates, respectively, are 7.30%, 6.82%, and 7.22%. For comparison purposes, the after-tax rates using Eq. (12-2) are

$$9,500 - 2,000(P/A \ i,5) + (1-.40)[1,000-200(A/G \ i,5)](P/A \ i,5)$$
$$i = k_d = 7.99\%$$
$$9,500 = (1-.40)(1,000)(P/A \ i,5) + 10,000(P/F \ i,5)$$
$$i = k_d = 7.23\%$$
$$9,500 = (1-.40)[1,000(P/F \ i,1) + 836(P/F \ i,2) + 656(P/F \ i,3) +$$
$$458(P/F \ i,4) + 240(P/F \ i,5)] + [1,638(P/F \ i,1) + \ ... \ +$$
$$2,398(P/F \ i,5)]$$
$$9,500 = 2,238(P/F \ i,1) + 2,304(P/F \ i,2) + 2,376(P/F \ i,3) +$$
$$2,455(P/F \ i,4) + 2,542(P/F \ i,5)$$
$$i = k_d = 7.87\%$$

The values for this case ($9,500) are summarized in Table 12-2.

TABLE 12-2
Costs of Debt Capital
(P = $9,500)

	Constant Principal	Constant Interest	Constant Payment
Before-tax	12.16%	11.37%	12.04%
Approximate After-tax	7.30%	6.82%	7.22%
After-tax	7.99%	7.23%	7.87%

TABLE 12-3
Debt Payment Methods
(Actually Received = $10,000)

(a) Constant Principal			(b) Constant Interest		
EOY	Principal	Interest	EOY	Principal	Interest
0	-	-	0	-	-
1	$2,105	$1,053	1	-	$1,053
2	2,105	842	2	-	1,053
3	2,105	631	3	-	1,053
4	2,105	420	4	-	1,053
5	2,105	209	5	$10,526	1,053

(c) Constant Payment

$$A = (10,526) \, A/P \, 10,5 = 2,777$$

EOY	Payment	Unpaid Principal	Interest	Principal Paid
0	-	$10,526	-	-
1	$2,777	8,802	$1,053	$1,724
2	2,777	6,905	880	1,897
3	2,777	4,818	691	2,086
4	2,777	2,523	482	2,295
5	2,777	0	252	2,525

For the case of receiving $10,000, the debt and interest payments for the three methods are given in Table 12-3. The before-tax rates for these three methods are

$$10,000 = 2,105 \ (P/A \ i,5) + [1,053 - 211(A/G \ i,5)](P/A \ i,5)$$
$$i = 12.16\%$$
$$10,000 = 1,053(P/A \ i,5) + 10,526(P/F \ i,5)$$
$$i = 11.37\%$$
$$10,000 = 2,777(P/A \ i,5)$$
$$i = 12.04\%$$

and the after-tax rates are

$$10,000 = 2,105(P/A \ i,5)+(1-.40)[1,053-211(A/G \ i,5)](P/A \ i,5)$$
$$i = k_d = 7.99\%$$
$$10,000 = (1-.40)(1,053)(P/A \ i,5) + 10,526(P/F \ i,5)$$
$$i = k_d = 7.23\%$$
$$10,000 = (1,724 + 632)(P/F \ i,1) + (1,897 + 528)(P/F \ i,2) +$$
$$(2,086 + 415) \ (P/F \ i,3) + (2,295 + 289) \ (P/F \ i,4) +$$
$$(2,525 + 150) \ (P/F \ i,5)$$
$$i = k_d = 7.87\%$$

A summary of these rates is given in Table 12-4.

TABLE 12-4
Costs of Debt Capital
(P = $10,000)

	Constant Principal	Constant Interest	Constant Payment
Before-tax	12.16%	11.37%	12.04%
Approximate After-tax	7.30%	6.82%	7.22%
After-tax	7.99%	7.23%	7.87%

A comparison of the results given in Tables 12-2 and 12-4 indicates that the same results are obtained in the case of discounting. However, it also shows that with discounting the actual rate of interest is higher than the stated rate (10%) and there is some difference between the approximate after-tax values and the actual after-tax values.

Bonds

The sale of bonds is another method for obtaining debt capital. The cost of capital for bonds is the actual rate of interest paid on the bond. It may or may not be the bond contractual rate because of the selling price of the bond and flotation costs. The after-tax cost of a fixed maturity bond, r, can be determined by Eq. (12-3)

$$P-S = \frac{kV(1-T)}{c}(P/A\frac{r}{c}, cn) + \frac{(P-V-S)T}{cn}(P/A\frac{r}{c}, cn) + V(P/F\frac{r}{c}, cn) \quad (12-3)$$

where

p	=	the selling price per bond
k	=	contractual rate on the bond
V	=	face value of the bond
kV/c	=	interest paid per period
r	=	cost of debt capital (a nominal rate)
c	=	number of interest periods per year
n	=	number of years to maturity of the bond
T	=	incremental tax rate on corporate income
S	=	selling cost per bond (brokerage fees per bond)
kV(1-T)/c	=	effective after tax interest cost
(P-V-S)T/cn	=	amortizations of difference between selling cn price, face value and selling expense per bond over the life of the bond. Under present tax laws, the amount (P-V-S) can be spread over the life of the bond and taken as an expense when P+S < V. When P+S > V the amount of (P-V-S) is income and is also spread over the life of the bond. This implies that the term (P-V-S) can be either negative or positive.

If T is set equal to zero in Eq. (12-3), the before-tax cost of the bond can be obtained.

Example 12-2

Determine the after-tax cost of a $1,000 bond that matures in ten years if the contractual rate is 10% and paid semiannually. Assume the selling price of the bond is $912, brokerage fees amount to $10 per bond, and the tax rate is 40%.

Substituting into Eq. (12-3) gives

$$912 - 10 = \frac{.10(1,000)(.6)}{2} (P/A \frac{r}{2}, 20)$$

$$+ \frac{(912 - 1,000 - 10)(.4)}{20} (P/A \frac{r}{2}, 20) + 1,000 (P/F \frac{r}{2}, 20)$$

$$r = 7\% \text{ compounded semiannually}$$

It is desirable to convert all cost of capital values to an effective annual rate, since it is in this context (annual basis) that they are used. The effective annual rate is

$$k_d = (1 + \frac{.07}{2})^2 - 1 = 7.12\% \text{ compounded yearly}$$

As a comparison the before-tax rate is

$$912 - 10 = \frac{.10(1,000)}{2} (P/A \frac{r}{2}, 20) + 1,000 (P/F \frac{r}{2}, 20)$$

$$r = 11.7\% \text{ compounded semiannually}$$

The effective annual rate is 12.04% which, if multiplied by (1-T) , gives as an approximate after-tax rate of 7.22%. This value is in close agreement with the 7.12% value. This is an approach that is often taken; that is, calculate the before-tax cost and then approximate the after-tax cost by multiplying by (1-T).

Bonds that include a provision for converting them to common stock are called *convertible bonds.* The conversion ratio specifies the number of common shares into which the bond is converted. Although convertible bonds have maturity dates, they are usually regarded as a means of selling common stock because they can be converted to common stock at the discretion of the company issuing the bond. The cost can be determined by Eq. (12-4)

$$P - S = \frac{kV(1-T)}{c} (P/A \frac{r}{c}, cx) \frac{(P - V - S)T}{cn} (P/A \frac{r}{c}, cx) + FR(P/F \frac{r}{c}, cx) \quad (12-4)$$

where the nomenclature is the same as before and

$x =$ estimated time, in years, at which bond is converted to common shares

$F =$ market value per share of common stock at the end of time x

$R =$ conversion ratio, the number of common stock received per bond

Note that the second term in Eq. (12-4) is divided by cn. This implies that the bond discount (or premium) is not deductible (or taxable) after the bond is converted to common stock.

Example 12-3 _____

Suppose the data in Example 12-2 is for a convertible bond and the conversion ratio is specified as 9. Also, it is estimated that the bond will be converted in five years, and at that time, the market price of a share of common stock is $110. What is the cost of this bond? Substituting into Eq. (12-4) gives

$$912 - 10 = \frac{.10(1,000)(.6)}{2} (P/A \frac{r}{2}, 10)$$

$$+ \frac{(912 - 1,000 - 10)(.4)}{20} (P/A \frac{r}{2}, 10) + 110(9) (P/F \frac{r}{2}, 10)$$

$$r = 7.84\% \text{ compounded semiannually}$$

which is an effective annual rate of 7.99%. _____

COST OF EQUITY CAPITAL

The principal sources of equity funds are from the sale of common stock and retained earnings.

The Cost of New Common Stock

An often-cited model for determining the cost of new common stock is the one proposed by Gordon and Shapiro [2]. Although their model is based on some questionable assumptions, it can provide a satisfactory estimate of the cost of equity funds if it is used with judgment.

The Gordon-Shapiro model is, essentially, a dividend valuation model; that is, the cost of a share of common stock to a company is the present value of the expected stream of dividends paid to the stockholder, or, expressed mathematically,

$$P_0 = D_0 + D_1 (1 + k_e)^{-1} + D_2(1 + k_e)^{-2} + \dots + D_t(1 + k_e)^{-t} + \dots \infty \quad (12\text{-}5)$$

$$P_0 = \sum_{t=0}^{\infty} \frac{D_t}{(1 + k_e)^t} \quad (12\text{-}6)$$

where

$P_0 =$ current market price of a share of common stock

$D_t =$ dividend per share paid in year t

$k_e =$ implied cost of the common stock

At this point, two assumptions are made in the Gordon-Shapiro model. One, a company is expected to retain a fraction, b, of its yearly after-tax earnings such that

$$b = \frac{Y_t - D_t}{Y_t} \qquad (12\text{-}7)$$

where Y_t is the earnings per share of common stock. Second a company is expected to earn a return, r, on its equity book value, B_t such that

$$r = \frac{Y_t}{B_t} \qquad (12\text{-}8)$$

For the sake of derivation purposes, the values of r and b are assumed constant; however, there is no reason why different values cannot be used in the final expression. It does not mean that r and b are permanent values.

As a result of these two assumptions, the dividends at time t are

$$D_t = (1 - b)\, Y_t \qquad (12\text{-}9)$$

Now it is required in the Gordon-Shapiro model that the retained earnings, bY_t, must earn a return of $r(bY_t)$. Consequently, the earnings for time t are

$$Y_0 = Y_0$$
$$Y_1 = Y_0 + r(bY_0)$$
$$Y_2 = Y_1 + r(bY_1)$$

$$\vdots \qquad \vdots \qquad \vdots$$

$$\vdots \qquad \vdots \qquad \vdots$$

$$Y_t = Y_{t-1} + r(bY_{t-1}) \qquad (12\text{-}10)$$

if Y_1 is substituted into Y_2, the result is

$$Y_2 = Y_0 + r(bY_0) + rb(Y_0 + rbY_0)$$
$$= Y_0 + 2rbY_0 + r2b^2 \qquad (12\text{-}11)$$
$$Y_2 = Y_0(1 + rb)^2$$

Generalizing Eq. (12-11), the earnings in time t are

$$Y_t = Y_0(1 + rb)^t \qquad (12\text{-}12)$$

Substituting Eq. (12-12) into Eq. (12-9) gives

$$D_t = Y_0 (1 - b)(1 + rb)_t \qquad (12\text{-}13)$$

and recognizing that $Y_0(1\text{-}b) = D_0$, Eq. (12-13) becomes

$$D_t = D_0(1 + rb)^t \qquad (12\text{-}14)$$

Substituting Eq. (12-14) into Eq. (12-6) gives

$$P_0 = \sum_{t=0}^{\infty} D_0(1 + rb)^t (1 + k_e)^{-t} \qquad (12\text{-}15)$$

In order to evaluate Eq. (12-15), it is necessary to convert the discrete interest factors to continuous interest factors in the following manner:

$$(1 + rb)^t \approx e^{rbt}$$
$$(1 + k_e)^{-t} \approx e^{-k_e t}$$

Equation (12-15) can now be written as

$$P_0 = \int_0^{\infty} D_0 e^{rbt - k_e t} dt = \int_0^{\infty} D_0 e^{-t(k_e - rb)} dt \qquad (12\text{-}16)$$

Performing the integration in Eq. (12-16) gives

$$P_0 = \frac{D_0}{k_e - rb} \qquad (12\text{-}17)$$

and solving for k_e gives the result

$$k_e = \frac{D_0}{P_0} + rb \qquad (12\text{-}18)$$

which is the same equation given in Chapter 5 with nomenclature changes. Equation (12-18) provides a means of estimating the cost of either common stock or retained earnings. The difference in the cost of common stock and retained earnings is due to flotation costs. Usually, common stock is sold at a price less than its current market value in order to encourage its sale. Also, there are usually selling expenses (brokerage fees). These flotation costs are the reason that the cost of common stock is higher than the cost of retained earnings. The usual adjustment for flotation costs is to express the flotation costs as a percentage of the market value per share(s). Then divide the cost of capital given by Eq. (12-18) by the term (1-s) to obtain the cost of common stock. Theoretically if the new common stock is sold to existing stockholders only the out-of-pocket selling expenses should be considered.

Example 12-4

A company is considering using new common stock and retained earnings to raise capital for new investments. The current market value for a share of common stock is $150. It is estimated that the selling costs will amount to $4.50 per share. The company's current financial report shows the following data:

total assets	= $46,000,000
after-tax earnings	= $ 3,744,000
liabilities	= $10,000,000
number of common stock	= 300,000 shares
dividends paid	= $ 2,619,000

It is desired to estimate the cost of capital from the sale of common stock and the use of retained earnings.

With the preceding data, it is possible to estimate the cost of retained earnings using Eq. (12-18). The dividend per share of common stock is

$$D_0 = \frac{2,619,000}{300,000} = \$8.73$$

and the earnings per share are

$$Y_0 = \frac{3,744,000}{300,000} = \$12.48$$

which implies the proportion of retained earnings is

$$b = \frac{12.48 - 8.73}{12.48} = 0.30$$

The book value per share of common stock is

$$B_0 = \frac{46,000,000 - 10,000,000}{300,000} = \$120$$

and the return is

$$r = \frac{12.48}{120} = 0.104$$

Substituting into Eq. (12-18), the cost of retained earnings is

$$k_e = \frac{8.73}{150} + (0.104)(0.30)$$

$$= .0894 = 8.94\%$$

For the cost of common stock, Eq. (12-18) is modified to reflect the flotation costs. The flotation cost ($4.50) is 3% of the selling price ($150). Therefore, the cost of common stock is

$$k_e = \frac{8.94}{1 - .03} = 9.22\%$$

As an extension to this problem, suppose the company sells the stock for $148.50 per share. For this case, the flotation costs are $1.50 ($150 - $148.50) plus $4.50 per share. Expressed as a percentage of the market value, the flotation costs are 4%. Therefore, the cost of common stock is

$$k_e = \frac{8.94}{1 - .04} = 9.31\%$$

Another method that is often used to estimate the cost of equity capital, is to rewrite Eq. (12-18) as

$$k_e = \frac{D_0}{P_0} + g \qquad\qquad (12\text{-}19)$$

Where the nomenclature is the same as before and g is the expected growth rate of dividends; that is, dividends are expected to grow a t a compound rate g forever. The usual procedure is to estimate g on the basis of past dividends or earnings; assuming, of course, that past dividends or earnings are believed to be meaningful for estimating the growth rate.

Example 12-5

Suppose the company is Example 12-4 has the earnings and growth rates shown in Table 12-5. The yearly growth rates are calculated in the following manner.

TABLE 12-5
Earnings Per Year for Example 12-5

Year	Earnings	Growth Rate
19X1	$3.010(10)^6$	-
19X2	$3.110(10)^6$	0.0332
19X3	$3.268(10)^6$	0.0508
19X4	$3.530(10)^6$	0.0802
19X5	$3.744(10)^6$	0.0606
Σ	$16.662(10)^6$	0.2248

$$g_1 = \frac{(3.110 - 3.010)(10)^6}{3.010(10)^6} = 0.0332$$

$$g_2 = \frac{(3.269 - 3.110)(10)^6}{3.0(10)^6} = 0.0508$$

Now, an average growth rate that might be used to estimate g in Eq. (12-19) is

$$g = \frac{0.2248}{4} = 0.0562$$

and the cost of capital (retained earnings) using Eq. (12-19) is

$$k_e = \frac{8.73}{150} + 0.0562 = 0.1144 = 11.44\%$$

It should be noted that estimating the growth rate on the basis of br may give different results than past earnings or dividends. If br = 5%, then this value might be considered representative of the growth rate. However, if br = 30%, then it is extremely unlikely that a company can grow at a 30% compound rate. In all probability, the growth rate will level off to a more normal rate (perhaps the growth rate of the national economy) as a company matures. What is involved, of course, is the use of judgment in the estimation of the growth rate; that is, the growth rate must be based on realistic estimates of the expected growth in future earnings.

Another Proposal

Solomon[6] suggests that the cost of a new issue of common stock is given by

$$k_e = \frac{E_a}{P} \qquad (12\text{-}20)$$

where

$E_a=$ average annual earnings per share with an adjustment for the growth of future earnings

$P=$ net amount received by the company from the sale of a share of common stock

There are similarities between Eqs. (12-20) and (12-18) that can be seen if Eq. (12-18) is written as

$$k_e = \frac{D_0}{P_0} + \frac{bY_0}{B_0} \qquad (12\text{-}21)$$

and Eq. (12-20) is written as

$$k_e = \frac{D+bY}{P} = \frac{D}{P} + \frac{bY}{P} \qquad (12\text{-}22)$$

The basic difference between Eqs. (12-21) and (12-22) is that one has the book value as the denominator of the second term and the other has the market value. These two equations would give the same values if the book and market values are identical. However, the usual case is that the market value is greater than the book value.

Gordon and Shapiro defend the use of book value on the basis that book value and not market value is used to measure a corporation's rate of return. For a more complete discussion of their defense of book value and their model in general, it is recommended that the Gordon-Shapiro article be studied. This book takes the point of view that the Gordon-Shapiro model can provide a satisfactory estimate of the cost of equity capital.

CAPITAL ASSET PRICING MODEL

The capital asset pricing model (CAPM) is another method for determining the cost of equity capital. It is based on a relationship between the expected return on a company's stock and the market risk of the company's stock. The CAPM can be expressed as

$$k_j = k_f + ß (k_m - k_f) \qquad (12\text{-}23)$$

where

k_j =   return on common stock

k_f =   risk-free rate of return available to investors such as the rate on U. S. Treasury Bonds.

k_m =   market rate of return for similar stocks (market portfolio)

β =   volatility of a company's stock relative to similar stocks in the market (β = 1.0 is the norm).

$(k_m\text{-}k_f)$ =   risk premium

Values of beta are available from several financial institutions. It is an expression of the responsiveness of a particular stock to a selected market portfolio of similar stocks. It is measured by the covariance of the required return on a company's stock (kj) and market rate of return, divided by the variance of the market return. If beta is less than one, the stock is less volatile and, theoretically, the required return for a particular stock is less. If beta is greater than one, the required return is larger.

If it is believed that historical data is a good predictor for the future, Eq. (12-22) can be written as

$$k_j = \overline{k_f} + \beta\,(\overline{k_m} - \overline{k_f})$$

(12-24)

where the bars above the components indicate average values and the value of β is calculated by

$$\beta = \frac{\text{cov}\,[(k_j - k_f),(k_m - k_f)]}{\text{var}\,(k_m - k_f)}$$

(12-25)

The following example shows the methodology involved in the calculation of Eq. (12-24) and (12-25). In this example it is assumed that the returns for a particular period of time, k_j, have been calculated for the company's and market's stock on the basis of

$$k_j = \frac{P_j - P_{j\text{-}1}}{P_{j\text{-}1}} + \frac{D_j}{P_{j\text{-}1}}$$

(12-26)

where

k_j =   return for period j

P_j =   closing market (stock) price at the end of period j

$P_{j\text{-}1}$ =   closing market (stock) price at the end of period (j-1)

D_j =   the dividend for the period j.

Example 12-6

The data necessary for the calculation of Eqs. (12-24) and (12-25) are given in columns one through four in Table 12-6. it is realized that the number of points used in this example may not be sufficient for statistical purposes. However, it is the methodology that is of concern in this example.

The calculations shown in Table 12-6 indicate a beta value of 1.105. Using this value and Eq. (12-24), the return for the company's common stock is

$$k_j = .08 + 1.105 \,(.16 - .08) = .1684 = 16.84\%$$

This value (16.84%) could be used as the company's cost of equity capital.

TABLE 12-6
CALCULATION FOR BETA (ß)
(EXAMPLE 12-6)

Year	Company Return k_j	Market Return k_m	Risk-Free Return k_f	$(k_j\text{-}k_f)$	$(k_m\text{-}k_f)$	$(k_j\text{-}k_f\text{-}A)$	$(k_m\text{-}k_f\text{-}B)$	$(k_m\text{-}k_f\text{-}B)^2$	$(k_j\text{-}k_f\text{-}A)(k_m\text{-}k_f\text{-}B)$
19X1	.25	.20	.06	.19	.14	.07	.06	.0036	.0042
19X2	-.10	-.08	.06	-.16	-.14	-.28	-.22	.0484	.0616
19X3	.30	.25	.08	.22	.17	.10	.09	.0081	.0090
19X4	.25	.25	.09	.16	.16	.04	.08	.0064	.0032
19X5	.30	.14	.09	.21	.05	.09	-.03	.0009	-.0027
19X6	.20	.20	.10	.10	.10	-.02	.02	.0004	-.0004
Σ	1.20	.96	.480	.72	.48	–	–	.0678	.0749
Avg	.20	.16	.080	.12	.08	–	–	–	–

$$\text{Var } (k_m - k_f) = \frac{.0678}{6\text{-}1} = .01356 \qquad ß = \frac{.01498}{.01356} = 1.105$$

$$\text{Cov } [(k_j\text{-}k_f),(k_m\text{-}k_f)] = \frac{.0749}{6\text{-}1} = .01498 \qquad A = .12 \qquad B = .08$$

COST OF PREFERRED STOCK

Preferred stock has some of the characteristics of bonds and some of the characteristics of equity capital. Like a bond, preferred stock pays a stated amount to the stockholder that is equal to its face value times a specified contractual rate. Also, preferred stockholders have a higher priority than common stockholders on earnings in cases of liquidation. Unlike bonds, preferred stock has no maturity date and its dividends are not tax deductible. Also, the payment of a preferred stock dividend is at the discretion of management. Consequently, unlike bonds, there is no risk of legal bankruptcy if the dividends are not paid. As a result of these considerations, the cost of preferred stock, k_p, is

$$k_p = \frac{rV}{P_0} \qquad\qquad (12\text{-}27)$$

where

$\quad r = \quad$ contractual rate

$\quad v = \quad$ face value of preferred stock

$\quad P_0 = \quad$ amount received from the sale of a share of preferred stock

As an example, the cost of capital for a 9%, $100 share of preferred stock selling for $98 a share with selling costs of $5 per share is

$$k_p = \frac{(0.09)(100)}{(98\text{-}5)} = 0.097 = 9.7\%$$

WEIGHTED COST OF CAPITAL

Once the cost of capital is determined for each source of funds, it is possible to calculate a weighted cost of capital using Eq. (12-1) provided the weighting factors (w_i) are known. At this point, it is important to understand that it is the marginal cost of capital that is to be determined since capital is raised incrementally to invest in new projects. It is the cost of this new capital that should be used in evaluating new projects. Methods have already been presented for determining the marginal costs from different sources of funds. The next step is to determine the weighting system.

Essentially, the weights must correspond to the future financing plans of the company. In actuality, new capital is raised in "blocks" and strict proportions from the various sources cannot be maintained. For example, a company may finance with retained earnings in one instance and entirely with debt in another instance. However, in the long run, companies are able to finance in some proportional manner. It is these future proportions of funds that should be used as the weights.

Example 12-7

Suppose a company is going to raise $20 million for new investments and the cost of capital from each source and the proportions shown in Table 12-7 are planned. Using Eq. (12-1), the before-tax cost of capital, k_b, is

$$k_b = 0.3(8) + 0.4(13) + 0.1(10) + 0.2(14) = 11.4\%$$

TABLE 12-7
Data for Example 12-7

	Incremental Cost of Capital	Proportion
Debt (before tax)	8%	0.30
Retained earnings	13%	0.40
Preferred stock	10%	0.10
Common stock	14%	0.20

The after-tax cost of capital, k_a, can be estimated by approximating the tax consideration (T = 40%) in the cost of the debt capital by the term (1 - T). For this example, k_a is

$$k_a = 0.3(8)(1 - 0.40) + 0.4(13) + 0.1(10) + 0.2(14) = 10.44\%$$

There are often questions regarding the basis of the proportions used to determine the weighted cost of capital. These questions center around whether the weights should be based on market values or book values. There is some disagreement on this point in the literature. This text takes the point of view that market values should be used because they, rather than book values, provide a better estimate of the market's value of the company.

Example 12-8

A company has decided it needs additional money for new projects. The present market values of their stocks and bonds are given in Table 12-8. It is planned to maintain the existing capital structure when raising the required money.

The proportions and costs of new capital are shown in Table 12-9. With this, the before-tax cost of capital is

$$k_b = .21(10) + .11(12) + .68(20) = 17.02\%$$

TABLE 12-8
Market Values and Numbers of Stocks and Bonds

Capital	Market value per Share (bond)	Number of Stocks or Bonds
Debt	$900	50,000
Preferred stock	80	300,000
Common stock	120	1,200,000

TABLE 12-9
Weighting Proportions
(Example 12-8)

Capital	Market Value of a Share (bond)	Number of Shares (bonds)	Amount	Proportion	Cost of Capital
Debt	$900	50,000	$45(10)^6$	0.21	10
Preferred stock	80	300,000	$24(10)^6$	0.11	12
Equity	120	1,200,000	$144(10)^6$	0.68	20
			$213(10)^6$		

and the after-tax (T = 40%) cost of capital is

$$k_a = .21(10) \ (1-.40) + .11(12) + .68(20) = 16.18\%$$

A Comment   In Example 12-8, there is no change in the capital structure of the company. However, if there are planned changes in the company's capital structure, it must be recognized that there can be discrepancies. This is because most component costs are based on the existing capital structure (market values) and it is not possible to measure directly the component costs until the desired capital structure is reached. Consequently, the component costs must be estimated taking into account the transition period.

COST OF DEPRECIATION

Depreciation allowances are an important source of funds. However, consideration of the cost of depreciation funds has been deferred until now because their cost is related to the weighted cost of capital. Unfortunately, it is sometimes thought that depreciation funds do not have a cost. This, of course, is not true. Depreciation funds have an opportunity cost similar to retained earnings. Consequently, depreciation funds should not be invested into capital assets unless they provide a return. Essentially, this return is the weighted cost of capital.

Example 12-9

If a company plans to finance its future projects with the mix of capital shown in Table 12-10, its before-tax weighted cost of capital is 12%. The major point that needs comment in regard to Table 12-10 is the cost of depreciation. This cost is determined in the following manner.

$$\frac{0.30}{0.80}(10) + \frac{0.35}{0.80}(12) + \frac{0.15}{0.80}(16) = 12\%$$

where, the value 0.80 is the sum of the proportions of debt, retained earnings, and common stock. It is being assumed that the alternative use to which the depreciation funds could be put to use are to repay debt (costing 10%), distribute dividends (costing 12%), and to repurchase common stock (costing 16%) implying an opportunity cost of 12%. It can be seen in Table 12-10 that the weighted cost of capital is exactly equal to the cost of depreciation funds. This is why the cost of depreciation funds does not directly enter into the calculation of a firm's cost of capital.

TABLE 12-10
Cost of Capital
(Example 12-9)

Source	Proportion of Capital	Cost Before Tax %	Weighted Average
Debt	0.30	10	3.0
Retained earnings	0.35	12	4.2
Common stock	0.15	16	2.4
Depreciation	0.20	12	2.4
			12.0

ESTIMATING THE COST OF CAPITAL FOR A COMPANY

In this section an example is presented that shows how certain values required in estimating the cost of capital are obtained from a company's financial report.

Example 12-10 _____

A company's financial report includes the balance sheets and income statement shown in Tables 12-11 and 12-12. In addition, the following information is obtained or estimated.

   1.   The company's common stock has a current market value of $30 a share. However, in order to insure future sales, common stock will be offered for $28 a share with brokerage fees amounting to $1.00 a share. The present number of common shares is 600,000 and the present dividend is $4 a share.

TABLE 12-11
Balance Sheet for the Company
(Example 12-10)

Assets		*Capitalization*	
At original cost		Common stock	$9,000,000
Plant A	$6,000,000	Retained earnings	3,000,000
Plant B	3,000,000	Total common equity	$12,000,000
Plant C	7,000,000	Preferred stock	1,000,000
Plant D	4,000,000	Long term debt	5,000,000
	$20,000,000	Current liabilities	
Less accumulated		Accounts payable	200,000
depreciation	3,000,000	Long-term debt due	
	$17,000,000	within 12 months	500,000
Current assets			$18,700,000
Cash	200,000		
Accounts receivable	500,000		
Inventories	1,000,000		
	$18,700,000		

TABLE 12-12
Income Statement for the Company
(Example 12-10)

Operating revenue	$11,140,000
Operating expenses and taxes	
Operation	2,500,000
Maintenance	1,000,000
Depreciation	500,000
Taxes other than federal	80,000
Federal taxes (T = 40%)	2,680,000
Total	6,760,000
Operating income	4,380,000
Interest	
Long-term debt interest	350,000
General interest	10,000
Total	360,000
Income before preferred dividends	4,020,000
Preferred dividends	900,000
Net income for common stock	3,120,000

2. Preferred stock has a current market value of $60 a share and there are 10,000 shares outstanding. Current market conditions indicate that in order to sell new preferred stock it would require a return of 10% on a $100 share. The selling price and brokerage fee, respectively, are estimated to be $100 and $3.00 a share.

3. The company's bonds were sold sometime ago and have a current market value of $850. The number of bonds outstanding is 10,000. If new bonds are issued, they will have a face value of $1,000, pay 8% semiannually, and mature in 10 years. New bonds can be sold for $950 with brokerage fees amounting to $10.00 per bond.

With the preceding information the incremental cost of capital from various sources can be calculated in the following manner.

Common Stock and Retained Earnings

The cost of new common stock is determined using Eq. (12-18). The data indicates $D_0 = \$4$ and $P_0 = \$30$. In order to determine the growth factor (rb), values for $Y_0, B_0,$ and b must be determined. The earnings per share are

$$Y_0 = \frac{3,120,000}{600,000} = \$5.20$$

and the book value per share is

$$B_0 = \frac{12,000,000}{600,000} = \$20.00$$

The book value per share can also be determined by taking the total assets and subtracting all liabilities (current and long term) as shown below:

$$B_0 = \frac{18,700,000 - (200,000 + 500,000 + 5,000,000 + 1,000,000)}{600,000} = \$20.00$$

With these values, the values of r and b can be determined.

$$r = \frac{Y_0}{B_0} = \frac{5.2}{20} = 0.26$$

$$b = \frac{Y_0 - D_0}{Y_0} = \frac{5.2 - 4.0}{5.2} = 0.23$$

Substituting into Eq. (12-18), the estimated cost of retained earnings is

$$k_e = \frac{4}{30} + (0.26)(0.23)$$
$$= 0.1931 = 19.31\%$$

The cost of the new common stock is obtained by adjusting the cost of retained earnings for the flotation costs. Assuming the common stock is to be offered to the general public, the flotation cost per share is

$$\frac{1 + 2}{30} = 0.10 = 10\%$$

Therefore, the cost of new stock is

$$k_e = \frac{19.31}{1 - .10} = 21.46\%$$

Preferred Stock

Using Eq. (12-28), the cost of preferred stock is

$$k_p = \frac{(0.1)(100)}{100 - 3} = 0.103 = 10.3\%$$

Debt

The before-tax cost of new debt capital is determined using Eq. (12-3) with $T = 0$. Evaluating this expression gives

$$(950 - 10) = \frac{0.08(1000)}{2} [PA \tfrac{r_d}{2}, 2(10)] + 1000 [PF \tfrac{r_d}{2}, 2(10)]$$

with the result $r_d = 9\%$ compounded semiannually or an effective annual cost of 9.2% (k_d). If the after-tax ($T = 40\%$) cost of debt is desired, it can be approximated by 9.2 (1 - 0.40)=5.52%, or determined exactly by using Eq. (12-3) with $T = 40\%$.

Weighted Average

If it is assumed that the company plans to raise capital in accordance with the present capital structure, its before-tax cost of capital is 17.01%. The calculations to obtain this value are shown in Table 12-13.

TABLE 12-13
Weight Cost of Capital
(Example 12-10)

Source	Market Value	Weight	Cost	Wtd Cost
Equity	30(600,000) = 18(10)^6	.664	20.92	13.89
Preferred stock	60(10,000) = 0.6(10)^6	.022	10.30	0.23
Debt	850(10,000) = 8.5(10)^6	.314	9.20	2.89
Total	27.1(10)^6			17.01

The cost of equity capital given in Table 12-12 is based on a weighted average of retained earnings and common stock. The weights are approximated using the current split between retained earnings and common stock (see Table 12-11); namely,

$$\frac{9}{12} (21.46) + \frac{3}{12} (19.31) = 20.92\%$$

The after-tax cost is obtained by multiplying the debt cost (9.2%) by (1-T). Assuming a tax rate of 40%, the after-tax cost is 15.85%.

LEVERAGE

The weighted cost of capital provides a basis for a discussion of an important financial concept called leverage. Essentially, leverage is the ratio of debt to the total value of the firm at market values. A major question in regard to leverage is, "What mix of debt and equity capital minimizes the weighted cost of capital?"

The traditional view of the effect of changes in leverage upon market value is shown in Figure 12-1. This figure shows

FIGURE 12-1
Leverage Versus Cost of Capital

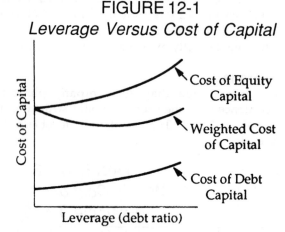

that as the leverage (debt ratio) increases, the cost of capital (k) decreases up to a point. Remember, the cost of capital is

$$k = w_d k_d + w_e k_e$$

After this point, the cost of capital starts to increase. These changes in the cost of capital are a direct result of the stockholders' and lenders' reactions to increases in leverage. In the beginning, the cost of capital decreases as the leverage increases because k_d is less than k_e and k_e is essentially constant. As leverage increases, past some point, k_e and k_d increase because stockholders and lenders demand a higher return as a result of the greater risk, resulting in a higher weighted cost of capital. This view of the effect of leverage on the cost of capital leads to the conclusion that some optimum point does exist. That is, there is some debt ratio that provides a minimum cost of capital. Determination of this optimum point, from a practical standpoint, is a difficult task. For it would be necessary to know how both k_e and k_d change as the debt ratio changes. This would require the prediction of the stockholders' and lenders' reactions to increases in leverage, a rather difficult task.

Another view of the cost of capital is taken by Modigliani and Miller. They believe that the cost of capital is independent of the capital structure. Thus, there is no "optimal" capital structure. This point of view is not considered in this text. For those who wish to pursue this view further the references listed at the end of this chapter provide a complete discussion.

COST OF CAPITAL AND MINIMUM ATTRACTIVE RATE OF RETURN

The incremental weighted average cost of capital provides a basis on which to evaluate investments. However, it is usually not used without some adjustment. The common procedure is to adjust (increase) the cost of capital to take into account risk. This procedure of using a risk-adjusted cost of capital as the MARR is objected to by many. They take the point of view that risk should be explicitly included in the analysis of investments through the use of probabilistic models or simulation. Nevertheless, a risk adjusted cost of capital figure is often used in practice. The amount of the risk adjustment usually depends on the type of project under consideration. Consequently, it is not unusual to find a company with several values for MARR. For example, a company might have a lower MARR for the expansion of existing facilities than the MARR for investments involving new products, the difference being a reflection of risk considerations between the two types of investments.

The cost of capital and, consequently, the MARR, may require adjustments over time as a result of changing conditions. For example, the supply and demand of funds varies with time, causing changes in the cost of debt and equity capital. For this reason and others, a company must monitor its cost of capital and make changes when necessary.

An Important Point   It must be remembered that the minimum attractive rate of return and its basis (cost-of-capital) are dependent upon the cash flow definition. This point is discussed in Chapters 5 and 6. That is, if total cash flows are used, the basis of MARR is the after-tax cost of capital. If operating cash flows are used, the basis is the before-tax cost of capital. If equity cash flows are used, the basis of MARR is the required return on equity. Also, equity cash flows require the use of a debt ratio. This debt ratio should be the debt ratio of the increment of money being raised for new projects.

REFERENCES

Gordon, M. J., *The Investment Financing, and Valuation of the Corporation*, Richard D. Irwin, Homewood, Ill., 1962.

Gordon, M. J. and E. Shapiro, "Capital Equipment Analysis: The Required Rate of Profit," *Management Science*, Vol. 3, October 1956, pp. 102-110.

Haley, C. W., and L. D. Schall, *The Theory of Financial Decisions*, McGraw-Hill Book Co., New York, 1973.

Lewellen, Wilbur, G., *The Cost of Capital*, Wadsworth Publishing Co., Inc., Belmont, Calif., 1969.

Robichek, A. A. and S. C. Myers, *Optimal Financial Decisions*, Prentice-Hall, Inc., Englewood Cliffs, NJ, 1965.

Solomon, Ezra, "Measuring a Company's Cost of Capital," *Journal of Business*, October 1955.

Van Horne, James C., *Financial Management and Policy*, 2nd ed., Prentice-hall, Inc., Englewood Cliffs, NJ, 1971.

Weston, J. F., and E. F. Brighan, *Essentials of Managerial Finance*, 3rd ed., The Dryden Press, Hinsdale, Ill., 1974.

PROBLEMS

12-1   A company is negotiating a loan of $100,000 with a bank. The bank has agreed to make the loan at an interest rate of 10% and a discount rate of 2%. If the loan is made on the basis of a 10-year period, determine the following:

(a)   The amount the company would actually receive as a result of this discount.

(b)   The yearly payments the company would make to the bank on the basis that the principal is to be paid in 10 equal installments.

(c)   The effective before-tax interest rate for the loan. Assume the company receives the amount in part (a).

(d)   An approximate after-tax interest rate [use part (c)] and the actual after-tax interest rate on the loan if the tax rate is 40%.

12-2 Rework Problem 12-1 on the basis that the principal will be paid back at the end of 10 years.

12-3 Rework Problem 12-1 on the basis that the company must have $100,000.

12-4 Rework Problem 12-2 on the basis that the company must have $100,000.

12-5 Based on the results of Problems 12-1 through 12-4, is it possible to make certain general comments regarding the rates of interest when money is borrowed?

12-6 A company is considering raising capital by issuing a series of fixed maturity bonds. The bonds have a face value of $1000, mature in five years, and pay 8% quarterly. It is estimated that the selling price of each bond to the general public will be $900 and brokerage fees will amount to $10 per bond. Determine the following:
(a) The company's before-tax cost of the bonds.
(b) The company's after-tax cost of the bonds if the tax rate is 40%. Compare this result with the approximate after-tax cost.

12-7 Rework Problem 12-6 assuming that the bond is a convertible bond. Also assume that the conversion ratio is 10, the bond will be converted in three years and the market value of a share of common stock at that time will be $110.

12-8 A company is considering raising some equity capital. The company's current financial reports show the following data.

total assets =	$20,000,000
liabilities =	$ 6,000,000
after-tax earnings =	$ 1,875,000
number of common stock =	100,000
dividends for common stock =	$ 1,500,000
current market price of common stock =	$187 per share

Determine the following:

(a) The estimated cost of capital through the sale of common stock. It is estimated that in order to insure its sale the stock will be sold for $183 per share and brokerage fees will amount to $5.00 per share. Use the Gordon-Shapiro model.

(b) The estimated cost of capital through the use of retained earnings.

(c) From the standpoint of the company, are there any tax considerations in parts (a) and (b)?

12-9 Using the data in Problem 12-8 and Solomon's approach [Eq. (12-20)], determine the cost of a new issue of common stock. Why is there a difference between this result and the result obtained in part (a) of Problem 12-8? Which one would you use? Why?

12-10 Suppose in Problem 12-8 the company's financial statements for the past six years indicated the following earnings. What is an estimate of the company's average growth rate?

Year	Earnings
19X7	$1,875,000
19X6	1,780,000
19X5	1,675,000
19X4	1,625,000
19X3	1,540,000
19X2	1,510,000
19X1	1,437,000

Also, determine the following

(a) The cost of capital for a new issue of common stock using the average growth rate.

(b) Compare the result of part (a) in this problem with the result of part (a) in Problem 12-8. Which one should be used?

12-11 Additional capital is to be raised by the sale of 8%, $100 preferred stock. The stock will be sold for $98 with flotation costs of $5 per share. Determine the cost of this preferred stock.

12-12 A company is going to raise capital at the costs and in the proportions shown in the following table:

Incremental Cost of Capital	Proportion
Equity 18%	0.50
Preferred stock 12%	0.10
Debt (before tax) 10%	0.40

Determine:
(a) The before-tax weighted cost of capital.
(b) The after-tax (T = 40%) weighted cost of capital.

12-13 A company is going to finance future projects on the basis of the capital costs and proportions shown below. The remaining proportion (10%) is to be obtained from depreciation reserves. Determine:
(a) The cost of depreciation funds.
(b) The before-tax weighted cost of capital.

Incremental Cost of Capital	Proportion
Equity 18%	0.40
Preferred stock 12%	0.20
Debt (before tax) 10%	0.30

12-14 Given the data in the following table, estimate the after-tax weighted cost of capital if the tax rate is 40%.

Capital	Cost	Market Value	#of Stocks or Bonds
Common stock	18%	$150	2,000,000
Preferred stock	12%	90	400,000
Debt (before tax)	10%	850	100,000

12-15 A company's financial statements show the following capitalization.

Common stock (1,000,000 shares)	$42(10)^6
Preferred stock (180,000 shares)	16(10)^6
Retained earnings	8(10)^6
Long-term debt (100,000 bonds)	34(10)^6
Current after-tax earnings	14(10)^6
Current dividends per share	12
Current market value of common	120

The company plans to raise additional capital for new investments under the following considerations.

(a) Common stock is expected to be sold for $115 per share in order to insure its sale and brokerage fees are expected to be $2 per share.

(b) Preferred stock is $100 per share and pays 12%. It is to be sold for $98 per share and brokerage fees are expected to be $2.00 per share. The current market value for preferred stock is $90 per share.

(c) Bonds have a face value of $1,000, pay 9% semiannually, and mature in ten years. The bonds are to be sold for $950 each. Brokerage fees are expected to be $10 per bond. The current market value of bonds is $950 per bond.

Determine the following:

(1) Cost of common stock.

(2) Cost of retained earnings.

(3) Cost of preferred stock.

(4) Cost of bonds (before tax).

(5) The incremental before-tax weighted cost of capital. Assume that the future and existing capital structure are to be the same.

(6) Estimate the cost of depreciation funds.

12-16 Using the data given below and Eq. (12-26), determine the yearly returns.

Year	Market Values of Common Stock	Dividends Per Share
19X0	$50	-
19X1	55	2
19X2	55	2
19X3	52	2
19X4	55	3
19X5	58	3
19X6	59	3
19X7	60	4
19X8	60	4
19X9	63	3

12-17 Using the data given below and the CAPM model, determine the company's cost of equity capital.

Year	Company's Return	Market Return	Risk-Free Rate
19X0	.20	.17	.11
19X1	.20	.18	.11
19X2	.19	.19	.10
19X3	.21	.19	.09
19X4	.22	.18	.08
19X5	.22	.17	.08
19X6	.19	.16	.08
19X7	.24	.18	.09
19X8	.24	.19	.09
19X9	.23	.18	.08

13

SOME PROBABILISTIC CONSIDERATIONS IN CASH FLOW MODELS

In the previous chapters, the models presented for the economic analysis of capital expenditures are based on a single value for the variables involved in a particular model. That is, the existence of variability in these values is not recognized. This chapter recognizes this variability by explicitly including it in the models considered. In considering these models, a knowledge of probability concepts and statistics is necessary and presupposes some knowledge in these areas. The usual beginning course in probability and statistics is considered to be sufficient for the material presented in this chapter.

The explicit inclusion of variability in cash flows models can be accomplished by either analytical or simulation approaches.

ANALYTICAL APPROACHES

In this section several basic analytical approaches to probabilistic cash flow models are presented. These approaches are based on the following fundamental relationships regarding the combination of random variables.

Sums of Random Variables

If $x_1, x_2, \ldots x_n$ are random variables and μ_i is the mean of the ith random variable, the expected value of the sum of these random values, μ_s, is

$$E(x_1 + x_2 + \ldots + x_n) = \mu_s = \sum_{i=1}^{n} \mu_i \tag{13-1}$$

and the variance of the sum, σ^2_s, is

$$V(x_1 + x_2 + \ldots + x_n) = \sigma^2_s = \sum_{i=1}^{n} \sigma^2_i + 2 \sum_{i=1}^{n-1} \sum_{j=i+1}^{n} \sigma_{ij} \tag{13-2}$$

Where, σ^2_i is the variance of the ith random variable and σ_{ij} are the covariance terms. A substitution often made for covariance terms is

$$\sigma_{ij} = r_{ij}\sigma_i\sigma_j \tag{13-3}$$

where r_{ij} is the correlation coefficient for the random variables x_i and x_j.

Difference of Two Random Variables

The expected value of the difference of two random variables, μ_D, is

$$E(x_i - x_j) = \mu_D = \mu_i - \mu_j \tag{13-4}$$

where x_i and x_j are the random variables and μ_i and μ_j are the means of the random variables. The variance of the difference of two random variables is

$$\sigma^2_D = \sigma^2_i + \sigma^2_j - 2\sigma_{ij} \tag{13-5}$$

Multiplication of Two Independent Random Variables

If two *independent* random variables are multiplied, the expected value of the product, μ_p, is

$$E(x_i x_j) = \mu_p = (\mu_i)(\mu_j) \tag{13-6}$$

and the variance, σ^2_p, is

$$V(x_i x_j) = \sigma^2_p = \mu^2_i \sigma^2_j + \mu^2_j \sigma^2_i + \sigma^2_j \sigma^2_i \tag{13-7}$$

A Random Variable Multiplied by a Constant

When a random variable x is multiplied by a constant, c, to give the random variable $z = cx$, the mean, μ_z, and variance σ^2_z of the product are

$$E(cx) = \mu_z = c\mu_x \tag{13-8}$$

$$V(cx) = \sigma^2_z = c^2 \sigma^2_x \tag{13-9}$$

The application of Eqs. (13-1) through (13-9) to probabilistic cash flow models is shown in the following examples.

Example 13-1

In this example the computation of the mean and standard deviation of the net present value distribution is shown for the situation depicted in Table 13-1.

TABLE 13-1
Mean and Variance of Cash Flows
(Example 13-1)

	Cash Flow	
Year	Mean	Variance
0	μ_0	σ^2_0
1	μ_1	σ^2_1
2	μ_2	σ^2_2
3	μ_3	σ^2_3
.	.	.
t	μ_t	σ^2_t
.	.	.
n	μ_n	σ^2_n

It is assumed in this example that the cash flows are independent. Also, the number of years, n, and minimum acceptable rate of return, k, are known with certainty. With these assumptions, the mean and variance of the net present value can be determined by applying some of the previously presented relationships for random variables.

Since k and n are constants, the discount factor, $(1 + k)^{-t}$ is also a constant, implying that Eqs. (13-8) and (13-9) are applicable. After discounting, Eqs. (13-1) through (13-5) are applicable since the sum and difference of random variables are involved. The difference is involved because the initial cash flow is assumed to be an outflow (the investment). With these considerations, the expected net present value and variance are

$$E(NPV) = \sum_{t=0}^{n} \mu_t (PFk,t) \tag{13-10}$$

$$V(NPV) = \sum_{t=0}^{n} \sigma_t^2 (PFk,2t) \tag{13-11}$$

As a numerical example of the use of Eqs. (13-10) and (13-11), consider the data given in Table 13-2. Using Eq. (13-10) and a minimum acceptable rate of return of 12%, the expected net present value is

$E(NPV) = -1500 + 1000(PF12,1) + 1000(PF12,2) + 2000(PF12,3) = \$1,609$

and the variance is

$$V(NPV) = (600)^2 + (700)2(PF12,2) + (700)^2(PF12,4)$$
$$+ (1000)^2(PF12,6) = 156.61(10)^4$$

The standard deviation of the net present value, $\sigma(NPV)$ is $\sqrt{156.61(10)^4} = \$1,251$.

TABLE 13-2
Means and Standard Deviations of Cash Flows (Example 13-1)

End of Year	Cash Flows Mean	Cash Flows Standard Deviation
0	-$1500	$600
1	1000	700
2	1000	700
3	2000	1000

Example 13-2 _____

In Example 13-1 it is assumed that the cash flows are independent. This assumption is not required. It is possible to determine the mean and variance of the net present value distribution when the cash flows are dependent. For the dependent case, the mean of the net present value does not change. It is the same as given by Eq. (13-10). In order to determine the variance of the net present value, Eq. (13-11) must be modified to include the covariance terms. This modification is shown in Eq. (13-12).

$$V(NPV) = \sum_{t=0}^{n} \sigma_t^2(PFk,2t) \pm 2 \sum_{t=0}^{n-1} \sum_{j=t+1}^{n} \sigma_{t,j}(PFk,(t+j)) \tag{13-12}$$

Substituting Eq. (13-3) for the covariance terms, Eq. (13-12) can be written as

$$V(NPV) = \sum_{t=0}^{n} \sigma_t^2(PFk,2t) \pm 2 \sum_{t=0}^{n-1} \sum_{j=t+1}^{n} r_{tj}\sigma_t\sigma_j(PFk,(t+j)) \tag{13-13}$$

The correct sign (plus or minus) in Eqs. (13-12) and (13-13) is determined by the relationship (addition or subtraction) involved between the random variables.

TABLE 13-3
Correlation Coefficients
(Example 13-2)

		j		
	0	1	2	3
0	–	.8	.5	.3
1		–	.7	.5
2			–	.6
3	(Symmetrical)			–

i = rows (0, 1, 2, 3)

As a numerical example, suppose the cash flows in Example 13-1 are dependent and it is believed the correlation coefficients given in Table 13-3 provide a correct representation of this dependency. For this case, the mean of the net present value distribution is the same as calculated previously, that is, $1,609. Using Eq. (13-13) the variance is

$$V(NPV)=(600)^2 + (700)^2(PF12,2) + (700)^2(PF12,4) +$$
$$(1000)^2(PF12,6) -2(.8)(600)(700)(PF12,1) -$$
$$2(.5)(600)(700)(PF12,2) -2(.3)(600)(1000)(PF12,3) +$$
$$2(.7)(700)(700)(PF12,3) +2(.5)(700)(1000)(PF12,4) +$$
$$2(.6)(700)(1000)(PF12,5) = 156.61(10)^4 + 21.88(10)^4$$
$$= 178.49(10)^4$$

and the standard deviation is

$$\sigma(NPV) = \sqrt{178.49(10)^4} = \$1,336$$

At this point it should be noted that a knowledge of the mean and variance (or standard deviation) of the net present value does not, by itself, provide a decision regarding the acceptability of a project (investment). They are simply an aid in the decision-making process. A subjective evaluation is still required. In the following discussion some additional uses of the mean and variance (or standard deviation) of the net present value are presented.

A Comment Example 13-2 suggests a computational problem; that is, the number of covariance terms that can exist in a large problem. In Example 13-2, there are six covariance terms when only four random variables are involved. In general, there can be $n(n-1)/2$ covariance terms. Consequently, for a problem with a large number of random variables (years) the number of covariance terms can be significant. A further discussion of covariance terms is given later.

Probability Statements

It is desirable in the decision-making process to be able to make probability statements regarding net present values. For example, it might be an aid in making a decision regarding the acceptability of a project to know the probability of the net present value being less than zero or within some specified interval. Without any knowledge or some assumption regarding the distribution of net present value, *exact* probability statements are not possible. However, it is possible to make *weak* probability statements using Tchebycheff's inequality. Mathematically, Tchebycheff's inequality can be expressed as

$$P(\mu - b\sigma \le X \le \mu + b\sigma) > 1 - \frac{1}{b^2} \qquad (13\text{-}14)$$

where

x = a random variable

μ = the expected value of x

σ = the standard deviation of x

b = a constant that is greater than 1

The application of Eq. (13-14) is shown in the following example.

Example 12-3

Suppose that the mean and standard deviation of the net present value distribution for a particular project are, respectively, $2,000 and $1,000. Using Tchebycheff's inequality the following statement is possible for $b = 2$.

The probability is greater than

$$1 - \frac{1}{(2)^2} = .75 = 75\%$$

that the net present value will fall within the interval

$$2000 \pm (2)(1000) = \$0 \text{ to } \$4000$$

Or, the probability is 25% or less that the actual net present value will fall outside the $0 to $4000 interval.

The phrases "greater than" and "or less" are the reasons that the probability statements given by Tchebycheff's inequality are often referred to as weak probability statements.

In this example the probability statements involve both tails of the probability distribution. It is also possible to make one-tailed probability statements by using the following relationships (see Reference 4).

$$P(X \leq \mu - k\sigma) \leq \frac{1}{1+k^2} \qquad \qquad (13\text{-}15)$$

$$P(X \geq \mu + k\sigma) \leq \frac{1}{1+k^2} \qquad \qquad (13\text{-}16)$$

As an example of the use of Eqs. (13-15) and (13-16), suppose the mean and standard deviation of the net present value distribution are, respectively, $2,000 and $1,000. Then, the following statements are possible.

The probability is equal to or less than

$$\frac{1}{1+(k)^2} = \frac{1}{1+(2)^2} = .20 = 20\%$$

that the actual net present value will be below

$$\mu - k\sigma = 2000 - 2(1000) = \$0$$

The probability is equal to or less than

$$\frac{1}{1+(k)^2} = \frac{1}{1+(2)^2} = .20 = 20\%$$

that the actual net present value will be greater than

$$\mu + k\sigma = 2000 + 2(1000) = \$4,000$$

There might be a tendency to combine Eqs. (13-15) and (13-16) in order to make probability statements regarding an interval. This is incorrect. Eq. (13-14) should be used for estimating interior probabilities since it establishes the lowest bound for interior probabilities.

Since Tchebycheff's inequality does not provide exact probability statements, a common approach is to assume that the net present value is normally distributed. In general, this assumption is hard to defend except in the case where the cash flows are known (or assumed) to be independent. In the independent case, a fairly strong argument can be presented for the assumption of normality on the basis of the central limit theorem. If it is decided (on some basis) that the net present value is normally distributed, the mean and standard deviation can be used to make exact probability statements and to calculate expected losses as shown in the following example.

Example 13-4

In this example the net present value is assumed to be normally distributed with a mean and standard deviation, respectively, of $2000 and $1000.

The determination of exact probability statements is a relatively simple matter with the assumption that the net present value is normally distributed. For example, the probability that the net present value is less than zero is

$$k_\alpha = \frac{0 - 2000}{1000} = -2.00$$

$$\alpha = .0228 = 2.28\%$$

There is another possible interpretation of this answer. By considering that a net present value less than zero is a loss, it is possible to interpret this answer as the probability of a loss.

Expected Loss and Gain

With the condition that the net present value is normally distributed, it is possible to calculate the expected loss (see also References 1 and 5) using Eq. (13-17).

$$EL = \sigma_{NPV} [L_N(D)] \qquad (13\text{-}17)$$

Where

EL = expected loss with a loss defined as the NPV < 0
σ_{NPV} = standard deviation of the net present value
$L_N(D)$ = unit normal loss integral given in the appendices

The unit normal loss integral as used in the context of Eq. (13-17) is

$$EL = \int_{-\infty}^{0} |X| f(X)dx \qquad (13\text{-}18)$$

where

X = all possible negative net present values, since an NPV < 0 is considered a loss
$f(X)$ = probability density function

As a result of the definition of the unit normal loss integral given by Eq. (13-18), it should be recognized that, in actuality, EL is negative. However, the negative sign is usually omitted because it is implied in the definition of a loss.

It is also possible to determine the expected loss given a loss occurs using Eq. (13-19)

$$EL \mid loss = \frac{EL}{\alpha} \qquad (13\text{-}19)$$

The expected gain, EG, can also be calculated using Eq. (13-20)

$$EG = \sigma (NPV) [L_N(-D)] \qquad (13\text{-}20)$$

where

$$L_N(-D) = [\frac{E(NPV)}{\sigma(NPV)} + L_N(D)] \qquad (13\text{-}21)$$

It should be noted that (remembering the EL is negative) EG + EL = E(NPV).

Example 13-5

For an expected net present value of $2,000 and standard deviation of $1,000, determine the expected loss, expected loss given a loss occurs, and the expected gain.

The expected loss is

$$EL = 1000 \, [0.008491] = \$8.491$$

The value in the brackets is obtained from the appendices in the following manner.

$$D = \frac{E(NPV)}{\sigma(NPV)} = \frac{2,000}{1,000} = 2.00$$

$$L_N(D) = 0.008491$$

The expected loss given a loss occurs is

$$EL \mid loss = \frac{8.491}{0.0228} = \$372.41$$

where the value 0.0228 is the probability of a loss.

Using Eqs. (13-20) and (13-21), the expected gain is

$$L_N(-D) = \frac{2000}{1000} + .008491$$

$$EG = 1000(2.008491) = \$2,008.491$$

Mean and Variance of Cash Flows

Up to this point the discussion is concerned with the determination and possible uses of the mean and variance of the net present value distribution. However, before these uses are possible, an intermediate step is required: the determination of the mean and variance of the cash flows. Therefore, the next examples are concerned with the development of analytical approaches for the determination of these quantities. Basically, these approaches are an application of the statistical theorems presented earlier in this chapter.

Example 13-6 _____

In this example the mean and variance of the cash flow equation shown as Eq. (13-22) is determined.

$$X_t = G_t - C_t - I_t - (G_t - C_t - D_t - I_t)T - K_t + L_t + B_t - Pt \qquad (13\text{-}22)$$

Initially, is assumed that all variables are independent and the tax rate T, is a constant. Of course, it is highly probable that many of the variables in Eq. (13-22) are not applicable for a particular year. For example, it is highly likely to have a capital expenditure, K, in earlier years and none in later years. Similarly, it is likely to have salvage values, L, only in later years.

Now in order to obtain the variance of Eq. (13-22) it is necessary to rewrite Eq. (13-22) as

$$X_t = G(1\text{-}T) - C(1\text{-}T) - I(1\text{-}T) + DT - K + L + B - P \qquad (13\text{-}23)$$

In this form, each term is independent since T is assumed to be a constant. This is the principal reason for assuming the tax rate (T) is a constant. That is, all the terms in Eq. (13-23) are independent. If T is allowed to be a random variable, the application of the statistical theorems presented previously is not possible.

The variance of Eq. (13-23) is

$$\sigma^2_{x_t} = \sigma^2_G(1\text{-}T)^2 + \sigma^2_C(1\text{-}T)^2 + \sigma^2_I(1\text{-}T)^2 + \sigma^2_D T^2 + \sigma^2_K + \sigma^2_L + \sigma^2_B + \sigma^2_P \quad (13\text{-}24)$$

and the mean is

$$\overline{X}_t = \overline{G}(1\text{-}T) - \overline{C}(1\text{-}T) - \overline{I}(1\text{-}T) + \overline{D}T - \overline{K} + \overline{L} + \overline{B} - \overline{P} \qquad (13\text{-}25)$$

With the means and variances determined by Eqs. (13-24) and (13-25), the mean and variance of the net present value could be determined by using Eqs. (13-10) and (13-11) assuming the number of years (n) is a constant.

Another approach to Example 13-6 is to discount the individual components in Eq. (13-23) in order to obtain the mean and variance of the net present value. This approach does have computational advantages when covariance terms are involved as shown in Example 13-7.

Example 13-7 _____

This example determines the mean and variance of the net present value for the situation depicted in Table 13-4 under the following conditions:

TABLE 13-4
Cash Flow Variables
(Example 13-7)

Year	Variables						
0		K_0	B_0				
1	G_1	C_1	I_1	D_1	T	P_1	
.	.	.	.	.	.	.	
.	.	.	.	.	.	.	
.	.	.	.	.	.	.	
t	G_t	C_t	I_t	D_t	T	P_t	
.	.	.	.	.	.	.	
.	.	.	.	.	.	.	
.	.	.	.	.	.	.	
n	G_n	C_n	I_n	D_n	T	P_n	L_n

1. The number of years, n, is known with certainty.
2. G, C, I, D, and P are all independent random variables.
3. The tax rate, T, and discount rate (minimum attractive rate of return) are constants.

The mean and variance of the net present value are the discounted sums of the various terms in Eqs. (13-24) and (13-25) as shown in Eqs. (13-26) and (13-27).

$$E(NPV) = (1-T) \sum_{t=1}^{n} \overline{G}_t(PFk,t) - (1-T)\sum_{t=1}^{n} \overline{C}_t(PFk,t)$$

$$-(1-T)\sum_{t=1}^{n} \overline{I}_t(PFk,t) + T\sum_{t=1}^{n} \overline{D}_t(PFk,t)$$

$$-\overline{K}_0 + \overline{B}_0 + \overline{L}(PFk,n) - \sum_{t=0}^{n} \overline{P}_t(PFk,t) \tag{13-26}$$

$$V(NPV) = (1-T)^2 \sum_{t=1}^{n} \sigma_{G_t}^2(PFk,2t) + (1-T)^2\sum_{t=1}^{n} \sigma_{C_t}^2(PFk,2t)$$

$$+ (1-T)^2\sum_{t=1}^{n} \sigma_{I_t}^2(PFk,2t) + T^2\sum_{t=1}^{n} \sigma_{D_t}^2(PFk,2t)$$

$$+\sigma_{K_0}^2 + \sigma_{B_0}^2 + \sigma_{L_n}^2 (PFk,2n) + \sum_{t=1}^{n} \sigma_{P_t}^2(PFk,2t) \tag{13-27}$$

In Example 13-6 and 13-7 all variables are assumed to be independent. If some of the variables are dependent, it is necessary to add the applicable covariance terms to determine the variance of the net present value. The expected value does not change. The manner in which covariance terms can be included is discussed in the next example.

Example 13-8 _____

If it is assumed there is a dependency between two variables *in the same time period (year)*, the covariance term is obtained using Eq. (13-13) and the constant term associated with a particular variable. For example, suppose in Eq. (13-23) that the gross income (G) and costs (C) are dependent. This would mean the term

$$-2r_{G,C}\sigma_G\sigma_C(1-T)^2 \tag{13-28}$$

would have to be added to Eq. (13-24). The negative sign is used because the *difference* of two random variables is involved. The constant term, $(1 - T)^2$ is involved because the two random variables (G and C) in Eq. (13-24) are both multiplied by the constant (1 - T) . As two further examples, the covariance term for a dependency between C and I is

$$+2r_{C,I}\sigma_C\sigma_I(1-T)^2 \tag{13-29}$$

and between G and D is

$$+2r_{G,D}\sigma_G\sigma_D(T)(1-T) \tag{13-30}$$

If the dependency occurs between random variables in different years, a discounting process is involved. For example, suppose that in Table 13-5, the gross incomes, G, are dependent and it is desired to obtain the present value of the variance of these three variables.

TABLE 13-5
Dependent Variables
(Example 13-8)

Year	Gross Income
0	-
1	$G_1 (1-T)$
2	$G_2 (1-T)$
3	$G_3 (1-T)$

The present value variance of the gross incomes, V(PV), in Table 13-5 is

$$V(PV) = \sigma_{G_1}^2 (1\text{-}T)^2(1+k)^{-2} + \sigma_{G_2}^2(1\text{-}T)^2(1\text{-}k)^{-4}$$
$$+ \sigma_{G_3}^2(1\text{-}T)^2(1+k)^{-6} + 2r_{G_1,G_1}\sigma_{G_1},\sigma_{G_2}(1\text{-}T)^2(1+k)^{-3}$$
$$2r_{G_1G_3}\sigma_{G_1}\sigma_{G_3}(1\text{-}T)^2(1+k)^{-4}$$
$$2r_{G_2G_3}\sigma_{G_2}\sigma_{G_3}(1\text{-}T)^2(1+k)^{-5}$$

This result can be generalized in the following manner.

$$V(PV) = \sum_{t=1}^{n} \sigma_t^2 (1+k)^{-2t} \pm 2 \sum_{t=1}^{n-1} \sum_{j=t+1}^{n} r_{t,j}\, \sigma_t\, \sigma_j (1+k)^{-(t+j)} \tag{13-31}$$

Eq. (13-31) does not include the constant terms. These terms are dependent upon the variables included in this equation.

A Comment From a theoretical standpoint the inclusion of dependencies in the determination of the mean and variance of the net present value is, of course, important since it is highly probable that dependencies do exist. However, from a practical standpoint, there are computational problems as mentioned earlier. These problems occur as a result of the number of covariance terms that can be involved in a problem of any magnitude. As a result, it is not unusual to find that assumptions are made of independence, perfect correlation, and/or equal distributions of random variables in probabilistic models. These assumptions greatly reduce the computational problems. However, they do so at the possible expense of the model. The reduction in computational problems is shown in the next example.

Example 13-9

Suppose that in Example 13-8, the following additional assumptions are made.

1. All random variables are perfectly correlated ($r_{ij} = 1$).
2. All random variables (G_t) are equally distributed.

$$\sigma_{G_1} = \sigma_{G_2} = \sigma_{G_3} = \sigma$$

With these assumptions and letting $x = 1/(1+k)$, the present value of the random variables in Table 13-5 is

$$V(PV) = \sigma^2 (1\text{-}T)^2 [x^2 + x^4 + x^6 + 2(x^3 + x^4 + x^5)] \tag{13-32}$$

The next example shows the development of a more complete probabilistic cash flow model using various simplifying assumptions.

Example 13-10

This example starts with the definition of cash flow given by Eq. (13-23). It assumes that the discount rate, k, and number of years of cash flow, n, are constants. In addition, other assumptions are made as expressions are developed for the components in Eq. (13-23). Initially, these expressions are developed without consideration of the discounting process and the constant terms of (1-T) and T.

First, it is assumed that the salvage value, L, can be expressed as a constant proportion, C_1 of the capital investment, K, and, therefore, the salvage value is

$$L = C_1 K \qquad (13\text{-}33)$$

The mean and variance of the salvage value are

$$\overline{L} = C_1\overline{K} \qquad (13\text{-}34)$$

$$\sigma^2_L = C^2_1\sigma^2_K \qquad (13\text{-}35)$$

If it is assumed that the yearly depreciation amounts, D_t, are equally distributed and are perfectly correlated, the total depreciation, d, is

$$d = K - L = K (1\text{-}C_1) \qquad (13\text{-}36)$$

and

$$K (1\text{-}C_1) = D_1 + D_2 + \dots + D_n = nD \qquad (13\text{-}37)$$

$$D = \frac{K(1 - C_1)}{n} \qquad (13\text{-}38)$$

The mean and variance of Eq. (13-38) are

$$\overline{D} = \frac{\overline{K}(1 - C_1)}{n} \qquad (13\text{-}39)$$

$$\sigma^2_D = \frac{\sigma^2_K(1 - C_1)^2}{n^2} \qquad (13\text{-}40)$$

The debt capital, B, is a constant proportion, C_2, of the capital investment (the debt ratio). Therefore,

$$B = C_2K \tag{13-41}$$

and

$$\bar{B} = C_2\bar{K} \tag{13-42}$$

$$\sigma_B^2 = C_2^2\sigma_K^2 \tag{13-43}$$

If it is assumed the yearly provisions for the recovery of debt capital, P, are equally distributed and perfectly correlated, then

$$B = C_2 \ K = P_1 + P_2 + ... + P_n = nP \tag{13-44}$$

$$P = \frac{C_2K}{n} \tag{13-45}$$

and the mean and variance of Eq. (13-45) are

$$\bar{P} = \frac{C_2\bar{K}}{n} \tag{13-46}$$

$$\sigma_p^2 = \frac{C_2^2\sigma_K^2}{n^2} \tag{13-47}$$

Assuming the cost of debt money, k_d, is a constant that is assessed on the unrecovered debt, the yearly interest, I_t, is

$$I_t = k_d [B - (t - 1) P] \tag{13-48}$$

$$= k_d [B - (t - 1) \frac{B}{n}] \tag{13-49}$$

$$= k_d [\frac{B}{n} (n - t + 1)] \tag{13-50}$$

Substituting Eq. (13-41) into Eq. (13-50) gives

$$I_t = k_d C_2 K [\frac{n-t+1}{n}] \tag{13-51}$$

and the mean and variance of Eq. (13-51) are

$$\bar{I} = \bar{K}[C_2 k_d \frac{n-t+1}{n}]^2 \tag{13-52}$$

$$\sigma_I^2 = \sigma_K^2 \, [C_2 \; k_d \tfrac{n-t-1}{n}]^2 \tag{13-53}$$

It is believed the assumptions made in the development of the preceding equations are plausible because of the nature of the variables involved. That is, the complete dependency of L, D, B, and I with K assumed in this example is not unreasonable. However when the gross incomes, G, and annual costs, C, are considered, it is more difficult to justify an assumption about the relationship of these two variables and yet provide the dependency that exists between these variables. It is highly likely that, in a particular year G and C are dependent. Also, it is likely that they are dependent from year to year. This leads to a high number of covariance terms. Consequently, it is necessary to make some plausible assumption regarding the relationship between G and C that reduces the number of covariance terms. Some possible ways are (1) assume independence, (2) assume that the costs are a constant proportion of gross income in a particular year and (3) assume a combination of independence and dependency. The second assumption is taken in this example because there is some basis for defending this assumption, since C in the cash flow equation is *the cost of goods sold*. Therefore, it is possible that for a particular year

$$C = C_3 G \tag{13-54}$$

or

$$G-C = G(1-C_3) \tag{13-55}$$

In this model, it is assumed that terms given by Eq. (13-55) are dependent from one time period to the next. The mean and variance of Eq. (13-55) are

$$\overline{G-C} = \overline{G}(1-C_3) \tag{13-56}$$

$$\sigma_{G-C}^2 = \sigma_G^2 \, (1-C_3)^2 \tag{13-57}$$

With these and the previous developed relationships, it is possible to obtain an expression for the variance of the net present value by substituting into Eq. (13-27) giving the result

$$V(NPV) = (1-T)^2(1-C_3)^2 \left[\sum_{t=1}^{n} \sigma_{G_t}^2 (P/Fk, 2t) + 2\sum_{t=1}^{n-1} \sum_{j=t+1}^{n} r_{G_t, G_j} \sigma_{G_t} \sigma_{G_j}(P/Fk, (t+j)) \right]$$

$$+ (1-T)^2 C_2^2 k_d^2 \sigma_K^2 \sum_{t=1}^{n} \left[\frac{n-t+1}{n} \right]^2 (P/Fk, 2t) + \frac{T^2 \sigma_K^2 (1-C_1)^2}{n^2} \sum_{t=1}^{n} (P/Fk, 2t) + \sigma_K^2 + C_2^2 \sigma_K^2$$

$$+ \frac{C_2^2 \sigma_K^2}{n^2} \sum_{t=1}^{n} (P/Fk, 2t) + C_1^2 \sigma_K^2 (P/Fk, 2n)$$

$$(13-58)$$

Substituting the expressions into Eq. (13-26) gives the expected net present value.

$$E(NPV) = (1-T)(1-C_3) \sum_{t=1}^{n} \overline{G}_t (P/Fk, t) - (1-T) C_2 k_d \overline{K} \sum_{t=1}^{n} \left[\frac{n-t+1}{n} \right] (P/Fk, t)$$

$$+ \frac{T\overline{K}(1-C_1)}{n} \sum_{t=1}^{n} (P/Fk, t) - \overline{K} + C_2 \overline{K}$$

$$- \frac{C_2 \overline{K}}{n} \sum_{t=1}^{n} (P/Fk, t) + C_1 \overline{K} (P/Fk, n)$$

$$(13-59)$$

The conditions and assumptions used in this example greatly reduce the estimating problems since most of the expressions are a function of the capital investment.

Note that since debt and principal are explicitly included in this example, the discount rate (k) is, in actuality, the cost of equity capital.

A PROBABILISTIC COST-VOLUME-PROFIT (C-V-P) MODEL

In Chapter 8 some deterministic C-V-P models are presented. In this section a probabilistic model is presented based on the work of Jaedicke and Robichek (see Reference 3).

The basic before-tax model presented in Chapter 8 is

$$P = V(S - C) - F \qquad\qquad (13-60)$$

If it is assumed that V, S, C, and F in Eq. 13-60 are independent random variables (Jaedicke and Robichek), expressions for the mean and variance of the profit can be determined using the statistical theorems presented earlier in this chapter. First Eq. (13-60) is rewritten as

$$P = VA - F \qquad\qquad (13-61)$$

where

$$A = S - C \qquad (13\text{-}62)$$

Applying Eq. (13-7) to Eq. (13-61), the variance of the profit is

$$\sigma_P^2 = \sigma_V^2 \, \overline{A}^2 + \sigma_A^2 \, \overline{V}^2 + \sigma_A^2 \sigma_V^2 + \sigma_F^2 \qquad (13\text{-}63)$$

and since

$$\overline{A} = \overline{S} - \overline{C} \qquad (13\text{-}64)$$

$$\sigma_A^2 = \sigma_S^2 + \sigma_C^2 \qquad (13\text{-}65)$$

Eq. (13-63) can be rewritten as

$$\sigma_P^2 = \sigma_V^2 (\overline{S} - \overline{C})^2 + (\sigma_S^2 + \sigma_C^2)\overline{V}^2 + \sigma_A^2 \sigma_V^2 + \sigma_F^2 \qquad (13\text{-}65)$$

The mean of the profit is

$$\overline{P} = \overline{V}(\overline{S} - \overline{C}) - \overline{F} \qquad (13\text{-}67)$$

Similar expressions can be obtained for the after tax profit, Pt, if the tax rate is assumed a constant and the tax and book depreciation are the same. The after tax profit is

$$P_t = (1 - T)\,[V(S - C) - F] \qquad (13\text{-}68)$$

Therefore, the mean and variance, respectively, of Eq. (13-68) are

$$\overline{P}_t = (1 - T)\,\overline{P} \qquad (13\text{-}69)$$

$$\sigma_{P_t}^2 = (1 - T)^2 \, \sigma_P^2 \qquad 13\text{-}70)$$

Where P and $\sigma^2 P$ are given by Eqs. (13-67) and (13-66). Note that the distribution of the profit is unknown. These expressions only give the mean and variance of the profit. If probability statements are desired, it is necessary to make some assumption about the distribution of the profit. A common assumption, although questionable, is that the profit is normally distributed. Or Tchebycheff's inequality can be used as shown in Example 13-3.

DECISION TREES

Another procedure sometimes used for the analysis of cash flow models with random elements is to use decision trees. The words "decision tree" could be considered a misnomer because, strictly speaking, they do not provide a decision regarding the acceptability of a project. Basically, a decision tree enumerates all the possible outcomes as shown in the following example.

Example 13-11 _____

Suppose a project has the initial investment and cash flow distributions shown in Figure 13-1. For the sake of simplicity, it is assumed that the cash flows are the same for each year and the life of the project is two years.

FIGURE 13-1
Cash Flow Distributions
(Example 13-11)

Initial Investment $X(10)^{-6}$ at $t = 0$	Cash flow per year $X(10)^{-6}$

With the data given in Figure 13-1, the decision tree shown in Figure 13-2 can be drawn. Each branch shows a possible outcome Also, the net present values for each branch and its probability can be calculated. For example, assuming the minimum acceptable rate of return is 15%, the net present value for the uppermost branch in Figure 13-2 is

NPV= 700,000(PF15,2) + 700,000(PF15,1) - 1,000,000 = 138,060

and the probability of this outcome is (. 6) (.3) (.3) = 0.054. With the NPV for each branch and its probability, it is possible to calculate the mean, E(NPV), and variance of the net present value, V(NPV), as shown below.

E(NPV)=138,060(.054)+213,680(.090)+...+563,220(.016) = $324,379

FIGURE 13-2
Decision Tree (Example 13-11)

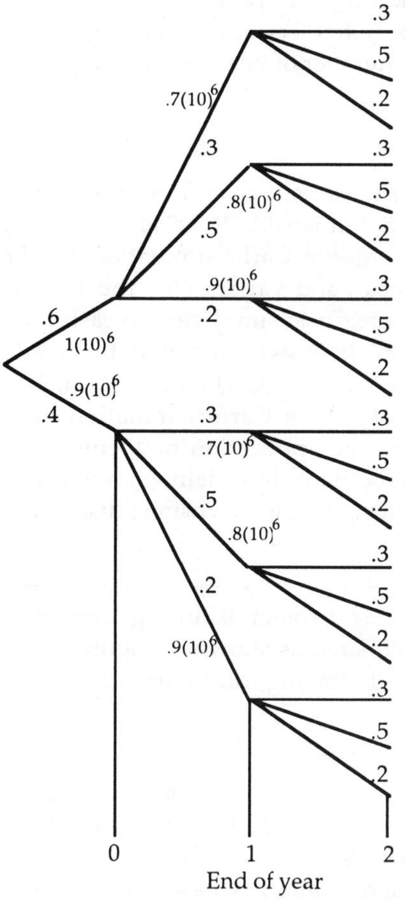

	NPV	Probability
$.7(10)^6$	138,060	.054
$.8(10)^6$	213,680	.090
$.9(10)^6$	289,300	.036
$.7(10)^6$	225,020	.090
$.8(10)^6$	300,640	.150
$.9(10)^6$	376,260	.060
$.7(10)^6$	311,980	.036
$.8(10)^6$	387,600	.060
$.9(10)^6$	463,220	.024
$.7(10)^6$	238,060	.036
$.8(10)^6$	313,680	.060
$.9(10)^6$	389,300	.024
$.7(10)^6$	325,020	.060
$.8(10)^6$	400,640	.100
$.9(10)^6$	476,260	.040
$.7(10)^6$	411,980	.024
$.8(10)^6$	487,980	.040
$.9(10)^6$	583,220	.016

End of year

$$V(NPV) = (138,060)^2 (.054) + (213,680)^2 (.090) + \dots$$
$$+ (563,220)^2 (.016) - (324,379)^2 \approx 1812.53(10)^8$$

Using these values in the decision-making process is strictly a matter of a subjective evaluation of the relative magnitude of the mean and variance of the net present value and the decision maker's attitude toward risk. In this particular case, there might be a tendency to consider the project acceptable since all the net present values are positive. However, in a case where there are several negative net present values, it may be more difficult to make a decision.

A Comment   A major disadvantage of using decision trees in the analysis of probabilistic cash flow models is that the number of computations can increase very rapidly. The number of end points (outcomes) on the decision tree becomes very large as the number of possible values and/or number of years increases.

SIMULATION

In the solution of probabilistic cash flow models it is sometimes found that a model is not amenable to an analytical approach. In these cases, the use of Monte Carlo simulation can be a valuable tool in obtaining the mean and variance of the net present value. The applications of Monte Carlo simulation to cash flow models are discussed in this section. It is assumed that the reader has some experience in the basics of Monte Carlo simulation. References that discuss the intricacies of Monte Carlo simulation are provided at the end of this chapter. The application of Monte Carlo simulation to cash flow models is, perhaps, best demonstrated through the use of a simple example with possible extensions discussed later.

Example 13-12 _____

Suppose a particular project is being considered and the variables have been estimated as shown in Figure 13-3. In addition, it has been decided the following information is applicable for this project.

1. Debt ratio = 30%.
2. The debt capital is to be recovered in equal installments over the life of the project and the cost of debt capital is 10%.
3. The tax depreciation is based on a MACRS model of five years.
4. The salvage values are obtained in the simulation.
5. The tax rate is assumed to be a constant value of 40% for each year.

Based on this data and the data given in Figure 13-3, one set (trial) of possible net cash flows is shown in Table 13-6. The procedure used to obtain these values is presented in the following discussion.

FIGURE 13-3
Distribution of Cash Flow Variables
(Example 13-12)

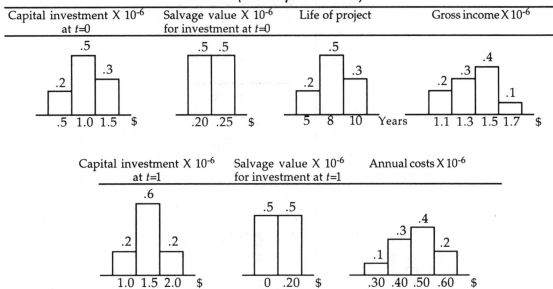

The first step is to generate three random numbers for, respectively, the life of the project, the capital investment for year zero, and the salvage value for this investment. Suppose these random numbers are 35, 54, and 43. Consequently, referring to the applicable distributions in Figure 13-3, the values for the life, investment, and salvage are, respectively, eight years, $1,000,000 and $200,000.

The next step is to generate two random numbers for the value of the capital expenditures occurring in year 1 and its salvage value. Assuming these values are 85 and 22, the investment in year 1 is $2,000,000 and its salvage value is zero. With this data it is possible to calculate the tax depreciation schedules, amount of debt capital, debt recovery, and interest. For example, the tax depreciation for the investments are calculated using the MACRS percentages and the values shown in Table 13-6 are obtained.

The amount of borrowed money is $1,000,000(.3) = $300,000, which occurs in year 0 and $2,000,000(.3) = $600,000 which occurs in year 1. Therefore, the debt recovery in years 1 through 8 is

TABLE 13-6
Simulation Values
(Example 13-12)

End of Year	Capital Investment and Salvage	Tax Depreciation for K_0	Tax Depreciation for K_1	Debt Recovery for K_0	Debt Recovery for K_1	Interest for K_0	Interest for K_1	RN G	Gross Income G	RN C	Costs C	Cash Flow X_k
0	-$1,000,000	-	-	-	-	-	-	-	-	-	-	-$700,000
1	-$2,000,000	$200,000	-	$37,500	-	$30,000	-	32	$1,300,000	05	$300,000	-775,500
2		320,000	$400,000	37,500	$85,714	26,250	$60,000	56	1,500,000	89	600,000	596,786
3		192,000	640,000	37,500	85,714	22,500	51,429	27	1,300,000	20	400,000	705,229
4		115,200	384,000	37,500	85,714	18,750	42,858	70	1,500,000	45	500,000	639,501
5		115,200	230,400	37,500	85,714	15,000	34,287	61	1,500,000	30	400,000	634,654
6		57,600	230,400	37,500	85,714	11,250	25,716	15	1,100,000	16	400,000	389,806
7		-	115,200	37,500	85,714	7,500	17,145	28	1,300,000	30	400,000	448,079
8	$L_0 = 200,000$	-	-	37,500	85,714	3,750	8,574	59	1,500,000	85	600,000	609,392
	$L_1 = 0$											

$$\frac{300,000}{8} = \$37,500$$

and in years 2 through 8 are

$$\frac{600,000}{7} = \$85,714$$

The interest is calculated on the basis of 10% on the unpaid balance.

Eight random numbers are now generated for the gross incomes and another eight random numbers for the annual costs. These values are shown in Table 13-6. After this, the net cash flows are calculated for each year using equity cash flows (debt recovery and interest are explicitly included). For example, the cash flows for years 0 and 1, 2, and 8 are

$$X_0 = -1,000,000 + .3(1,000,000)$$
$$= -\$700,000$$
$$X_1 = (1,300,000 - 300,000 - 30,000) - (1,300,000 - 300,000 -$$
$$\qquad 30,000 - 200,000)(.4) - 2,000,000 + 600,000 - 37,500$$
$$= -\$775,500$$
$$X_2 = (1,500,000 - 600,000 - 26,250 - 60,000)$$
$$\qquad -(1,500,000-60,000-26,260-60,000-320,000-400,000)(.4)$$
$$\qquad - 37,500 - 85,714$$
$$= \$596,786$$
$$X_8 = (1,500,000 - 600,000 - 3,750 - 8,574) - (1,500,000 - 600,000$$
$$\qquad - 3,750 - 8,574)(.4) - 37,500 - 85,714 + 200,000$$
$$= \$609,392.$$

Once the cash flows are determined, it is possible to calculate the internal rate of return, net present value, and payback period. For example, the net present value of the cash flows in Table 13-6 is $190,961 using a required return on equity of 25% (which could also be a random variable). Also, the internal rate of return is 30%.

The procedure just shown provides only one iteration and must be repeated many times. After this procedure is repeated many times it is possible to plot a frequency distribution similar to that shown in Figure 13-4. Or, the distribution of the internal rate of return or payback period can be plotted.

FIGURE 13-4
Frequency Distribution of Net Present Value

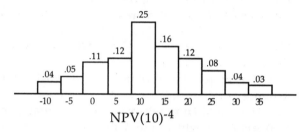

$$NPV(10)^{-4}$$

With a frequency distribution of net present value, such as shown in Figure 13-4, it is possible to make probability statements regarding the net present value. For example, defining a loss as a net present value of zero or less, the probability of a loss is

$$.04 + .05 + .11 = .20 = 20\%$$

The expected loss is

$$EL = .04(100,000) + .05(50,000) + .11(0) = \$6,500$$

where the negative sign is implied. Also, the expected loss given a loss occurs is

$$E1 \mid loss = \frac{6,500}{.04 + .05 + .11} = \$32,500$$

It is also possible to calculate the mean and variance of the net present value.

From a decision-making standpoint, a frequency distribution such as shown in Figure 13-4 is a valuable tool for evaluating a project.

Comments and Extensions   The simulation discussed in Example 13-12 is relatively simple. There are many possible extensions. For example the gross income could be simulated by estimating distributions for the selling price per unit and volume of yearly sales. The annual costs could be broken down into such components as material, labor, and overhead costs. Working capital considerations could also be included. In actuality, there are very few limitations in the simulation of cash flows except, perhaps, computer time. For, of course, Monte Carlo simulation is definitely computer oriented.

Note in Example 13-12 that the variables are assumed to be independent. This is not a requirement for it is entirely possible to include dependency between variables in Monte Carlo simulation. The problem when allowing dependency between variables is in the *estimation* and *expression* of the dependency; not in the Monte Carlo procedure itself. Some examples and discussion of including dependencies in the simulation of cash flows are given in references provided at the end of this chapter.

In this example, the assumed distributions are discrete. This, of course, is not a requirement. It is entirely possible to represent variables by continuous distributions.

A FINAL POINT

In this chapter it has been stated several times that probabilities, expected losses, and means and variances of the net present value do not, by themselves, provide a decision regarding the acceptability of a project. They simply provide a decision maker with additional quantitative information on which to evaluate a project. In the final analysis, the acceptability of a project will be decided by the decision maker's attitudes toward risk and the evaluation of intangible factors. There are, theoretically at least, methods for quantifying attitudes towards risk; for example, the concept of cardinal utility theory. A project will be accepted or rejected on the basis of the decision-maker's utility function.

REFERENCES

Canada, J. R., Intermediate Economic Analysis for Management and Engineering, Prentice-Hall, Inc., Englewood Cliffs, NJ, 1971.

Hillier, F. S., "The Derivation of Probabilistic Information for the Evaluation of Risky Investments," Management Science, April 1963.

Jaedicke, R. K., and A. A. Robichek, "Cost-Volume-Profit Analysis Under Conditions of Uncertainty," The Accounting Review, XXXIX, October 1964, pp. 917-926.

Marshall, A. W. and Olkin, I. "A One-Side Inequality of the Chebyshev Type," Annals of Mathematical Statistics, 1960.

Schlaifer, R., Probability and Statistics for Business Decisions, McGraw-Hill Book Co., New York, 1959.

Simulation References

Bonini, C. P., *Simulation of Information and Decision Systems in the Firm*, Prentice-Hall, Inc., Englewood Cliffs, NJ, 1963.

Hillier, F. S., and G. J. Lierberman, *Introduction to Operations Research*, Chap. 14, Holden-Day, Inc., San Francisco, 1968.

Mize, J. H., and J. F. Cox, *Essentials of Simulation*, Prentice-Hall, Inc., Englewood Cliffs, N. J., 1968.

Naylor, T. F., J. L. Balintfy, D. S. Burdick, and C. Kong, *Computer Simulation Techniques*, John Wiley & Sons, New York, 1966.

Schmidt, J. W., and R. E. Taylor, *Simulation and Analysis of Industrial Systems*, Richard D. Irwin, Inc., Homewood, Ill., 1970.

Tocher, K. D., *The Art of Simulation*, The English University Press, Ltd., London, 1963.

PROBLEMS

13-1   For the cash flow means and standard deviations shown below, determine the following assuming the minimum attractive rate of return is 12% and the net present value is normally distributed.

(a) The mean and standard deviation of the net present value.

(b) The probability of a loss.

(c) The expected loss.

(d) The expected loss given that a loss occurs.

(e) The expected gain.

End of	Cash Flow	
Year	Mean	Standard Deviation
0	-$300,000	$30,000
1	70,000	7,000
2	80,000	10,000
3	80,000	10,000
4	80,000	10,000
5	80,000	10,000
6	50,000	12,000
7	50,000	12,000
8	50,000	12,000

13-2   If the mean and standard deviation of the net present value are, respectively, $50,000 and $30,000, and there is no knowledge about the distribution of net present value, determine the following:
   (a) The probability that the net present value will fall outside the plus and minus three sigma limits. What are these limits?
   (b) The probability that there will be a loss.

13-3   Consider the definition of cash flow, X_t, shown below and determine the following.
   (a) The mean and variance of the cash flow if the tax rate is a constant and all other variables are independent and random.
   (b) The same as part (b) only S, C, and M are dependent.
   (c) What additional term would have to be added in part (b) if I and B are dependent?

$$X_t = (VS - VC - VM - H - I)$$
$$- (VS - VC - VM - H - I - D)T - K + L - P + B$$

where

X_t	= cash flow in year t	I	= interest
V	= volume of sales	D	= depreciation
S	= selling price per unit	T	= tax rate
C	= labor costs per unit	K	= capital investment
M	= material costs per unit	L	= salvage value
H	= overhead	P	= debt recovery
B	= debt capital		

13-4   For the situation depicted below and the following conditions, derive expressions for the mean and variance of the net present value.
(a) n and T are constants.
(b) The discount rate is a constant.
(c) $G_t, C_t, D_t, K_0, K_1, L_0, L_1$ are random variables.
(d) K_0 and L_0 are dependent.
(e) K_1 and L_1 are dependent.
(f) The gross incomes, G_t are dependent for the first X years.
(g) The costs, C_t, are dependent for the first X years.
(h) The depreciations, D_t, are dependent for the first X years.
(i) All other variables are independent.

End of Year Variables

0	K_0				
1	G_1	C_1	D_1	T	K_1
2	G_2	C_2	D_2	T	
.	.	.	.	.	.
.	.	.	.	.	.
t	G_t	C_t	Dt	T	
.	.	.	.	.	.
.	.	.	.	.	.
n	G_n	C_n	D_n	T	L_0, L_1

13-5   For a particular capital investment the data shown below has been estimated. Based on this data, determine the mean and standard deviation of the net present value assuming all variables are independent.

	Mean	Standard Deviation
Capital investment in year zero	$300,000	$40,000
Life of project	10 years	0
Depreciation (years 1-10)	$ 40,000	0
Minimum acceptable return	15%	0
Annual gross income (years 1-10)	$170,000	$30,000
Annual costs (years 1-10)	$ 50,000	$10,000
Tax rate	40%	0

13-6   Suppose in Example 13-10, the yearly distributions of gross income are the same and perfectly correlated. What is the mean and variance of the net present value.

13-7   Using the results obtained in Problem 13-6 and the following data, determine the mean and standard deviation of the net present value.

	Mean	Standard Deviation
Capital investment in year zero	$300,000	$40,000
Life of project	4 years	0
Annual gross income (years 1-10)	$170,000	$30,000
Annual costs (% of gross income)	30%	0
Cost of debt capital	10%	0
Cost of equity capital	15%	0
Tax rate	40%	0
Debt ratio	30%	0
Salvage value (% of capital investment)	5%	0

13-8   Past data indicates that the mean and standard deviation of *yearly sales*, respectively, are $120,000 and $24,000. Assuming the distribution of monthly sales is normally distributed and equal, determine the probability of monthly sales being less than $5,000 under the conditions:
(a) monthly sales are independent.
(b) monthly sales are perfectly correlated.

13-9   Using the data given below for a particular capital investment, determine the following based on the cash flow definition:

$$X_t = (G - C) - (G - C - D)T - K_t$$

(a) A decision tree showing all cash flow elements (gross income, costs, etc.).
(b) The net present value for all possible outcomes and their respective probabilities.
(c) The probability of a loss for this investment.
(d) What major assumption is implied in parts (a) and (b)?

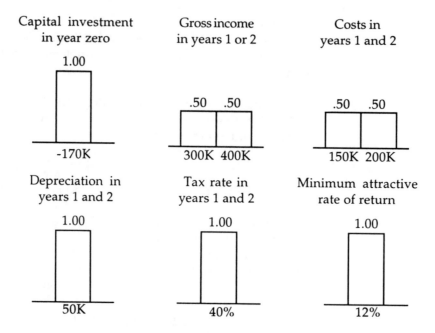

13-10 Listed below are the necessary data for a C-V-P model. Assuming the variables are independent and the profit is normally distributed, determine the probability of at least breaking even based on a before-tax analysis.

Variable	Mean	Standard Deviation
Volume of sales per unit	60,000	8,000
Selling price per units	$ 80	$7
Variable cost per unit	$ 35	$4
Fixed costs per year	$1,900,000	$200,000

13-11 Repeat Problem 13-10 on an after-tax basis assuming a tax rate of 40% assuming the tax and book depreciation are the same.

13-12 Assume that in the C-V-P model considered in this chapter the selling price (S) and variable costs (C) are dependent and that all other variables are independent. Derive expressions for the mean and variance of the profit based on these assumptions.

13-13   Assume in Problem 13-11 that the selling price and variable costs are dependent and the correlation coefficient that measures this dependency is .5. Determine the probability of at least breaking even with this assumption.

13-14   Repeat Example 13-12 using the same conditions and the following random numbers.

$$\text{life} = 19$$
$$\text{capital investment in year zero} = 85$$
$$\text{salvage value} = 10$$
$$\text{capital investment in year one} = 16$$
$$\text{salvage value} = 32$$

End of	Random Numbers[a]	
Year	Gross Income	Costs
1	45	26
2	65	27
3	06	75
4	59	87
5	33	37
6	17	45
7	13	19
8	44	16

[a]There may be more than needed.

13-15   The Monte Carlo simulation of a particular capital investment has given the frequency distribution shown below.

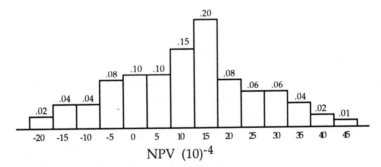

Determine the following:
(a) The probability of a loss. Define a loss as the NPV < 0 since a discrete distribution is involved.

      (b) The expected loss.

      (c) The expected loss given that a loss occurs.

      (d) The mean and variance of the net present value.

13-16 How should the investment tax credit be included in (a) Example 13-10 and (b) in Problem 13-14.

13-17 Suppose in the simulation of a capital investment, it is assumed that the gross incomes and costs in the same year are dependent. Give some ways that it might be included.

14

NEUMANN-MORGENSTERN UTILITY THEORY

Suppose a person is given a choice between the two gambles shown below:

Gamble A		Gamble B	
$4	$p_1 = 1$	$10	$p_2 = 1/2$
		$ 0	$1 - p_2 = 1/2$

That is, if A is chosen, the person receives $4 for sure ($p_1 = 1$). If B is chosen, a coin is tossed and if it is heads ($p_2 = 1/2$) the person receives $10. If the coin is tails, the person receives nothing. Which gamble is the person's choice? Only the person involved knows the answer to this question. It is perhaps safe to say that a fair sized number of persons might choose B. However, if the magnitudes of the dollar values are increased significantly, say by a factor of 10^6, then it is also probably safe to say that the number of persons choosing B is significantly less. It is important to note that if a choice is based on maximizing expected monetary values, Gamble B is the choice in either case. This points out, intuitively at least, that decisions of this type are not necessarily based upon the criterion of maximizing expected values. Of course, if it is known that a choice between Gambles A and B is available many times, there might be a tendency to pick B due to its higher expected monetary value. However, specific financial opportunities are, by far, one-time propositions. Consequently, decisions are not necessarily based on the criterion of maximum expected monetary values. Rather, they are based on some other criterion.

As early as 1738, Bernoulli [1] expressed the idea that persons do not, necessarily, maximize expected monetary values. However, it was not until 1944 that a basis for expressing a decision-maker's preference (aversion) for monetary returns under conditions of risk became available. In a monumental work, von Neumann and Morgenstern [11] provide a basis upon which it is possible to construct a utility function and rank monetary returns on the basis of an expected utility criterion. Consequently, this chapter is concerned with the basics and some uses of the utility theory advanced by Neumann and Morgenstern (N-M).

THE BASICS

A utility function for a particular decision-maker can be constructed by proposing certain gambles (sometimes called lotteries) to the decision-maker. However before this is done, two set points must be established. These two points are set arbitrarily, but should be chosen such that the range of monetary values usually encountered by the decision-maker is covered. These set points can be established arbitrarily because utility is measured on a relative scale. This is analogous to having different freezing and boiling points on thermometers (Fahrenheit and Centigrade).

As an example of the construction of a utility function, the following two set points are established for a decision-maker:

$$0 \text{ utiles} = \$0$$
$$100 \text{ utiles} = \$500,000.$$

Utiles are a fictitious units that reflect the relative worth of monetary values. These two set points are shown in Figure 14-1.

FIGURE 14-1
A Utility Function

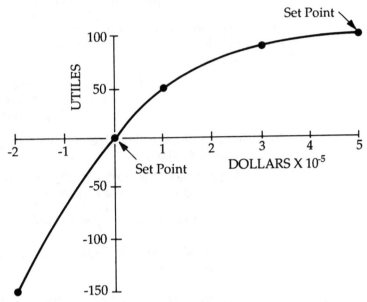

The next step is to propose gambles to the decision-maker in order to establish other points. For example, the decision-maker is given the two gambles

Gamble A	Gamble B
$100,000 $p_1 = 1$	$500,000 $p_2 = ?$
	$0 $1-p_2$

and asked, at what probability, p_2, are they indifferent between the gains (returns) in gambles A and B? Suppose the decision-maker's answer is $p_2 = 0.50$. This implies the decision-maker's utility for a gain of $100,000 is

$$1U(\$100,000) = .5U(\$500,000) + (1-.5)U(\$0)$$
$$U(\$100,000) = .5(100) + .5(0) = 50 \text{ utiles.}$$

As another example, the decision-maker says that at $p_2 = 0.90$ they are indifferent between the gambles

Gamble A	Gamble B
$300,000 $p_1 = 1$	$500,000 $p_2 = ?$
	$0 $1-p_2$

This means that the decision-maker's utility for $300,000 is

$$U(\$300{,}000) = (0.9)U(\$500{,}000) + (0.1)U(\$0)$$
$$= (0.9)(100) + (0.1)(0) = 90 \text{ utiles.}$$

These two points are plotted in Figure 14-1.

In order to determine the utility of losses, gambles such as the following are proposed.

Gamble A		Gamble B	
$0	$p_1 = 1$	$500,000	$p_2 = ?$
		-$200,000	$(1-p_2)$

Suppose the decision-maker gives the answer $p_2 = 0.60$, then the utility for a loss of $200,000 is

$$U(\$0) = .6\ U(\$500{,}000) + (1-.6)\ U\ (-\$200{,}000)$$
$$0 = .6(100) + .4\ U(-\$200{,}000)$$
$$U(\$-200{,}000) = \frac{60}{.4} = -150 \text{ utiles}$$

which provides another point in Figure 14-1. The points are then joined with a smooth curve.

Some Comments   Of course the five points used in determining the utility function are not enough. Many more points are needed to establish a utility function. In establishing these points, answers to a proposed gamble must be consistent with past answers. If an answer is not consistent, the inconsistency is pointed out to the decision-maker and they must "correct" the answer.

The procedure just outlined for establishing a utility function is based on certain fundamental assumptions inherent in the concept of utility theory. These assumptions are discussed in a subsequent section.

The shape of the curve shown in Figure 14-1 should not be generalized. Utility functions can have several shapes as discussed later.

BASIC ASSUMPTIONS INVOLVED IN N-M UTILITY THEORY

N-M utility theory is based on the following axioms (sometimes called the axioms of rational human behavior).

1.   *Alternatives are transitive:* That is, if X is preferred to Y and Y is preferred to Z, then X is preferred to Z.

2. *For any two alternatives, a decision-maker can decide which one he prefers or that he is indifferent to them:* This may seem obvious. However, finding the exact point of indifference can be difficult. It does imply that a decision-maker is capable and willing to make consistent decisions.

3. *For purposes of analysis, two gambles may be substituted for each other if the decision-maker is indifferent to the two gambles:* This implies, of course, that the utility of both gambles are equal.

4. *If X is preferred to Y, and Y is preferred to Z, then a gamble involving X and Z can be defined which results in indifference between Y for certain:* This is a basic assumption used in establishing points for a utility function. For example, if X = $500, 000, Y = $100, 000, and Z = $0, then it is obvious that X is preferred to Y and it is preferred to Z. Therefore, based on this axiom, it is possible to assign some value to p which makes Y = p(X) + (1-p)Z true.

5. *If two gambles have the same outcomes but the probabilities for the outcomes are different, then the preferred gamble is the one with the most favorable outcome.* This simply means that for the two gambles shown in Table 14-1, Gamble A is preferred.

TABLE 14-1
Axiom 5

Gamble A	Gamble B
$500,000 p = .8	$500,000 p = .6
$100,000 p = .2	$100,000 p = .4

6. *If Gamble X is preferred to Gamble Y, then it is possible to define a Gamble X + Z that is preferred to the Gamble Y + Z. Provided, the probabilities for X and Y are the same and the probability of Z is less than one:* Mathematically, this means that p(X) + (1-p)Z is preferred to p(Y) + (1-p)Z.

7. *The expected utility of a gamble is the sum of the utility of its components:* That is, the utility of Gamble X is

$$U(X) = \sum_{i=1}^{n} p_i U(X_i)$$

(14-1)

where,

$$n \quad = \text{number of components in Gamble } X,$$
$$U(X_i) \quad = \text{utility of component } X_i$$
$$p_i \quad = \text{probability of component } X_i.$$

Some Examples   Some examples of the use of an utility function are presented in this section. More involved uses are presented later.

Example 14-1

A decision-maker with the utility function shown in Figure 14-1 is faced with the two gambles shown in Table 14-2. Which gamble is the decision-maker's choice? In order to answer this question, the utility for each monetary value is obtained from Figure 14-1 and the expected utility for each gamble is calculated in the following manner.

$$E[U(A)] = .8U(\$200,000) + .2U(\$O)$$
$$= .8(72) + .2(0) = 57.6 \text{ utiles.}$$
$$E[U(B)] = .7U(\$400,000) + .3U(-\$100,000)$$
$$= .7(97) + .3(-100) = 37.9 \text{ utiles.}$$

In this case, Gamble A is the decision-maker's choice since its expected utility is the largest.

TABLE 14-2
Gambles (Example 14-1)

Gamble A		Gamble B	
$200,000	$p_1 = .8$	$400,000	$p_2 = .7$
$0	$(1-p_1) = .2$	-$100,000	$(1-p_2) = .3$

A Comment In Example 14-1, Gamble A is specified on the basis of its having the higher expected utility. This is a basic premise in N-M utility theory. That is, decision-makers maximize utility and not expected values. For, if expected values are maximized, the decision is Gamble B since its expected value is the largest as shown in the following calculations.

$$E(A) = .8(200,000) + .2(0) = \$160,000$$
$$E(B) = .7(400,000) + .3(-100,000) = \$250,000.$$

It should be remembered that N-M utility theory not only considers the probabilities involved in gambles but also implies a consideration of the magnitude of the involved monetary values. As an example, suppose the monetary values in Table 14-2 are all divided by ten and the probabilities remain the same. Then, the expected utilities for each gamble using Figure 14-1 are

$E[U(A)] = .8U(\$20,000) + .2U(\$0)$
$= .8(11) + (.2) (0) = 8.8$ utiles
$E[U(B)] = .7U(\$40,000) + 3(-\$10,000)$ a
$= .7(22) + .3(-12) = 11.8$ utiles

which indicates that Gamble B is selected and also points out that the magnitudes of the monetary values are an important factor in the decision process as well as the probabilities.

Example 14-2 _____

A project has the estimated cash flows shown in Table 14-3. Assuming the decision-maker's utility function is given by Figure 14-1 and the minimum acceptable rate of return is 12%, determine if the project is acceptable.

This problem is basically a "decision tree" problem. The decision tree is shown in Figure 14-2 where the numbers refer to a particular branch. In order to determine if the project is acceptable, the net present values and probabilities for each branch are calculated. These values are shown in Table 14-4 and are calculated in the following manner. For branch 1, the net present value is

$NPV_1 = -400,000 + 300,000(PF\ 12,1) + 400,000(PF\ 12,2) = \$186,750$

and the probability is

$$(0.3)(0.3)(1) = .09.$$

TABLE 14-3
Cash Flows (Example 14-2)

End of Year	Cash Flow	Probability
0	-$400,000	1.0
1	300,000	0.3
	200,000	0.5
	100,000	0.2
2	400,000	0.3
	300,000	0.4
	250,000	0.3

FIGURE 14-2
A Decision Tree
(Example 14-2)

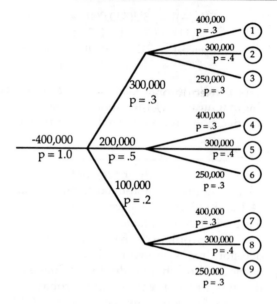

TABLE 14-4
NPV and Expected Utility
(Example 14-2)

Branch	Net Present Value	Utility	Probability	Expected Utility
1	186,750	70	0.09	6.30
2	107,030	52	0.12	6.24
3	67,170	35	0.09	3.15
4	97,460	48	0.15	7.20
5	17,740	10	0.20	2.00
6	-22,120	-15	0.15	-2.25
7	8,170	5	0.06	0.30
8	-71,550	-45	0.08	-3.60
9	-111,410	-75	0.06	-4.50
				$\Sigma = 14.84$

The utility for each net present value shown in Table 14-4 is determined using Figure 14-1. The expected utility for each branch is determined by multiplying the utility of a branch by the probability of the branch. The sum of the expected utilities, which is the expected utility of the project, is 14.84. This result indicates the project is acceptable since it is greater than the utility of "doing nothing" which is zero.

A Comment   A question can be raised regarding the method used to obtain the solution in Example 14-2. Namely, is it correct to use discounted future monetary values in order to obtain the utility of the project since N-M utility theory is based on probabilistic gains in the present-time? The answer to this question is yes, provided it is assumed that the discount rate is a constant over time. With this assumption, equivalent amounts are obtained and the variation in net present values is only a result of the changes in the cash flows from predicted values. This assumption of a constant discount rate is made in future discussions of N-M utility theory.

SHAPES OF UTILITY FUNCTIONS

A utility function can have a different shape than that shown in Figure 14-1. Some of the reported shapes are shown in Figure 14-3.

FIGURE 14-3
Shapes of Utility Functions

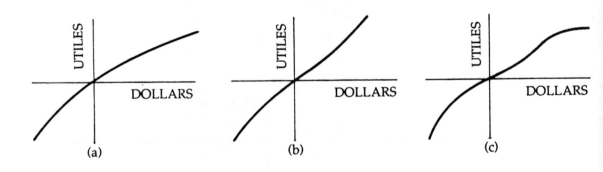

(a)   (b)   (c)

There is experimental evidence (see Grayson [8] and Swalm [14]) of the existence of shapes shown in Figures 14-3a and 14-3b. Friedman and Savage [7] demonstrated and Markowitz [10] argued the existence of the complex utility function shown in Figure 14-3c. No one shape can be said to be more correct than another since utility theory does not specify any particular form for a utility function. The "correct" shape is strictly dependent upon an individual's risk attitudes. However, at this point, one generalization can be made about utility functions and this is shown in Figure 14-3; namely, the slope of the utility function must be greater than zero. In other words, there is always greater utility for greater amounts of money. All of the curves in Figure 14-3 pass through the origin. This is not a requirement for a utility function. Although it is, perhaps, more convenient from a decision standpoint; namely, a project is acceptable if it has a positive utility. Otherwise, the utility of a project must be compared with the alternative of doing nothing ($0) (see Figure 14-4). Of course, any utility function can be made to pass through the origin, without loss of generality, by translating the axes. Since, as mentioned previously, utility is measured on a relative scale.

The shape of the utility function in a particular monetary range determines expression of whether a decision-maker has a risk preference or risk aversion. For example, in Figure 14-5,

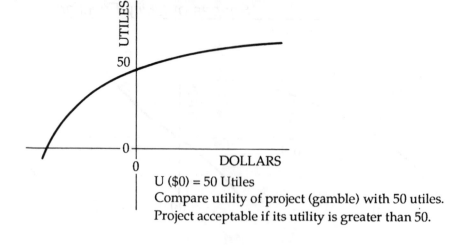

FIGURE 14-4
A Utility Function with U(0) ≠ 0

U ($0) = 50 Utiles
Compare utility of project (gamble) with 50 utiles.
Project acceptable if its utility is greater than 50.

FIGURE 14-5
A Utility Function with Risk Preference and Risk Aversion

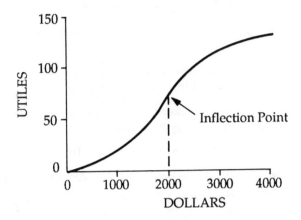

the decision-maker has a risk preference in the monetary range 0 to 2,000 and a risk aversion in the range 2,000 to 4,000 dollars. Risk preference means that the decision-maker prefers a gamble instead of an amount for certain (p = 1.0) that is equal to the expected value of the gamble. For example, using the utility function shown in Figure 14-5, the decision-maker prefers the gamble

$2,000   p = 0.6
$1,000   p = .4

to a certainty amount of

2,000(.6) + 1,000(.4) = $1,600.

Since the utility of the gamble is

U = .6 U($2,000) + .4U($1,000)
= .6(60) + .4(15) = 42 utiles

and the utility of $1,600 is 35 utiles. In other words, the decision-maker desires to take the gamble in the hope that things will "go well" and that a $2,000 gain will be realized even though the probability of this is 0.6. For risk aversion, the converse of this is true. That is, the decision-maker prefers the certainty amount. For example, given the gamble

> 4,000   p = .6
> 2,000   p = .4

the decision-maker prefers the amount

$$4,000(.6) + 2,000(.4) = \$3,200$$

to the gamble since the utility of \$3,200 is 117 utiles and the utility of the gamble is only

$$U = .6\ U(\$4,000) + .4U(\$2,000)$$
$$= .6\ (125) + .4(60) = 99\ \text{utiles}.$$

A decision-maker's risk premium, RP, can be expressed by a dollar amount using the equation

$$RP = (\text{expected monetary value}) - (\text{monetary equivalent}) \qquad (14\text{-}2)$$

For example, in the preceding two cases the risk premiums are

$$RP = 1,600 - 1,700 = -\$100$$
$$RP = 3,200 - 2,600 = \$600$$

Where the \$1,700 and \$2,600 values are obtained from Figure 14-5 using, respectively, 42 and 99 utiles. A negative result in Eq. (14-2) indicates risk preference while a positive result indicates risk aversion.

Consideration of Eq. (14-2) leads to the fact that a linear utility function results in the maximization of expected values since the risk premium is zero. That is, the utility for a gamble and the utility for the expected amount of the gamble are equal. For example, consider the gamble

> 2,000   p = .6
> 1,000   p = .4

and the utility function given in Figure 14-6. The expected value of the gamble is

$$E(G) = 2,000\ (.6) + 1,000\ (.4) = \$1,600$$

and the expected utility of the gamble is

$$E[U(G)] = .6(60) + .4(30) = 48\ \text{utiles}.$$

Therefore, the risk premium using Eq. (14-2) is

$$RP = 1,600 - 1,600 = 0.$$

FIGURE 14-6
A Linear Utility Function

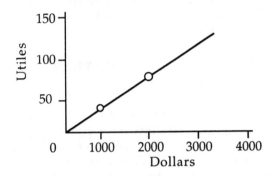

The inflection point in Figure 14-5 is described by Siegel [12] as an individual's level of aspiration. That is, the individual feels unsuccessful when less than this amount of money ($2,000 in Figure 14-5) is received and feels successful if more than this amount is received.

Some Comments   At this point, some additional comments are required regarding N-M utility theory. First, there are more uses of N-M utility theory than those just described. These additional uses are presented in a later section.

Although the assumptions underlying N-M utility theory may appear to be "innocent" there are many questions regarding its basis and practical use. N-M utility theory does assume that people are rational beings. Is this true? There are some who question this basic assumption. Once a utility function is established, does it change with the passage of time? Intuitively, it appears that it would. For if a decision-maker has made favorable decisions in the past, there may be a tendency to take more risks now and in the future. Conversely, if there have been some bad decisions in the past, there may be a tendency to become more conservative (risk averse).

Another point, a utility function is not, necessarily, a normative function; that is, it shows how an individual makes decisions not how the individual *should* make decisions. Also, an individual's utility function may or may not agree with a company's or a group's (stockholders) utility function. This brings up another question. Can an individual with one utility function be trained to use another's utility function?

Despite these questions and reservations, this text takes the point of view that the N-M utility theory is an important topic in the study of economic analysis. For, it does provide an understanding of how decisions are made and how decisions will be made under conditions of risk.

MATHEMATICAL APPROXIMATIONS OF UTILITY FUNCTIONS

Previously, an example is given for the construction of a utility function. This example uses five points joined by a "free-hand" curve. This is the approach used by some of the earlier investigators such as Grayson [8] and Swalm [14]. Another approach is to simply hypothesize an expected utility function. For example, one that is sometimes suggested is

$$E(U) = \mu - A\sigma^2 \tag{14-3}$$

where,

$$
\begin{array}{ll}
E(U) & = \text{expected utility} \\
\mu & = \text{expected return} \\
\sigma^2 & = \text{variance of the return} \\
A & = \text{a positive constant (sometimes called a coefficient} \\
& \quad \text{of risk aversion)}
\end{array}
$$

A third approach is to approximate a utility function with some mathematical function. Representing utility functions in this manner are considered approximations because some mathematical functions do not exhibit the requirements of a positive slope in all monetary ranges. Also, utility theory does not provide, as previously mentioned, any mathematical function that is theoretically correct. Consequently, the procedure is to assume some mathematical function that seems to best fit the data. Four mathematical functions are considered in this section: (1) a parabola, (2) negative exponential, (3) a third degree polynomial, and (4) a fourth degree polynomial.

A Parabola   Suppose it is decided to represent a utility function by the parabola

$$U = AX^2 + BX \tag{14-4}$$

where,

X = the return (a random variable)

A,B = constants

Eq. (14-4) assumes the utility function passes through the origin. This can be accomplished by defining $U = 0$ at $X = 0$. As mentioned earlier, this results in no loss of generality.

Since N-M utility theory assumes the maximization of *expected* utility, the expected value of Eq. (14-4) is needed. Therefore, taking the expected value of Eq. (14-4) gives

$$E(U) = AE(X^2) + BE(X). \qquad (14\text{-}5)$$

Now, the expected value of the random variable X is the mean.

$$E(X) = \mu \qquad (14\text{-}6)$$

Also, the definition of the variance is

$$\sigma^2 = E(X^2) - \mu^2 \qquad (14\text{-}7)$$

and, consequently,

$$E(X^2) = \sigma^2 + \mu^2. \qquad (14\text{-}8)$$

Substituting Eqs. (14-6) and (14-8) into Eq. (14-5) gives

$$E(U) = A(\sigma^2 + \mu^2) + B\mu. \qquad (14\text{-}9)$$

Eq. (14-9) gives the expected utility of the random return X when the utility function is assumed to be a parabola.

FIGURE 14-7
A Parabolic Utility Function

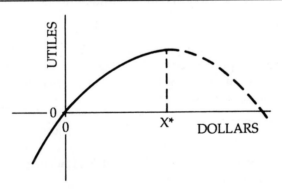

In order to be a valid utility function, Eq. (14-4) must possess certain characteristics. Namely, it must be concave with respect to the abscissa as shown in Figure 14-7.

For if it were convex, this would imply an increasing utility for decreasing monetary returns; which, of course, is not reasonable. Since Eq. (14-4) must be concave, this requires that A and B in Eq. (14-4) must be, respectively, negative and positive. These coefficients are determined from a regression analysis of the responses given by the decision-maker to a series of proposed gambles.

Figure (14-7) also implies that the use of a quadratic to approximate a utility function is limited to a particular range of monetary values. Since, for values greater than X* (shown in Figure 14-7) the utility function has a negative slope. This is contrary to the basic requirement that a utility function must increase with increasing monetary returns. The value of X* is obtained by differentiating Eq. (14-4) and setting the derivation equal to zero. That is,

$$X^* = \frac{B}{2A} \tag{14-10}$$

It should be noted that the use of a quadratic to represent a utility function implies risk-avoidance in the entire range of monetary returns.

A Negative Exponential   Freund [6] uses a negative exponential to approximate a utility function and thus avoids the limiting problem involved with a parabolic approximation. Mathematically, Freund's utility function is

$$U = 1 - e^{-AX} \tag{14-11}$$

where A is a positive constant. Eq. (14-11) is shown in Figure 14-8 and implies risk-aversion over the entire monetary range.

Freund states that Eq. (14-11) leads to an expected utility function of the form

$$E(U) = \mu - \frac{A}{2}\sigma^2 \tag{14-12}$$

based on the assumption that X is normally distributed. Bussey [3] derives the expression

FIGURE 14-8
An Exponential Utility Function

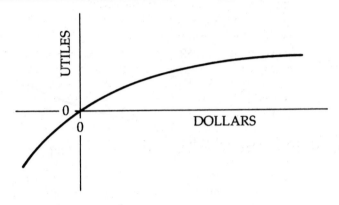

$$E(U) = 1 - \exp[-(A\mu - \frac{A^2\sigma^2}{2})]$$ (14-13)

from Eq. (14-11) and shows that Freund's form, Eq. (14-12), leads to the same relative ranking of choices. However when the expected utility of a particular project is desired, it is best to use Eq. (14-13).

A Cubic Polynomial   A cubic polynomial of the form

$$U = AX^3 + BX^2 + CX$$ (14-14)

was proposed as an approximation for a utility function in 1969 by Levy (8). This approximation allows for both risk-preference and risk-avoidance as shown in Figure 14-9. Now in order to define an expected utility criterion, the expected value of Eq. (14-13) is taken with the result

$$E(U) = AE(X^3) + BE(X^2) + CE(X).$$ (14-15)

The third moment of a random variable, M_3, is defined as

$$M_3 = E(X^3) - 3E(X^2)E(X) + 2[E(X)]^3.$$ (14-15)

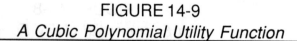

FIGURE 14-9
A Cubic Polynomial Utility Function

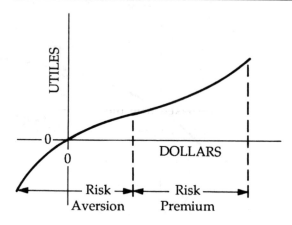

Substituting Eqs. (14-6) and (14-8) into Eq. (14-16) and rearranging gives

$$E(X^3) = M_3 + 3(\mu^2 + \sigma^2)\mu - 2\mu^3 = M_3 + 3\sigma^2\mu + \mu^3. \qquad (14\text{-}18)$$

Substituting Eqs. (14—6), (14-8) and (14-17) into Eq. (14-15) gives the expected utility as

$$E(U) = A(M_3 + 3\sigma^2\mu + \mu^3) + B(\mu^2 + \sigma^2) + C\mu. \qquad (14\text{-}18)$$

In order for a cubic polynomial to be a valid approximation for a utility function, the following conditions for the coefficients must be satisfied [2][9].

1. The values of A and C must be positive.
2. The value of B must be negative.
3. The inequality $B^2 < 3AC$ must be satisfied.

A Quartic Polynomial The use of a cubic polynomial to approximate a utility function implies a risk-preference in the area of large monetary values (see Figure 14-9). Intuitively, at least, this might seem doubtful. For, it might be more reasonable to expect a decision-maker to become a risk-avoider when monetary values become large and the level of aspiration (see Figure 14-5) has been reached. This point is suggested by Markowitz [10], Chernoff and Moses [5], and Siegel [12]. As a result, Stevens and Bussey [13] suggest the use of a quartic polynomial as an approximation for a utility function which they later use to solve a capital budgeting problem [4].

The use of a quartic polynomial as proposed by Stevens and Bussey [14] implies a utility function of the form

$$U = AX^4 + BX^3 + CX^2 + DX. \tag{14-19}$$

In order to define an expected utility function, the expected value of Eq. (14-18) is taken with the result

$$E(U) = AE(X^4) + BE(X^3) + CE(X^2) + DE(X). \tag{14-20}$$

The fourth moment, M4, is defined by

$$M_4 = E(X^4) - 4E(X^3)E(X) + 6E(X^2)[E(X)]^2 - 3(E(X))^4 \tag{14-21}$$

Substituting Eqs. (14-17), (14-8), and (14-6) into Eq. (14-21) and simplifying gives

$$E(X^4) = M_4 + 4\mu M_3 + 6\sigma^2\mu^2 + \mu^4. \tag{14-22}$$

Substituting Eqs. (14-6), (14-8), (14-17), and (14-22) in Eq. (14-20) gives as the expected utility function

$$E(U) = A(M_4 + 4\mu M_3 + 6\sigma^2\mu^2 + \mu^4)$$
$$+ B(M_3 + 3\sigma^2\mu + \mu^3) + C(\sigma^2 + \mu^2) + D\mu. \tag{14-23}$$

In order for Eq. (14-19) to be a valid utility function it must have the following characteristics [13]:

1. The coefficients B and D must be positive.
2. The coefficients A and C must be negative.

With these requirements, this implies the utility function shown in Figure 14-10. This figure also implies a limitation in the use of a quartic polynomial as an approximation of a utility function. That is, after the point X^*, the approximation is not valid since the slope is negative. This value (X^*) is obtained by taking the first derivation of Eq. (14-19), setting it equal to zero, and finding the positive root.

Figure 14-10 shows that a quartic approximation provides for risk avoidance in the negative return range up to X_1, risk preference in the range of X_1 to x X_2 and risk avoidance in the range X_2 to X^*.

FIGURE 14-10
A Quartic Utility Function

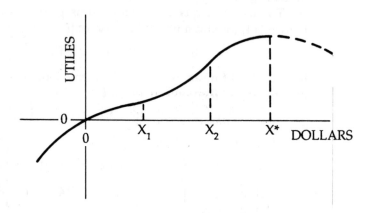

DEFINITION OF A RETURN

In the previous discussions of approximations for utility functions, the random variable X is defined as a monetary return. In terms of project selection and capital budgeting problems the definition of a return must be more specific. This text takes the point of view that the random variable for purposes of project selection and capital budgeting problems is the net present value. Consequently, the mean, variance, and higher moments involved in the expected utility functions are the moments of the net present value distribution.

SOME USES OF UTILITY FUNCTIONS

Once the points for a utility function are determined as a result of a decision-maker's replies to series of proposed gambles, a mathematical function that seems to describe the data is hypothesized. Then, the coefficients for the utility function are determined using regressions analysis. In turn, these coefficients can be used to completely specify the expected utility function.

With the expected utility function completely defined, it is a relatively simple matter to determine the acceptability of a single project (investment). All that is required is to substitute the required moments into the expected utility function and if the expected utility is positive, the project is acceptable. This assumes the utility function passes through the origin. If the utility function does not pass through the origin, the expected utility of the project must be greater than the utility of doing nothing ($0) in order to be acceptable.

In the case of a set of mutually exclusive projects, the project with the highest expected utility is the choice. Provided, of course, the utility of the chosen project is greater than that of doing nothing. Some problems are given at the end of this chapter which demonstrate these uses. Utility theory can also be used as a basis for solutions to capital budgeting problems. This extension is left as an exercise (see Problem 14-9).

REFERENCES

Bernoulli, Daniel, "Exposition of a New Theory of the Measurement of Risk," *Econometrica*, 1954, pp. 23-36.

Bussey, Lynn, E. , "Capital Budgeting Project Analysis and Selection with Complex Utility Functions," Unpublished Ph.D. Dissertation, Oklahoma State University, Stillwater, Oklahoma, 1970.

Bussey, Lynn, E., *The Economic Analysis of Industrial Projects*, Prentice-Hall, Inc., Englewood Cliffs, N. J., 1978.

Bussey, Lynn, E., and G. T. Stevens, Jr., "A Solution Methodology for Probabilistic Capital Budgeting Using Complex Utility Functions," *The Engineering Economist*, 21(2) 1975, pp. 89-109.

Chernoff, H. and L. E. Moses, *Elementary Decision Theory*, John Wiley & Sons, New York, NY, 1959.

Freund, Rudolf J., "The Introduction of Risk into a Programming Model," *Econometrica*, 24(3), July 1956, pp. 253-263.

Friedman, Milton, and L. J. Savage, "The Utility Analysis of Choices Involving Risk", *Journal of Political Economy*, Apr, 1948, pp. 279-304.

Grayson, C. Jackson, Jr., *Decisions Under Uncertainty: Drilling Decisions by Oil and Gas Operators*, Division of Research, Graduate School of Business Administration, Harvard University, Boston, Mass., 1960.

Levy, H., "A Utility Function Depending on the First Three Moments," *The Journal of Finance*, Sept. 1969, pp. 715-720.

Markowitz, Harry M., *Portfolio Selection: Efficient Diversification of Investments*, Cowles Foundation Monograph, 16, John Wiley & Sons, New York, NY, 1959.

Neumann, John von and Oskar Morgenstern, *Theory of Games and Economic Behavior*, 2nd Ed., University Press Princeton, NJ, 1947.

Siegel, Sidney, "Level of Aspiration and Decision Making," *Psychological Review*, 64, 1957, pp. 253-262.

Stevens, Jr., G. T., and Lynn E. Bussey, "Quartic Polynomials as Approximations to Complex Utility Functions: A Technical Note," *The Engineering Economist.* 19(2), 1974, pp. 127-138.

Swalm, Ralph O., "Utility Theory: Insights into Risk Taking," *Harvard Business Review*, Nov.-Dec., 1966.

PROBLEMS

14-1 A decision-maker's utility function is defined by the following points.

Dollars	Utilities
300,000	90
200,000	80
100,000	60
50,000	40
20,000	20
0	0
-10,000	-20
-40,000	-100
-50,000	-150

Plot the decision-maker's utility function and answer the following questions.

(a) Over what range of monetary values is the decision-maker a risk-taker or risk-avoider?

(b) Given the gambles below, which one would the decision-maker choose?

	Gamble A		Gamble B	
	100,000	p = .5	250,000	p = .7
	20,000	p = .5	-30,000	p = .3

(c)   In Part b, if the decision-maker has a linear utility function, which gamble would be the choice?

14-2   A decision-maker's utility function is given by the following points.

Dollars	Utiles
200,000	38
125,000	36
100,000	33
75,000	28
55,000	20
37,500	10
20,000	4
0	0
-5,000	-1
-15,000	-5
-20,000	-8
-25,000	-12
-35,000	-20
-42,500	-30

Plot the decision-maker's utility function and answer the following questions.
(a)   Over what range of monetary values is the decision-maker a risk-taker or risk-avoider?
(b)   Estimate the decision-maker's "level of aspiration."
(c)   Given the gambles shown below, which one would the decision-maker choose?

Gamble A		Gamble B		Gamble C	
$80,000	p=.5	$125,000	p=.5	$200,000	p=.6
30,000	p=.3	0	p=.5	-25,000	p=.4
-15,000	p=.2				

(d)   In Part c if the decision-maker has a linear utility function, which gamble would be the choice?

14-3 If the following two set points have been established for a utility function

Dollars	Utiles
$0	0
$100,000	50

Answer the following questions:
a) What question would you propose to determine a decision-maker's utility for $25,000?
b) What question would you propose to determine a decision-maker's utility for a loss of $50,000?

14-4 Using the utility function given in Problem 14-2, what is a decision-maker's risk premium for the following gambles
a) $55,000   p=.5
   $ 0   p=.5
b) $200,000   p=.4
   20,000   p=.6
Which premiums show a risk preference (aversion)?

14-5 If a project has the estimated cash flows shown below, determine if the project is acceptable using the utility function given in Problem 14-2 and a discount rate of 10%.

End of Year	Cash Flow	Probability
0	-100,000	p = .3
	-120,000	p = .7
1	120,000	p = .8
	0	p = .2
2	100,000	p = .5
	150,000	p = .5

14-6 The simulation of a project (capital expenditure) has given the following distribution of net present value (NPV).

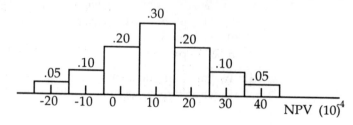

It has been determined that a decision-maker's utility function is a parabola of the form

$$U = -0.05X^2 + 5.5X$$

where X is in dollars multiplied by 10^{-4}. Determine the decision-maker's expected utility for the project.

14-7 Repeat Problem 14-6 using the following utility function

$$U = 1 - e^{-.5(10)^{-5}x}$$

14-8 The simulation of a particular capital investment has resulted in the distribution of NPV shown below:

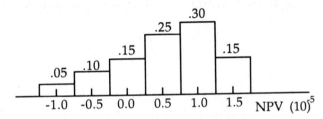

If the decision-maker's expected utility function is

$$U = -0.1X^4 + 2.5X^3 - 20X^2 + 50X$$

where X is dollars times 10^{-5}, determine:
(a) the decision-maker's expected utility for this particular capital investment.
(b) is the investment acceptable to the decision-maker?

14-9 Four projects have the following data:

Project	$E(NPV)(10)^{-5}$	$V(NPV)10^{-10}$	$M_3(10)^{-15}$	$M_4(10)^{-20}$
1	0.55	0.4725	-0.126	0.1685
2	1.00	0.5200	0.000	3.0000
3	0.75	0.3200	0.150	1.2000
4	1.50	0.6200	0.000	1.4000

Using the utility function given in Problem 14-8, determine the following:
(a) Which project will be selected if the projects are mutually exclusive?

(b) Which projects will be picked if the projects are independent?

(c) The capital expenditures associated with each project are deterministic with values of $K_1 = \$10(10)^6$, $K_2 = \$15(10)^6$, $K_3 = \$8(10)^6$, and $K_4 = \$6(10)^6$ and there is a limit on the amount of money that can be spent on capital expenditures (a budget restriction) of $\$25(10)^6$. Assuming the projects are independent, which ones will be selected?

15

DECISIONS UNDER UNCERTAINTY

This chapter considers various criteria for making choices under conditions of uncertainty. The basic difference between decisions under risk and uncertainty is that with uncertainty the probabilities of outcomes cannot be estimated. The various criteria are presented in the following discussion.

THE MAXIMIN OR MINIMAX

The basic difference between the maximin or minimax depends on whether the outcomes of the alternatives are incomes (returns, profits, revenues) or outflows (costs). If they are incomes, the maximin criterion is appropriate. If they are costs, the minimax is appropriate. In either case, these criteria are pessimistic and conservative.

For the maximin criterion, the smallest return for each alternative is compared and from these values the alternative with the highest value is selected. Mathematically, the maximin criterion can be expressed as

$$(\max)_i \, [(\min)_j, P_{ij}] \tag{15-1}$$

The nomenclature used in Eq. (15-1) is shown in Table 15-1.

TABLE 15-1
General Form for Contingencies and Alternatives

Alt.	Contingency					
	1	2	.	.	.	*j*
1	P_{11}	P_{23}	.	.	.	P_{1j}
2	P_{21}	P_{22}	.	.	.	P_{2j}
.	.	.	.	.	.	.
.	.	.	.	.	.	.
.	.	.	.	.	.	.
i	P_{i1}	P_{i2}	.	.	.	P_{ij}

This table shows that there are i alternatives and j contingencies. The P_{ji} term in this table implies that if alternative i is picked and if contingency j occurs, the outcome is P_{ij}.

Example 15-1 _____

Suppose the values in Table 15-2 represent net present values for four alternatives under three contingencies. Determine the alternative that is chosen under the maximin criterion. Using Eq. (15-1) the smallest j values for each alternative are

Alt.	
1	20
2	21
3	19
4	18

Therefore, the choice is alternative 2 (the maximum i value). If there is a tie at this point, either alternative is the choice.

The minimax criterion is the reverse of the maximin criterion and is expressed mathematically by Eq. (15-2)

$$(\min)_i \, [(\max)_j, C_{ij}] \tag{15-2}$$

where the C_{ij} term represents the cost of alternative i if contingency j occurs. The use of Eq. (15-2) is shown in the next example.

TABLE 15-2
Present Values
(Example 15-1)

Alt.	Contingency 1	2	3
1	20	23	25
2	21	26	22
3	24	22	19
4	18	28	21

Example 15-2 _____

If the values in Table 15-3 represent costs, determine which

TABLE 15-3
Cost Values
(Example 15-2)

Alt.	Contingency 1	2	3	4
1	200	100	150	250
2	190	180	220	200
3	150	200	125	270

alternative is selected under the minimax criterion. Using Eq. (15-2), the maximum j values are

Alt.	
1	250
2	220
3	270

Therefore, the choice is alternative 2 (the minimum i value).

THE MAXIMAX OR MINIMIN

Each of these criterion is based on complete optimism. The maximax criterion is expressed mathematically as

$$(\max)_i \, [(\max)_j, P_{ij}] \qquad (15\text{-}3)$$

The use of Eq. (15-3) is shown in the next example.

Example 15-3

Using the data in Example 15-1, what alternative is selected using the maximax criterion?

Using Eq. (15-3), the largest j value is chosen for each alternative giving the results

Alt.	
1	25
2	26
3	24
4	28

Therefore, the choice is alternative 4 (the maximum i value).

The minimum criterion is used for costs and is the reverse of the maximax criterion. It is expressed mathematically as

$$(\min)_i \, [(\min)_j , C_{ij}] \qquad (15\text{-}4)$$

The use of Eq. (15-4) is shown in the next example.

Example 15-4

Using the data in Example 15-2, what alternative is selected using the minimum criterion. Applying Eq. (15-4) to the data in Table 15-3, the minimum j values for each alternative are

Alt.	
1	100
2	180
3	125

Therefore, the choice is alternative 1 (the minimum i value).

THE HURWICZ PRINCIPLE

This criterion is sometimes called the maxim or minim depending on whether returns or costs are involved. It allows for the selection of an alternative between the position of complete pessimism (maximin/minimax) and complete optimism (maximax/minimin).

For incomes (returns), the Hurwicz principle is expressed mathematically as

$$H_i = \beta[(\max)_j , P_{ij}] + (1\text{-}\beta) \, [(\min)_j , P_{ij}] \qquad (15\text{-}5)$$

where $0 \le \beta \le 1$ and β is an index that reflects an attitude between pessimism and optimism. A β value of zero is extreme pessimism and a β value of one is extreme optimism. For costs, the Hurwicz principle is expressed as

$$H(i) = \beta\,[(min)_j\,,C_{ij}] + (1-\beta)[(max)_j,\,C_{ij}] \qquad (15\text{-}6)$$

The use of Eqs. (15-5) and (15-6) is shown in the next example.

Example 15-5

Using the Hurwicz principle, determine the selected alternative if (a) the data in Example 15-1 is used ($\beta = 0.4$) and (b) the data in Example 15-2 is used ($\beta = .4$).

For part (a), Eq. (15-5) gives

$$H_1 = (.4)(25) + (.6)(20) = 22.0$$
$$H_2 = (.4)(26) + (.6)(21) = 23.0$$
$$H_3 = (.4)(24) + (.6)(19) = 21.0$$
$$H_4 = (.4)(28) + (.6)(18) = 22.0$$

and selecting the largest value, alternative 2 is the solution.

For Part (b), Eq. (15-6) gives

$$H_1 = (.4)(100) + (.6)(250) = 190$$
$$H_2 = (.4)(180) + (.6)(220) = 204$$
$$H_3 = (.4)(125) + (.6)(270) = 212$$

Identifying the smallest value, alternative 1 is selected.

THE LAPLACE PRINCIPLE

This criterion assumes that the probabilities of the contingencies are equal. It is sometimes referred to as the principle of insufficient reason. For revenues (incomes), this criterion is

$$(max)_i\,[\frac{1}{k}\sum_{j=1}^{k} P_{ij}] \qquad (15\text{-}7)$$

where k is the number of contingencies (future events) Eq. (15-7) is the expected value and, consequently, the alternative with the largest value is selected.

For costs, the Laplace principle is

$$(\min)_i \left[\frac{1}{k}\sum_{j=1}^{k} C_{ij}\right]$$

(15-8)

and the alternative with the smallest value is selected. The application of Eqs. (15-7) and (15-8) is shown in the next example.

Example 15-6 _____

Using the Laplace principle, determine the selected alternative if (a) the data in Example 15-1 is used and (b) the data in Example 15-2 is used.

For Part (a), the expected values of the alternatives are

$E_1 = 1/3\ (20 + 23 + 25) = 22.67$
$E_2 = 1/3\ (21 + 26 + 22) = 23.00$
$E_3 = 1/3\ (24 + 22 + 19) = 21.67$
$E_4 = 1/3\ (18 + 28 + 21) = 22.33$

Since alternative 2 has the highest value, it is selected. For Part (b), the expected values are

$E_1 = 1/4\ (200 + 100 + 150 + 250) = 175.00$
$E_2 = 1/4\ (190 + 180 + 220 + 200) = 197.50$
$E_3 = 1/4\ (150 + 200 + 125 + 270) = 186.25$

Since alternative 1 has the lowest value, it is selected.

THE MINIMAX REGRET

This criterion is sometimes called the Savage Principle. It is based on the assumption that the *difference* between the actual outcome and the outcome that would have occurred, if the future (contingency) was known with certainty, is the primary concern. The first step for the criterion is to convert the values in the income or cost matrix to regret values. This is accomplished by using Eq. (15-9) for income values and Eq. (15-10) for cost values

$$[(\max)_i, P_{ij}] - P_{ij}$$

(15-9)

$$C_{ij} - [(\min)_i, C_{ij}]$$

(15-10)

Once a regret matrix has been the determined, Eq. (15-11)is used to select an alternative on the basis of incomes. Eq. (15-12) is used for cost data.

$$(\min)_i(\max)_j \{[(\max)_i, P_{ij}] - P_{ij}\} \qquad (15\text{-}11)$$
$$(\min)_i(\max)_j \{C_{ij} - [(\min)_i, C_{ij}]\} \qquad (15\text{-}12)$$

The application of these equations is shown in the following example.

Example 15-7 _____

Using the minimax regret criterion, determine the selected alternative for (a) the data in Example 15-1 and (b) the data in Example 15-2.

For part (a), the determination of the regret matrix is shown in Table 15-4. The largest values in Table 15-4 for each alternative are

Alt.	
1	5
2	3
3	6
4	6

Consequently, alternative 2 is selected since it has the smallest value (minimum regret).

For Part (b), the regret matrix is shown in Table 15-5. The largest values for each alternative are

Alt.	
1	50
2	95
3	100

Therefore, the selection is alternative 1 since it has the smallest value (minimum regret).

TABLE 15-4
Regret Matrix for Income (Example 15-7)

Alt.	Contingency 1	2	3
1	24-20=4	28-23=5	25-25=0
2	24-21=3	28-26=2	25-22=3
3	24-24=0	28-22=6	25-19=6
4	24-18=6	28-28=0	25-21=4

TABLE 15-5
Regret Matrix for Costs (Example 15-7)

Alt.	Contingency			
	1	2	3	4
1	200-150=50	100-100=0	150-125=25	250-200=50
2	190-150=40	180-100=80	220-125=95	200-200=0
3	150-150=0	200-100=100	125-125=0	270-200=70

There is an inconsistency when using the minimax regret criterion. That is, the selected alternative can change for a particular set of values when another alternative is added. *Even though, the added alternative is not the selected alternative.* For example, if a fifth alternative is added to Table 15-2 with the contingency values of 24, 34, and 18, the regret matrix changes to Table 15-6 and Alternative 4 is selected.

TABLE 15-6
Addition of Alternative to Table 15-2

Alt.	Contingency			
	1	2	3	Max j
1	24-20=4	34-23=11	25-25=0	11
2	24-21=3	34-26=8	25-22=3	8
3	24-24=0	34-22=12	25-19=6	12
4	24-18=6	34-28=6	25-21=4	6
5	24-24=0	34-34=0	25-18=7	7

The point is, the selected project has been changed from alternative 2 to 4 by adding a new alternative that is not the selected alternative.

Some Comments It is pointed out that there is no requirement that various criterion give the same selection of an alternative. Different criterion will give different solutions. Also, there is no simple answer to the question, which criterion is correct? However, a consideration of the various criterion gives some insight to the decision process.

PROBLEMS

15-1 Assuming the values given in the following matrix are revenues (incomes), determine the alternative that would be selected under the following criteria: (a) maximin, (b) maximax, (c) Hurwicz ($\beta=0.4$), (d) Laplace, and (e) minimax regret

Alt.	Contingency				
	1	2	3	4	5
1	152	220	140	128	180
2	170	125	135	162	195
3	148	171	158	136	218
4	169	179	145	183	163

15-2 Assuming the values (given in the following matrix are costs, determine the alternative that would be selected under the following criteria: (a) minimax, (b) minimin, (c) Hurwicz ($\beta=0.6$), (d) Laplace, and (e) minimax regret

Alt.	Contingency			
	1	2	3	4
1	100	128	95	115
2	108	118	120	100
3	88	120	107	122
4	98	112	130	98
5	118	100	125	106

15-3 Assuming the values given in the following matrix are revenues, determine the alternative that would be selected under the following criteria: (a) maximin, (b) maximax, Hurwicz ($\beta = .4$), (d) Laplace, and (e) minimax regret

Alt.	Contingency		
	1	2	3
1	5	3	0
2	-1	7	2
3	3	4	-2

15-4   Assuming the values given in the following matrix are costs, determine the alternative that would be selected under the following criteria: (a) minimax, (b) minimin, (c) Hurwicz ($\beta = 0.4$), (d) Laplace, and (e) minimax regret.

Alt.	Contingency		
	1	2	3
1	6	3	-2
2	4	0	5
3	-3	1	0

APPENDIX

A

DISCRETE INTEREST FACTORS

Table A.1. $\frac{1}{2}$% Interest Factors for Annual Compounding Interest

	Single Payment		Equal Payment Series				Uniform gradient-series factor
	Compound-amount factor	Present-worth factor	Compound-amount factor	Sinking-fund factor	Present-worth factor	Capital-recovery factor	
n	To find F Given P F/P i,n	To find P Given F P/F i,n	To find F Given A F/A i,n	To find A Given F A/F i,n	To find P Given A P/A i,n	To find A Given P A/P i,n	To find A Given G A/G i,n
1	1.005	0.9950	1.000	1.0000	0.9950	1.0050	0.0000
2	1.010	0.9901	2.005	0.4988	1.9851	0.5038	0.4988
3	1.015	0.9852	3.015	0.3317	2.9703	0.3367	0.9967
4	1.020	0.9803	4.030	0.2481	3.9505	0.2531	1.4938
5	1.025	0.9754	5.050	0.1980	4.9259	0.2030	1.9900
6	1.030	0.9705	6.076	0.1646	5.8964	0.1696	2.4855
7	1.036	0.9657	7.106	0.1407	6.8621	0.1457	2.9801
8	1.041	0.9609	8.141	0.1228	7.8230	0.1278	3.4738
9	1.046	0.9561	9.182	0.1089	8.7791	0.1139	3.9668
10	1.051	0.9514	10.228	0.0978	9.7304	0.1028	4.4589
11	1.056	0.9466	11.279	0.0887	10.6770	0.0937	4.9501
12	1.062	0.9419	12.336	0.0811	11.6189	0.0861	5.4406
13	1.067	0.9372	13.397	0.0747	12.5562	0.0797	5.9302
14	1.072	0.9326	14.464	0.0691	13.4887	0.0741	6.4190
15	1.078	0.9279	15.537	0.0644	14.4166	0.0694	6.9069
16	1.083	0.9233	16.614	0.0602	15.3399	0.0652	7.3940
17	1.088	0.9187	17.697	0.0565	16.2586	0.0615	7.8803
18	1.094	0.9141	18.786	0.0532	17.1728	0.0582	8.3658
19	1.099	0.9096	19.880	0.0503	18.0824	0.0553	8.8504
20	1.105	0.9051	20.979	0.0477	18.9874	0.0527	9.3342
21	1.110	0.9006	22.084	0.0453	19.8880	0.0503	9.8172
22	1.116	0.8961	23.194	0.0431	20.7841	0.0481	10.2993
23	1.122	0.8916	24.310	0.0411	21.6757	0.0461	10.7806
24	1.127	0.8872	25.432	0.0393	22.5629	0.0443	11.2611
25	1.133	0.8828	26.559	0.0377	23.4456	0.0427	11.7407
26	1.138	0.8784	27.692	0.0361	24.3240	0.0411	12.2195
27	1.144	0.8740	28.830	0.0347	25.1980	0.0397	12.6975
28	1.150	0.8697	29.975	0.0334	26.0677	0.0384	13.1747
29	1.156	0.8653	31.124	0.0321	26.9330	0.0371	13.6510
30	1.161	0.8610	32.280	0.0310	27.7941	0.0360	14.1265
31	1.167	0.8568	33.441	0.0299	28.6508	0.0349	14.6012
32	1.173	0.8525	34.609	0.0289	29.5033	0.0339	15.0750
33	1.179	0.8483	35.782	0.0280	30.3515	0.0330	15.5480
34	1.185	0.8440	36.961	0.0271	31.1956	0.0321	16.0202
35	1.191	0.8398	38.145	0.0262	32.0354	0.0312	16.4915
40	1.221	0.8191	44.159	0.0227	36.1722	0.0277	18.8358
45	1.252	0.7990	50.324	0.0199	40.2072	0.0249	21.1595
50	1.283	0.7793	56.645	0.0177	44.1428	0.0227	23.4624
55	1.316	0.7601	63.126	0.0159	47.9815	0.0209	25.7447
60	1.349	0.7414	69.770	0.0143	51.7256	0.0193	28.0064
65	1.383	0.7231	76.582	0.0131	55.3775	0.0181	30.2475
70	1.418	0.7053	83.566	0.0120	58.9394	0.0170	32.4680
75	1.454	0.6879	90.727	0.0110	62.4137	0.0160	34.6679
80	1.490	0.6710	98.068	0.0102	65.8023	0.0152	36.8474
85	1.528	0.6545	105.594	0.0095	69.1075	0.0145	39.0065
90	1.567	0.6384	113.311	0.0088	72.3313	0.0138	41.1451
95	1.606	0.6226	121.222	0.0083	75.4757	0.0133	43.2633
100	1.647	0.6073	129.334	0.0077	78.5427	0.0127	45.3613

G.J. Thuesen/W.J Fabrycky, *Engineering Economy*, 7e, © 1989, pp. 643-698. Reprinted by permission of Prentice-Hall, Inc., Englewood Cliffs, NJ.

Table A.2. $\dfrac{3}{4}$% Interest Factors for Annual Compounding Interest

	Single Payment		Equal Payment Series				Uniform gradient-series factor
	Compound-amount factor	Present-worth factor	Compound-amount factor	Sinking-fund factor	Present-worth factor	Capital-recovery factor	
n	To find F Given P F/P i, n	To find P Given F P/F i, n	To find F Given A F/A i, n	To find A Given F A/F i, n	To find P Given A P/A i, n	To find A Given P A/P i, n	To find A Given G A/G i, n
1	1.008	0.9926	1.000	1.0000	0.9926	1.0075	0.0000
2	1.015	0.9852	2.008	0.4981	1.9777	0.5056	0.4981
3	1.023	0.9778	3.023	0.3309	2.9556	0.3384	0.9950
4	1.030	0.9706	4.045	0.2472	3.9261	0.2547	1.4907
5	1.038	0.9633	5.076	0.1970	4.8894	0.2045	1.9851
6	1.046	0.9562	6.114	0.1636	5.8456	0.1711	2.4782
7	1.054	0.9491	7.159	0.1397	6.7946	0.1472	2.9701
8	1.062	0.9420	8.213	0.1218	7.7366	0.1293	3.4608
9	1.070	0.9350	9.275	0.1078	8.6716	0.1153	3.9502
10	1.078	0.9280	10.344	0.0967	9.5996	0.1042	4.4384
11	1.086	0.9211	11.422	0.0876	10.5207	0.0951	4.9253
12	1.094	0.9142	12.508	0.0800	11.4349	0.0875	5.4110
13	1.102	0.9074	13.601	0.0735	12.3424	0.0810	5.8954
14	1.110	0.9007	14.703	0.0680	13.2430	0.0755	6.3786
15	1.119	0.8940	15.814	0.0632	14.1370	0.0707	6.8606
16	1.127	0.8873	16.932	0.0591	15.0243	0.0666	7.3413
17	1.135	0.8807	18.059	0.0554	15.9050	0.0629	7.8207
18	1.144	0.8742	19.195	0.0521	16.7792	0.0596	8.2989
19	1.153	0.8677	20.339	0.0492	17.6468	0.0567	8.7759
20	1.161	0.8612	21.491	0.0465	18.5080	0.0540	9.2517
21	1.170	0.8548	22.652	0.0442	19.3628	0.0517	9.7261
22	1.179	0.8484	23.822	0.0420	20.2112	0.0495	10.1994
23	1.188	0.8421	25.001	0.0400	21.0533	0.0475	10.6714
24	1.196	0.8358	26.188	0.0382	21.8892	0.0457	11.1422
25	1.205	0.8296	27.385	0.0365	22.7188	0.0440	11.6117
26	1.214	0.8234	28.590	0.0350	23.5422	0.0425	12.0800
27	1.224	0.8173	29.805	0.0336	24.3595	0.0411	12.5470
28	1.233	0.8112	31.028	0.0322	25.1707	0.0397	13.0128
29	1.242	0.8052	32.261	0.0310	25.9759	0.0385	13.4774
30	1.251	0.7992	33.503	0.0299	26.7751	0.0374	13.9407
31	1.261	0.7932	34.754	0.0288	27.5683	0.0363	14.4028
32	1.270	0.7873	36.015	0.0278	28.3557	0.0353	14.8636
33	1.280	0.7815	37.285	0.0268	29.1371	0.0343	15.3232
34	1.289	0.7757	38.565	0.0259	29.9128	0.0334	15.7816
35	1.299	0.7699	39.854	0.0251	30.6827	0.0326	16.2387
40	1.348	0.7417	46.446	0.0215	34.4469	0.0290	18.5058
45	1.400	0.7145	53.290	0.0188	38.0732	0.0263	20.7421
50	1.453	0.6883	60.394	0.0166	41.5665	0.0241	22.9476
55	1.508	0.6630	67.769	0.0148	44.9316	0.0223	25.1223
60	1.566	0.6387	75.424	0.0133	48.1734	0.0208	27.2665
65	1.625	0.6153	83.371	0.0120	51.2963	0.0195	29.3801
70	1.687	0.5927	91.620	0.0109	54.3046	0.0184	31.4634
75	1.751	0.5710	100.183	0.0100	57.2027	0.0175	33.5163
80	1.818	0.5501	109.073	0.0092	59.9945	0.0167	35.5391
85	1.887	0.5299	118.300	0.0085	62.6838	0.0160	37.5318
90	1.959	0.5105	127.879	0.0078	65.2746	0.0153	39.4946
95	2.034	0.4917	137.823	0.0073	67.7704	0.0148	41.4277
100	2.111	0.4737	148.145	0.0068	70.1746	0.0143	43.3311

G.J. Thuesen/W.J Fabrycky, *Engineering Economy*, 7e, © 1989, pp. 643–698.
Reprinted by permission of Prentice-Hall, Inc., Englewood Cliffs, NJ.

Table A.3. 1% Interest Factors for Annual Compounding Interest

	Single Payment		Equal Payment Series				Uniform gradient-series factor
	Compound-amount factor	Present-worth factor	Compound-amount factor	Sinking-fund factor	Present-worth factor	Capital-recovery factor	
n	To find F Given P F/P i,n	To find P Given F P/F i,n	To find F Given A F/A i,n	To find A Given F A/F i,n	To find P Given A P/A i,n	To find A Given P A/P i,n	To find A Given G A/G i,n
1	1.010	0.9901	1.000	1.0000	0.9901	1.0100	0.0000
2	1.020	0.9803	2.010	0.4975	1.9704	0.5075	0.4975
3	1.030	0.9706	3.030	0.3300	2.9410	0.3400	0.9934
4	1.041	0.9610	4.060	0.2463	3.9020	0.2563	1.4876
5	1.051	0.9515	5.101	0.1960	4.8534	0.2060	1.9801
6	1.062	0.9421	6.152	0.1626	5.7955	0.1726	2.4710
7	1.072	0.9327	7.214	0.1386	6.7282	0.1486	2.9602
8	1.083	0.9235	8.286	0.1207	7.6517	0.1307	3.4478
9	1.094	0.9143	9.369	0.1068	8.5660	0.1168	3.9337
10	1.105	0.9053	10.462	0.0956	9.4713	0.1056	4.4179
11	1.116	0.8963	11.567	0.0865	10.3676	0.0965	4.9005
12	1.127	0.8875	12.683	0.0789	11.2551	0.0889	5.3815
13	1.138	0.8787	13.809	0.0724	12.1338	0.0824	5.8607
14	1.149	0.8700	14.947	0.0669	13.0037	0.0769	6.3384
15	1.161	0.8614	16.097	0.0621	13.8651	0.0721	6.8143
16	1.173	0.8528	17.258	0.0580	14.7179	0.0680	7.2887
17	1.184	0.8444	18.430	0.0543	15.5623	0.0643	7.7613
18	1.196	0.8360	19.615	0.0510	16.3983	0.0610	8.2323
19	1.208	0.8277	20.811	0.0481	17.2260	0.0581	8.7017
20	1.220	0.8196	22.019	0.0454	18.0456	0.0554	9.1694
21	1.232	0.8114	23.239	0.0430	18.8570	0.0530	9.6354
22	1.245	0.8034	24.472	0.0409	19.6604	0.0509	10.0998
23	1.257	0.7955	25.716	0.0389	20.4558	0.0489	10.5626
24	1.270	0.7876	26.973	0.0371	21.2434	0.0471	11.0237
25	1.282	0.7798	28.243	0.0354	22.0232	0.0454	11.4831
26	1.295	0.7721	29.526	0.0339	22.7952	0.0439	11.9409
27	1.308	0.7644	30.821	0.0325	23.5596	0.0425	12.3971
28	1.321	0.7568	32.129	0.0311	24.3165	0.0411	12.8516
29	1.335	0.7494	33.450	0.0299	25.0658	0.0399	13.3045
30	1.348	0.7419	34.785	0.0288	25.8077	0.0388	13.7557
31	1.361	0.7346	36.133	0.0277	26.5423	0.0377	14.2052
32	1.375	0.7273	37.494	0.0267	27.2696	0.0367	14.6532
33	1.389	0.7201	38.869	0.0257	27.9897	0.0357	15.0995
34	1.403	0.7130	40.258	0.0248	28.7027	0.0348	15.5441
35	1.417	0.7059	41.660	0.0240	29.4086	0.0340	15.9871
40	1.489	0.6717	48.886	0.0205	32.8347	0.0305	18.1776
45	1.565	0.6391	56.481	0.0177	36.0945	0.0277	20.3273
50	1.645	0.6080	64.463	0.0155	39.1961	0.0255	22.4363
55	1.729	0.5785	72.852	0.0137	42.1472	0.0237	24.5049
60	1.817	0.5505	81.670	0.0123	44.9550	0.0223	26.5333
65	1.909	0.5237	90.937	0.0110	47.6266	0.0210	28.5217
70	2.007	0.4983	100.676	0.0099	50.1685	0.0199	30.4703
75	2.109	0.4741	110.913	0.0090	52.5871	0.0190	32.3793
80	2.217	0.4511	121.672	0.0082	54.8882	0.0182	34.2492
85	2.330	0.4292	132.979	0.0075	57.0777	0.0175	36.0801
90	2.449	0.4084	144.863	0.0069	59.1609	0.0169	37.8725
95	2.574	0.3886	157.354	0.0064	61.1430	0.0164	39.6265
100	2.705	0.3697	170.481	0.0059	63.0289	0.0159	41.3426

G.J. Thuesen/W.J Fabrycky, *Engineering Economy*, 7e, © 1989, pp. 643-698. Reprinted by permission of Prentice-Hall, Inc., Englewood Cliffs, NJ.

Table A.4. $1\frac{1}{4}\%$ Interest Factors for Annual Compounding Interest

n	Single Payment		Equal Payment Series				Uniform gradient-series factor
	Compound-amount factor	Present-worth factor	Compound-amount factor	Sinking-fund factor	Present-worth factor	Capital-recovery factor	
	To find F Given P $F/P\ i, n$	To find P Given F $P/F\ i, n$	To find F Given A $F/A\ i, n$	To find A Given F $A/F\ i, n$	To find P Given A $P/A\ i, n$	To find A Given P $A/P\ i, n$	To find A Given G $A/G\ i, n$
1	1.013	0.9877	1.000	1.0001	0.9877	1.0126	0.0000
2	1.025	0.9755	2.013	0.4970	1.9631	0.5095	0.4932
3	1.038	0.9635	3.038	0.3293	2.9265	0.3418	0.9895
4	1.051	0.9516	4.076	0.2454	3.8780	0.2579	1.4830
5	1.064	0.9398	5.127	0.1951	4.8177	0.2076	1.9729
6	1.077	0.9282	6.191	0.1616	5.7459	0.1741	2.4618
7	1.091	0.9168	7.268	0.1376	6.6627	0.1501	2.9491
8	1.105	0.9055	8.359	0.1197	7.5680	0.1322	3.4330
9	1.118	0.8943	9.463	0.1057	8.4623	0.1182	3.9158
10	1.132	0.8832	10.582	0.0946	9.3454	0.1071	4.3960
11	1.147	0.8723	11.714	0.0854	10.2177	0.0979	4.8744
12	1.161	0.8616	12.860	0.0778	11.0792	0.0903	5.3506
13	1.175	0.8509	14.021	0.0714	11.9300	0.0839	5.8248
14	1.190	0.8404	15.196	0.0659	12.7704	0.0784	6.2968
15	1.205	0.8300	16.386	0.0611	13.6004	0.0736	6.7669
16	1.220	0.8198	17.591	0.0569	14.4201	0.0694	7.2350
17	1.235	0.8097	18.811	0.0532	15.2298	0.0657	7.7009
18	1.251	0.7997	20.046	0.0499	16.0293	0.0624	8.1645
19	1.266	0.7898	21.296	0.0470	16.8191	0.0595	8.6264
20	1.282	0.7801	22.563	0.0444	17.5991	0.0569	9.0861
21	1.298	0.7704	23.845	0.0420	18.3695	0.0545	9.5439
22	1.314	0.7609	25.143	0.0398	19.1303	0.0523	9.9993
23	1.331	0.7515	26.457	0.0378	19.8818	0.0503	10.4528
24	1.347	0.7423	27.788	0.0360	20.6240	0.0485	10.9044
25	1.364	0.7331	29.135	0.0344	21.3570	0.0469	11.3539
26	1.381	0.7240	30.499	0.0328	22.0810	0.0453	11.8012
27	1.399	0.7151	31.880	0.0314	22.7960	0.0439	12.2465
28	1.416	0.7063	33.279	0.0301	23.5022	0.0426	12.6898
29	1.434	0.6976	34.695	0.0289	24.1998	0.0414	13.1311
30	1.452	0.6889	36.128	0.0277	24.8886	0.0402	13.5703
31	1.470	0.6804	37.580	0.0267	25.5690	0.0392	14.0074
32	1.488	0.6720	39.050	0.0257	26.2410	0.0382	14.4425
33	1.507	0.6637	40.538	0.0247	26.9047	0.0372	14.8756
34	1.526	0.6555	42.045	0.0238	27.5601	0.0363	15.3066
35	1.545	0.6475	43.570	0.0230	28.2075	0.0355	15.7357
40	1.644	0.6085	51.489	0.0195	31.3266	0.0320	17.8503
45	1.749	0.5718	59.915	0.0167	34.2578	0.0292	19.9144
50	1.861	0.5374	68.880	0.0146	37.0125	0.0271	21.9284
55	1.980	0.5050	78.421	0.0128	39.6013	0.0253	23.8925
60	2.107	0.4746	88.573	0.0113	42.0342	0.0238	25.8072
65	2.242	0.4460	99.375	0.0101	44.3206	0.0226	27.6730
70	2.386	0.4192	110.870	0.0091	46.4693	0.0216	29.4902
75	2.539	0.3939	123.101	0.0082	48.4886	0.0207	31.2594
80	2.702	0.3702	136.116	0.0074	50.3862	0.0199	32.9812
85	2.875	0.3479	149.965	0.0067	52.1696	0.0192	34.6560
90	3.059	0.3270	164.701	0.0061	53.8456	0.0186	36.2844
95	3.255	0.3073	180.382	0.0056	55.4207	0.0181	37.8671
100	3.463	0.2888	197.067	0.0051	56.9009	0.0176	39.4048

G.J. Thuesen/W.J Fabrycky, *Engineering Economy*, 7e, © 1989, pp. 643–698.
Reprinted by permission of Prentice-Hall, Inc., Englewood Cliffs, NJ.

Table A.5. $1\frac{1}{2}$% Interest Factors for Annual Compounding Interest

n	Single Payment		Equal Payment Series				Uniform gradient-series factor
	Compound-amount factor	Present-worth factor	Compound-amount factor	Sinking-fund factor	Present-worth factor	Capital-recovery factor	
	To find F Given P F/P i, n	To find P Given F P/F i, n	To find F Given A F/A i, n	To find A Given F A/F i, n	To find P Given A P/A i, n	To find A Given P A/P i, n	To find A Given G A/G i, n
1	1.015	0.9852	1.000	1.0000	0.9852	1.0150	0.0000
2	1.030	0.9707	2.015	0.4963	1.9559	0.5113	0.4963
3	1.046	0.9563	3.045	0.3284	2.9122	0.3434	0.9901
4	1.061	0.9422	4.091	0.2445	3.8544	0.2595	1.4814
5	1.077	0.9283	5.152	0.1941	4.7827	0.2091	1.9702
6	1.093	0.9146	6.230	0.1605	5.6972	0.1755	2.4566
7	1.110	0.9010	7.323	0.1366	6.5982	0.1516	2.9405
8	1.127	0.8877	8.433	0.1186	7.4859	0.1336	3.4219
9	1.143	0.8746	9.559	0.1046	8.3605	0.1196	3.9008
10	1.161	0.8617	10.703	0.0934	9.2222	0.1084	4.3772
11	1.178	0.8489	11.863	0.0843	10.0711	0.0993	4.8512
12	1.196	0.8364	13.041	0.0767	10.9075	0.0917	5.3227
13	1.214	0.8240	14.237	0.0703	11.7315	0.0853	5.7917
14	1.232	0.8119	15.450	0.0647	12.5434	0.0797	6.2582
15	1.250	0.7999	16.682	0.0600	13.3432	0.0750	6.7223
16	1.269	0.7880	17.932	0.0558	14.1313	0.0708	7.1839
17	1.288	0.7764	19.201	0.0521	14.9077	0.0671	7.6431
18	1.307	0.7649	20.489	0.0488	15.6726	0.0638	8.0997
19	1.327	0.7536	21.797	0.0459	16.4262	0.0609	8.5539
20	1.347	0.7425	23.124	0.0433	17.1686	0.0583	9.0057
21	1.367	0.7315	24.471	0.0409	17.9001	0.0559	9.4550
22	1.388	0.7207	25.838	0.0387	18.6208	0.0537	9.9018
23	1.408	0.7100	27.225	0.0367	19.3309	0.0517	10.3462
24	1.430	0.6996	28.634	0.0349	20.0304	0.0499	10.7881
25	1.451	0.6892	30.063	0.0333	20.7196	0.0483	11.2276
26	1.473	0.6790	31.514	0.0317	21.3986	0.0467	11.6646
27	1.495	0.6690	32.987	0.0303	22.0676	0.0453	12.0992
28	1.517	0.6591	34.481	0.0290	22.7267	0.0440	12.5313
29	1.540	0.6494	35.999	0.0278	23.3761	0.0428	12.9610
30	1.563	0.6398	37.539	0.0266	24.0158	0.0416	13.3883
31	1.587	0.6303	39.102	0.0256	24.6462	0.0406	13.8131
32	1.610	0.6210	40.688	0.0246	25.2671	0.0396	14.2355
33	1.634	0.6118	42.299	0.0237	25.8790	0.0387	14.6555
34	1.659	0.6028	43.933	0.0228	26.4817	0.0378	15.0731
35	1.684	0.5939	45.592	0.0219	27.0756	0.0369	15.4882
40	1.814	0.5513	54.268	0.0184	29.9159	0.0334	17.5277
45	1.954	0.5117	63.614	0.0157	32.5523	0.0307	19.5074
50	2.105	0.4750	73.683	0.0136	34.9997	0.0286	21.4277
55	2.268	0.4409	84.530	0.0118	37.2715	0.0268	23.2894
60	2.443	0.4093	96.215	0.0104	39.3803	0.0254	25.0930
65	2.632	0.3799	108.803	0.0092	41.3378	0.0242	26.8392
70	2.835	0.3527	122.364	0.0082	43.1549	0.0232	28.5290
75	3.055	0.3274	136.973	0.0073	44.8416	0.0223	30.1631
80	3.291	0.3039	152.711	0.0066	46.4073	0.0216	31.7423
85	3.545	0.2821	169.665	0.0059	47.8607	0.0209	33.2676
90	3.819	0.2619	187.930	0.0053	49.2099	0.0203	34.7399
95	4.114	0.2431	207.606	0.0048	50.4622	0.0198	36.1602
100	4.432	0.2256	228.803	0.0044	51.6247	0.0194	37.5295

G.J. Thuesen/W.J Fabrycky, *Engineering Economy*, 7e, © 1989, pp. 643-698.
Reprinted by permission of Prentice-Hall, Inc., Englewood Cliffs, NJ.

Table A.6.   2% Interest Factors for Annual Compounding Interest

	Single Payment		Equal Payment Series				Uniform gradient-series factor
	Compound-amount factor	Present-worth factor	Compound-amount factor	Sinking-fund factor	Present-worth factor	Capital-recovery factor	
n	To find F Given P F/P i, n	To find P Given F P/F i, n	To find F Given A F/A i, n	To find A Given F A/F i, n	To find P Given A P/A i, n	To find A Given P A/P i, n	To find A Given G A/G i, n
1	1.020	0.9804	1.000	1.0000	0.9804	1.0200	0.0000
2	1.040	0.9612	2.020	0.4951	1.9416	0.5151	0.4951
3	1.061	0.9423	3.060	0.3268	2.8839	0.3468	0.9868
4	1.082	0.9239	4.122	0.2426	3.8077	0.2626	1.4753
5	1.104	0.9057	5.204	0.1922	4.7135	0.2122	1.9604
6	1.126	0.8880	6.308	0.1585	5.6014	0.1785	2.4423
7	1.149	0.8706	7.434	0.1345	6.4720	0.1545	2.9208
8	1.172	0.8535	8.583	0.1165	7.3255	0.1365	3.3961
9	1.195	0.8368	9.755	0.1025	8.1622	0.1225	3.8681
10	1.219	0.8204	10.950	0.0913	8.9826	0.1113	4.3367
11	1.243	0.8043	12.169	0.0822	9.7869	0.1022	4.8021
12	1.268	0.7885	13.412	0.0746	10.5754	0.0946	5.2643
13	1.294	0.7730	14.680	0.0681	11.3484	0.0881	5.7231
14	1.319	0.7579	15.974	0.0626	12.1063	0.0826	6.1786
15	1.346	0.7430	17.293	0.0578	12.8493	0.0778	6.6309
16	1.373	0.7285	18.639	0.0537	13.5777	0.0737	7.0799
17	1.400	0.7142	20.012	0.0500	14.2919	0.0700	7.5256
18	1.428	0.7002	21.412	0.0467	14.9920	0.0667	7.9681
19	1.457	0.6864	22.841	0.0438	15.6785	0.0638	8.4073
20	1.486	0.6730	24.297	0.0412	16.3514	0.0612	8.8433
21	1.516	0.6598	25.783	0.0388	17.0112	0.0588	9.2760
22	1.546	0.6468	27.299	0.0366	17.6581	0.0566	9.7055
23	1.577	0.6342	28.845	0.0347	18.2922	0.0547	10.1317
24	1.608	0.6217	30.422	0.0329	18.9139	0.0529	10.5547
25	1.641	0.6095	32.030	0.0312	19.5235	0.0512	10.9745
26	1.673	0.5976	33.671	0.0297	20.1210	0.0497	11.3910
27	1.707	0.5859	35.344	0.0283	20.7069	0.0483	11.8043
28	1.741	0.5744	37.051	0.0270	21.2813	0.0470	12.2145
29	1.776	0.5631	38.792	0.0258	21.8444	0.0458	12.6214
30	1.811	0.5521	40.568	0.0247	22.3965	0.0447	13.0251
31	1.848	0.5413	42.379	0.0236	22.9377	0.0436	13.4257
32	1.885	0.5306	44.227	0.0226	23.4683	0.0426	13.8230
33	1.922	0.5202	46.112	0.0217	23.9886	0.0417	14.2172
34	1.961	0.5100	48.034	0.0208	24.4986	0.0408	14.6083
35	2.000	0.5000	49.994	0.0200	24.9986	0.0400	14.9961
40	2.208	0.4529	60.402	0.0166	27.3555	0.0366	16.8885
45	2.438	0.4102	71.893	0.0139	29.4902	0.0339	18.7034
50	2.692	0.3715	84.579	0.0118	31.4236	0.0318	20.4420
55	2.972	0.3365	98.587	0.0102	33.1748	0.0302	22.1057
60	3.281	0.3048	114.052	0.0088	34.7609	0.0288	23.6961
65	3.623	0.2761	131.126	0.0076	36.1975	0.0276	25.2147
70	4.000	0.2500	149.978	0.0067	37.4986	0.0267	26.6632
75	4.416	0.2265	170.792	0.0059	38.6771	0.0259	28.0434
80	4.875	0.2051	193.772	0.0052	39.7445	0.0252	29.3572
85	5.383	0.1858	219.144	0.0046	40.7113	0.0246	30.6064
90	5.943	0.1683	247.157	0.0041	41.5869	0.0241	31.7929
95	6.562	0.1524	278.085	0.0036	42.3800	0.0236	32.9189
100	7.245	0.1380	312.232	0.0032	43.0984	0.0232	33.9863

G.J. Thuesen/W.J Fabrycky, *Engineering Economy*, 7e, © 1989, pp. 643-698. Reprinted by permission of Prentice-Hall, Inc., Englewood Cliffs, NJ.

Table A.7. 3% Interest Factors for Annual Compounding Interest

	Single Payment		Equal Payment Series				Uniform gradient-series factor
	Compound-amount factor	Present-worth factor	Compound-amount factor	Sinking-fund factor	Present-worth factor	Capital-recovery factor	
n	To find F Given P F/P i,n	To find P Given F P/F i,n	To find F Given A F/A i,n	To find A Given F A/F i,n	To find P Given A P/A i,n	To find A Given P A/P i,n	To find A Given G A/G i,n
1	1.030	0.9709	1.000	1.0000	0.9709	1.0300	0.0000
2	1.061	0.9426	2.030	0.4926	1.9135	0.5226	0.4926
3	1.093	0.9152	3.091	0.3235	2.8286	0.3535	0.9803
4	1.126	0.8885	4.184	0.2390	3.7171	0.2690	1.4631
5	1.159	0.8626	5.309	0.1884	4.5797	0.2184	1.9409
6	1.194	0.8375	6.468	0.1546	5.4172	0.1846	2.4138
7	1.230	0.8131	7.662	0.1305	6.2303	0.1605	2.8819
8	1.267	0.7894	8.892	0.1125	7.0197	0.1425	3.3450
9	1.305	0.7664	10.159	0.0984	7.7861	0.1284	3.8032
10	1.344	0.7441	11.464	0.0872	8.5302	0.1172	4.2565
11	1.384	0.7224	12.808	0.0781	9.2526	0.1081	4.7049
12	1.426	0.7014	14.192	0.0705	9.9540	0.1005	5.1485
13	1.469	0.6810	15.618	0.0640	10.6350	0.0940	5.5872
14	1.513	0.6611	17.086	0.0585	11.2961	0.0885	6.0211
15	1.558	0.6419	18.599	0.0538	11.9379	0.0838	6.4501
16	1.605	0.6232	20.157	0.0496	12.5611	0.0796	6.8742
17	1.653	0.6050	21.762	0.0460	13.1661	0.0760	7.2936
18	1.702	0.5874	23.414	0.0427	13.7535	0.0727	7.7081
19	1.754	0.5703	25.117	0.0398	14.3238	0.0698	8.1179
20	1.806	0.5537	26.870	0.0372	14.8775	0.0672	8.5229
21	1.860	0.5376	28.676	0.0349	15.4150	0.0649	8.9231
22	1.916	0.5219	30.537	0.0328	15.9369	0.0628	9.3186
23	1.974	0.5067	32.453	0.0308	16.4436	0.0608	9.7094
24	2.033	0.4919	34.426	0.0291	16.9356	0.0591	10.0954
25	2.094	0.4776	36.459	0.0274	17.4132	0.0574	10.4768
26	2.157	0.4637	38.553	0.0259	17.8769	0.0559	10.8535
27	2.221	0.4502	40.710	0.0246	18.3270	0.0546	11.2256
28	2.288	0.4371	42.931	0.0233	18.7641	0.0533	11.5930
29	2.357	0.4244	45.219	0.0221	19.1885	0.0521	11.9558
30	2.427	0.4120	47.575	0.0210	19.6005	0.0510	12.3141
31	2.500	0.4000	50.003	0.0200	20.0004	0.0500	12.6678
32	2.575	0.3883	52.503	0.0191	20.3888	0.0491	13.0169
33	2.652	0.3770	55.078	0.0182	20.7658	0.0482	13.3616
34	2.732	0.3661	57.730	0.0173	21.1318	0.0473	13.7018
35	2.814	0.3554	60.462	0.0165	21.4872	0.0465	14.0375
40	3.262	0.3066	75.401	0.0133	23.1148	0.0433	15.6502
⏵45	3.782	0.2644	92.720	0.0108	24.5187	0.0408	17.1556
50	4.384	0.2281	112.797	0.0089	25.7298	0.0389	18.5575
55	5.082	0.1968	136.072	0.0074	26.7744	0.0374	19.8600
60	5.892	·0.1697	163.053	0.0061	27.6756	0.0361	21.0674
65	6.830	0.1464	194.333	0.0052	28.4529	0.0352	22.1841
70	7.918	0.1263	230.594	0.0043	29.1234	0.0343	23.2145
75	9.179	0.1090	272.631	0.0037	29.7018	0.0337	24.1634
80	10.641	0.0940	321.363	0.0031	30.2008	0.0331	25.0354
85	12.336	0.0811	377.857	0.0027	30.6312	0.0327	25.8349
90	14.300	0.0699	443.349	0.0023	31.0024	0.0323	26.5667
95	16.578	0.0603	519.272	0.0019	31.3227	0.0319	27.2351
100	19.219	0.0520	607.288	0.0017	31.5989	0.0317	27.8445

G.J. Thuesen/W.J Fabrycky, *Engineering Economy*, 7e, © 1989, pp. 643-698. Reprinted by permission of Prentice-Hall, Inc., Englewood Cliffs, NJ.

Table A.8.　　4% Interest Factors for Annual Compounding Interest

	Single Payment		Equal Payment Series				Uniform gradient-series factor
	Compound-amount factor	Present-worth factor	Compound-amount factor	Sinking-fund factor	Present-worth factor	Capital-recovery factor	
n	To find F Given P F/P i,n	To find P Given F P/F i,n	To find F Given A F/A i,n	To find A Given F A/F i,n	To find P Given A P/A i,n	To find A Given P A/P i,n	To find A Given G A/G i,n
1	1.040	0.9615	1.000	1.0000	0.9615	1.0400	0.0000
2	1.082	0.9246	2.040	0.4902	1.8861	0.5302	0.4902
3	1.125	0.8890	3.122	0.3204	2.7751	0.3604	0.9739
4	1.170	0.8548	4.246	0.2355	3.6299	0.2755	1.4510
5	1.217	0.8219	5.416	0.1846	4.4518	0.2246	1.9216
6	1.265	0.7903	6.633	0.1508	5.2421	0.1908	2.3857
7	1.316	0.7599	7.898	0.1266	6.0021	0.1666	2.8433
8	1.369	0.7307	9.214	0.1085	6.7328	0.1485	3.2944
9	1.423	0.7026	10.583	0.0945	7.4353	0.1345	3.7391
10	1.480	0.6756	12.006	0.0833	8.1109	0.1233	4.1773
11	1.539	0.6496	13.486	0.0742	8.7605	0.1142	4.6090
12	1.601	0.6246	15.026	0.0666	9.3851	0.1066	5.0344
13	1.665	0.6006	16.627	0.0602	9.9857	0.1002	5.4533
14	1.732	0.5775	18.292	0.0547	10.5631	0.0947	5.8659
15	1.801	0.5553	20.024	0.0500	11.1184	0.0900	6.2721
16	1.873	0.5339	21.825	0.0458	11.6523	0.0858	6.6720
17	1.948	0.5134	23.698	0.0422	12.1657	0.0822	7.0656
18	2.026	0.4936	25.645	0.0390	12.6593	0.0790	7.4530
19	2.107	0.4747	27.671	0.0361	13.1339	0.0761	7.8342
20	2.191	0.4564	29.778	0.0336	13.5903	0.0736	8.2091
21	2.279	0.4388	31.969	0.0313	14.0292	0.0713	8.5780
22	2.370	0.4220	34.248	0.0292	14.4511	0.0692	8.9407
23	2.465	0.4057	36.618	0.0273	14.8569	0.0673	9.2973
24	2.563	0.3901	39.083	0.0256	15.2470	0.0656	9.6479
25	2.666	0.3751	41.646	0.0240	15.6221	0.0640	9.9925
26	2.772	0.3607	44.312	0.0226	15.9828	0.0626	10.3312
27	2.883	0.3468	47.084	0.0212	16.3296	0.0612	10.6640
28	2.999	0.3335	49.968	0.0200	16.6631	0.0600	10.9909
29	3.119	0.3207	52.966	0.0189	16.9837	0.0589	11.3121
30	3.243	0.3083	56.085	0.0178	17.2920	0.0578	11.6274
31	3.373	0.2965	59.328	0.0169	17.5885	0.0569	11.9371
32	3.508	0.2851	62.701	0.0160	17.8736	0.0560	12.2411
33	3.648	0.2741	66.210	0.0151	18.1477	0.0551	12.5396
34	3.794	0.2636	69.858	0.0143	18.4112	0.0543	12.8325
35	3.946	0.2534	73.652	0.0136	18.6646	0.0536	13.1199
40	4.801	0.2083	95.026	0.0105	19.7928	0.0505	14.4765
45	5.841	0.1712	121.029	0.0083	20.7200	0.0483	15.7047
50	7.107	0.1407	152.667	0.0066	21.4822	0.0466	16.8123
55	8.646	0.1157	191.159	0.0052	22.1086	0.0452	17.8070
60	10.520	0.0951	237.991	0.0042	22.6235	0.0442	18.6972
65	12.799	0.0781	294.968	0.0034	23.0467	0.0434	19.4909
70	15.572	0.0642	364.290	0.0028	23.3945	0.0428	20.1961
75	18.945	0.0528	448.631	0.0022	23.6804	0.0422	20.8206
80	23.050	0.0434	551.245	0.0018	23.9154	0.0418	21.3719
85	28.044	0.0357	676.090	0.0015	24.1085	0.0415	21.8569
90	34.119	0.0293	817.983	0.0012	24.2673	0.0412	22.2826
95	41.511	0.0241	1012.785	0.0010	24.3978	0.0410	22.6550
100	50.505	0.0198	1237.624	0.0008	24.5050	0.0408	22.9800

G.J. Thuesen/W.J Fabrycky, *Engineering Economy*, 7e, © 1989, pp. 643-698. Reprinted by permission of Prentice-Hall, Inc., Englewood Cliffs, NJ.

Table A.9. **5% Interest Factors for Annual Compounding Interest**

	Single Payment		Equal Payment Series				Uniform gradient-series factor
	Compound-amount factor	Present-worth factor	Compound-amount factor	Sinking-fund factor	Present-worth factor	Capital-recovery factor	
n	To find F Given P F/P i,n	To find P Given F P/F i,n	To find F Given A F/A i,n	To find A Given F A/F i,n	To find P Given A P/A i,n	To find A Given P A/P i,n	To find A Given G A/G i,n
1	1.050	0.9524	1.000	1.0000	0.9524	1.0500	0.0000
2	1.103	0.9070	2.050	0.4878	1.8594	0.5378	0.4878
3	1.158	0.8638	3.153	0.3172	2.7233	0.3672	0.9675
4	1.216	0.8227	4.310	0.2320	3.5460	0.2820	1.4391
5	1.276	0.7835	5.526	0.1810	4.3295	0.2310	1.9025
6	1.340	0.7462	6.802	0.1470	5.0757	0.1970	2.3579
7	1.407	0.7107	8.142	0.1228	5.7864	0.1728	2.8052
8	1.477	0.6768	9.549	0.1047	6.4632	0.1547	3.2445
9	1.551	0.6446	11.027	0.0907	7.1078	0.1407	3.6758
10	1.629	0.6139	12.587	0.0795	7.7217	0.1295	4.0991
11	1.710	0.5847	14.207	0.0704	8.3064	0.1204	4.5145
12	1.796	0.5568	15.917	0.0628	8.8633	0.1128	4.9219
13	1.886	0.5303	17.713	0.0565	9.3936	0.1065	5.3215
14	1.980	0.5051	19.599	0.0510	9.8987	0.1010	5.7133
15	2.079	0.4810	21.579	0.0464	10.3797	0.0964	6.0973
16	2.183	0.4581	23.658	0.0423	10.8378	0.0923	6.4736
17	2.292	0.4363	25.840	0.0387	11.2741	0.0887	6.8423
18	2.407	0.4155	28.132	0.0356	11.6896	0.0856	7.2034
19	2.527	0.3957	30.539	0.0328	12.0853	0.0828	7.5569
20	2.653	0.3769	33.066	0.0303	12.4622	0.0803	7.9030
21	2.786	0.3590	35.719	0.0280	12.8212	0.0780	8.2416
22	2.925	0.3419	38.505	0.0260	13.1630	0.0760	8.5730
23	3.072	0.3256	41.430	0.0241	13.4886	0.0741	8.8971
24	3.225	0.3101	44.502	0.0225	13.7987	0.0725	9.2140
25	3.386	0.2953	47.727	0.0210	14.0940	0.0710	9.5238
26	3.556	0.2813	51.113	0.0196	14.3752	0.0696	9.8266
27	3.733	0.2679	54.669	0.0183	14.6430	0.0683	10.1224
28	3.920	0.2551	58.403	0.0171	14.8981	0.0671	10.4114
29	4.116	0.2430	62.323	0.0161	15.1411	0.0661	10.6936
30	4.322	0.2314	66.439	0.0151	15.3725	0.0651	10.9691
31	4.538	0.2204	70.761	0.0141	15.5928	0.0641	11.2381
32	4.765	0.2099	75.299	0.0133	15.8027	0.0633	11.5005
33	5.003	0.1999	80.064	0.0125	16.0026	0.0625	11.7566
34	5.253	0.1904	85.067	0.0118	16.1929	0.0618	12.0063
35	5.516	0.1813	90.320	0.0111	16.3742	0.0611	12.2498
40	7.040	0.1421	120.800	0.0083	17.1591	0.0583	13.3775
45	8.985	0.1113	159.700	0.0063	17.7741	0.0563	14.3644
50	11.467	0.0872	209.348	0.0048	18.2559	0.0548	15.2233
55	14.636	0.0683	272.713	0.0037	18.6335	0.0537	15.9665
60	18.679	0.0535	353.584	0.0028	18.9293	0.0528	16.6062
65	23.840	0.0420	456.798	0.0022	19.1611	0.0522	17.1541
70	30.426	0.0329	588.529	0.0017	19.3427	0.0517	17.6212
75	38.833	0.0258	756.654	0.0013	19.4850	0.0513	18.0176
80	49.561	0.0202	971.229	0.0010	19.5965	0.0510	18.3526
85	63.254	0.0158	1245.087	0.0008	19.6838	0.0508	18.6346
90	80.730	0.0124	1594.607	0.0006	19.7523	0.0506	18.8712
95	103.035	0.0097	2040.694	0.0005	19.8059	0.0505	19.0689
100	131.501	0.0076	2610.025	0.0004	19.8479	0.0504	19.2337

G.J. Thuesen/W.J Fabrycky, *Engineering Economy*, 7e, © 1989, pp. 643-698. Reprinted by permission of Prentice-Hall, Inc., Englewood Cliffs, NJ.

Table A.10. 6% Interest Factors for Annual Compounding Interest

	Single Payment		Equal Payment Series				Uniform gradient-series factor
	Compound-amount factor	Present-worth factor	Compound-amount factor	Sinking-fund factor	Present-worth factor	Capital-recovery factor	
n	To find F Given P F/P i,n	To find P Given F P/F i,n	To find F Given A F/A i,n	To find A Given F A/F i,n	To find P Given A P/A i,n	To find A Given P A/P i,n	To find A Given G A/G i,n
1	1.060	0.9434	1.000	1.0000	0.9434	1.0600	0.0000
2	1.124	0.8900	2.060	0.4854	1.8334	0.5454	0.4854
3	1.191	0.8396	3.184	0.3141	2.6730	0.3741	0.9612
4	1.262	0.7921	4.375	0.2286	3.4651	0.2886	1.4272
5	1.338	0.7473	5.637	0.1774	4.2124	0.2374	1.8836
6	1.419	0.7050	6.975	0.1434	4.9173	0.2034	2.3304
7	1.504	0.6651	8.394	0.1191	5.5824	0.1791	2.7676
8	1.594	0.6274	9.897	0.1010	6.2098	0.1610	3.1952
9	1.689	0.5919	11.491	0.0870	6.8017	0.1470	3.6133
10	1.791	0.5584	13.181	0.0759	7.3601	0.1359	4.0220
11	1.898	0.5268	14.972	0.0668	7.8869	0.1268	4.4213
12	2.012	0.4970	16.870	0.0593	8.3839	0.1193	4.8113
13	2.133	0.4688	18.882	0.0530	8.8527	0.1130	5.1920
14	2.261	0.4423	21.015	0.0476	9.2950	0.1076	5.5635
15	2.397	0.4173	23.276	0.0430	9.7123	0.1030	5.9260
16	2.540	0.3937	25.673	0.0390	10.1059	0.0990	6.2794
17	2.693	0.3714	28.213	0.0355	10.4773	0.0955	6.6240
18	2.854	0.3504	30.906	0.0324	10.8276	0.0924	6.9597
19	3.026	0.3305	33.760	0.0296	11.1581	0.0896	7.2867
20	3.207	0.3118	36.786	0.0272	11.4699	0.0872	7.6052
21	3.400	0.2942	39.993	0.0250	11.7641	0.0850	7.9151
22	3.604	0.2775	43.392	0.0231	12.0416	0.0831	8.2166
23	3.820	0.2618	46.996	0.0213	12.3034	0.0813	8.5099
24	4.049	0.2470	50.816	0.0197	12.5504	0.0797	8.7951
25	4.292	0.2330	54.865	0.0182	12.7834	0.0782	9.0722
26	4.549	0.2198	59.156	0.0169	13,0032	0.0769	9.3415
27	4.822	0.2074	63.706	0.0157	13.2105	0.0757	9.6030
28	5.112	0.1956	68.528	0.0146	13.4062	0.0746	9.8568
29	5.418	0.1846	73.640	0.0136	13.5907	0.0736	10.1032
30	5.744	0 1741	79.058	0.0127	13.7648	0.0727	10.3422
31	6.088	0.1643	84.802	0.0118	13.9291	0.0718	10.5740
32	6.453	0.1550	90.890	0.0110	14.0841	0.0710	10.7988
33	6.841	0.1462	97.343	0.0103	14.2302	0.0703	11.0166
34	7.251	0.1379	104.184	0.0096	14.3682	0.0696	11.2276
35	7.686	0.1301	111.435	0.0090	14.4983	0.0690	11.4319
40	10.286	0.0972	154.762	0.0065	15.0463	0.0665	12.3590
45	13.765	0.0727	212.744	0.0047	15.4558	0.0647	13.1413
50	18.420	0.0543	290.336	0.0035	15.7619	0.0635	13.7964
55	24.650	0.0406	394.172	0.0025	15.9906	0.0625	14.3411
60	32.988	0.0303	533.128	0.0019	16.1614	0.0619	14.7910
65	44.145	0.0227	719.083	0.0014	16.2891	0.0614	15.1601
70	59.076	0.0169	967.932	0.0010	16.3846	0.0610	15.4614
75	79.057	0.0127	1300.949	0.0008	16.4559	0.0608	15.7058
80	105.796	0.0095	1746.600	0.0006	16.5091	0.0606	15.9033
85	141.579	0.0071	2342.982	0.0004	16.5490	0.0604	16.0620
90	189.465	0.0053	3141.075	0.0003	16.5787	0.0603	16.1891
95	253.546	0.0040	4209.104	0.0002	16.6009	0.0602	16.2905
100	339.302	0.0030	5638.368	0.0002	16.6176	0.0602	16.3711

G.J. Thuesen/W.J Fabrycky, *Engineering Economy*, 7e, © 1989, pp. 643-698. Reprinted by permission of Prentice-Hall, Inc., Englewood Cliffs, NJ.

Table A.11. **7% Interest Factors for Annual Compounding Interest**

	Single Payment		Equal Payment Series				Uniform gradient-series factor
	Compound-amount factor	Present-worth factor	Compound-amount factor	Sinking-fund factor	Present-worth factor	Capital-recovery factor	
n	To find F Given P F/P i,n	To find P Given F P/F i,n	To find F Given A F/A i,n	To find A Given F A/F i,n	To find P Given A P/A i,n	To find A Given P A/P i,n	To find A Given G A/G i,n
1	1.070	0.9346	1.000	1.0000	0.9346	1.0700	0.0000
2	1.145	0.8734	2.070	0.4831	1.8080	0.5531	0.4831
3	1.225	0.8163	3.215	0.3111	2.6243	0.3811	0.9549
4	1.311	0.7629	4.440	0.2252	3.3872	0.2952	1.4155
5	1.403	0.7130	5.751	0.1739	4.1002	0.2439	1.8650
6	1.501	0.6664	7.163	0.1398	4.7665	0.2098	2.3032
7	1.606	0.6228	8.654	0.1156	5.3893	0.1856	2.7304
8	1.718	0.5820	10.260	0.0975	5.9713	0.1675	3.1466
9	1.838	0.5439	11.978	0.0835	6.5152	0.1535	3.5517
10	1.967	0.5084	13.816	0.0724	7.0236	0.1424	3.9461
11	2.105	0.4751	15.784	0.0634	7.4987	0.1334	4.3296
12	2.252	0.4440	17.888	0.0559	7.9427	0.1259	4.7025
13	2.410	0.4150	20.141	0.0497	8.3577	0.1197	5.0649
14	2.579	0.3878	22.550	0.0444	8.7455	0.1144	5.4167
15	2.759	0.3625	25.129	0.0398	9.1079	0.1098	5.7583
16	2.952	0.3387	27.888	0.0359	9.4467	0.1059	6.0897
17	3.159	0.3166	30.840	0.0324	9.7632	0.1024	6.4110
18	3.380	0.2959	33.999	0.0294	10.0591	0.0994	6.7225
19	3.617	0.2765	37.379	0.0268	10.3356	0.0968	7.0242
20	3.870	0.2584	40.996	0.0244	10.5940	0.0944	7.3163
21	4.141	0.2415	44.865	0.0223	10.8355	0.0923	7.5990
22	4.430	0.2257	49.006	0.0204	11.0613	0.0904	7.8725
23	4.741	0.2110	53.436	0.0187	11.2722	0.0887	8.1369
24	5.072	0.1972	58.177	0.0172	11.4693	0.0872	8.3923
25	5.427	0.1843	63.249	0.0158	11.6536	0.0858	8.6391
26	5.807	0.1722	68.676	0.0146	11.8258	0.0846	8.8773
27	6.214	0.1609	74.484	0.0134	11.9867	0.0834	9.1072
28	6.649	0.1504	80.698	0.0124	12.1371	0.0824	9.3290
29	7.114	0.1406	87.347	0.0115	12.2777	0.0815	9.5427
30	7.612	0.1314	94.461	0.0106	12.4091	0.0806	9.7487
31	8.145	0.1228	102.073	0.0098	12.5318	0.0798	9.9471
32	8.715	0.1148	110.218	0.0091	12.6466	0.0791	10.1381
33	9.325	0.1072	118.933	0.0084	12.7538	0.0784	10.3219
34	9.978	0.1002	128.259	0.0078	12.8540	0.0778	10.4987
35	10.677	0.0937	138.237	0.0072	12.9477	0.0772	10.6687
40	14.974	0.0668	199.635	0.0050	13.3317	0.0750	11.4234
45	21.002	0.0476	285.749	0.0035	13.6055	0.0735	12.0360
50	29.457	0.0340	406.529	0.0025	13.8008	0.0725	12.5287
55	41.315	0.0242	575.929	0.0017	13.9399	0.0717	12.9215
60	57.946	0.0173	813.520	0.0012	14.0392	0.0712	13.2321
65	81.273	0.0123	1146.755	0.0009	14.1099	0.0709	13.4760
70	113.989	0.0088	1614.134	0.0006	14.1604	0.0706	13.6662
75	159.876	0.0063	2269.657	0.0005	14.1964	0.0705	13.8137
80	224.234	0.0045	3189.063	0.0003	14.2220	0.0703	13.9274
85	314.500	0.0032	4478.576	0.0002	14.2403	0.0702	14.0146
90	441.103	0.0023	6287.185	0.0002	14.2533	0.0702	14.0812
95	618.670	0.0016	8823.854	0.0001	14.2626	0.0701	14.1319
100	867.716	0.0012	12381.662	0.0001	14.2693	0.0701	14.1703

G.J. Thuesen/W.J Fabrycky, *Engineering Economy*, 7e, © 1989, pp. 643-698.
Reprinted by permission of Prentice-Hall, Inc., Englewood Cliffs, NJ.

Table A.12.   8% Interest Factors for Annual Compounding Interest

	Single Payment		Equal Payment Series				Uniform gradient-series factor
	Compound-amount factor	Present-worth factor	Compound-amount factor	Sinking-fund factor	Present-worth factor	Capital-recovery factor	
n	To find F Given P F/P i,n	To find P Given F P/F i,n	To find F Given A F/A i,n	To find A Given F A/F i,n	To find P Given A P/A i,n	To find A Given P A/P i,n	To find A Given G A/G i,n
1	1.080	0.9259	1.000	1.0000	0.9259	1.0800	0.0000
2	1.166	0.8573	2.080	0.4808	1.7833	0.5608	0.4808
3	1.260	0.7938	3.246	0.3080	2.5771	0.3880	0.9488
4	1.360	0.7350	4.506	0.2219	3.3121	0.3019	1.4040
5	1.469	0.6806	5.867	0.1705	3.9927	0.2505	1.8465
6	1.587	0.6302	7.336	0.1363	4.6229	0.2163	2.2764
7	1.714	0.5835	8.923	0.1121	5.2064	0.1921	2.6937
8	1.851	0.5403	10.637	0.0940	5.7466	0.1740	2.0985
9	1.999	0.5003	12.488	0.0801	6.2469	0.1601	3.4910
10	2.159	0.4632	14.487	0.0690	6.7101	0.1490	3.8713
11	2.332	0.4289	16.645	0.0601	7.1390	0.1401	4.2395
12	2.518	0.3971	18.977	0.0527	7.5361	0.1327	4.5958
13	2.720	0.3677	21.495	0.0465	7.9038	0.1265	4.9402
14	2.937	0.3405	24.215	0.0413	8.2442	0.1213	5.2731
15	3.172	0.3153	27.152	0.0368	8.5595	0.1168	5.5945
16	3.426	0.2919	30.324	0.0330	8.8514	0.1130	5.9046
17	3.700	0.2703	33.750	0.0296	9.1216	0.1096	6.2038
18	3.996	0.2503	37.450	0.0267	9.3719	0.1067	6.4920
19	4.316	0.2317	41.446	0.0241	9.6036	0.1041	6.7697
20	4.661	0.2146	45.762	0.0219	9.8182	0.1019	7.0370
21	5.034	0.1987	50.423	0.0198	10.0168	0.0998	7.2940
22	5.437	0.1840	55.457	0.0180	10.2008	0.0980	7.5412
23	5.871	0.1703	60.893	0.0164	10.3711	0.0964	7.7786
24	6.341	0.1577	66.765	0.0150	10.5288	0.0950	8.0066
25	6.848	0.1460	73.106	0.0137	10.6748	0.0937	8.2254
26	7.396	0.1352	79.954	0.0125	10.8100	0.0925	8.4352
27	7.988	0.1252	87.351	0.0115	10.9352	0.0915	8.6363
28	8.627	0.1159	95.339	0.0105	11.0511	0.0905	8.8289
29	9.317	0.1073	103.966	0.0096	11.1584	0.0896	9.0133
30	10.063	0.0994	113.283	0.0088	11.2578	0.0888	9.1897
31	10.868	0.0920	123.346	0.0081	11.3498	0.0881	9.3584
32	11.737	0.0852	134.214	0.0075	11.4350	0.0875	9.5197
33	12.676	0.0789	145.951	0.0069	11.5139	0.0869	9.6737
34	13.690	0.0731	158.627	0.0063	11.5869	0.0863	9.8208
35	14.785	0.0676	172.317	0.0058	11.6546	0.0858	9.9611
40	21.725	0.0460	259.057	0.0039	11.9246	0.0839	10.5699
45	31.920	0.0313	386.506	0.0026	12.1084	0.0826	11.0447
50	46.902	0.0213	573.770	0.0018	12.2335	0.0818	11.4107
55	68.914	0.0145	848.923	0.0012	12.3186	0.0812	11.6902
60	101.257	0.0099	1253.213	0.0008	12.3766	0.0808	11.9015
65	148.780	0.0067	1847.248	0.0006	12.4160	0.0806	12.0602
70	218.606	0.0046	2720.080	0.0004	12.4428	0.0804	12.1783
75	321.205	0.0031	4002.557	0.0003	12.4611	0.0803	12.2658
80	471.955	0.0021	5886.935	0.0002	12.4735	0.0802	12.3301
85	693.456	0.0015	8655.706	0.0001	12.4820	0.0801	12.3773
90	1018.915	0.0010	12723.939	0.0001	12.4877	0.0801	12.4116
95	1497.121	0.0007	18701.507	0.0001	12.4917	0.0801	12.4365
100	2199.761	0.0005	27484.516	0.0001	12.4943	0.0800	12.4545

G.J. Thuesen/W.J Fabrycky, *Engineering Economy*, 7e, © 1989, pp. 643-698.
Reprinted by permission of Prentice-Hall, Inc., Englewood Cliffs, NJ.

Table A.13.   9% Interest Factors for Annual Compounding Interest

	Single Payment		Equal Payment Series				Uniform gradient-series factor
	Compound-amount factor	Present-worth factor	Compound-amount factor	Sinking-fund factor	Present-worth factor	Capital-recovery factor	
n	To find F Given P F/P i, n	To find P Given F P/F i, n	To find F Given A F/A i, n	To find A Given F A/F i, n	To find P Given A P/A i, n	To find A Given P A/P i, n	To find A Given G A/G i, n
1	1.090	0.9174	1.000	1.0000	0.9174	1.0900	0.0000
2	1.188	0.8417	2.090	0.4785	1.7591	0.5685	0.4785
3	1.295	0.7722	3.278	0.3051	2.5313	0.3951	0.9426
4	1.412	0.7084	4.573	0.2187	3.2397	0.3087	1.3925
5	1.539	0.6499	5.985	0.1671	3.8897	0.2571	1.8282
6	1.677	0.5963	7.523	0.1329	4.4859	0.2229	2.2498
7	1.828	0.5470	9.200	0.1087	5.0330	0.1987	2.6574
8	1.993	0.5019	11.028	0.0907	5.5348	0.1807	3.0512
9	2.172	0.4604	13.021	0.0768	5.9953	0.1668	3.4312
10	2.367	0.4224	15.193	0.0658	6.4177	0.1558	3.7978
11	2.580	0.3875	17.560	0.0570	6.8052	0.1470	4.1510
12	2.813	0.3555	20.141	0.0497	7.1607	0.1397	4.4910
13	3.066	0.3262	22.953	0.0436	7.4869	0.1336	4.8182
14	3.342	0.2993	26.019	0.0384	7.7862	0.1284	5.1326
15	3.642	0.2745	29.361	0.0341	8.0607	0.1241	5.4346
16	3.970	0.2519	33.003	0.0303	8.3126	0.1203	5.7245
17	4.328	0.2311	36.974	0.0271	8.5436	0.1171	6.0024
18	4.717	0.2120	41.301	0.0242	8.7556	0.1142	6.2687
19	5.142	0.1945	46.018	0.0217	8.9501	0.1117	6.5236
20	5.604	0.1784	51.160	0.0196	9.1286	0.1096	6.7675
21	6.109	0.1637	56.765	0.0176	9.2923	0.1076	7.0006
22	6.659	0.1502	62.873	0.0159	9.4424	0.1059	7.2232
23	7.258	0.1378	69.532	0.0144	9.5802	0.1044	7.4358
24	7.911	0.1264	76.790	0.0130	9.7066	0.1030	7.6384
25	8.623	0.1160	84.701	0.0118	9.8226	0.1018	7.8316
26	9.399	0.1064	93.324	0.0107	9.9290	0.1007	8.0156
27	10.245	0.0976	102.723	0.0097	10.0266	0.0997	8.1906
28	11.167	0.0896	112.968	0.0089	10.1161	0.0989	8.3572
29	12.172	0.0822	124.135	0.0081	10.1983	0.0981	8.5154
30	13.268	0.0754	136.308	0.0073	10.2737	0.0973	8.6657
31	14.462	0.0692	149.575	0.0067	10.3428	0.0967	8.8083
32	15.763	0.0634	164.037	0.0061	10.4063	0.0961	8.9436
33	17.182	0.0582	179.800	0.0056	10.4645	0.0956	9.0718
34	18.728	0.0534	196.982	0.0051	10.5178	0.0951	9.1933
35	20.414	0.0490	215.711	0.0046	10.5668	0.0946	9.3083
40	31.409	0.0318	337.882	0.0030	10.7574	0.0930	9.7957
45	48.327	0.0207	525.859	0.0019	10.8812	0.0919	10.1603
50	74.358	0.0135	815.084	0.0012	10.9617	0.0912	10.4295
55	114.408	0.0088	1260.092	0.0008	11.0140	0.0908	10.6261
60	176.031	0.0057	1944.792	0.0005	11.0480	0.0905	10.7683
65	270.846	0.0037	2998.288	0.0003	11.0701	0.0903	10.8702
70	416.730	0.0024	4619.223	0.0002	11.0845	0.0902	10.9427
75	641.191	0.0016	7113.232	0.0002	11.0938	0.0902	10.9940
80	986.552	0.0010	10950.574	0.0001	11.0999	0.0901	11.0299
85	1517.932	0.0007	16854.800	0.0001	11.1038	0.0901	11.0551
90	2335.527	0.0004	25939.184	0.0001	11.1064	0.0900	11.0726
95	3593.497	0.0003	39916.635	0.0000	11.1080	0.0900	11.0847
100	5529.041	0.0002	61422.675	0.0000	11.1091	0.0900	11.0930

G.J. Thuesen/W.J Fabrycky, *Engineering Economy*, 7e, © 1989, pp. 643-698.
Reprinted by permission of Prentice-Hall, Inc., Englewood Cliffs, NJ.

Table A.14.   10% Interest Factors for Annual Compounding Interest

n	Single Payment		Equal Payment Series				Uniform gradient-series factor
	Compound-amount factor	Present-worth factor	Compound-amount factor	Sinking-fund factor	Present-worth factor	Capital-recovery factor	
	To find F Given P F/P i,n	To find P Given F P/F i,n	To find F Given A F/A i,n	To find A Given F A/F i,n	To find P Given A P/A i,n	To find A Given P A/P i,n	To find A Given G A/G i,n
1	1.100	0.9091	1.000	1.0000	0.9091	1.1000	0.0000
2	1.210	0.8265	2.100	0.4762	1.7355	0.5762	0.4762
3	1.331	0.7513	3.310	0.3021	2.4869	0.4021	0.9366
4	1.464	0.6830	4.641	0.2155	3.1699	0.3155	1.3812
5	1.611	0.6209	6.105	0.1638	3.7908	0.2638	1.8101
6	1.772	0.5645	7.716	0.1296	4.3553	0.2296	2.2236
7	1.949	0.5132	9.487	0.1054	4.8684	0.2054	2.6216
8	2.144	0.4665	11.436	0.0875	5.3349	0.1875	3.0045
9	2.358	0.4241	13.579	0.0737	5.7590	0.1737	3.3724
10	2.594	0.3856	15.937	0.0628	6.1446	0.1628	3.7255
11	2.853	0.3505	18.531	0.0540	6.4951	0.1540	4.0641
12	3.138	0.3186	21.384	0.0468	6.8137	0.1468	4.3884
13	3.452	0.2897	24.523	0.0408	7.1034	0.1408	4.6988
14	3.798	0.2633	27.975	0.0358	7.3667	0.1358	4.9955
15	4.177	0.2394	31.772	0.0315	7.6061	0.1315	5.2789
16	4.595	0.2176	35.950	0.0278	7.8237	0.1278	5.5493
17	5.054	0.1979	40.545	0.0247	8.0216	0.1247	5.8071
18	5.560	0.1799	45.599	0.0219	8.2014	0.1219	6.0526
19	6.116	0.1635	51.159	0.0196	8.3649	0.1196	6.2861
20	6.728	0.1487	57.275	0.0175	8.5136	0.1175	6.5081
21	7.400	0.1351	64.003	0.0156	8.6487	0.1156	6.7189
22	8.140	0.1229	71.403	0.0140	8.7716	0.1140	6.9189
23	8.954	0.1117	79.543	0.0126	8.8832	0.1126	7.1085
24	9.850	0.1015	88.497	0.0113	8.9848	0.1113	7.2881
25	10.835	0.0923	98.347	0.0102	9.0771	0.1102	7.4580
26	11.918	0.0839	109.182	0.0092	9.1610	0.1092	7.6187
27	13.110	0.0763	121.100	0.0083	9.2372	0.1083	7.7704
28	14.421	0.0694	134.210	0.0075	9.3066	0.1075	7.9137
29	15.863	0.0630	148.631	0.0067	9.3696	0.1067	8.0489
30	17.449	0.0573	164.494	0.0061	9.4269	0.1061	8.1762
31	19.194	0.0521	181.943	0.0055	9.4790	0.1055	8.2962
32	21.114	0.0474	201.138	0.0050	9.5264	0.1050	8.4091
33	23.225	0.0431	222.252	0.0045	9.5694	0.1045	8.5152
34	25.548	0.0392	245.477	0.0041	9.6086	0.1041	8.6149
35	28.102	0.0356	271.024	0.0037	9.6442	0.1037	8.7086
40	45.259	0.0221	442.593	0.0023	9.7791	0:1023	9.0962
45	72.890	0.0137	718.905	0.0014	9.8628	0.1014	9.3741
50	117.391	0.0085	1163.909	0.0009	9.9148	0.1009	9.5704
55	189.059	0.0053	1880.591	0.0005	9.9471	0.1005	9.7075
60	304.482	0.0033	3034.816	0.0003	9.9672	0.1003	9.8023
65	490.371	0.0020	4893.707	0.0002	9.9796	0.1002	9.8672
70	789.747	0.0013	7887.470	0.0001	9.9873	0.1001	9.9113
75	1271.895	0.0008	12708.954	0.0001	9.9921	0.1001	9.9410
80	2048.400	0.0005	20474.002	0.0001	9.9951	0.1001	9.9609
85	3298.969	0.0003	32979.690	0.0000	9.9970	0.1000	9.9742
90	5313.023	0.0002	53120.226	0.0000	9.9981	0.1000	9.9831
95	8556.676	0.0001	85556.760	0.0000	9.9988	0.1000	9.9889
100	13780.612	0.0001	137796.123	0.0000	9.9993	0.1000	9.9928

G.J. Thuesen/W.J Fabrycky, *Engineering Economy*, 7e, © 1989, pp. 643-698.
Reprinted by permission of Prentice-Hall, Inc., Englewood Cliffs, NJ.

Table A.15.   12% Interest Factors for Annual Compounding Interest

	Single Payment		Equal Payment Series				Uniform gradient-series factor
	Compound-amount factor	Present-worth factor	Compound-amount factor	Sinking-fund factor	Present-worth factor	Capital-recovery factor	
n	To find F Given P F/P i, n	To find P Given F P/F i, n	To find F Given A F/A i, n	To find A Given F A/F i, n	To find P Given A P/A i, n	To find A Given P A/P i, n	To find A Given G A/G i, n
1	1.120	0.8929	1.000	1.0000	0.8929	1.1200	0.0000
2	1.254	0.7972	2.120	0.4717	1.6901	0.5917	0.4717
3	1.405	0.7118	3.374	0.2964	2.4018	0.4164	0.9246
4	1.574	0.6355	4.779	0.2092	3.0374	0.3292	1.3589
5	1.762	0.5674	6.353	0.1574	3.6048	0.2774	1.7746
6	1.974	0.5066	8.115	0.1232	4.1114	0.2432	2.1721
7	2.211	0.4524	10.089	0.0991	4.5638	0.2191	2.5515
8	2.476	0.4039	12.300	0.0813	4.9676	0.2013	2.9132
9	2.773	0.3606	14.776	0.0677	5.3283	0.1877	3.2574
10	3.106	0.3220	17.549	0.0570	5.6502	0.1770	3.5847
11	3.479	0.2875	20.655	0.0484	5.9377	0.1684	3.8953
12	3.896	0.2567	24.133	0.0414	6.1944	0.1614	4.1897
13	4.364	0.2292	28.029	0.0357	6.4236	0.1557	4.4683
14	4.887	0.2046	32.393	0.0309	6.6282	0.1509	4.7317
15	5.474	0.1827	37.280	0.0268	6.8109	0.1468	4.9803
16	6.130	0.1631	42.753	0.0234	6.9740	0.1434	5.2147
17	6.866	0.1457	48.884	0.0205	7.1196	0.1405	5.4353
18	7.690	0.1300	55.750	0.0179	7.2497	0.1379	5.6427
19	8.613	0.1161	63.440	0.0158	7.3658	0.1358	5.8375
20	9.646	0.1037	72.052	0.0139	7.4695	0.1339	6.0202
21	10.804	0.0926	81.699	0.0123	7.5620	0.1323	6.1913
22	12.100	0.0827	92.503	0.0108	7.6447	0.1308	6.3514
23	13.552	0.0738	104.603	0.0096	7.7184	0.1296	6.5010
24	15.179	0.0659	118.155	0.0085	7.7843	0.1285	6.6407
25	17.000	0.0588	133.334	0.0075	7.8431	0.1275	6.7708
26	19.040	0.0525	150.334	0.0067	7.8957	0.1267	6.8921
27	21.325	0.0469	169.374	0.0059	7.9426	0.1259	7.0049
28	23.884	0.0419	190.699	0.0053	7.9844	0.1253	7.1098
29	26.750	0.0374	214.583	0.0047	8.0218	0.1247	7.2071
30	29.960	0.0334	241.333	0.0042	8.0552	0.1242	7.2974
31	33.555	0.0298	271.293	0.0037	8.0850	0.1237	7.3811
32	37.582	0.0266	304.848	0.0033	8.1116	0.1233	7.4586
33	42.092	0.0238	342.429	0.0029	8.1354	0.1229	7.5303
34	47.143	0.0212	384.521	0.0026	8.1566	0.1226	7.5965
35	52.800	0.0189	431.664	0.0023	8.1755	0.1223	7.6577
40	93.051	0.0108	767.091	0.0013	8.2438	0.1213	7.8988
45	163.988	0.0061	1358.230	0.0007	8.2825	0.1207	8.0572
50	289.002	0.0035	2400.018	0.0004	8.3045	0.1204	8.1597

G.J. Thuesen/W.J Fabrycky, *Engineering Economy*, 7e, © 1989, pp. 643-698.
Reprinted by permission of Prentice-Hall, Inc., Englewood Cliffs, NJ.

Table A.16.   15% Interest Factors for Annual Compounding Interest

	Single Payment		Equal Payment Series				Uniform gradient-series factor
	Compound-amount factor	Present-worth factor	Compound-amount factor	Sinking-fund factor	Present-worth factor	Capital-recovery factor	
n	To find *F* Given *P* $F/P \ \ i,n$	To find *P* Given *F* $P/F \ \ i,n$	To find *F* Given *A* $F/A \ \ i,n$	To find *A* Given *F* $A/F \ \ i,n$	To find *P* Given *A* $P/A \ \ i,n$	To find *A* Given *P* $A/P \ \ i,n$	To find *A* Given *G* $A/G \ \ i,n$
1	1.150	0.8696	1.000	1.0000	0.8696	1.1500	0.0000
2	1.323	0.7562	2.150	0.4651	1.6257	0.6151	0.4651
3	1.521	0.6575	3.473	0.2880	2.2832	0.4380	0.9071
4	1.749	0.5718	4.993	0.2003	2.8550	0.3503	1.3263
5	2.011	0.4972	6.742	0.1483	3.3522	0.2983	1.7228
6	2.313	0.4323	8.754	0.1142	3.7845	0.2642	2.0972
7	2.660	0.3759	11.067	0.0904	4.1604	0.2404	2.4499
8	3.059	0.3269	13.727	0.0729	4.4873	0.2229	2.7813
9	3.518	0.2843	16.786	0.0596	4.7716	0.2096	3.0922
10	4.046	0.2472	20.304	0.0493	5.0188	0.1993	3.3832
11	4.652	0.2150	24.349	0.0411	5.2337	0.1911	3.6550
12	5.350	0.1869	29.002	0.0345	5.4206	0.1845	3.9082
13	6.153	0.1625	34.352	0.0291	5.5832	0.1791	4.1438
14	7.076	0.1413	40.505	0.0247	5.7245	0.1747	4.3624
15	8.137	0.1229	47.580	0.0210	5.8474	0.1710	4.5650
16	9.358	0.1069	55.717	0.0180	5.9542	0.1680	4.7523
17	10.761	0.0929	65.075	0.0154	6.0472	0.1654	4.9251
18	12.375	0.0808	75.836	0.0132	6.1280	0.1632	5.0843
19	14.232	0.0703	88.212	0.0113	6.1982	0.1613	5.2307
20	16.367	0.0611	102.444	0.0098	6.2593	0.1598	5.3651
21	18.822	0.0531	118.810	0.0084	6.3125	0.1584	5.4883
22	21.645	0.0462	137.632	0.0073	6.3587	0.1573	5.6010
23	24.891	0.0402	159.276	0.0063	6.3988	0.1563	5.7040
24	28.625	0.0349	184.168	0.0054	6.4338	0.1554	5.7979
25	32.919	0.0304	212.793	0.0047	6.4642	0.1547	5.8834
26	37.857	0.0264	245.712	0.0041	6.4906	0.1541	5.9612
27	43.535	0.0230	283.569	0.0035	6.5135	0.1535	6.0319
28	50.066	0.0200	327.104	0.0031	6.5335	0.1531	6.0960
29	57.575	0.0174	377.170	0.0027	6.5509	0.1527	6.1541
30	66.212	0.0151	434.745	0.0023	6.5660	0.1523	6.2066
31	76.144	0.0131	500.957	0.0020	6.5791	0.1520	6.2541
32	87.565	0.0114	577.100	0.0017	6.5905	0.1517	6.2970
33	100.700	0.0099	664.666	0.0015	6.6005	0.1515	6.3357
34	115.805	0.0086	765.365	0.0013	6.6091	0.1513	6.3705
35	133.176	0.0075	881.170	0.0011	6.6166	0.1511	6.4019
40	267.864	0.0037	1779.090	0.0006	6.6418	0.1506	6.5168
45	538.769	0.0019	3585.128	0.0003	6.6543	0.1503	6.5830
50	1083.657	0.0009	7217.716	0.0002	6.6605	0.1501	6.6205

G.J. Thuesen/W.J Fabrycky, *Engineering Economy*, 7e, © 1989, pp. 643-698.
Reprinted by permission of Prentice-Hall, Inc., Englewood Cliffs, NJ.

Table A.17.   20% Interest Factors for Annual Compounding Interest

	Single Payment		Equal Payment Series				Uniform gradient-series factor
	Compound-amount factor	Present-worth factor	Compound-amount factor	Sinking-fund factor	Present-worth factor	Capital-recovery factor	
n	To find F Given P F/P i,n	To find P Given F P/F i,n	To find F Given A F/A i,n	To find A Given F A/F i,n	To find P Given A P/A i,n	To find A Given P A/P i,n	To find A Given G A/G i,n
1	1.200	0.8333	1.000	1.0000	0.8333	1.2000	0.0000
2	1.440	0.6945	2.200	0.4546	1.5278	0.6546	0.4546
3	1.728	0.5787	3.640	0.2747	2.1065	0.4747	0.8791
4	2.074	0.4823	5.368	0.1863	2.5887	0.3863	1.2742
5	2.488	0.4019	7.442	0.1344	2.9906	0.3344	1.6405
6	2.986	0.3349	9.930	0.1007	3.3255	0.3007	1.9788
7	3.583	0.2791	12.916	0.0774	3.6046	0.2774	2.2902
8	4.300	0.2326	16.499	0.0606	3.8372	0.2606	2.5756
9	5.160	0.1938	20.799	0.0481	4.0310	0.2481	2.8364
10	6.192	0.1615	25.959	0.0385	4.1925	0.2385	3.0739
11	7.430	0.1346	32.150	0.0311	4.3271	0.2311	3.2893
12	8.916	0.1122	39.581	0.0253	4.4392	0.2253	3.4841
13	10.699	0.0935	48.497	0.0206	4.5327	0.2206	3.6597
14	12.839	0.0779	59.196	0.0169	4.6106	0.2169	3.8175
15	15.407	0.0649	72.035	0.0139	4.6755	0.2139	3.9589
16	18.488	0.0541	87.442	0.0114	4.7296	0.2114	4.0851
17	22.186	0.0451	105.931	0.0095	4.7746	0.2095	4.1976
18	26.623	0.0376	128.117	0.0078	4.8122	0.2078	4.2975
19	31.948	0.0313	154.740	0.0065	4.8435	0.2065	4.3861
20	38.338	0.0261	186.688	0.0054	4.8696	0.2054	4.4644
21	46.005	0.0217	225.026	0.0045	4.8913	0.2045	4.5334
22	55.206	0.0181	271.031	0.0037	4.9094	0.2037	4.5942
23	66.247	0.0151	326.237	0.0031	4.9245	0.2031	4.6475
24	79.497	0.0126	392.484	0.0026	4.9371	0.2026	4.6943
25	95.396	0.0105	471.981	0.0021	4.9476	0.2021	4.7352
26	114.475	0.0087	567.377	0.0018	4.9563	0.2018	4.7709
27	137.371	0.0073	681.853	0.0015	4.9636	0.2015	4.8020
28	164.845	0.0061	819.223	0.0012	4.9697	0.2012	4.8291
29	197.814	0.0051	984.068	0.0010	4.9747	0.2010	4.8527
30	237.376	0.0042	1181.882	0.0009	4.9789	0.2009	4.8731
31	284.852	0.0035	1419.258	0.0007	4.9825	0.2007	4.8908
32	341.822	0.0029	1704.109	0.0006	4.9854	0.2006	4.9061
33	410.186	0.0024	2045.931	0.0005	4.9878	0.2005	4.9194
34	492.224	0.0020	2456.118	0.0004	4.9899	0.2004	4.9308
35	590.668	0.0017	2948.341	0.0003	4.9915	0.2003	4.9407
40	1469.772	0.0007	7343.858	0.0002	4.9966	0.2001	4.9728
45	3657.262	0.0003	18281.310	0.0001	4.9986	0.2001	4.9877
50	9100.438	0.0001	45497.191	0.0000	4.9995	0.2000	4.9945

G.J. Thuesen/W.J Fabrycky, *Engineering Economy*, 7e, © 1989, pp. 643-698.
Reprinted by permission of Prentice-Hall, Inc., Englewood Cliffs, NJ.

Table A.18.   25% Interest Factors for Annual Compounding Interest

	Single Payment		Equal Payment Series				Uniform gradient-series factor
	Compound-amount factor	Present-worth factor	Compound-amount factor	Sinking-fund factor	Present-worth factor	Capital-recovery factor	
n	To find F Given P F/P i,n	To find P Given F P/F i,n	To find F Given A F/A i,n	To find A Given F A/F i,n	To find P Given A P/A i,n	To find A Given P A/P i,n	To find A Given G A/G i,n
1	1.250	0.8000	1.000	1.0000	0.8000	1.2500	0.0000
2	1.563	0.6400	2.250	0.4445	1.4400	0.6945	0.4445
3	1.953	0.5120	3.813	0.2623	1.9520	0.5123	0.8525
4	2.441	0.4096	5.766	0.1735	2.3616	0.4235	1.2249
5	3.052	0.3277	8.207	0.1219	2.6893	0.3719	1.5631
6	3.815	0.2622	11.259	0.0888	2.9514	0.3388	1.8683
7	4.768	0.2097	15.073	0.0664	3.1611	0.3164	2.1424
8	5.960	0.1678	19.842	0.0504	3.3289	0.3004	2.3873
9	7.451	0.1342	25.802	0.0388	3.4631	0.2888	2.6048
10	9.313	0.1074	33.253	0.0301	3.5705	0.2801	2.7971
11	11.642	0.0859	42.566	0.0235	3.6564	0.2735	2.9663
12	14.552	0.0687	54.208	0.0185	3.7251	0.2685	3.1145
13	18.190	0.0550	68.760	0.0146	3.7801	0.2646	3.2438
14	22.737	0.0440	86.949	0.0115	3.8241	0.2615	3.3560
15	28.422	0.0352	109.687	0.0091	3.8593	0.2591	3.4530
16	35.527	0.0282	138.109	0.0073	3.8874	0.2573	3.5366
17	44.409	0.0225	173.636	0.0058	3.9099	0.2558	3.6084
18	55.511	0.0180	218.045	0.0046	3.9280	0.2546	3.6698
19	69.389	0.0144	273.556	0.0037	3.9424	0.2537	3.7222
20	86.736	0.0115	342.945	0.0029	3.9539	0.2529	3.7667
21	108.420	0.0092	429.681	0.0023	3.9631	0.2523	3.8045
22	135.525	0.0074	538.101	0.0019	3.9705	0.2519	3.8365
23	169.407	0.0059	673.626	0.0015	3.9764	0.2515	3.8634
24	211.758	0.0047	843.033	0.0012	3.9811	0.2512	3.8861
25	264.698	0.0038	1054.791	0.0010	3.9849	0.2510	3.9052
26	330.872	0.0030	1319.489	0.0008	3.9879	0.2508	3.9212
27	413.590	0.0024	1650.361	0.0006	3.9903	0.2506	3.9346
28	516.988	0.0019	2063.952	0.0005	3.9923	0.2505	3.9457
29	646.235	0.0016	2580.939	0.0004	3.9938	0.2504	3.9551
30	807.794	0.0012	3227.174	0.0003	3.9951	0.2503	3.9628
31	1009.742	0.0010	4034.968	0.0003	3.9960	0.2503	3.9693
32	1262.177	0.0008	5044.710	0.0002	3.9968	0.2502	3.9746
33	1577.722	0.0006	6306.887	0.0002	3.9975	0.2502	3.9791
34	1972.152	0.0005	7884.609	0.0001	3.9980	0.2501	3.9828
35	2465.190	0.0004	9856.761	0.0001	3.9984	0.2501	3.9858

G.J. Thuesen/W.J Fabrycky, *Engineering Economy*, 7e, © 1989, pp. 643-698. Reprinted by permission of Prentice-Hall, Inc., Englewood Cliffs, NJ.

Table A.19.   **30% Interest Factors for Annual Compounding Interest**

	Single Payment		Equal Payment Series				Uniform gradient-series factor
	Compound-amount factor	Present-worth factor	Compound-amount factor	Sinking-fund factor	Present-worth factor	Capital-recovery factor	
n	To find F Given P F/P i, n	To find P Given F P/F i, n	To find F Given A F/A i, n	To find A Given F A/F i, n	To find P Given A P/A i, n	To find A Given P A/P i, n	To find A Given G A/G i, n
1	1.300	0.7692	1.000	1.0000	0.7692	1.3000	0.0000
2	1.690	0.5917	2.300	0.4348	1.3610	0.7348	0.4348
3	2.197	0.4552	3.990	0.2506	1.8161	0.5506	0.8271
4	2.856	0.3501	6.187	0.1616	2.1663	0.4616	1.1783
5	3.713	0.2693	9.043	0.1106	2.4356	0.4106	1.4903
6	4.827	0.2072	12.756	0.0784	2.6428	0.3784	1.7655
7	6.275	0.1594	17.583	0.0569	2.8021	0.3569	2.0063
8	8.157	0.1226	23.858	0.0419	2.9247	0.3419	2.2156
9	10.605	0.0943	32.015	0.0312	3.0190	0.3312	2.3963
10	13.786	0.0725	42.620	0.0235	3.0915	0.3235	2.5512
11	17.922	0.0558	56.405	0.0177	3.1473	0.3177	2.6833
12	23.298	0.0429	74.327	0.0135	3.1903	0.3135	2.7952
13	30.288	0.0330	97.625	0.0103	3.2233	0.3103	2.8895
14	39.374	0.0254	127.913	0.0078	3.2487	0.3078	2.9685
15	51.186	0.0195	167.286	0.0060	3.2682	0.3060	3.0345
16	66.542	0.0150	218.472	0.0046	3.2832	0.3046	3.0892
17	86.504	0.0116	285.014	0.0035	3.2948	0.3035	3.1345
18	112.455	0.0089	371.518	0.0027	3.3037	0.3027	3.1718
19	146.192	0.0069	483.973	0.0021	3.3105	0.3021	3.2025
20	190.050	0.0053	630.165	0.0016	3.3158	0.3016	3.2276
21	247.065	0.0041	820.215	0.0012	3.3199	0.3012	3.2480
22	321.184	0.0031	1067.280	0.0009	3.3230	0.3009	3.2646
23	417.539	0.0024	1388.464	0.0007	3 3254	0.3007	3.2781
24	542.801	0.0019	1806.003	0.0006	3.3272	0.3006	3.2890
25	705.641	0.0014	2348.803	0.0004	3.3286	0.3004	3.2979
26	917.333	0.0011	3054.444	0.0003	3.3297	0.3003	3.3050
27	1192.533	0.0008	3971.778	0.0003	3.3305	0.3003	3.3107
28	1550.293	0.0007	5164.311	0.0002	3.3312	0.3002	3.3153
29	2015.381	0.0005	6714.604	0.0002	3.3317	0.3002	3.3189
30	2619.996	0.0004	8729.985	0.0001	3.3321	0.3001	3.3219
31	3405.994	0.0003	11349.981	0.0001	3.3324	0.3001	3.3242
32	4427.793	0.0002	14755.975	0.0001	3.3326	0.3001	3.3261
33	5756.130	0.0002	19183.768	0.0001	3.3328	0.3001	3.3276
34	7482.970	0.0001	24939.899	0.0001	3.3329	0.3001	3.3288
35	9727.860	0.0001	32422.868	0.0000	3.3330	0.3000	3.3297

G.J. Thuesen/W.J Fabrycky, *Engineering Economy*, 7e, © 1989, pp. 643-698.
Reprinted by permission of Prentice-Hall, Inc., Englewood Cliffs, NJ.

Table A.20.   40% Interest Factors for Annual Compounding Interest

	Single Payment		Equal Payment Series				Uniform gradient-series factor
	Compound-amount factor	Present-worth factor	Compound-amount factor	Sinking-fund factor	Present-worth factor	Capital-recovery factor	
n	To find F Given P $F/P\ i, n$	To find P Given F $P/F\ i, n$	To find F Given A $F/A\ i, n$	To find A Given F $A/F\ i, n$	To find P Given A $P/A\ i, n$	To find A Given P $A/P\ i, n$	To find A Given G $A/G\ i, n$
1	1.400	0.7143	1.000	1.0001	0.7143	1.4001	0.0000
2	1.960	0.5103	2.400	0.4167	1.2245	0.8167	0.4167
3	2.744	0.3645	4.360	0.2294	1.5890	0.6294	0.7799
4	3.842	0.2604	7.104	0.1408	1.8493	0.5408	1.0924
5	5.378	0.1860	10.946	0.0914	2.0352	0.4914	1.3580
6	7.530	0.1329	16.324	0.0613	2.1680	0.4613	1.5811
7	10.541	0.0949	23.853	0.0420	2.2629	0.4420	1.7664
8	14.758	0.0678	34.395	0.0291	2.3306	0.4291	1.9186
9	20.661	0.0485	49.153	0.0204	2.3790	0.4204	2.0423
10	28.925	0.0346	69.814	0.0144	2.4136	0.4144	2.1420
11	40.496	0.0247	98.739	0.0102	2.4383	0.4102	2.2215
12	56.694	0.0177	139.234	0.0072	2.4560	0.4072	2.2846
13	79.371	0.0126	195.928	0.0052	2.4686	0.4052	2.3342
14	111.120	0.0090	275.299	0.0037	2.4775	0.4037	2.3729
15	155.568	0.0065	386.419	0.0026	2.4840	0.4026	2.4030
16	217.794	0.0046	541.986	0.0019	2.4886	0.4019	2.4262
17	304.912	0.0033	759.780	0.0014	2.4918	0.4014	2.4441
18	426.877	0.0024	1064.691	0.0010	2.4942	0.4010	2.4578
19	597.627	0.0017	1491.567	0.0007	2.4959	0.4007	2.4682
20	836.678	0.0012	2089.195	0.0005	2.4971	0.4005	2.4761
21	1171.348	0.0009	2925.871	0.0004	2.4979	0.4004	2.4821
22	1639.887	0.0007	4097.218	0.0003	2.4985	0.4003	2.4866
23	2295.842	0.0005	5737.105	0.0002	2.4990	0.4002	2.4900
24	3214.178	0.0004	8032.945	0.0002	2.4993	0.4002	2.4926
25	4499.847	0.0003	11247.110	0.0001	2.4995	0.4001	2.4945
26	6299.785	0.0002	15746.960	0.0001	2.4997	0.4001	2.4959
27	8819.695	0.0002	22046.730	0.0001	2.4998	0.4001	2.4970
28	12347.570	0.0001	30866.430	0.0001	2.4998	0.4001	2.4978
29	17286.590	0.0001	43213.990	0.0001	2.4999	0.4001	2.4984
30	24201.230	0.0001	60500.580	0.0001	2.4999	0.4001	2.4988

G.J. Thuesen/W.J Fabrycky, *Engineering Economy*, 7e, © 1989, pp. 643-698.
Reprinted by permission of Prentice-Hall, Inc., Englewood Cliffs, NJ.

Table A.21. **50% Interest Factors for Annual Compounding Interest**

	Single Payment		Equal Payment Series				Uniform gradient-series factor
	Compound-amount factor	Present-worth factor	Compound-amount factor	Sinking-fund factor	Present-worth factor	Capital-recovery factor	
n	To find F Given P $F/P\,i,n$	To find P Given F $P/F\,i,n$	To find F Given A $F/A\,i,n$	To find A Given F $A/F\,i,n$	To find P Given A $P/A\,i,n$	To find A Given P $A/P\,i,n$	To find A Given G $A/G\,i,n$
1	1.500	0.6667	1.000	1.0000	0.6667	1.5000	0.0001
2	2.250	0.4445	2.500	0.4000	1.1112	0.9001	0.4001
3	3.375	0.2963	4.750	0.2106	1.4075	0.7106	0.7369
4	5.063	0.1976	8.125	0.1231	1.6050	0.6231	1.0154
5	7.594	0.1317	13.188	0.0759	1.7367	0.5759	1.2418
6	11.391	0.0878	20.781	0.0482	1.8245	0.5482	1.4226
7	17.086	0.0586	32.172	0.0311	1.8830	0.5311	1.5649
8	25.629	0.0391	49.258	0.0204	1.9220	0.5204	1.6752
9	38.443	0.0261	74.887	0.0134	1.9480	0.5134	1.7597
10	57.665	0.0174	113.330	0.0089	1.9654	0.5089	1.8236
11	86.498	0.0116	170.995	0.0059	1.9769	0.5059	1.8714
12	129.746	0.0078	257.493	0.0039	1.9846	0.5039	1.9068
13	194.620	0.0052	387.239	0.0026	1.9898	0.5026	1.9329
14	291.929	0.0035	581.858	0.0018	1.9932	0.5018	1.9519
15	437.894	0.0023	873.788	0.0012	1.9955	0.5012	1.9657
16	656.841	0.0016	1311.681	0.0008	1.9970	0.5008	1.9757
17	985.261	0.0011	1968.522	0.0006	1.9980	0.5006	1.9828
18	1477.891	0.0007	2953.783	0.0004	1.9987	0.5004	1.9879
19	2216.837	0.0005	4431.671	0.0003	1.9991	0.5003	1.9915
20	3325.256	0.0004	6648.511	0.0002	1.9994	0.5002	1.9940
21	4987.882	0.0003	9973.765	0.0002	1.9996	0.5002	1.9958
22	7481.824	0.0002	14961.640	0.0001	1.9998	0.5001	1.9971
23	11222.730	0.0001	22443.470	0.0001	1.9999	0.5001	1.9980
24	16834.100	0.0001	33666.210	0.0001	1.9999	0.5001	1.9986
25	25251.160	0.0001	50500.330	0.0001	2.0000	0.5001	1.9991

G.J. Thuesen/W.J Fabrycky, *Engineering Economy*, 7e, © 1989, pp. 643-698. Reprinted by permission of Prentice-Hall, Inc., Englewood Cliffs, NJ.

APPENDIX

B

CONVERSION OF NOMINAL RATES TO EFFECTIVE RATES

Table B.1. **Effective Interest Rates Corresponding to Nominal Rate r**

r	Compounding Frequency					
	Semi-annually $\left(1+\frac{r}{2}\right)^2 -1$	Quarterly $\left(1+\frac{r}{4}\right)^4 -1$	Monthly $\left(1+\frac{r}{12}\right)^{12} -1$	Weekly $\left(1+\frac{r}{52}\right)^{52} -1$	Daily $\left(1+\frac{r}{365}\right)^{365} -1$	Continuously $\left(1+\frac{r}{\infty}\right)^{\infty} -1$
.01	.010025	.010038	.010046	.010049	.010050	.010050
.02	.020100	.020151	.020184	.020197	.020200	.020201
.03	.030225	.030339	.030416	.030444	.030451	.030455
.04	.040400	.040604	.040741	.040793	.040805	.040811
.05	.050625	.050945	.051161	.051244	.051261	.051271
.06	.060900	.061364	.061678	.061797	.061799	.061837
.07	.071225	.071859	.072290	.072455	.072469	.072508
.08	.081600	.082432	.082999	.083217	.083246	.083287
.09	.092025	.093083	.093807	.094085	.094132	.094174
.10	.102500	.103813	.104713	.105060	.105126	.105171
.11	.113025	.114621	.115718	.116144	.116231	.116278
.12	.123600	.125509	.126825	.127336	.127447	.127497
.13	.134225	.136476	.138032	.138644	.138775	.138828
.14	.144900	.147523	.149341	.150057	.150217	.150274
.15	.155625	.158650	.160755	.161582	.161773	.161834
.16	.166400	.169859	.172270	.173221	.173446	.173511
.17	.177225	.181148	.183891	.184974	.185235	.185305
.18	.188100	.192517	.195618	.196843	.197142	.197217
.19	.199025	.203971	.207451	.208828	.209169	.209250
.20	.210000	.215506	.219390	.220931	.221316	.221403
.21	.221025	.227124	.231439	.233153	.233584	.233678
.22	.232100	.238825	.243596	.245494	.245976	.246077
.23	.243225	.250609	.255863	.257957	.258492	.258600
.24	.254400	.262477	.268242	.270542	.271133	.271249
.25	.265625	.274429	.280731	.283250	.283901	.284025
.26	.276900	.286466	.293333	.296090	.296796	.296930
.27	.288225	.298588	.306050	.309049	.309821	.309964
.28	.299600	.310796	.318880	.322135	.322976	.323130
.29	.311025	.323089	.331826	.335350	.336264	.336428
.30	.322500	.335469	.344889	.348693	.349684	.349859
.31	.334025	.347936	.358068	.362168	.363238	.363425
.32	.345600	.360489	.371366	.375775	.376928	.377128
.33	.357225	.373130	.384784	.389515	.390756	.390968
.34	.368900	.385859	.398321	.403389	.404722	.404948
.35	.380625	.398676	.411979	.417399	.418827	.419068

G.J. Thuesen/W.J Fabrycky, *Engineering Economy*, 7e, © 1989, pp. 643-698. Reprinted by permission of Prentice-Hall, Inc., Englewood Cliffs, NJ.

APPENDIX

C

CONTINUOUS INTEREST FACTORS

Table C.1. 1% Interest Factors for Continuous Compounding Interest

	Single Payment		Equal Payment Series				Uniform gradient-series factor
	Compound-amount factor	Present-worth factor	Compound-amount factor	Sinking-fund factor	Present-worth factor	Capital-recovery factor	
n	To find F Given P F/P r,n	To find P Given F P/F r,n	To find F Given A F/A r,n	To find A Given F A/F r,n	To find P Given A P/A r,n	To find A Given P A/P r,n	To find A Given G A/G r,n
1	1.010	0.9901	1.000	1.0000	0.9901	1.0101	0.0000
2	1.020	0.9802	2.010	0.4975	1.9703	0.5076	0.4975
3	1.030	0.9705	3.030	0.3300	2.9407	0.3401	0.9933
4	1.041	0.9608	4.061	0.2463	3.9015	0.2563	1.4875
5	1.051	0.9512	5.102	0.1960	4.8527	0.2061	1.9800
6	1.062	0.9418	6.153	0.1625	5.7945	0.1726	2.4708
7	1.073	0.9324	7.215	0.1386	6.7269	0.1487	2.9600
8	1.083	0.9231	8.287	0.1207	7.6500	0.1307	3.4475
9	1.094	0.9139	9.370	0.1067	8.5639	0.1168	3.9334
10	1.105	0.9048	10.465	0.0956	9.4688	0.1056	4.4175
11	1.116	0.8958	11.570	0.0864	10.3646	0.0965	4.9000
12	1.128	0.8869	12.686	0.0788	11.2515	0.0889	5.3809
13	1.139	0.8781	13.814	0.0724	12.1296	0.0825	5.8600
14	1.150	0.8694	14.952	0.0669	12.9990	0.0769	6.3376
15	1.162	0.8607	16.103	0.0621	13.8597	0.0722	6.8134
16	1.174	0.8522	17.264	0.0579	14.7118	0.0680	7.2876
17	1.185	0.8437	18.438	0.0542	15.5555	0.0643	7.7601
18	1.197	0.8353	19.623	0.0510	16.3908	0.0610	8.2310
19	1.209	0.8270	20.821	0.0480	17.2177	0.0581	8.7002
20	1.221	0.8187	22.030	0.0454	18.0365	0.0555	9.1677
21	1.234	0.8106	23.251	0.0430	18.8470	0.0531	9.6336
22	1.246	0.8025	24.485	0.0409	19.6496	0.0509	10.0978
23	1.259	0.7945	25.731	0.0389	20.4441	0.0489	10.5604
24	1.271	0.7866	26.990	0.0371	21.2307	0.0471	11.0213
25	1.284	0.7788	28.261	0.0354	22.0095	0.0454	11.4806
26	1.297	0.7711	29.545	0.0339	22.7806	0.0439	11.9381
27	1.310	0.7634	30.842	0.0324	23.5439	0.0425	12.3941
28	1.323	0.7558	32.152	0.0311	24.2997	0.0412	12.8484
29	1.336	0.7483	33.475	0.0299	25.0480	0.0399	13.3010
30	1.350	0.7408	34.811	0.0287	25.7888	0.0388	13.7520
31	1.363	0.7335	36.161	0.0277	26.5223	0.0377	14.2013
32	1.377	0.7262	37.525	0.0267	27.2484	0.0367	14.6490
33	1.391	0.7189	38.902	0.0257	27.9673	0.0358	15.0950
34	1.405	0.7118	40.293	0.0248	28.6791	0.0349	15.5394
35	1.419	0.7047	41.698	0.0240	29.3838	0.0340	15.9821
40	1.492	0.6703	48.937	0.0204	32.8034	0.0305	18.1711
45	1.568	0.6376	56.548	0.0177	36.0563	0.0277	20.3190
50	1.649	0.6065	64.548	0.0155	39.1505	0.0256	22.4261
55	1.733	0.5770	72.959	0.0137	42.0939	0.0238	24.4926
60	1.822	0.5488	81.802	0.0122	44.8936	0.0223	26.5187
65	1.916	0.5221	91.097	0.0110	47.5569	0.0210	28.5045
70	2.014	0.4966	100.869	0.0099	50.0902	0.0200	30.4505
75	2.117	0.4724	111.142	0.0090	52.5000	0.0191	32.3567
80	2.226	0.4493	121.942	0.0082	54.7922	0.0183	34.2235
85	2.340	0.4274	133.296	0.0075	56.9727	0.0176	36.0513
90	2.460	0.4066	145.232	0.0069	59.0468	0.0169	37.8402
95	2.586	0.3868	157.779	0.0063	61.0198	0.0164	39.5907
100	2.718	0.3679	170.970	0.0059	62.8965	0.0159	41.3032

G.J. Thuesen/W.J Fabrycky, *Engineering Economy*, 7e, © 1989, pp. 643-698.
Reprinted by permission of Prentice-Hall, Inc., Englewood Cliffs, NJ.

Table C.2. 2% Interest Factors for Continuous Compounding Interest

n	Single Payment		Equal Payment Series				Uniform gradient-series factor
	Compound-amount factor	Present-worth factor	Compound-amount factor	Sinking-fund factor	Present-worth factor	Capital-recovery factor	
	To find F Given P F/P r,n	To find P Given F P/F r,n	To find F Given A F/A r,n	To find A Given F A/F r,n	To find P Given A P/A r,n	To find A Given P A/P r,n	To find A Given G A/G r,n
1	1.020	0.9802	1.000	1.0000	0.9802	1.0202	0.0000
2	1.041	0.9608	2.020	0.4950	1.9410	0.5152	0.4950
3	1.062	0.9418	3.061	0.3267	2.8828	0.3469	0.9867
4	1.083	0.9231	4.123	0.2426	3.8059	0.2628	1.4750
5	1.105	0.9048	5.206	0.1921	4.7107	0.2123	1.9600
6	1.128	0.8869	6.311	0.1585	5.5976	0.1787	2.4417
7	1.150	0.8694	7.439	0.1344	6.4670	0.1546	2.9200
8	1.174	0.8522	8.589	0.1164	7.3191	0.1366	3.3951
9	1.197	0.8353	9.763	0.1024	8.1544	0.1226	3.8667
10	1.221	0.8187	10.960	0.0913	8.9731	0.1115	4.3351
11	1.246	0.8025	12.181	0.0821	9.7757	0.1023	4.8002
12	1.271	0.7866	13.427	0.0745	10.5623	0.0947	5.2619
13	1.297	0.7711	14.699	0.0680	11.3333	0.0882	5.7203
14	1.323	0.7558	15.995	0.0625	12.0891	0.0827	6.1754
15	1.350	0.7408	17.319	0.0578	12.8299	0.0780	6.6272
16	1.377	0.7262	18.668	0.0536	13.5561	0.0738	7.0757
17	1.405	0.7118	20.046	0.0499	14.2679	0.0701	7.5209
18	1.433	0.6977	21.451	0.0466	14.9655	0.0668	7.9628
19	1.462	0.6839	22.884	0.0437	15.6494	0.0639	8.4015
20	1.492	0.6703	24.346	0.0411	16.3197	0.0613	8.8368
21	1.522	0.6571	25.838	0.0387	16.9768	0.0589	9.2688
22	1.553	0.6440	27.360	0.0366	17.6208	0.0568	9.6976
23	1.584	0.6313	28.913	0.0346	18.2521	0.0548	10.1231
24	1.616	0.6188	30.497	0.0328	18.8709	0.0530	10.5453
25	1.649	0.6065	32.113	0.0312	19.4774	0.0514	10.9643
26	1.682	0.5945	33.762	0.0296	20.0719	0.0498	11.3801
27	1.716	0.5828	35.444	0.0282	20.6547	0.0484	11.7925
28	1.751	0.5712	37.160	0.0269	21.2259	0.0471	12.2018
29	1.786	0.5599	38.910	0.0257	21.7858	0.0459	12.6078
30	1.822	0.5488	40.696	0.0246	22.3346	0.0448	13.0106
31	1.859	0.5380	42.518	0.0235	22.8725	0.0437	13.4102
32	1.896	0.5273	44.377	0.0225	23.3998	0.0427	13.8065
33	1.935	0.5169	46.274	0.0216	23.9167	0.0418	14.1997
34	1.974	0.5066	48.209	0.0208	24.4233	0.0410	14.5897
35	2.014	0.4966	50.182	0.0199	24.9199	0.0401	14.9765
40	2.226	0.4493	60.666	0.0165	27.2591	0.0367	16.8630
45	2.460	0.4066	72.253	0.0139	29.3758	0.0341	18.6714
50	2.718	0.3679	85.058	0.0118	31.2910	0.0320	20.4028
55	3.004	0.3329	99.210	0.0101	33.0240	0.0303	22.0588
60	3.320	0.3012	114.850	0.0087	34.5921	0.0289	23.6409
65	3.669	0.2725	132.135	0.0076	36.0109	0.0278	25.1507
70	4.055	0.2466	151.238	0.0066	37.2947	0.0268	26.5899
75	4.482	0.2231	172.349	0.0058	38.4564	0.0260	27.9604
80	4.953	0.2019	195.682	0.0051	39.5075	0.0253	29.2640
85	5.474	0.1827	221.468	0.0045	40.4585	0.0247	30.5028
90	6.050	0.1653	249.966	0.0040	41.3191	0.0242	31.6786
95	6.686	0.1496	281.461	0.0036	42.0978	0.0238	32.7937
100	7.389	0.1353	316.269	0.0032	42.8024	0.0234	33.8499

G.J. Thuesen/W.J Fabrycky, *Engineering Economy*, 7e, © 1989, pp. 643-698.
Reprinted by permission of Prentice-Hall, Inc., Englewood Cliffs, NJ.

Table C.3.   **3% Interest Factors for Continuous Compounding Interest**

	Single Payment		Equal Payment Series				Uniform gradient-series factor
	Compound-amount factor	Present-worth factor	Compound-amount factor	Sinking-fund factor	Present-worth factor	Capital-recovery factor	
n	To find F Given P F/P r,n	To find P Given F P/F r,n	To find F Given A F/A r,n	To find A Given F A/F r,n	To find P Given A P/A r,n	To find A Given P A/P r,n	To find A Given G A/G r,n
1	1.030	0.9705	1.000	1.0000	0.9705	1.0305	0.0000
2	1.062	0.9418	2.030	0.4925	1.9122	0.5230	0.4925
3	1.094	0.9139	3.092	0.3234	2.8262	0.3538	0.9800
4	1.128	0.8869	4.186	0.2389	3.7131	0.2693	1.4625
5	1.162	0.8607	5.314	0.1882	4.5738	0.2186	1.9400
6	1.197	0.8353	6.476	0.1544	5.4090	0.1849	2.4126
7	1.234	0.8106	7.673	0.1303	6.2196	0.1608	2.8801
8	1.271	0.7866	8.907	0.1123	7.0063	0.1427	3.3427
9	1.310	0.7634	10.178	0.0983	7.7696	0.1287	3.8003
10	1.350	0.7408	11.488	0.0871	8.5105	0.1175	4.2529
11	1.391	0.7189	12.838	0.0779	9.2294	0.1084	4.7006
12	1.433	0.6977	14.229	0.0703	9.9271	0.1007	5.1433
13	1.477	0.6771	15.662	0.0639	10.6041	0.0943	5.5811
14	1.522	0.6571	17.139	0.0584	11.2612	0.0888	6.0139
15	1.568	0.6376	18.661	0.0536	11.8988	0.0841	6.4419
16	1.616	0.6188	20.229	0.0494	12.5176	0.0799	6.8650
17	1.665	0.6005	21.845	0.0458	13.1181	0.0762	7.2831
18	1.716	0.5828	23.511	0.0425	13.7008	0.0730	7.6964
19	1.768	0.5655	25.227	0.0397	14.2663	0.0701	8.1049
20	1.822	0.5488	26.995	0.0371	14.8152	0.0675	8.5085
21	1.878	0.5326	28.817	0.0347	15.3477	0.0652	8.9072
22	1.935	0.5169	30.695	0.0326	15.8646	0.0630	9.3012
23	1.994	0.5016	32.629	0.0307	16.3662	0.0611	9.6904
24	2.054	0.4868	34.623	0.0289	16.8529	0.0593	10.0748
25	2.117	0.4724	36.678	0.0273	17.3253	0.0577	10.4545
26	2.181	0.4584	38.795	0.0258	17.7837	0.0562	10.8294
27	2.248	0.4449	40.976	0.0244	18.2286	0.0549	11.1996
28	2.316	0.4317	43.224	0.0231	18.6603	0.0536	11.5652
29	2.387	0.4190	45.540	0.0220	19.0792	0.0524	11.9261
30	2.460	0.4066	47.927	0.0209	19.4858	0.0513	12.2823
31	2.535	0.3946	50.387	0.0199	19.8803	0.0503	12.6339
32	2.612	0.3829	52.921	0.0189	20.2632	0.0494	12.9810
33	2.691	0.3716	55.533	0.0180	20.6348	0.0485	13.3235
34	2.773	0.3606	58.224	0.0172	20.9954	0.0476	13.6614
35	2.858	0.3499	60.998	0.0164	21.3453	0.0469	13.9948
40	3.320	0.3012	76.183	0.0131	22.9459	0.0436	15.5953
45	3.857	0.2593	93.826	0.0107	24.3235	0.0411	17.0874
50	4.482	0.2231	114.324	0.0088	25.5092	0.0392	18.4750
55	5.207	0.1921	138.140	0.0072	26.5297	0.0377	19.7623
60	6.050	0.1653	165.809	0.0060	27.4081	0.0365	20.9538
65	7.029	0.1423	197.957	0.0051	28.1642	0.0355	22.0540
70	8.166	0.1225	235.307	0.0043	28.8149	0.0347	23.0677
75	9.488	0.1054	278.702	0.0036	29.3750	0.0341	23.9996
80	11.023	0.0907	329.119	0.0030	29.8570	0.0335	24.8543
85	12.807	0.0781	387.696	0.0026	30.2720	0.0330	25.6368
90	14.880	0.0672	455.753	0.0022	30.6291	0.0327	26.3516
95	17.288	0.0579	534.823	0.0019	30.9365	0.0323	27.0033
100	20.086	0.0498	626.690	0.0016	31.2010	0.0321	27.5963

G.J. Thuesen/W.J Fabrycky, *Engineering Economy*, 7e, © 1989, pp. 643-698. Reprinted by permission of Prentice-Hall, Inc., Englewood Cliffs, NJ.

Table C.4.   4% Interest Factors for Continuous Compounding Interest

	Single Payment		Equal Payment Series				Uniform gradient-series factor
	Compound-amount factor	Present-worth factor	Compound-amount factor	Sinking-fund factor	Present-worth factor	Capital-recovery factor	
n	To find F Given P F/P r,n	To find P Given F P/F r,n	To find F Given A F/A r,n	To find A Given F A/F r,n	To find P Given A P/A r,n	To find A Given P A/P r,n	To find A Given G A/G r,n
1	1.041	0.9608	1.000	1.0000	0.9608	1.0408	0.0000
2	1.083	0.9231	2.041	0.4900	1.8839	0.5308	0.4900
3	1.128	0.8869	3.124	0.3201	2.7708	0.3609	0.9734
4	1.174	0.8522	4.252	0.2352	3.6230	0.2760	1.4500
5	1.221	0.8187	5.425	0.1843	4.4417	0.2251	1.9201
6	1.271	0.7866	6.647	0.1505	5.2283	0.1913	2.3835
7	1.323	0.7558	7.918	0.1263	5.9841	0.1671	2.8402
8	1.377	0.7262	9.241	0.1082	6.7103	0.1490	3.2904
9	1.433	0.6977	10.618	0.0942	7.4079	0.1350	3.7339
10	1.492	0.6703	12.051	0.0830	8.0783	0.1238	4.1709
11	1.553	0.6440	13.543	0.0738	8.7223	0.1147	4.6013
12	1.616	0.6188	15.096	0.0663	9.3411	0.1071	5.0252
13	1.682	0.5945	16.712	0.0598	9.9356	0.1007	5.4425
14	1.751	0.5712	18.394	0.0644	10.5068	0.0952	5.8534
15	1.822	0.5488	20.145	0.0497	11.0556	0.0905	6.2578
16	1.896	0.5273	21.967	0.0455	11.5829	0.0863	6.6558
17	1.974	0.5066	23.863	0.0419	12.0895	0.0827	7.0474
18	2.054	0.4868	25.837	0.0387	12.5763	0.0795	7.4326
19	2.138	0.4677	27.892	0.0359	13.0440	0.0767	7.8114
20	2.226	0.4493	30.030	0.0333	13.4933	0.0741	8.1840
21	2.316	0.4317	32.255	0.0310	13.9250	0.0718	8.5503
22	2.411	0.4148	34.572	0.0289	14.3398	0.0697	8.9105
23	2.509	0.3985	36.983	0.0270	14.7383	0.0679	9.2644
24	2.612	0.3829	39.492	0.0253	15.1212	0.0661	9.6122
25	2.718	0.3679	42.104	0.0238	15.4891	0.0646	9.9539
26	2.829	0.3535	44.822	0.0223	15.8425	0.0631	10.2896
27	2.945	0.3396	47.651	0.0210	16.1821	0.0618	10.6193
28	3.065	0.3263	50.596	0.0198	16.5084	0.0606	10.9431
29	3.190	0.3135	53.661	0.0186	16.8219	0.0595	11.2609
30	3.320	0.3012	56.851	0.0176	17.1231	0.0584	11.5730
31	3.456	0.2894	60.171	0.0166	17.4125	0.0574	11.8792
32	3.597	0.2780	63.626	0.0157	17.6905	0.0565	12.1797
33	3.743	0.2671	67.223	0.0149	17.9576	0.0557	12.4746
34	3.896	0.2567	70.966	0.0141	18.2143	0.0549	12.7638
35	4.055	0.2466	74.863	0.0134	18.4609	0.0542	13.0475
40	4.953	0.2019	96.862	0.0103	19.5562	0.0511	14.3845
45	6.050	0.1653	123.733	0.0081	20.4530	0.0489	15.5918
50	7.389	0.1353	156.553	0.0064	21.1872	0.0472	16.6775
55	9.025	0.1108	196.640	0.0051	21.7883	0.0459	17.6498
60	11.023	0.0907	245.601	0.0041	22.2805	0.0449	18.5172
65	13.464	0.0743	305.403	0.0033	22.6834	0.0441	19.2882
70	16.445	0.0608	378.445	0.0027	23.0133	0.0435	19.9710
75	20.086	0.0498	467.659	0.0021	23.2834	0.0430	20.5737
80	24.533	0.0408	576.625	0.0017	23.5045	0.0426	21.1038
85	29.964	0.0334	709.717	0.0014	23.6856	0.0422	21.5687
90	36.598	0.0273	872.275	0.0012	23.8338	0.0420	21.9751
95	44.701	0.0224	1070.825	0.0009	23.9552	0.0418	22.3295
100	54.598	0.0183	1313.333	0.0008	24.0545	0.0416	22.6376

G.J. Thuesen/W.J Fabrycky, *Engineering Economy*, 7e, © 1989, pp. 643-698. Reprinted by permission of Prentice-Hall, Inc., Englewood Cliffs, NJ.

Table C.5.   5% Interest Factors for Continuous Compounding Interest

	Single Payment		Equal Payment Series				Uniform gradient-series factor
	Compound-amount factor	Present-worth factor	Compound-amount factor	Sinking-fund factor	Present-worth factor	Capital-recovery factor	
n	To find *F* Given *P* F/P r, n	To find *P* Given *F* P/F r, n	To find *F* Given *A* F/A r, n	To find *A* Given *F* A/F r, n	To find *P* Given *A* P/A r, n	To find *A* Given *P* A/P r, n	To find *A* Given *G* A/G r, n
1	1.051	0.9512	1.000	1.0000	0.9512	1.0513	0.0000
2	1.105	0.9048	2.051	0.4875	1.8561	0.5388	0.4875
3	1.162	0.8607	3.156	0.3168	2.7168	0.3681	0.9667
4	1.221	0.8187	4.318	0.2316	3.5355	0.2829	1.4376
5	1.284	0.7788	5.540	0.1805	4.3143	0.2318	1.9001
6	1.350	0.7408	6.824	0.1466	5.0551	0.1978	2.3544
7	1.419	0.7047	8.174	0.1224	5.7598	0.1736	2.8004
8	1.492	0.6703	9.593	0.1043	6.4301	0.1555	3.2382
9	1.568	0.6376	11.084	0.0902	7.0678	0.1415	3.6678
10	1.649	0.6065	12.653	0.0790	7.6743	0.1303	4.0892
11	1.733	0.5770	14.301	0.0699	8.2513	0.1212	4.5025
12	1.822	0.5488	16.035	0.0624	8.8001	0.1136	4.9077
13	1.916	0.5221	17.857	0.0560	9.3221	0.1073	5.3049
14	2.014	0.4966	19.772	0.0506	9.8187	0.1019	5.6941
15	2.117	0.4724	21.786	0.0459	10.2911	0.0972	6.0753
16	2.226	0.4493	23.903	0.0418	10.7404	0.0931	6.4487
17	2.340	0.4274	26.129	0.0383	11.1678	0.0896	6.8143
18	2.460	0.4066	28.468	0.0351	11.5744	0.0864	7.1721
19	2.586	0.3868	30.928	0.0323	11.9611	0.0836	7.5222
20	2.718	0.3679	33.514	0.0298	12.3290	0.0811	7.8646
21	2.858	0.3499	36.232	0.0276	12.6789	0.0789	8.1996
22	3.004	0.3329	39.090	0.0256	13.0118	0.0769	8.5270
23	3.158	0.3166	42.094	0.0238	13.3284	0.0750	8.8471
24	3.320	0.3012	45.252	0.0221	13.6296	0.0734	9.1599
25	3.490	0.2865	48.572	0.0206	13.9161	0.0719	9.4654
26	3.669	0.2725	52.062	0.0192	14.1887	0.0705	9.7638
27	3.857	0.2593	55.732	0.0180	14.4479	0.0692	10.0551
28	4.055	0.2466	59.589	0.0168	14.6945	0.0681	10.3395
29	4.263	0.2346	63.644	0.0157	14.9291	0.0670	10.6170
30	4.482	0.2231	67.907	0.0147	15.1522	0.0660	10.8877
31	4.711	0.2123	72.389	0.0138	15.3645	0.0651	11.1517
32	4.953	0.2019	77.101	0.0130	15.5664	0.0643	11.4091
33	5.207	0.1921	82.054	0.0122	15.7584	0.0635	11.6601
34	5.474	0.1827	87.261	0.0115	15.9411	0.0627	11.9046
35	5.755	0.1738	92.735	0.0108	16.1149	0.0621	12.1429
40	7.389	0.1353	124.613	0.0080	16.8646	0.0593	13.2435
45	9.488	0.1054	165.546	0.0061	17.4485	0.0573	14.2024
50	12.183	0.0821	218.105	0.0046	17.9032	0.0559	15.0329
55	15.643	0.0639	285.592	0.0035	18.2573	0.0548	15.7480
60	20.086	0.0498	372.247	0.0027	18.5331	0.0540	16.3604
65	25.790	0.0388	483.515	0.0021	18.7479	0.0533	16.8822
70	33.115	0.0302	626.385	0.0016	18.9152	0.0529	17.3245
75	42.521	0.0235	809.834	0.0012	19.0455	0.0525	17.6979
80	54.598	0.0183	1045.387	0.0010	19.1469	0.0522	18.0116
85	70.105	0.0143	1347.843	0.0008	19.2260	0.0520	18.2742
90	90.017	0.0111	1736.205	0.0006	19.2875	0.0519	18.4931
95	115.584	0.0087	2234.871	0.0005	19.3354	0.0517	18.6751
100	148.413	0.0067	2875.171	0.0004	19.3728	0.0516	18.8258

G.J. Thuesen/W.J Fabrycky, *Engineering Economy*, 7e, © 1989, pp. 643-698. Reprinted by permission of Prentice-Hall, Inc., Englewood Cliffs, NJ.

Table C.6.   6% Interest Factors for Continuous Compounding Interest

	Single Payment		Equal Payment Series				Uniform gradient-series factor
	Compound-amount factor	Present-worth factor	Compound-amount factor	Sinking-fund factor	Present-worth factor	Capital-recovery factor	
n	To find F Given P F/P r, n	To find P Given F P/F r, n	To find F Given A F/A r, n	To find A Given F A/F r, n	To find P Given A P/A r, n	To find A Given P A/P r, n	To find A Given G A/G r, n
1	1.062	0.9418	1.000	1.0000	0.9418	1.0618	0.0000
2	1.128	0.8869	2.062	0.4850	1.8287	0.5469	0.4850
3	1.197	0.8353	3.189	0.3136	2.6640	0.3754	0.9600
4	1.271	0.7866	4.387	0.2280	3.4506	0.2898	1.4251
5	1.350	0.7408	5.658	0.1768	4.1914	0.2386	1.8802
6	1.433	0.6977	7.008	0.1427	4.8891	0.2045	2.3254
7	1.522	0.6571	8.441	0.1185	5.5461	0.1803	2.7607
8	1.616	0.6188	9.963	0.1004	6.1649	0.1622	3.1862
9	1.716	0.5828	11.579	0.0864	6.7477	0.1482	3.6020
10	1.822	0.5488	13.295	0.0752	7.2965	0.1371	4.0080
11	1.935	0.5169	15.117	0.0662	7.8133	0.1280	4.4044
12	2.054	0.4868	17.052	0.0587	8.3001	0.1205	4.7912
13	2.181	0.4584	19.106	0.0523	8.7585	0.1142	5.1685
14	2.316	0.4317	21.288	0.0470	9.1902	0.1088	5.5363
15	2.460	0.4066	23.604	0.0424	9.5968	0.1042	5.8949
16	2.612	0.3829	26.064	0.0384	9.9797	0.1002	6.2442
17	2.773	0.3606	28.676	0.0349	10.3403	0.0967	6.5845
18	2.945	0.3396	31.449	0.0318	10.6799	0.0936	6.9157
19	3.127	0.3198	34.393	0.0291	10.9997	0.0909	7.2379
20	3.320	0.3012	37.520	0.0267	11.3009	0.0885	7.5514
21	3.525	0.2837	40.840	0.0245	11.5845	0.0863	7.8562
22	3.743	0.2671	44.366	0.0225	11.8517	0.0844	8.1525
23	3.975	0.2516	48.109	0.0208	12.1032	0.0826	8.4403
24	4.221	0.2369	52.084	0.0192	12.3402	0.0810	8.7199
25	4.482	0.2231	56.305	0.0178	12.5633	0.0796	8.9913
26	4.759	0.2101	60.786	0.0165	12.7734	0.0783	9.2546
27	5.053	0.1979	65.545	0.0153	12.9713	0.0771	9.5101
28	5.366	0.1864	70.598	0.0142	13.1577	0.0760	9.7578
29	5.697	0.1755	75.964	0.0132	13.3332	0.0750	9.9980
30	6.050	0.1653	81.661	0.0123	13.4985	0.0741	10.2307
31	6.424	0.1557	87.711	0.0114	13.6542	0.0732	10.4561
32	6.821	0.1466	94.135	0.0106	13.8008	0.0725	10.6743
33	7.243	0.1381	100.956	0.0099	13.9389	0.0718	10.8855
34	7.691	0.1300	108.198	0.0093	14.0689	0.0711	11.0899
35	8.166	0.1225	115.889	0.0086	14.1914	0.0705	11.2876
40	11.023	0.0907	162.091	0.0062	14.7046	0.0680	12.1809
45	14.880	0.0672	224.458	0.0045	15.0849	0.0663	12.9295
50	20.086	0.0498	308.645	0.0032	15.3665	0.0651	13.5519
55	27.113	0.0369	422.285	0.0024	15.5752	0.0642	14.0654
60	36.598	0.0273	575.683	0.0017	15.7298	0.0636	14.4862
65	49.402	0.0203	782.748	0.0013	15.8443	0.0631	14.8288
70	66.686	0.0150	1062.257	0.0010	15.9292	0.0628	15.1060
75	90.017	0.0111	1439.555	0.0007	15.9920	0.0625	15.3291
80	121.510	0.0082	1948.854	0.0005	16.0386	0.0624	15.5078
85	164.022	0.0061	2636.336	0.0004	16.0731	0.0622	15.6503
90	221.406	0.0045	3564.339	0.0003	16.0986	0.0621	15.7633
95	298.867	0.0034	4817.012	0.0002	16.1176	0.0621	15.8527
100	403.429	0.0025	6507.944	0.0002	16.1316	0.0620	15.9232

G.J. Thuesen/W.J Fabrycky, *Engineering Economy*, 7e, © 1989, pp. 643-698.
Reprinted by permission of Prentice-Hall, Inc., Englewood Cliffs, NJ.

Table C.7.   7% Interest Factors for Continuous Compounding Interest

	Single Payment		Equal Payment Series				Uniform gradient-series factor
	Compound-amount factor	Present-worth factor	Compound-amount factor	Sinking-fund factor	Present-worth factor	Capital-recovery factor	
n	To find F Given P F/P r,n	To find P Given F P/F r,n	To find F Given A F/A r,n	To find A Given F A/F r,n	To find P Given A P/A r,n	To find A Given P A/P r,n	To find A Given G A/G r,n
1	1.073	0.9324	1.000	1.0000	0.9324	1.0725	0.0000
2	1.150	0.8694	2.073	0.4825	1.8018	0.5550	0.4825
3	1.234	0.8106	3.223	0.3103	2.6123	0.3828	0.9534
4	1.323	0.7558	4.456	0.2244	3.3681	0.2969	1.4126
5	1.419	0.7047	5.780	0.1730	4.0728	0.2455	1.8603
6	1.522	0.6571	7.199	0.1389	4.7299	0.2114	2.2965
7	1.632	0.6126	8.721	0.1147	5.3425	0.1872	2.7211
8	1.751	0.5712	10.353	0.0966	5.9137	0.1691	3.1344
9	1.878	0.5326	12.104	0.0826	6.4463	0.1551	3.5364
10	2.014	0.4966	13.981	0.0715	6.9429	0.1440	3.9272
11	2.160	0.4630	15.995	0.0625	7.4059	0.1350	4.3069
12	2.316	0.4317	18.155	0.0551	7.8376	0.1276	4.6756
13	2.484	0.4025	20.471	0.0489	8.2401	0.1214	5.0334
14	2.664	0.3753	22.955	0.0436	8.6154	0.1161	5.3804
15	2.858	0.3499	25.620	0.0390	8.9654	0.1161	5.7168
16	3.065	0.3263	28.478	0.0351	9.2917	0.1076	6.0428
17	3.287	0.3042	31.542	0.0317	9.5959	0.1042	6.3585
18	3.525	0.2837	34.829	0.0287	9.8795	0.1012	6.6640
19	3.781	0.2645	38.355	0.0261	10.1440	0.0986	6.9596
20	4.055	0.2466	42.136	0.0237	10.3906	0.0963	7.2453
21	4.349	0.2299	46.191	0.0217	10.6205	0.0942	7.5215
22	4.665	0.2144	50.540	0.0198	10.8349	0.0923	7.7882
23	5.003	0.1999	55.205	0.0181	11.0348	0.0906	8.0456
24	5.366	0.1864	60.208	0.0166	11.2212	0.0891	8.2940
25	5.755	0.1738	65.573	0.0153	13.3949	0.0878	8.5335
26	6.172	0.1620	71.328	0.0140	11.5570	0.0865	8.7643
27	6.619	0.1511	77.500	0.0129	11.7080	0.0854	8.9867
28	7.099	0.1409	84.119	0.0119	11.8489	0.0844	9.2009
29	7.614	0.1313	91.218	0.0110	11.9802	0.0835	9.4070
30	8.166	0.1225	98.833	0.0101	12.1027	0.0826	9.6052
31	8.758	0.1142	106.999	0.0094	12.2169	0.0819	9.7958
32	9.393	0.1065	115.757	0.0086	12.3233	0.0812	9.9790
33	10.047	0.0993	125.150	0.0080	12.4226	0.0805	10.1550
34	10.805	0.0926	135.225	0.0074	12.5151	0.0799	10.3239
35	11.588	0.0863	146.030	0.0069	12.6014	0.0794	10.4860
40	16.445	0.0608	213.006	0.0047	12.9529	0.0772	11.2017
45	23.336	0.0429	308.049	0.0033	13.2006	0.0758	11.7769
50	33.115	0.0302	442.922	0.0023	13.3751	0.0748	12.2347
55	46.993	0.0213	634.316	0.0016	13.4981	0.0741	12.5957
60	66.686	0.0150	905.916	0.0011	13.5847	0.0736	12.8781
65	94.632	0.0106	1291.336	0.0008	13.6458	0.0733	13.0974
70	134.290	0.0075	1838.272	0.0006	13.6889	0.0731	13.2664
75	190.566	0.0053	2614.412	0.0004	13.7192	0.0729	13.3959
80	270.426	0.0037	3715.807	0.0003	13.7406	0.0728	13.4946
85	383.753	0.0026	5278.761	0.0002	13.7556	0.0727	13.5695
90	544.572	0.0019	7496.698	0.0001	13.7662	0.0727	13.6260
95	772.784	0.0013	10644.100	0.0001	13.7737	0.0726	13.6685
100	1096.633	0.0009	15110.476	0.0001	13.7790	0.0726	13.7003

G.J. Thuesen/W.J Fabrycky, *Engineering Economy*, 7e, © 1989, pp. 643-698.
Reprinted by permission of Prentice-Hall, Inc., Englewood Cliffs, NJ.

Table C.8.　　8% Interest Factors for Continuous Compounding Interest

n	Single Payment		Equal Payment Series				Uniform gradient-series factor
	Compound-amount factor	Present-worth factor	Compound-amount factor	Sinking-fund factor	Present-worth factor	Capital-recovery factor	
	To find F Given P F/P r,n	To find P Given F P/F r,n	To find F Given A F/A r,n	To find A Given F A/F r,n	To find P Given A P/A r,n	To find A Given P A/P r,n	To find A Given G A/G r,n
1	1.083	0.9231	1.000	1.0000	0.9231	1.0833	0.0000
2	1.174	0.8522	2.083	0.4800	1.7753	0.5633	0.4800
3	1.271	0.7866	3.257	0.3071	2.5619	0.3903	0.9467
4	1.377	0.7262	4.528	0.2209	3.2880	0.3041	1.4002
5	1.492	0.6703	5.905	0.1694	3.9584	0.2526	1.8405
6	1.616	0.6188	7.397	0.1352	4.5772	0.2185	2.2676
7	1.751	0.5712	9.013	0.1110	5.1484	0.1942	2.6817
8	1.896	0.5273	10.764	0.0929	5.6757	0.1762	3.0829
9	2.054	0.4868	12.660	0.0790	6.1624	0.1623	3.4713
10	2.226	0.4493	14.715	0.0680	6.6117	0.1513	3.8470
11	2.411	0.4148	16.940	0.0590	7.0265	0.1423	4.2102
12	2.612	0.3829	19.351	0.0517	7.4094	0.1350	4.5611
13	2.829	0.3535	21.963	0.0455	7.7629	0.1288	4.8998
14	3.065	0.3263	24.792	0.0403	8.0891	0.1236	5.2265
15	3.320	0.3012	27.857	0.0359	8.3903	0.1192	5.5415
16	3.597	0.2780	31.177	0.0321	8.6684	0.1154	5.8449
17	3.896	0.2567	34.774	0.0288	8.9250	0.1121	6.1369
18	4.221	0.2369	38.670	0.0259	9.1620	0.1092	6.4178
19	4.572	0.2187	42.891	0.0233	9.3807	0.1066	6.6879
20	4.953	0.2019	47.463	0.0211	9.5826	0.1044	6.9473
21	5.366	0.1864	52.416	0.0191	9.7689	0.1024	7.1963
22	5.812	0.1721	57.781	0.0173	9.9410	0.1006	7.4352
23	6.297	0.1588	63.594	0.0157	10.0998	0.0990	7.6642
24	6.821	0.1466	69.890	0.0143	10.2464	0.0976	7.8836
25	7.389	0.1353	76.711	0.0130	10.3818	0.0963	8.0937
26	8.004	0.1249	84.100	0.0119	10.5067	0.0952	8.2948
27	8.671	0.1153	92.105	0.0109	10.6220	0.0942	8.4870
28	9.393	0.1065	100.776	0.0099	10.7285	0.0932	8.6707
29	10.176	0.0983	110.169	0.0091	10.8267	0.0924	8.8461
30	11.023	0.0907	120.345	0.0083	10.9175	0.0916	9.0136
31	11.941	0.0838	131.368	0.0076	11.0012	0.0909	9.1734
32	12.936	0.0773	143.309	0.0070	11.0785	0.0903	9.3257
33	14.013	0.0714	156.245	0.0064	11.1499	0.0897	9.4708
34	15.180	0.0659	170.258	0.0059	11.2157	0.0892	9.6090
35	16.445	0.0608	185.439	0.0054	11.2765	0.0887	9.7405
40	24.533	0.0408	282.547	0.0035	11.5173	0.0868	10.3069
45	36.598	0.0273	427.416	0.0023	11.6786	0.0856	10.7426
50	54.598	0.0183	643.535	0.0016	11.7868	0.0849	11.0738
55	81.451	0.0123	965.947	0.0010	11.8593	0.0843	11.3230
60	121.510	0.0082	1446.928	0.0007	11.9079	0.0840	11.5088
65	181.272	0.0055	2164.469	0.0005	11.9404	0.0838	11.6461
70	270.426	0.0037	3234.913	0.0003	11.9623	0.0836	11.7469
75	403.429	0.0025	4831.828	0.0002	11.9769	0.0835	11.8203
80	601.845	0.0017	7214.146	0.0002	11.9867	0.0834	11.8735
85	897.847	0.0011	10768.146	0.0001	11.9933	0.0834	11.9119
90	1339.431	0.0008	16070.091	0.0001	11.9977	0.0834	11.9394
95	1998.196	0.0005	23979.664	0.0001	12.0007	0.0833	11.9591
100	2980.958	0.0004	35779.360	0.0000	12.0026	0.0833	11.9731

G.J. Thuesen/W.J Fabrycky, *Engineering Economy*, 7e, © 1989, pp. 643-698. Reprinted by permission of Prentice-Hall, Inc., Englewood Cliffs, NJ.

Table C.9.   9% Interest Factors for Continuous Compounding Interest

n	Single Payment		Equal Payment Series				Uniform gradient-series factor
	Compound-amount factor	Present-worth factor	Compound-amount factor	Sinking-fund factor	Present-worth factor	Capital-recovery factor	
	To find F Given P F/P r,n	To find P Given F P/F r,n	To find F Given A F/A r,n	To find A Given F A/F r,n	To find P Given A P/A r,n	To find A Given P A/P r,n	To find A Given G A/G r,n
1	1.094	0.9139	1.000	1.0000	0.9139	1.0942	0.0000
2	1.197	0.8353	2.094	0.4775	1.7492	0.5717	0.4775
3	1.310	0.7634	3.291	0.3038	2.5126	0.3980	0.9401
4	1.433	0.6977	4.601	0.2173	3.2103	0.3115	1.3878
5	1.568	0.6376	6.035	0.1657	3.8479	0.2599	1.8206
6	1.716	0.5828	7.603	0.1315	4.4306	0.2257	2.2388
7	1.878	0.5326	9.319	0.1073	4.9632	0.2015	2.6424
8	2.054	0.4868	11.197	0.0893	5.4500	0.1835	3.0316
9	2.248	0.4449	13.251	0.0755	5.8948	0.1697	3.4065
10	2.460	0.4066	15.499	0.0645	6.3014	0.1587	3.7674
11	2.691	0.3716	17.959	0.0557	6.6730	0.1499	4.1145
12	2.945	0.3396	20.650	0.0484	7.0126	0.1426	4.4479
13	3.222	0.3104	23.594	0.0424	7.3230	0.1366	4.7680
14	3.525	0.2837	26.816	0.0373	7.6066	0.1315	5.0750
15	3.857	0.2593	30.342	0.0330	7.8658	0.1271	5.3691
16	4.221	0.2369	34.199	0.0293	8.1028	0.1234	5.6507
17	4.618	0.2165	38.420	0.0260	8.3193	0.1202	5.9201
18	5.053	0.1979	43.038	0.0232	8.5172	0.1174	6.1776
19	5.529	0.1809	48.091	0.0208	8.6981	0.1150	6.4234
20	6.050	0.1653	53.620	0.0187	8.8634	0.1128	6.6579
21	6.619	0.1511	59.670	0.0168	9.0144	0.1109	6.8815
22	7.243	0.1381	66.289	0.0151	9.1525	0.1093	7.0945
23	7.925	0.1262	73.532	0.0136	9.2787	0.1078	7.2972
24	8.671	0.1153	81.457	0.0123	9.3940	0.1065	7.4900
25	9.488	0.1054	90.128	0.0111	9.4994	0.1053	7.6732
26	10.381	0.0963	99.616	0.0100	9.5958	0.1042	7.8471
27	11.359	0.0880	109.997	0.0091	9.6838	0.1033	8.0122
28	12.429	0.0805	121.356	0.0083	9.7643	0.1024	8.1686
29	13.599	0.0735	133.784	0.0075	9.8378	0.1017	8.3169
30	14.880	0.0672	147.383	0.0068	9.9050	0.1010	8.4572
31	16.281	0.0614	162.263	0.0062	9.9664	0.1003	8.5900
32	17.814	0.0561	178.544	0.0056	10.0225	0.0998	8.7155
33	19.492	0.0513	196.358	0.0051	10.0739	0.0993	8.8341
34	21.328	0.0469	215.850	0.0046	10.1207	0.0988	8.9460
35	23.336	0.0429	237.178	0.0042	10.1636	0.0984	9.0516
40	36.598	0.0273	378.004	0.0027	10.3285	0.0968	9.4950
45	57.397	0.0174	598.863	0.0017	10.4336	0.0959	9.8207
50	90.017	0.0111	945.238	0.0011	10.5007	0.0952	10.0569
55	141.175	0.0071	1488.463	0.0007	10.5434	0.0949	10.2263
60	221.406	0.0045	2340.410	0.0004	10.5707	0.0946	10.3464
65	347.234	0.0029	3676.528	0.0003	10.5880	0.0945	10.4309
70	544.572	0.0019	5771.978	0.0002	10.5991	0.0944	10.4898
75	854.059	0.0012	9058.298	0.0001	10.6062	0.0943	10.5307
80	1339.431	0.0008	14212.274	0.0001	10.6107	0.0943	10.5588
85	2100.646	0.0005	22295.318	0.0001	10.6136	0.0942	10.5781
90	3294.468	0.0003	34972.053	0.0000	10.6154	0.0942	10.5913
95	5166.754	0.0002	54853.132	0.0000	10.6166	0.0942	10.6002
100	8103.084	0.0001	86032.870	0.0000	10.6173	0.0942	10.6063

G.J. Thuesen/W.J Fabrycky, *Engineering Economy*, 7e, © 1989, pp. 643-698.
Reprinted by permission of Prentice-Hall, Inc., Englewood Cliffs, NJ.

Table C.10. 10% Interest Factors for Continuous Compounding Interest

	Single Payment		Equal Payment Series				Uniform gradient-series factor
	Compound-amount factor	Present-worth factor	Compound-amount factor	Sinking-fund factor	Present-worth factor	Capital-recovery factor	
n	To find F Given P $F/P \ r,n$	To find P Given F $P/F \ r,n$	To find F Given A $F/A \ r,n$	To find A Given F $A/F \ r,n$	To find P Given A $P/A \ r,n$	To find A Given P $A/P \ r,n$	To find A Given G $A/G \ r,n$
1	1.105	0.9048	1.000	1.0000	0.9048	1.1052	0.0000
2	1.221	0.8187	2.105	0.4750	1.7236	0.5802	0.4750
3	1.350	0.7408	3.327	0.3006	2.4644	0.4058	0.9335
4	1.492	0.6703	4.676	0.2138	3.1347	0.3190	1.3754
5	1.649	0.6065	6.168	0.1621	3.7412	0.2673	1.8009
6	1.822	0.5488	7.817	0.1279	4.2901	0.2331	2.2101
7	2.014	0.4966	9.639	0.1038	4.7866	0.2089	2.6033
8	2.226	0.4493	11.653	0.0858	5.2360	0.1910	2.9806
9	2.460	0.4066	13.878	0.0721	5.6425	0.1772	3.3423
10	2.718	0.3679	16.338	0.0612	6.0104	0.1664	3.6886
11	3.004	0.3329	19.056	0.0525	6.3433	0.1577	4.0198
12	3.320	0.3012	22.060	0.0453	6.6445	0.1505	4.3362
13	3.669	0.2725	25.381	0.0394	6.9170	0.1446	4.6381
14	4.055	0.2466	29.050	0.0344	7.1636	0.1396	4.9260
15	4.482	0.2231	33.105	0.0302	7.3867	0.1354	5.2001
16	4.953	0.2019	37.587	0.0266	7.5886	0.1318	5.4608
17	5.474	0.1827	42.540	0.0235	7.7713	0.1287	5.7086
18	6.050	0.1653	48.014	0.0208	7.9366	0.1260	5.9437
19	6.686	0.1496	54.063	0.0185	8.0862	0.1237	6.1667
20	7.389	0.1353	60.749	0.0165	8.2215	0.1216	6.3780
21	8.166	0.1225	68.138	0.0147	8.3440	0.1199	6.5779
22	9.025	0.1108	76.305	0.0131	8.4548	0.1183	6.7669
23	9.974	0.1003	85.330	0.0117	8.5550	0.1169	6.9454
24	11.023	0.0907	95.304	0.0105	8.6458	0.1157	7.1139
25	12.183	0.0821	106.327	0.0094	8.7279	0.1146	7.2727
26	13.464	0.0743	118.509	0.0084	8.8021	0.1136	7.4223
27	14.880	0.0672	131.973	0.0076	8.8693	0.1128	7.5631
28	16.445	0.0608	146.853	0.0068	8.9301	0.1120	7.6954
29	18.174	0.0550	163.297	0.0061	8.9852	0.1113	7.8198
30	20.086	0.0498	181.472	0.0055	9.0349	0.1107	7.9365
31	22.198	0.0451	201.557	0.0050	9.0800	0.1101	8.0459
32	24.533	0.0408	223.755	0.0045	9.1208	0.1097	8.1485
33	27.113	0.0369	248.288	0.0040	9.1576	0.1092	8.2446
34	29.964	0.0334	275.400	0.0036	9.1910	0.1088	8.3345
35	33.115	0.0302	305.364	0.0033	9.2212	0.1085	8.4185
40	54.598	0.0183	509.629	0.0020	9.3342	0.1071	8.7620
45	90.017	0.0111	846.404	0.0012	9.4027	0.1064	9.0028
50	148.413	0.0067	1401.653	0.0007	9.4443	0.1059	9.1692
55	244.692	0.0041	2317.104	0.0004	9.4695	0.1056	9.2826
60	403.429	0.0025	3826.427	0.0003	9.4848	0.1054	9.3592
65	665.142	0.0015	6314.879	0.0002	9.4940	0.1053	9.4105
70	1096.633	0.0009	10417.644	0.0001	9.4997	0.1053	9.4445
75	1808.042	0.0006	17181.959	0.0001	9.5031	0.1052	9.4668
80	2980.958	0.0004	28334.430	0.0001	9.5052	0.1052	9.4815
85	4914.769	0.0002	46721.745	0.0000	9.5064	0.1052	9.4910
90	8103.084	0.0001	77037.303	0.0000	9.5072	0.1052	9.4972
95	13359.727	0.0001	127019.209	0.0000	9.5076	0.1052	9.5012
100	22026.466	0.0001	209425.440	0.0000	9.5079	0.1052	9.5038

G.J. Thuesen/W.J Fabrycky, *Engineering Economy*, 7e, © 1989, pp. 643-698. Reprinted by permission of Prentice-Hall, Inc., Englewood Cliffs, NJ.

Table C.11.   12% Interest Factors for Continuous Compounding Interest

	Single Payment		Equal Payment Series				Uniform
	Compound-amount factor	Present-worth factor	Compound-amount factor	Sinking-fund factor	Present-worth factor	Capital-recovery factor	gradient-series factor
n	To find F Given P F/P r, n	To find P Given F P/F r, n	To find F Given A F/A r, n	To find A Given F A/F r, n	To find P Given A P/A r, n	To find A Given P A/P r, n	To find A Given G A/G r, n
1	1.128	0.8869	1.000	1.0000	0.8869	1.1275	0.0000
2	1.271	0.7866	2.128	0.4700	1.6736	0.5975	0.4700
3	1.433	0.6977	3.399	0.2942	2.3712	0.4217	0.9202
4	1.616	0.6188	4.832	0.2070	2.9900	0.3345	1.3506
5	1.822	0.5488	6.448	0.1551	3.5388	0.2826	1.7615
6	2.054	0.4868	8.270	0.1209	4.0256	0.2484	2.1531
7	2.316	0.4317	10.325	0.0969	4.4573	0.2244	2.5257
8	2.612	0.3829	12.641	0.0791	4.8402	0.2066	2.8796
9	2.945	0.3396	15.253	0.0656	5.1798	0.1931	3.2153
10	3.320	0.3012	18.197	0.0550	5.4810	0.1825	3.5332
11	3.743	0.2671	21.518	0.0465	5.7481	0.1740	3.8337
12	4.221	0.2369	25.261	0.0396	5.9850	0.1671	4.1174
13	4.759	0.2101	29.482	0.0339	6.1952	0.1614	4.3848
14	5.366	0.1864	34.241	0.0292	6.3815	0.1567	4.6364
15	6.050	0.1653	39.606	0.0253	6.5468	0.1528	4.8728
16	6.821	0.1466	45.656	0.0219	6.6935	0.1494	5.0947
17	7.691	0.1300	52.477	0.0191	6.8235	0.1466	5.3025
18	8.671	0.1153	60.167	0.0166	6.9388	0.1441	5.4969
19	9.777	0.1023	68.838	0.0145	7.0411	0.1420	5.6785
20	11.023	0.0907	78.615	0.0127	7.1318	0.1402	5.8480
21	12.429	0.0805	89.638	0.0112	7.2123	0.1387	6.0058
22	14.013	0.0714	102.067	0.0098	7.2836	0.1373	6.1528
23	15.800	0.0633	116.080	0.0086	7.3469	0.1361	6.2893
24	17.814	0.0561	131.880	0.0076	7.4031	0.1351	6.4160
25	20.086	0.0498	149.694	0.0067	7.4528	0.1342	6.5334
26	22.646	0.0442	169.780	0.0059	7.4970	0.1334	6.6422
27	25.534	0.0392	192.426	0.0052	7.5362	0.1327	6.7428
28	28.789	0.0347	217.960	0.0046	7.5709	0.1321	6.8358
29	32.460	0.0308	246.749	0.0041	7.6017	0.1316	6.9215
30	36.598	0.0273	279.209	0.0036	7.6290	0.1311	7.0006
31	41.264	0.0242	315.807	0.0032	7.6533	0.1307	7.0734
32	46.525	0.0215	357.071	0.0028	7.6748	0.1303	7.1404
33	52.457	0.0191	403.597	0.0025	7.6938	0.1300	7.2020
34	59.145	0.0169	456.054	0.0022	7.7107	0.1297	7.2586
35	66.686	0.0150	515.200	0.0020	7.7257	0.1294	7.3105
40	121.510	0.0082	945.203	0.0011	7.7788	0.1286	7.5114
45	221.406	0.0045	1728.720	0.0006	7.8079	0.1281	7.6392
50	403.429	0.0025	3156.382	0.0003	7.8239	0.1278	7.7191

G.J. Thuesen/W.J Fabrycky, *Engineering Economy*, 7e, © 1989, pp. 643-698.
Reprinted by permission of Prentice-Hall, Inc., Englewood Cliffs, NJ.

Table C.12.   15% Interest Factors for Continuous Compounding Interest

n	Single Payment		Equal Payment Series				Uniform gradient-series factor
	Compound-amount factor	Present-worth factor	Compound-amount factor	Sinking-fund factor	Present-worth factor	Capital-recovery factor	
	To find F Given P F/P r,n	To find P Given F P/F r,n	To find F Given A F/A r,n	To find A Given F A/F r,n	To find P Given A P/A r,n	To find A Given P A/P r,n	To find A Given G A/G r,n
1	1.162	0.8607	1.000	1.0000	0.8607	1.1618	0.0000
2	1.350	0.7408	2.162	0.4626	1.6015	0.6244	0.4626
3	1.568	0.6376	3.512	0.2848	2.2392	0.4466	0.9004
4	1.822	0.5488	5.080	0.1969	2.7880	0.3587	1.3137
5	2.117	0.4724	6.902	0.1449	3.2603	0.3067	1.7029
6	2.460	0.4066	9.019	0.1109	3.6669	0.2727	2.0685
7	2.858	0.3499	11.479	0.0871	4.0168	0.2490	2.4110
8	3.320	0.3012	14.336	0.0698	4.3180	0.2316	2.7311
9	3.857	0.2593	17.657	0.0566	4.5773	0.2185	3.0295
10	4.482	0.2231	21.514	0.0465	4.8004	0.2083	3.3070
11	5.207	0.1921	25.996	0.0385	4.9925	0.2003	3.5645
12	6.050	0.1653	31.203	0.0321	5.1578	0.1939	3.8028
13	7.029	0.1423	37.252	0.0269	5.3000	0.1887	4.0228
14	8.166	0.1225	44.281	0.0226	5.4225	0.1844	4.2255
15	9.488	0.1054	52.447	0.0191	5.5279	0.1809	4.4119
16	11.023	0.0907	61.935	0.0162	5.6186	0.1780	4.5829
17	12.807	0.0781	72.958	0.0137	5.6967	0.1756	4.7394
18	14.880	0.0672	85.765	0.0117	5.7639	0.1735	4.8823
19	17.288	0.0579	100.645	0.0099	5.8217	0.1718	5.0127
20	20.086	0.0498	117.933	0.0085	5.8715	0.1703	5.1313
21	23.336	0.0429	138.018	0.0073	5.9144	0.1691	5.2390
22	27.113	0.0369	161.354	0.0062	5.9513	0.1680	5.3367
23	31.500	0.0318	188.467	0.0053	5.9830	0.1672	5.4251
24	36.598	0.0273	219.967	0.0046	6.0103	0.1664	5.5050
25	42.521	0.0235	256.566	0.0039	6.0339	0.1657	5.5771
26	49.402	0.0203	299.087	0.0034	6.0541	0.1652	5.6420
27	57.397	0.0174	348.489	0.0029	6.0715	0.1647	5.7004
28	66.686	0.0150	405.886	0.0025	6.0865	0.1643	5.7529
29	77.478	0.0129	472.573	0.0021	6.0994	0.1640	5.8000
30	90.017	0.0111	550.051	0.0018	6.1105	0.1637	5.8422
31	104.585	0.0096	640.068	0.0016	6.1201	0.1634	5.8799
32	121.510	0.0082	744.653	0.0014	6.1283	0.1632	5.9136
33	141.175	0.0071	866.164	0.0012	6.1354	0.1630	5.9438
34	164.022	0.0061	1007.339	0.0010	6.1415	0.1628	5.9706
35	190.566	0.0053	1171.361	0.0009	6.1467	0.1627	5.9945
40	403.429	0.0025	2486.673	0.0004	6.1639	0.1622	6.0798
45	854.059	0.0012	5271.188	0.0002	6.1719	0.1620	6.1264
50	1808.042	0.0006	11166.008	0.0001	6.1758	0.1619	6.1515

G.J. Thuesen/W.J Fabrycky, *Engineering Economy*, 7e, © 1989, pp. 643-698.
Reprinted by permission of Prentice-Hall, Inc., Englewood Cliffs, NJ.

Table C.13.   20% Interest Factors for Continuous Compounding Interest

n	Single Payment		Equal Payment Series				Uniform gradient-series factor
	Compound-amount factor	Present-worth factor	Compound-amount factor	Sinking-fund factor	Present-worth factor	Capital-recovery factor	
	To find F Given P F/P r,n	To find P Given F P/F r,n	To find F Given A F/A r,n	To find A Given F A/F r,n	To find P Given A P/A r,n	To find A Given P A/P r,n	To find A Given G A/G r,n
1	1.221	0.8187	1.000	1.0000	0.8187	1.2214	0.0000
2	1.492	0.6703	2.221	0.4502	1.4891	0.6716	0.4502
3	1.822	0.5488	3.713	0.2693	2.0379	0.4907	0.8676
4	2.226	0.4493	5.535	0.1807	2.4872	0.4021	1.2528
5	2.718	0.3679	7.761	0.1289	2.8551	0.3503	1.6068
6	3.320	0.3012	10.479	0.0954	3.1563	0.3168	1.9306
7	4.055	0.2466	13.799	0.0725	3.4029	0.2939	2.2255
8	4.953	0.2019	17.854	0.0560	3.6048	0.2774	2.4929
9	6.050	0.1653	22.808	0.0439	3.7701	0.2653	2.7344
10	7.389	0.1353	28.857	0.0347	3.9054	0.2561	2.9515
11	9.025	0.1108	36.246	0.0276	4.0162	0.2490	3.1460
12	11.023	0.0907	45.271	0.0221	4.1069	0.2435	3.3194
13	13.464	0.0743	56.294	0.0178	4.1812	0.2392	3.4736
14	16.445	0.0608	69.758	0.0143	4.2420	0.2357	3.6102
15	20.086	0.0498	86.203	0.0116	4.2918	0.2330	3.7307
16	24.533	0.0408	106.288	0.0094	4.3326	0.2308	3.8368
17	29.964	0.0334	130.821	0.0077	4.3659	0.2291	3.9297
18	36.598	0.0273	160.785	0.0062	4.3933	0.2276	4.0110
19	44.701	0.0224	197.383	0.0051	4.4156	0.2265	4.0819
20	54.598	0.0183	242.084	0.0041	4.4339	0.2255	4.1435
21	66.686	0.0150	296.683	0.0034	4.4489	0.2248	4.1970
22	81.451	0.0123	363.369	0.0028	4.4612	0.2242	4.2432
23	99.484	0.0101	444.820	0.0023	4.4713	0.2237	4.2831
24	121.510	0.0082	544.304	0.0018	4.4795	0.2232	4.3175
25	148.413	0.0067	665.814	0.0015	4.4862	0.2229	4.3471
26	181.272	0.0055	814.228	0.0012	4.4917	0.2226	4.3724
27	221.406	0.0045	995.500	0.0010	4.4963	0.2224	4.3942
28	270.426	0.0037	1216.906	0.0008	4.5000	0.2222	4.4127
29	330.300	0.0030	1487.333	0.0007	4.5030	0.2221	4.4286
30	403.429	0.0025	1817.632	0.0006	4.5055	0.2220	4.4421
31	492.749	0.0020	2221.061	0.0005	4.5075	0.2219	4.4536
32	601.845	0.0017	2713.810	0.0004	4.5092	0.2218	4.4634
33	735.095	0.0014	3315.655	0.0003	4.5105	0.2217	4.4717
34	897.847	0.0011	4050.750	0.0003	4.5116	0.2217	4.4788
35	1096.633	0.0009	4948.598	0.0002	4.5125	0.2216	4.4847
40	2980.958	0.0004	13459.444	0.0001	4.5152	0.2215	4.5032
45	8103.084	0.0001	36594.322	0.0000	4.5161	0.2214	4.5111
50	22026.466	0.0001	99481.443	0.0000	4.5165	0.2214	4.5144

G.J. Thuesen/W.J Fabrycky, *Engineering Economy*, 7e, © 1989, pp. 643-698.
Reprinted by permission of Prentice-Hall, Inc., Englewood Cliffs, NJ.

Table C.14.   25% Interest Factors for Continuous Compounding Interest

	Single Payment		Equal Payment Series				Uniform gradient-series factor
	Compound-amount factor	Present-worth factor	Compound-amount factor	Sinking-fund factor	Present-worth factor	Capital-recovery factor	
n	To find F Given P F/P r, n	To find P Given F P/F r, n	To find F Given A F/A r, n	To find A Given F A/F r, n	To find P Given A P/A r, n	To find A Given P A/P r, n	To find A Given G A/G r, n
1	1.284	0.7788	1.000	1.0000	0.7788	1.2840	0.0000
2	1.649	0.6065	2.284	0.4378	1.3853	0.7219	0.4378
3	2.117	0.4724	3.933	0.2543	1.8577	0.5383	0.8351
4	2.718	0.3679	6.050	0.1653	2.2256	0.4493	1.1929
5	3.490	0.2865	8.768	0.1141	2.5121	0.3981	1.5131
6	4.482	0.2231	12.258	0.0816	2.7352	0.3656	1.7975
7	5.755	0.1738	16.740	0.0597	2.9090	0.3438	2.0486
8	7.389	0.1353	22.495	0.0445	3.0443	0.3285	2.2687
9	9.488	0.1054	29.884	0.0335	3.1497	0.3175	2.4605
10	12.183	0.0821	39.371	0.0254	3.2318	0.3094	2.6266
11	15.643	0.0639	51.554	0.0194	3.2957	0.3034	2.7696
12	20.086	0.0498	67.197	0.0149	3.3455	0.2989	2.8921
13	25.790	0.0388	87.282	0.0115	3.3843	0.2955	2.9964
14	33.115	0.0302	113.072	0.0089	3.4145	0.2929	3.0849
15	42.521	0.0235	146.188	0.0069	3.4380	0.2909	3.1596
16	54.598	0.0183	188.709	0.0053	3.4563	0.2893	3.2223
17	70.105	0.0143	243.307	0.0041	3.4706	0.2881	3.2748
18	90.017	0.0111	313.413	0.0032	3.4817	0.2872	3.3186
19	115.584	0.0087	403.430	0.0025	3.4904	0.2865	3.3550
20	148.413	0.0067	519.014	0.0019	3.4971	0.2860	3.3851
21	190.566	0.0053	667.427	0.0015	3.5023	0.2855	3.4100
22	244.692	0.0041	857.993	0.0012	3.5064	0.2852	3.4305
23	314.191	0.0032	1102.685	0.0009	3.5096	0.2849	3.4474
24	403.429	0.0025	1416.876	0.0007	3.5121	0.2847	3.4612
25	518.013	0.0019	1820.305	0.0006	3.5140	0.2846	3.4725
26	665.142	0.0015	2338.318	0.0004	3.5155	0.2845	3.4817
27	854.059	0.0012	3003.459	0.0003	3.5167	0.2844	3.4892
28	1096.633	0.0009	3857.518	0.0003	3.5176	0.2843	3.4953
29	1408.105	0.0007	4954.151	0.0002	3.5183	0.2842	3.5002
30	1808.042	0.0006	6362.256	0.0002	3.5189	0.2842	3.5042
31	2321.572	0.0004	8170.298	0.0001	3.5193	0.2842	3.5075
32	2980.958	0.0004	10491.871	0.0001	3.5196	0.2841	3.5101
33	3827.626	0.0003	13472.829	0.0001	3.5199	0.2841	3.5122
34	4914.769	0.0002	17300.455	0.0001	3.5201	0.2841	3.5139
35	6310.688	0.0002	22215.223	0.0001	3.5203	0.2841	3.5153

G.J. Thuesen/W.J Fabrycky, *Engineering Economy*, 7e, © 1989, pp. 643-698.
Reprinted by permission of Prentice-Hall, Inc., Englewood Cliffs, NJ.

Table C.15.   30% Interest Factors for Continuous Compounding Interest

n	Single Payment		Equal Payment Series				Uniform gradient-series factor
	Compound-amount factor	Present-worth factor	Compound-amount factor	Sinking-fund factor	Present-worth factor	Capital-recovery factor	
	To find F Given P F/P r, n	To find P Given F P/F r, n	To find F Given A F/A r, n	To find A Given F A/F r, n	To find P Given A P/A r, n	To find A Given P A/P r, n	To find A Given G A/G r, n
1	1.350	0.7408	1.000	1.0000	0.7408	1.3499	0.0000
2	1.822	0.5488	2.350	0.4256	1.2896	0.7754	0.4256
3	2.460	0.4066	4.172	0.2397	1.6962	0.5896	0.8030
4	3.320	0.3012	6.632	0.1508	1.9974	0.5007	1.1343
5	4.482	0.2231	9.952	0.1005	2.2205	0.4504	1.4222
6	6.050	0.1653	14.433	0.0693	2.3858	0.4192	1.6701
7	8.166	0.1225	20.483	0.0488	2.5083	0.3987	1.8815
8	11.023	0.0907	28.649	0.0349	2.5990	0.3848	2.0602
9	14.880	0.0672	39.672	0.0252	2.6662	0.3751	2.2099
10	20.086	0.0498	54.552	0.0183	2.7160	0.3682	2.3343
11	27.113	0.0369	74.638	0.0134	2.7529	0.3633	2.4371
12	36.598	0.0273	101.750	0.0098	2.7802	0.3597	2.5212
13	49.402	0.0203	138.349	0.0072	2.8004	0.3571	2.5897
14	66.686	0.0150	187.751	0.0053	2.8154	0.3552	2.6452
15	90.017	0.0111	254.437	0.0039	2.8266	0.3538	2.6898
16	121.510	0.0082	344.454	0.0029	2.8348	0.3528	2.7255
17	164.022	0.0061	465.965	0.0022	2.8409	0.3520	2.7540
18	221.406	0.0045	629.987	0.0016	2.8454	0.3515	2.7766
19	298.867	0.0034	851.393	0.0012	2.8487	0.3510	2.7945
20	403.429	0.0025	1150.261	0.0009	2.8512	0.3507	2.8086
21	544.572	0.0018	1553.689	0.0007	2.8531	0.3505	2.8197
22	735.095	0.0014	2098.261	0.0005	2.8544	0.3503	2.8283
23	992.275	0.0010	2833.356	0.0004	2.8554	0.3502	2.8351
24	1339.431	0.0008	3825.631	0.0003	2.8562	0.3501	2.8404
25	1808.042	0.0006	5165.062	0.0002	2.8567	0.3501	2.8445
26	2440.602	0.0004	6973.104	0.0002	2.8571	0.3500	2.8476
27	3294.468	0.0003	9413.706	0.0001	2.8574	0.3500	2.8501
28	4447.067	0.0002	12708.174	0.0001	2.8577	0.3499	2.8520
29	6002.912	0.0002	17155.241	0.0001	2.8578	0.3499	2.8535
30	8103.084	0.0001	23158.153	0.0001	2.8580	0.3499	2.8546
31	10938.019	0.0001	31261.237	0.0000	2.8580	0.3499	2.8555
32	14764.782	0.0001	42199.257	0.0000	2.8581	0.3499	2.8561
33	19930.370	0.0001	56964.038	0.0000	2.8582	0.3499	2.8566
34	26903.186	0.0001	76894.409	0.0000	2.8582	0.3499	2.8570
35	36315.503	0.0000	103797.595	0.0000	2.8582	0.3499	2.8573

G.J. Thuesen/W.J Fabrycky, *Engineering Economy*, 7e, © 1989, pp. 643-698.
Reprinted by permission of Prentice-Hall, Inc., Englewood Cliffs, NJ.

APPENDIX

D

FUNDS FLOW FACTORS

Table D.1.   Funds Flow Conversion Factors

r	$\dfrac{e^r - 1}{r}$ $(A/\bar{A}\ r)$
1	1.005020
2	1.010065
3	1.015150
4	1.020270
5	1.025422
6	1.030608
7	1.035831
8	1.041088
9	1.046381
10	1.051709
11	1.057073
12	1.062474
13	1.067910
14	1.073384
15	1.078894
16	1.084443
17	1.090028
18	1.095652
19	1.101313
20	1.107014
21	1.112752
22	1.118530
23	1.124347
24	1.130204
25	1.136101
26	1.142038
27	1.148016
28	1.154035
29	1.160094
30	1.166196
31	1.172339
32	1.178524
33	1.184751
34	1.191022
35	1.197335
36	1.203692
37	1.210093
38	1.216538
39	1.223027
40	1.229561

G.J. Thuesen/W.J Fabrycky, *Engineering Economy*, 7e, © 1989, pp. 643-698.
Reprinted by permission of Prentice-Hall, Inc., Englewood Cliffs, NJ.

APPENDIX

E

COMPUTER PROGRAM FOR INTERNAL RATE OF RETURN

A computer program for determining the internal rate of return is provided in this appendix. The input data consists of the yearly cash flows and number of years. This program uses a beginning of the year conversion.

```
      $JOB
      C
      C
      C
      C         INTERNAL RATE OF RETURN
   1            DIMENSION PV(50),CF(50)
   2            READ(5,10) N,(CF(I),I=1,N)
   3         10 FORMAT(I5,/,(F15.2))
   4            WRITE(6,20) (I,CF(I),I=1,N)
   5         20 FORMAT(1H1,4X,'PERIOD',6X,'     CASH FLOW ',//,(/,4X,I6,6X,F15.2))
   6            WRITE(6,30)
   7         30 FORMAT(////,1X,'ITERATION',6X,'  RATE CF RETURN',//)
   8            ERROR=CF(1)*.00001
   9            ITER=1
  10            RATE=1.
  11            IFLAG=1
  12            PV(1)=CF(1)
  13            IF(PV(1)) 1,2,2
  14          1 DO 40 J=2,N
  15            PV(J)=PV(J-1)*(1.0+RATE)+CF(J)
  16            IF(PV(J)+ERROR) 40,40,50
  17         40 CONTINUE
  18            WRITE(6,60) ITER,RATE
  19         60 FORMAT(/,1X,I9,6X,F16.5)
  20            ITER=ITER+1
  21            IF(PV(N)-ERROR) 35,55,55
  22         35 IFLAG=0
  23            M=N
  24         11 ARATE=PV(1)
  25            MK=M-1
  26            ML=MK-1
  27            IF(ML) 45,15,45
  28         45 DO 17 I=2,MK
  29         17 ARATE=ARATE*(1.+RATE)+PV(I)
  30         15 RATE=RATE-PV(M)/ARATE
  31            GO TO 1
  32         50 IF(IFLAG) 55,19,46
  33         46 M=J
  34            GO TO 11
  35          2 J=1
  36         19 WRITE(6,21)
  37         21 FORMAT(///,2X,'NC SINGLE FEASIBLE SOLUTION EXISTS.')
  38         55 WRITE(6,18)
  39         18 FORMAT(1H1)
  40            STOP
  41            END

      $ENTRY
```

Reprinted, by permission from G.T. Stevens, Jr., *Economic and Financial Analysis of Capital Investments*, p. 351. Copyright © 1979 by John Wiley and Sons, Inc.

APPENDIX

F

COMPUTER PROGRAM FOR MINIMAL ANNUAL REVENUE REQUIREMENTS

A computer program is provided for determining the minimum annual revenue requirements. Three depreciation models are possible: (1) straight line, (2) SYD, and (3) DDB with a switch over to straight-line.

```
      $ JOB
      C
      C
      C
      C
      C
      C       MINIMUM ANNUAL REVENUE REQUIREMENT BY FLOW THROUGH METHOD
   1          REAL INITC,INVTCR,NB,NT,INC
   2          DIMENSION DEPB(50),DEPS(50),DEPT(50),DTX(50),TXC(50),AMTXC(50),
             1CAPINV(50),FD(50),FE(50),TAX(50),COST(50),RN(50),CAPINT(50)
             2,SDEPT(50)
      C       INPUT DATA ENTERED AS FOLLOW;
      C       "INITC" REPRESENTS INITIAL INVESTMENT COST.
   3          READ(5,5000) INITC
      C       "SALV" REPRESENTS THE SALVAGE VALUE AT THE END OF THE USEFUL LIFE.
   4          READ(5,5000) SALV
      C       "TXSALV" REPRESENTS THE ESTIMATED SALVAGE VALUE FOR TAX PURPOSE.
   5          READ(5,5000) TXSALV
      C       "NB" REPRESENTS THE USEFUL LIFE FOR BOOK PURPOSE.
   6          READ(5,5000) NB
      C       "NT" REPRESENTS THE USEFUL LIFE FOR TAX PURPOSE.
   7          READ(5,5000) NT
      C       "RE" REPRESENTS THE RATE OF RETURN ON EQUITY.
   8          READ(5,5000) RE
      C       "RD" REPRESENTS THE RATE OF RETURN ON DEBT.
   9          READ(5,5000) RD
      C       "DR" REPRESENTS THE RATIO OF DEBT PORTION.
  10          READ(5,5000) DR
      C       "T" REPRESENTS THE TAX RATE.
  11          READ(5,5000) T
      C       "CAPIRA" REPRESENTS THE CAPITAL INTEREST RATE.
  12          READ(5,5000) CAPIRA
      C       "INVTCR" REPRESENTS THE INVESTMENT TAX CREDIT RATE.
  13          READ(5,5000) INVTCR
      C       "BDEP" REPRESENTS THE BOOK DEPRECIATION METHOD.
  14          READ(5,5000) BDEP
      C       "TDEP" REPRESENTS THE TAX DEPRECIATION METHOD.
  15          READ(5,5000) TDEP
  16          IF(NB.GE.NT) GO TO 31
  17          N=NT
  18          K=NB
  19          GO TO 32
  20       31 N=NB
  21          K=NT
  22       32 READ(5,5000) (COST(I),I=1,N)
  23          CAP=INITC
  24          CALL SLDEP(DEPS,INITC,SALV,NB,NT)
      C       CHOOSE APPROPRIATE DEPRECIATION METHOD FOR BOOK AND TAX PURPOSES
      C       FROM THE SUBROUTINES.
      C       SUBROUTINE "SLDEP" REPRESENTS THE STRAIGHT LINE DEPRECIATION
      C       METHOD.( BDEP OR TDEP AS 1.)
      C       SUBROUTINE "SYDEP" REPRESENTS THE SUM-OF-THE -YEARS-DIGITS METHOD.
      C       ( BDEP OR TDEP AS 2.)
      C       SUBROUTINE "DDBDEP" REPRESENTS THE DOUBLE DECLINING BALANCE
      C       DEPRECIATION METHOD.( BDEP OR TDEP AS 3.)
      C       "DEPB" REPRESENTS BOOK DEPRECIATION AMOUNT FOR A PARTICULAR YEAR
      C       "DEPS" REPRESENTS THE STRAIGHT LINE DEPRECIATION AMOUNT FOR A
      C       PARTICULAR YEAR.
      C       "DEPT" REPRESENTS TAX DEPRECIATION AMOUNT FOR A PARTICULAR
      C       YEAR.
      C       "CAP" REPRESENTS CAPITALIZED INVESTMENT COST FOR NORMALIZING
```

```
        C       METHOD
        C       THIS "CAP" ALSO REPRESENTS INITIAL INVESTMENT COST FOR
        C       FLOW THROUGH METHOD.
25              IBDEP=BDEP
26              ITDEP=TDEP
27              GO TO (111,222,333),IBDEP
28        111 CALL SLDEP(DEPB,CAP,SALV,NB,NT)
29              GO TO 1234
30        222 CALL SYDDEP(DEPB,CAP,SALV,NB,NT)
31              GO TO 1234
32        333 CALL DDBDEP(DEPB,CAP,SALV,NB,NT)
33       1234 GO TO (1111,2222,3333),ITDEP
34       1111 CALL SLDEP(DEPT,INITC,TXSALV,NB,NT)
35              GO TO 4321
36       2222 CALL SYDDEP(DEPT,INITC,TXSALV,NB,NT)
37              GO TO 4321
38       3333 CALL DDBDEP(DEPT,INITC,TXSALV,NB,NT)
39       4321 TXC(1)=INITC*INVTCR
40              DO 200 I=2,N
41              TXC(I)=0.
42        200 CAPINT(I)=0.
43              CAPINT(1)=INITC*CAPIRA
44              DO 500 I=1,N
45              AMTXC(I)=TXC(1)/NB
46              IF(I.EQ.1) GO TO 300
47              XCAP=CAPINV(I-1)
48              GO TO 400
49        300 XCAP=CAP
50        400 CONTINUE
51              DTX(I)=(DEPT(I)-DEPS(I))*T
52              CAPINV(I)=XCAP-DEPB(I)
53              FD(I)=XCAP*DR*RD
54              FE(I)=XCAP*(1.-DR)*RE
55              TAX(I)=(T/(1.-T))*(FE(I)+DEPB(I)-DEPT(I))-TXC(I)/(1.-T)
56              RN(I)=DEPB(I)+FD(I)+FE(I)+CAPINT(I)+TAX(I)+COST(I)
57        500 CONTINUE
58              IF(NT.GT.NB) GO TO 663
59              GO TO 670
60        663 SDEPT(1)=DEPT(1)
61              DO 655 I=2,K
62              SDEPT(I)=DEPT(I)+SDEPT(I-1)
63              TXBV=INITC-SDEPT(I)
64        655 CONTINUE
65              TAX(K)=(T/(1.-T))*(FE(K)+DEPB(K)-DEPT(K))-TXC(K)/(1.-T)+(SALV-TXBV
                1)*(T/(1.-T))
66              RN(K)=DEPB(K)+FD(K)+FE(K)+CAPINT(K)+TAX(K)+COST(K)
67              M=NB+1
68              DO 665 I=M,N
69              CAPINV(I)=0.0
70              FD(I)=0.0
71              FE(I)=0.0
72              TAX(I)=0.0
73              RN(I)=0.0
74        665 CONTINUE
75        670 WRITE(6,6000)
76              DO 700 I=1,N
77              WRITE(6,6100) I,DEPB(I),DEPS(I),DEPT(I),TXC(I)
78        700 CONTINUE
79              WRITE(6,6200) CAP
80              DO 800 I=1,N
81              WRITE(6,6100) I,CAPINV(I),CAPINT(I),FD(I),FE(I)
```

```
 82      800 CONTINUE
 83          WRITE(6,6201)
 84          DO 801 I=1,N
 85          WRITE(6,6100) I,TAX(I),COST(I),RN(I)
 86      801 CONTINUE
 87     5000 FORMAT(F10.0)
 88     6100 FORMAT(I5,5F12.2)
 89     6200 FORMAT(/,1X,'YEAR     CAP INV     CAP INT  RET ON DEBT    RET ON EQT
          1Y',/,5X,F12.2)
 90     6201 FORMAT(33X,'ANNUAL COST OR',/,1X,'YEAR       TAX       OPRT.COST
          1MIN ANN REV')
 91     6000 FORMAT(1H1,' YEAR',,' BOOK DEP ',' S.L DEP ',' TAX DEP ',
          1'   TAX CREDIT')
 92          WRITE(6,3900)
 93     3900 FORMAT(/,5X,'MIN. ANNUAL REV. REQMT BY FLOW THROUGH METHOD')
 94          WRITE(6,4000) INITC,SALV,NB,NT,RE,RD,DR,T,CAPIRA,INVTCR,TXSALV
 95     4000 FORMAT(///,1X,'INPUT DATA;',///,1X,'INITIAL INVESTMENT COST=',F10.2
          1,5X,'SALVAGE VALUE=',F10.2,/,1X,'NO. OF USEFUL LIFE FOR BOOK PURPO
          1SE=',F5.0,/,1X,'NO. OF USEFUL LIFE FOR TAX PURPOSE=',F5.0,/,1X,
          2'RATE OF RETURN ON EQUITY=',F5.3,3X,'RATE OF RETURN ON DEBT=',
          3F5.3,/,1X,'DEBT RATIO=',F5.3,5X,'TAX RATE=',F5.3,5X,/,1X,
          4'CAPITAL INTEREST RATE=',F5.3,5X,'INVESTMENT TAX CREDIT RATE='
          5,F5.3,5X,/,1X,'TAX SALVAGE VALUE=',F10.2)
 96          GO TO (555,666,777),IBDEP
 97      555 WRITE(6,8000)
 98     8000 FORMAT(/,1X,'BOOK DEP. METHOD ; STRAIGHT LINE DEP.')
 99          GO TO 8301
100      666 WRITE(6,8100)
101     8100 FORMAT(/,1X,'BOOK DEP. METHOD ; SUM OF THE YEARS DIGITS DEP.')
102          GO TO 8301
103      777 WRITE(6,8200)
104     8200 FORMAT(/,1X,'BOOK DEP. METHOD ; DOUBLE DECLINING BALANCE DEP.')
105     8301 GO TO(999,805,705),ITDEP
106      999 WRITE(6,8400)
107     8400 FORMAT(/,1X,'TAX DEP. METHOD ; STRAIGHT LINE DEP.')
108          GO TO 8402
109      805 WRITE(6,8500)
110     8500 FORMAT(/,1X,'TAX DEP. METHOD ; SUM OF THE YEARS DIGITS DEP.')
111          GO TO 8402
112      705 WRITE(6,8600)
113     8600 FORMAT(/,1X,'TAX DEP. METHOD ; DOUBLE DECLINING BALANCE DEP.')
114     8402 WRITE(6,4500) (COST(I),I=1,N)
115     4500 FORMAT(/,2X,'COST DATA;',/,(2X,5(F13.1),/))
116          STOP
117          END

118          SUBROUTINE DDBDEP(DEP,INC,SALV,NX,NY)
119          REAL INC,NX,NY
120          DIMENSION DEP(50),BV(50),RBVSL(50),SDEP(50)
121          IF(NX.GE.NY) GO TO 1561
122          N=NY
123          K=NX
124          GO TO 116
125     1561 N=NX
126          K=NY
127      116 D=2./NY
128          BV(1)=INC*(1.-D)**1.
129          DEP(1)=INC-BV(1)
130          RBVSL(1)=(INC-SALV)/NY
131          SDEP(1)=DEP(1)
132          P=INC-SALV
```

Reprinted, by permission from G.T. Stevens, Jr., *Economic and Financial Analysis of Capital Investments*, p. 351. Copyright © 1979 by John Wiley and Sons, Inc.

```
133              M=0
134              DO 200 I=2,N
135              IF(NY.GT.NX) K=N
136              IF(I.LE.K) GO TO 220
137              GO TO 210
138         220 AI=I
139              IF(M.EQ.1) GO TO 205
140              BV(I)=INC*(1.-D)**AI
141              ADEP=BV(I-1)
142              DEP(I)=ADEP-BV(I)
143              IF(I.EQ.K) GO TO 900
144              RBVSL(I)=(BV(I)-SALV)/(NY-AI)
145              IF(DEP(I).LE.RRVSL(I-1)) GO TO 600
146              IF(M.EQ.0) DEP(I)=ADEP-BV(I)
147              GO TO 250
148         205 IF(M.EQ.1) DEP(I)=RBVSL(II)
149              GO TO 250
150         600 IF(M.EQ.1) GO TO 205
151              M=1
152              II=I-1
153              GO TO 205
154         900 SDEP(I)=DEP(I)+SDEP(I-1)
155              IF(SDEP(I).LT.P) DEP(I)=P-(INC-SDEP(I))
156              DEP(I)=INC-SDEP(I-1)-SALV
157              GO TO 200
158         210 DEP(I)=0.
159              GO TO 200
160         250 SDEP(I)=DEP(I)+SDEP(I-1)
161              IF(SDEP(I).LT.P) GO TO 200
162              DEP(I)=P-SDEP(I-1)
163              JI=I+1
164              DO 255 L=JI,N
165         255 DEP(L)=0.
166              GO TO 70
167         200 CONTINUE
168          70 RETURN
169              END

170              SUBROUTINE SLDEP(DEP,INC,SALV,NX,NY)
171              REAL INC,NX,NY
172              DIMENSION DEP(50)
173              IF(NX.GE.NY) GO TO 1564
174              N=NY
175              K=NX
176              GO TO 115
177        1564 N=NX
178              K=NY
179         115 DO 200 I=1,N
180              IF(I.GT.NX) GO TO 210
181              DEP(I)=(INC-SALV)/NX
182              GO TO 200
183         210 DEP(I)=0.0
184         200 CONTINUE
185              RETURN
186              END
```

Reprinted, by permission from G.T. Stevens, Jr., *Economic and Financial Analysis of Capital Investments*, p. 351. Copyright © 1979 by John Wiley and Sons, Inc.

```
187          SUBROUTINE SYDDEP(DEP,INC,SALV,NX,NY)
188          REAL INC,NX,NY
189          DIMENSION DEP(50)
190          IF(NX.GE.NY) GO TO 1562
191          N=NY
192          K=NX
193          GO TO 117
194     1562 N=NX
195          K=NY
196          DO 200 I=1,N
197          IF(I.LE.K) GO TO 220
198          GO TO 210
199      220 DEP(I)=2.*(NY-I+1.)/NY/(NY+1.)*(INC-SALV)
200          GO TO 200
201      210 DEP(I)=0.
202      200 CONTINUE
203          GO TO 230
204      117 DO 201 I=1,N
205          DEP(I)=2.*(NY-I+1.)/NY/(NY+1.)*(INC-SALV)
206      201 CONTINUE
207      230 RETURN
208          END

        $ENTRY
```

APPENDIX

G

AREA UNDER NORMAL CURVE

Table G.1.   Area Under the Normal Curve

Proportion of total area under the curve that is under the portion of the curve from $-\infty$ to $\dfrac{X_i - \bar{X}'}{\sigma'}$. ($X_i$ represents any desired value of the variable X)

$\dfrac{X_i - \bar{X}'}{\sigma'}$	0.09	0.08	0.07	0.06	0.05	0.04	0.03	0.02	0.01	0.00
−3.5	0.00017	0.00017	0.00018	0.00019	0.00019	0.00020	0.00021	0.00022	0.00022	0.00023
−3.4	0.00024	0.00025	0.00026	0.00027	0.00028	0.00029	0.00030	0.00031	0.00033	0.00034
−3.3	0.00035	0.00036	0.00038	0.00039	0.00040	0.00042	0.00043	0.00045	0.00047	0.00048
−3.2	0.00050	0.00052	0.00054	0.00056	0.00058	0.00060	0.00062	0.00064	0.00066	0.00069
−3.1	0.00071	0.00074	0.00076	0.00079	0.00082	0.00085	0.00087	0.00090	0.00094	0.00097
−3.0	0.00100	0.00104	0.00107	0.00111	0.00114	0.00118	0.00122	0.00126	0.00131	0.00135
−2.9	0.0014	0.0014	0.0015	0.0015	0.0016	0.0016	0.0017	0.0017	0.0018	0.0019
−2.8	0.0019	0.0020	0.0021	0.0021	0.0022	0.0023	0.0023	0.0024	0.0025	0.0026
−2.7	0.0026	0.0027	0.0028	0.0029	0.0030	0.0031	0.0032	0.0033	0.0034	0.0035
−2.6	0.0036	0.0037	0.0038	0.0039	0.0040	0.0041	0.0043	0.0044	0.0045	0.0047
−2.5	0.0048	0.0049	0.0051	0.0052	0.0054	0.0055	0.0057	0.0059	0.0060	0.0062
−2.4	0.0064	0.0066	0.0068	0.0069	0.0071	0.0073	0.0075	0.0078	0.0080	0.0082
−2.3	0.0084	0.0087	0.0089	0.0091	0.0094	0.0096	0.0099	0.0102	0.0104	0.0107
−2.2	0.0110	0.0113	0.0116	0.0119	0.0122	0.0125	0.0129	0.0132	0.0136	0.0139
−2.1	0.0143	0.0146	0.0150	0.0154	0.0158	0.0162	0.0166	0.0170	0.0174	0.0179
−2.0	0.0183	0.0188	0.0192	0.0197	0.0202	0.0207	0.0212	0.0217	0.0222	0.0228
−1.9	0.0233	0.0239	0.0244	0.0250	0.0256	0.0262	0.0268	0.0274	0.0281	0.0287
−1.8	0.0294	0.0301	0.0307	0.0314	0.0322	0.0329	0.0336	0.0344	0.0351	0.0359
−1.7	0.0367	0.0375	0.0384	0.0392	0.0401	0.0409	0.0418	0.0427	0.0436	0.0446
−1.6	0.0455	0.0465	0.0475	0.0485	0.0495	0.0505	0.0516	0.0526	0.0537	0.0548
−1.5	0.0559	0.0571	0.0582	0.0594	0.0606	0.0618	0.0630	0.0643	0.0655	0.0668
−1.4	0.0681	0.0694	0.0708	0.0721	0.0735	0.0749	0.0764	0.0778	0.0793	0.0808
−1.3	0.0823	0.0838	0.0853	0.0869	0.0885	0.0901	0.0918	0.0934	0.0951	0.0968
−1.2	0.0985	0.1003	0.1020	0.1038	0.1057	0.1075	0.1093	0.1112	0.1131	0.1151
−1.1	0.1170	0.1190	0.1210	0.1230	0.1251	0.1271	0.1292	0.1314	0.1335	0.1357
−1.0	0.1379	0.1401	0.1423	0.1446	0.1469	0.1492	0.1515	0.1539	0.1562	0.1587
−0.9	0.1611	0.1635	0.1660	0.1685	0.1711	0.1736	0.1762	0.1788	0.1814	0.1841
−0.8	0.1867	0.1894	0.1922	0.1949	0.1977	0.2005	0.2033	0.2061	0.2090	0.2119
−0.7	0.2148	0.2177	0.2207	0.2236	0.2266	0.2297	0.2327	0.2358	0.2389	0.2420
−0.6	0.2451	0.2483	0.2514	0.2546	0.2578	0.2611	0.2643	0.2676	0.2709	0.2743
−0.5	0.2776	0.2810	0.2843	0.2877	0.2912	0.2946	0.2981	0.3015	0.3050	0.3085
−0.4	0.3121	0.3156	0.3192	0.3228	0.3264	0.3300	0.3336	0.3372	0.3409	0.3446
−0.3	0.3483	0.3520	0.3557	0.3594	0.3632	0.3669	0.3707	0.3745	0.3783	0.3821
−0.2	0.3859	0.3897	0.3936	0.3974	0.4013	0.4052	0.4090	0.4129	0.4168	0.4207
−0.1	0.4247	0.4286	0.4325	0.4364	0.4404	0.4443	0.4483	0.4522	0.4562	0.4602
−0.0	0.4641	0.4681	0.4721	0.4761	0.4801	0.4840	0.4880	0.4920	0.4960	0.5000

Table G.1. (continued)   **Area Under the Normal Curve**

$\frac{X_i-\bar{X}}{\sigma}$	0.00	0.01	0.02	0.03	0.04	0.05	0.06	0.07	0.08	0.09
+0.0	0.5000	0.5040	0.5080	0.5120	0.5160	0.5199	0.5239	0.5279	0.5319	0.5359
+0.1	0.5398	0.5438	0.5478	0.5517	0.5557	0.5596	0.5636	0.5675	0.5714	0.5753
+0.2	0.5793	0.5832	0.5871	0.5910	0.5948	0.5987	0.6026	0.6064	0.6103	0.6141
+0.3	0.6179	0.6217	0.6255	0.6293	0.6331	0.6368	0.6406	0.6443	0.6480	0.6517
+0.4	0.6554	0.6591	0.6628	0.6664	0.6700	0.6736	0.6772	0.6808	0.6844	0.6879
+0.5	0.6915	0.6950	0.6985	0.7019	0.7054	0.7088	0.7123	0.7157	0.7190	0.7224
+0.6	0.7257	0.7291	0.7324	0.7357	0.7389	0.7422	0.7454	0.7486	0.7517	0.7549
+0.7	0.7580	0.7611	0.7642	0.7673	0.7704	0.7734	0.7764	0.7794	0.7823	0.7852
+0.8	0.7881	0.7910	0.7939	0.7967	0.7995	0.8023	0.8051	0.8079	0.8106	0.8133
+0.9	0.8159	0.8186	0.8212	0.8238	0.8264	0.8289	0.8315	0.8340	0.8365	0.8389
+1.0	0.8413	0.8438	0.8461	0.8485	0.8508	0.8531	0.8554	0.8577	0.8599	0.8621
+1.1	0.8643	0.8665	0.8686	0.8708	0.8729	0.8749	0.8770	0.8790	0.8810	0.8830
+1.2	0.8849	0.8869	0.8888	0.8907	0.8925	0.8944	0.8962	0.8980	0.8997	0.9015
+1.3	0.9032	0.9049	0.9066	0.9082	0.9099	0.9115	0.9131	0.9147	0.9162	0.9177
+1.4	0.9192	0.9207	0.9222	0.9236	0.9251	0.9265	0.9279	0.9292	0.9306	0.9319
+1.5	0.9332	0.9345	0.9357	0.9370	0.9382	0.9394	0.9406	0.9418	0.9429	0.9441
+1.6	0.9452	0.9463	0.9474	0.9484	0.9495	0.9505	0.9515	0.9525	0.9535	0.9545
+1.7	0.9554	0.9564	0.9573	0.9582	0.9591	0.9599	0.9608	0.9616	0.9625	0.9633
+1.8	0.9641	0.9649	0.9656	0.9664	0.9671	0.9678	0.9686	0.9693	0.9699	0.9706
+1.9	0.9713	0.9719	0.9726	0.9732	0.9738	0.9744	0.9750	0.9756	0.9761	0.9767
+2.0	0.9773	0.9778	0.9783	0.9788	0.9793	0.9798	0.9803	0.9808	0.9812	0.9817
+2.1	0.9821	0.9826	0.9830	0.9834	0.9838	0.9842	0.9846	0.9850	0.9854	0.9857
+2.2	0.9861	0.9864	0.9868	0.9871	0.9875	0.9878	0.9881	0.9884	0.9887	0.9890
+2.3	0.9893	0.9896	0.9898	0.9901	0.9904	0.9906	0.9909	0.9911	0.9913	0.9916
+2.4	0.9918	0.9920	0.9922	0.9925	0.9927	0.9929	0.9931	0.9932	0.9934	0.9936
+2.5	0.9938	0.9940	0.9941	0.9943	0.9945	0.9946	0.9948	0.9949	0.9951	0.9952
+2.6	0.9953	0.9955	0.9956	0.9957	0.9959	0.9960	0.9961	0.9962	0.9963	0.9964
+2.7	0.9965	0.9966	0.9967	0.9968	0.9969	0.9970	0.9971	0.9972	0.9973	0.9974
+2.8	0.9974	0.9975	0.9976	0.9977	0.9977	0.9978	0.9979	0.9979	0.9980	0.9981
+2.9	0.9981	0.9982	0.9983	0.9983	0.9984	0.9984	0.9985	0.9985	0.9986	0.9986
+3.0	0.99865	0.99869	0.99874	0.99878	0.99882	0.99886	0.99889	0.99893	0.99896	0.99900
+3.1	0.99903	0.99906	0.99910	0.99913	0.99915	0.99918	0.99921	0.99924	0.99926	0.99929
+3.2	0.99931	0.99934	0.99936	0.99938	0.99940	0.99942	0.99944	0.99946	0.99948	0.99950
+3.3	0.99952	0.99953	0.99955	0.99957	0.99958	0.99960	0.99961	0.99962	0.99964	0.99965
+3.4	0.99966	0.99967	0.99969	0.99970	0.99971	0.99972	0.99973	0.99974	0.99975	0.99976
+3.5	0.99977	0.99978	0.99978	0.99979	0.99980	0.99981	0.99981	0.99982	0.99983	0.99983

Reprinted, by permission from G.T. Stevens, Jr., *Economic and Financial Analysis of Capital Investments*, p. 351. Copyright © 1979 by John Wiley and Sons, Inc.

APPENDIX

H

UNIT NORMAL
LOSS INTEGRAL

Table H.1.   Unit Normal Loss Integral

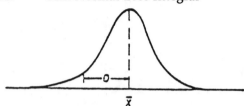

D	.00	.01	.02	.03	.04	.05	.06	.07	.08	.09
.0	.3989	.3940	.3890	.3841	.3793	.3744	.3697	.3649	.3602	.3556
.1	.3509	.3464	.3418	.3373	.3328	.3284	.3240	.3197	.3154	.3111
.2	.3069	.3027	.2986	.2944	.2904	.2863	.2824	.2784	.2745	.2706
.3	.2668	.2630	.2592	.2555	.2518	.2481	.2445	.2409	.2374	.2339
.4	.2304	.2270	.2236	.2203	.2169	.2137	.2104	.2072	.2040	.2009
.5	.1978	.1947	.1917	.1887	.1857	.1828	.1799	.1771	.1742	.1714
.6	.1687	.1659	.1633	.1606	.1580	.1554	.1528	.1503	.1478	.1453
.7	.1429	.1405	.1381	.1358	.1334	.1312	.1289	.1267	.1245	.1223
.8	.1202	.1181	.1160	.1140	.1120	.1100	.1080	.1061	.1042	.1023
.9	.1004	.09860	.09680	.09503	.09328	.09156	.08986	.08819	.08654	.08491
1.0	.08332	.08174	.08019	.07866	.07716	.07568	.07422	.07279	.07138	.06999
1.1	.06862	.06727	.06595	.06465	.06336	.06210	.06086	.05964	.05844	.05726
1.2	.05610	.05496	.05384	.05274	.05165	.05059	.04954	.04851	.04750	.04650
1.3	.04553	.04457	.04363	.04270	.04179	.04090	.04002	.03916	.03831	.03748
1.4	.03667	.03587	.03508	.03431	.03356	.03281	.03208	.03137	.03067	.02998
1.5	.02931	.02865	.02800	.02736	.02674	.02612	.02552	.02494	.02436	.02380
1.6	.02324	.02270	.02217	.02165	.02114	.02064	.02015	.01967	.01920	.01874
1.7	.01829	.01785	.01742	.01699	.01658	.01617	.01578	.01539	.01501	.01464
1.8	.01428	.01392	.01357	.01323	.01290	.01257	.01226	.01195	.01164	.01134
1.9	.01105	.01077	.01049	.01022	$.0^{2}9957$	$.0^{2}9698$	$.0^{2}9445$	$.0^{2}9198$	$.0^{2}8957$	$.0^{2}8721$
2.0	$.0^{2}8491$	$.0^{2}8266$	$.0^{2}8046$	$.0^{2}7832$	$.0^{2}7623$	$.0^{2}7418$	$.0^{2}7219$	$.0^{2}7024$	$.0^{2}6835$	$.0^{2}6649$
2.1	$.0^{2}6468$	$.0^{2}6292$	$.0^{2}6120$	$.0^{2}5952$	$.0^{2}5788$	$.0^{2}5628$	$.0^{2}5472$	$.0^{2}5320$	$.0^{2}5172$	$.0^{2}5028$
2.2	$.0^{2}4887$	$.0^{2}4750$	$.0^{2}4616$	$.0^{2}4486$	$.0^{2}4358$	$.0^{2}4235$	$.0^{2}4114$	$.0^{2}3996$	$.0^{2}3882$	$.0^{2}3770$
2.3	$.0^{2}3662$	$.0^{2}3556$	$.0^{2}3453$	$.0^{2}3352$	$.0^{2}3255$	$.0^{2}3159$	$.0^{2}3067$	$.0^{2}2977$	$.0^{2}2889$	$.0^{2}2804$
2.4	$.0^{2}2720$	$.0^{2}2640$	$.0^{2}2561$	$.0^{2}2484$	$.0^{2}2410$	$.0^{2}2337$	$.0^{2}2267$	$.0^{2}2199$	$.0^{2}2132$	$.0^{2}2067$
2.5	$.0^{2}2004$	$.0^{2}1943$	$.0^{2}1883$	$.0^{2}1826$	$.0^{2}1769$	$.0^{2}1715$	$.0^{2}1662$	$.0^{2}1610$	$.0^{2}1560$	$.0^{2}1511$
2.6	$.0^{2}1464$	$.0^{2}1418$	$.0^{2}1373$	$.0^{2}1330$	$.0^{2}1288$	$.0^{2}1247$	$.0^{2}1207$	$.0^{2}1169$	$.0^{2}1132$	$.0^{2}1095$
2.7	$.0^{2}1060$	$.0^{2}1026$	$.0^{3}9928$	$.0^{3}9607$	$.0^{3}9295$	$.0^{3}8992$	$.0^{3}8699$	$.0^{3}8414$	$.0^{3}8138$	$.0^{3}7870$
2.8	$.0^{3}7611$	$.0^{3}7359$	$.0^{3}7115$	$.0^{3}6879$	$.0^{3}6650$	$.0^{3}6428$	$.0^{3}6213$	$.0^{3}6004$	$.0^{3}5802$	$.0^{3}5606$
2.9	$.0^{3}5417$	$.0^{3}5233$	$.0^{3}5055$	$.0^{3}4883$	$.0^{3}4716$	$.0^{3}4555$	$.0^{3}4398$	$.0^{3}4247$	$.0^{3}4101$	$.0^{3}3959$
3.0	$.0^{3}3822$	$.0^{3}3689$	$.0^{3}3560$	$.0^{3}3436$	$.0^{3}3316$	$.0^{3}3199$	$.0^{3}3087$	$.0^{3}2978$	$.0^{3}2873$	$.0^{3}2771$
3.1	$.0^{3}2673$	$.0^{3}2577$	$.0^{3}2485$	$.0^{3}2396$	$.0^{3}2311$	$.0^{3}2227$	$.0^{3}2147$	$.0^{3}2070$	$.0^{3}1995$	$.0^{3}1922$
3.2	$.0^{3}1852$	$.0^{3}1785$	$.0^{3}1720$	$.0^{3}1657$	$.0^{3}1596$	$.0^{3}1537$	$.0^{3}1480$	$.0^{3}1426$	$.0^{3}1373$	$.0^{3}1322$
3.3	$.0^{3}1273$	$.0^{3}1225$	$.0^{3}1179$	$.0^{3}1135$	$.0^{3}1093$	$.0^{3}1051$	$.0^{3}1012$	$.0^{4}9734$	$.0^{4}9365$	$.0^{4}9009$
3.4	$.0^{4}8666$	$.0^{4}8335$	$.0^{4}8016$	$.0^{4}7709$	$.0^{4}7413$	$.0^{4}7127$	$.0^{4}6852$	$.0^{4}6587$	$.0^{4}6331$	$.0^{4}6085$
3.5	$.0^{4}5848$	$.0^{4}5620$	$.0^{4}5400$	$.0^{4}5188$	$.0^{4}4984$	$.0^{4}4788$	$.0^{4}4599$	$.0^{4}4417$	$.0^{4}4242$	$.0^{4}4073$
3.6	$.0^{4}3911$	$.0^{4}3755$	$.0^{4}3605$	$.0^{4}3460$	$.0^{4}3321$	$.0^{4}3188$	$.0^{4}3059$	$.0^{4}2935$	$.0^{4}2816$	$.0^{4}2702$
3.7	$.0^{4}2592$	$.0^{4}2486$	$.0^{4}2385$	$.0^{4}2287$	$.0^{4}2193$	$.0^{4}2103$	$.0^{4}2016$	$.0^{4}1933$	$.0^{4}1853$	$.0^{4}1776$
3.8	$.0^{4}1702$	$.0^{4}1632$	$.0^{4}1563$	$.0^{4}1498$	$.0^{4}1435$	$.0^{4}1375$	$.0^{4}1317$	$.0^{4}1262$	$.0^{4}1208$	$.0^{4}1157$
3.9	$.0^{4}1108$	$.0^{4}1061$	$.0^{4}1016$	$.0^{5}9723$	$.0^{5}9307$	$.0^{5}8908$	$.0^{5}8525$	$.0^{5}8158$	$.0^{5}7806$	$.0^{5}7469$
4.0	$.0^{5}7145$	$.0^{5}6835$	$.0^{5}6538$	$.0^{5}6253$	$.0^{5}5980$	$.0^{5}5718$	$.0^{5}5468$	$.0^{5}5227$	$.0^{5}4997$	$.0^{5}4777$
4.1	$.0^{5}4566$	$.0^{5}4364$	$.0^{5}4170$	$.0^{5}3985$	$.0^{5}3807$	$.0^{5}3637$	$.0^{5}3475$	$.0^{5}3319$	$.0^{5}3170$	$.0^{5}3027$
4.2	$.0^{5}2891$	$.0^{5}2760$	$.0^{5}2635$	$.0^{5}2516$	$.0^{5}2402$	$.0^{5}2292$	$.0^{5}2188$	$.0^{5}2088$	$.0^{5}1992$	$.0^{5}1901$
4.3	$.0^{5}1814$	$.0^{5}1730$	$.0^{5}1650$	$.0^{5}1574$	$.0^{5}1501$	$.0^{5}1431$	$.0^{5}1365$	$.0^{5}1301$	$.0^{5}1241$	$.0^{5}1183$
4.4	$.0^{5}1127$	$.0^{5}1074$	$.0^{5}1024$	$.0^{6}9756$	$.0^{6}9296$	$.0^{6}8857$	$.0^{6}8437$	$.{}^{*}8037$	$.0^{6}7655$	$.0^{6}7290$

Reprinted, by permission from *Probability and Statistics for Business Decisions* by R. Schlaifer, McGraw-Hill, Inc., 1959, pp.706-707.
Copyright © 1979 by McGraw-Hill, Inc.

INDEX